Brief Contents

Contents

Foreword

Surely there can be no crime that inspires greater anguish among the general public than sexual crimes, especially violent sexual offenses. Sexual violation is deeply troubling to us all, and most of us carry around an image of depraved strangers who assault their victims in wanton moments of lustful violence. And we can imagine the nefarious pedophile, unnaturally sexually attracted to children. These images understandably distress us, and we want protection from these repulsing violations of our sexual and personal safety.

It is good to remember that among active criminals, these repulsive sex crimes are rarities. Indeed, even among those who have been committed for sexual crimes, the wanton serial rapist and perverse pedophiliac are rare. One of the antidotes to widespread distress about sex crimes is to get good information about them. With good, accurate, and up-to-date information about sex crimes, we can learn to moderate the unreasonable fears that fuel overreactions and ineffective policies, and we can become more clear about the kinds of strategic thinking that will lead to greater public safety in this important area of personal security.

That is why I am delighted to announce the publication of *Sexual Offenses and Offenders: Theory, Practice, and Policy* by Karen J. Terry, the newest contribution to the *Wadsworth Contemporary Issues in Crime and Justice Series*. The *Contemporary Issues Series* is devoted to furthering our understanding of important issues in crime and justice by providing an in-depth treatment of topics that are neglected or insufficiently discussed in today's textbooks. *Sexual Offenses and Offenders: Theory, Practice, and Policy* is an excellent example of the kind of work the series was designed to promote.

This book covers virtually every aspect of sexual offending, and promises to leave its reader with a deeper and more reliable expertise about sex crimes throughout history and in contemporary society. Professor Terry's text is so packed with information that it will come to be seen as the most authoritative introductory text on the subject available in the market. Those who read it will know the latest information about the nature of sex criminality, and how to prevent and control repeat sexual victimization.

Among the many important contributions this book makes to the literature on sexual criminality, three stand out. First, the text places our understanding of sex crimes directly within a social context. Since the 1800s, there has been a public awareness of and reaction to sex crimes, almost always fueled by a particularly dramatic and public sex crime that speaks to the public consciousness. This powerful social context means that public policy about sex crimes is topically driven by extreme events that dominate the news, and the realities that apply to the less rare kinds of sexual victimization can get lost in the public outcry.

Second, much is not known about sexual offenders, and this text paints a more complex, nuanced portrait of the problem than does the popular media or the public imagination. We know that both psychological and social factors play a role in the onset and duration of sex crimes, that most sexual criminality plays out in behavior cycles in which victims are "groomed" by offenders, and that distortions of thinking precipitate criminal events. This growing expertise on the etiology of sex crimes means that what has been, for most of history, a mysterious social aberration is now better understood as a maladaptive form of development.

Third, this growing knowledge has helped to develop better methods of treatment and relapse prevention. While the myth about sex offenders is that they cannot be changed, a new and impressive body of research shows that for many (if not most) sex offenders, treatment can eliminate reoccurrences of sexual victimization. This is especially possible for two reasons. For one thing, recent studies show that sex offenders have lower-than-expected rates of recidivism. For another, coordinated efforts of police, corrections, and treatment providers develop a cocoon of support and control that can prevent recidivism entirely, so long as the systems of support and control remain active and alert.

Professor Terry delivers these three contributions with authority and assurance. Where research studies exist to illuminate a particular issue, she describes them. Where a point can be supported by the words of those who have been convicted of sex crimes, she provides rich detail from her own personal research files. This is at once a book that summarizes the vast body of work that exists on the topic and offers new data published here for the first time.

As Professor Terry's book makes apparent, there is a great deal of misunderstanding about sex offenders today, and stemming from this has been an active legislative agenda trying to deal with public outrage about violent sex crime. Some of this legislation may have been counterproductive to the aims of public safety, and almost all of it is based, at least in part, on myths about the prevention and control of repeat sex crimes. While much needs to be done about the problem of sexual victimization, some of what has been done may need to be undone. Those who read this book will find themselves with a strong foundation for a future agenda of action.

Todd R. Clear
Series Editor

Preface

Most books on sexual offending cover a specific topic area related to offenses, offenders, or victims, such as treatment, management, or victimization. The aim of this book is to provide a comprehensive overview of psychological, sociological, and legal issues related to sexual offending. With the growing number of criminal justice and criminology classes, as well as classes specifically devoted to the topic of sexual offending, this book can fill the gap that currently exists in the market. Additionally, it should be used as a basis for research on offenses and offenders, as it combines both an extensive literature review and some unique primary data.

The purpose of this book is twofold. First, it addresses the literature on sexual offending, including characteristics and typologies of offenders and current treatment and management practices. Second, it analyzes the policies that address sex offenders, including reasons for the implementation of these policies and their likely future. The theoretical literature and empirical research on sex offenders is vast, much of it comprised of conflicting results that seem to be influenced by the population of offenders studied, their location, and the researchers studying them. One result of these studies is the depiction of an atypical group of offenders: they tend to be older and more educated than other types of offenders; many are either married or cohabiting at the time of their offenses; the basis of their offending behavior is often considered to be psychological in nature; and their acts are considered to be among the most detestable in the criminal justice system (O'Connell, Leberg, & Donaldson, 1990; West, 1987). Politicians, the public, other types of offenders, and correctional officers alike scorn them (Akerstrom, 1986; Prison Reform Trust, 1990, 1991), and their lives are sometimes in danger if the nature of their offenses is disclosed to those in the community or in prison.

In addition to the literature on sexual offending, this book contains excerpts from interviews with sex offenders incarcerated in the English prison system who participated in a cognitive-behavioral treatment program. I conducted 85 interviews, resulting in approximately 250 hours of discussions with sex offenders on their offenses, their treatment, their self-professed reasons for committing the offenses, how they initiated (and, for some, maintained) contact with the victims, and why they will not (or will) commit the offenses again. I conducted these interviews prior to the offenders' participation in a treatment program and shortly after they completed the program. The aim of the study was to determine the efficacy of cognitive-behavioral treatment at reducing their cognitive distortions. (For a detailed explanation of the methodology and results of this study, see Terry and Mitchell, 2001.) The sex offenders in this study committed a variety of sexual or sexually motivated acts against children and adults, including murder. Some offenders had extensive histories of deviant behavior, both sexual and nonsexual; others were convicted of only one offense. They ranged in age from 19 to 63 (at the time of the interviews), and their sentences ranged from three years to life in prison. All had some characteristics in common, such as cognitive distortions, but they constitute a heterogeneous group of individuals in every other way. All those interviewed were adult male offenders. Because of this, and because most literature on sexual offending is based on the same population, the majority of this book focuses on adult male offenders. Only Chapter 6 explores the population of juvenile offenders and Chapter 12 female offenders, each of which comprise their own body of research.

This book is divided into three parts. Part I is an analysis of the sex offender and victim populations. It contains information about statistics on offending and victimization, typologies of offenders, and causes of offending. Part II looks at how sex offenders are dealt with in society; specifically, it focuses on treatment, management, and legislation implemented in the 1990s. The management and care of sex offenders in prison and in the community is a topical issue today, with new approaches to containment theory evolving for more appropriate systems of supervision. Part III of the book looks at special populations of offenders and where research regarding sex offenders is headed in the 21st century.

ACKNOWLEDGMENTS

I would like to thank all the reviewers of this text who helped to shape its development:

Tim App, Northeastern University

Allan Barnes, University of Alaska–Anchorage

Shawna Cleary, University of Central Oklahoma

Sue Cote, Sacramento State University

Karin Dudash, Cameron University

Bob Glazier, University of Houston

Mark Hansel, Minnesota State University, Moorhead

Patricia Harris, University of Texas at San Antonio

Scott Hedlund, Pierce College

Eric Jensen, University of Idaho

Glen Kercher, Sam Houston State University

Deborah Laufersweiler-Dwyer, University of Arkansas, Little Rock

Alan McEvoy, Wittenburg University

Heather Melton, University of Utah

Jody Miller, University of Missouri

Dwight Noble, Indiana University

Callie Rennison, University of Missouri–St. Louis

Isaac T. Van Patten, Radford University

I owe many thanks to some wonderful people at Cambridge University, who assisted me at the outset of this research as well as through the publication process. Adrian Grounds's assistance was invaluable, as he helped me to establish relationships throughout the English prison system. Helen, Stuart, and the rest of the library staff were so helpful and supportive, as were so many other faculty members, particularly Alison Liebling and Lorraine Gelsthorpe. And, of course, I am forever indebted to Ed Mitchell for all of his last-minute help at Heathrow Airport.

I also appreciate the support of my colleagues in the Department of Law, Police Science and Criminal Justice Administration at John Jay College of Criminal Justice. Many thanks in particular to Heath Grant, who has been there for me as a friend and colleague for the past five years. Maki Haberfeld, chair of the department, has also been very encouraging throughout the publication process. I would also like to thank Jim Levine, dean of Graduate Studies, and Gerald Lynch, past president of John Jay College, for their support for my research over the past two years. It has been a pleasure working with them both.

Finally, I would like to thank Sabra Horne, who devoted so much effort to helping me throughout the publication process, and to Steve Perreault, for being there every night when I get home.

PART I

❖

Sexual Offenses, Offenders, and Victims

1

Sexual Offenses
and Offenders

Nothing is so prone to contaminate—under certain circumstances,
even to exhaust—the source of all noble and ideal sentiments, which
arise from a normally developed sexual instinct, as the practice of
masturbation in one's early years. It despoils the unfolding bud of perfume
and beauty, and leaves behind only the coarse, animal desire for sexual
satisfaction. If an individual, thus depraved, reaches the age of maturity, there
is lacking in him that aesthetic, ideal, pure and free impulse that draws the
opposite sexes together. The glow of sensual sensibility wanes, and attraction
toward the opposite sex is weakened. This defect in the morals, character,
fantasy and instinct of the youthful masturbator, male or female, in an
unfavorable manner, even causing, under certain circumstances, desire for
the opposite sex to become entirely absent; thus masturbation becomes
preferable to the natural mode of sexual satisfaction.

— Krafft-Ebing (1886/1965): 241

As we enter the 21st century, there are few groups of individuals who are
less understood or tolerated than sex offenders. Though they have been
of considerable interest to researchers throughout the 20th century,
they have, in the past two decades, brought about a resurgence of intense public and political interest. This interest has been characterized by a vast increase
in both the reporting of sex offenses and in the incapacitation of offenders. It is

unlikely that significantly more sexual offenses are being committed than before, particularly when considering the recent plummet of violent crime throughout the United States. Rather, the perception of sex offenders is likely the effect of "socially constructed realities" influenced by the existing social and political ideologies (Jenkins, 1998: 4). Several emotionally charged cases of child sexual abuse were highly publicized in the 1980s and 1990s, regenerating public intolerance for sexual offenders. This is similar to attitudes in the 1930s, when sexual psychopathy laws emerged to incapacitate those defined as "unfortunate but dangerous wretches" (Robson, 1999: 2). Empirical research has increasingly shown that sex offenders constitute a heterogeneous population of individuals for whom a one-size-fits-all policy will not be effective. Nonetheless, these one-size-fits-all policies regarding the incapacitation of sexual offenders have gone full circle since the beginning of the century.

Because 99 percent of convicted sex offenders eventually return to the community, it is important to determine what best reduces their risk of recidivism. Research has focused on three areas in particular: (1) why sex offenders begin to commit sexually deviant behavior, (2) how best to treat that behavior, and (3) how to manage offenders once they are in the community. The unfortunate reality is that most sex offenders do not participate in extensive treatment programs. There are many reasons for this, beginning with the decline of the "rehabilitative ideal" in the 1970s. Since that time, many people have considered the focus on rehabilitation for offenders—particularly sex offenders—futile and unnecessary. Politicians, the public, and the courts alike are often opposed to the allocation of funds for sex offender treatment programs, as these programs require an immense appropriation of resources for a single category of offenders (Holmes, 1991). These tough-on-crime-and-criminals attitudes have been consolidated by the increasingly conservative attitudes of the Supreme Court justices, who focus on the incapacitation of offenders rather than their rehabilitation. Yet another reason for the lack of participation in treatment is that most sex offenders do not want to participate in treatment. Seventy-three percent of the rapists interviewed in one study stated that they either did not want or need treatment, but 41 percent of those said they would participate if they were expected to do so (Grubin & Gunn, 1990).

Empirical research has also been conducted to analyze attitudes toward deviant sexual behavior and determine who is likely to offend or reoffend. Some controlled studies have produced dismaying results: in one study, for example, 1 in 4 men admitted to using coercion in a sexual relationship (Koss, Gidycz, & Wisniewski, 1987). Yet another researcher (Malamuth, 1981) found that 35 percent of male students in a university research sample admitted to the hypothetical likelihood of committing rape if they thought it would go undetected. Feminist researchers have long stated that men who commit acts are the norm in male-dominated social cultures, and the question should be asked, "Why do some men *not* offend?" rather than why some men *do* (Herman, 1990). Before addressing the issue of why people commit sexual offenses and how best to prevent them, we must first discuss the nature and scope of sex crimes.

WHAT IS A SEXUAL OFFENSE?

Richard von Krafft-Ebing made the statement at the beginning of this chapter approximately 100 years ago. At that time, masturbation, homosexuality, and other common sexual practices were not only condemned, but were also considered pathological and loathsome. Attitudes toward sexual behavior are structured through social and political ideologies, and they have changed drastically throughout the centuries. Some harmful sexual acts are—and should continue to be—illegal in nearly every community. One such example is rape, which constitutes a violation of the person and can cause irreparable harm both physically and psychologically. In describing rape, the Policy Advisory Committee on Sexual Offences in England states that

> rape involves a severe degree of emotional and psychological trauma; it may be described as a violation which in effect obliterates the personality of the victim. . . . Rape is also unpleasant because it involves such intimate proximity between the offender and the victim. . . . (Criminal Law Revision Committee, 1984)

The legally and socially accepted boundaries of other sexual behaviors, however, are not as clear, and sexual violence is not unique to any one culture or historical period (Stermac, Segal, & Gillis, 1990). Sexual behaviors other than those for the purposes of procreation (for example, homosexuality, incest, adultery, masturbation, bestiality, and sexual activity with children) have vacillated among social acceptance, stigmatization, and illegality.

Sexual offenses vary across time and cultures, and even across various jurisdictions in the United States. There are generally three categories of sexual acts that are criminalized today:

1. *Sexual Acts with Contact* Most sexual offenses are within this category, where there is touching of the intimate parts of the body either without the consent of the victim or when one person is incapable of consenting under the law (for example, a person who has not yet reached the age of consent in that state, a person who is not conscious, a person who is dead). This category involves all contact acts, from touching over the clothes to forced sexual intercourse.

2. *Noncontact Sexual Behavior* This involves acts that are for the purpose of sexual gratification, but no contact is made between the perpetrator and the victim (for example, exposure of the genitals, voyeurism, telling children to perform sexual acts).

3. *Viewing, Possessing, or Producing Child Pornography* This third category includes any act involving the filming or photographing of a child that is for the purpose of sexually gratifying an adult. This may include sexual contact with children or just the sexual exploitation of children in photos and film.

There are some offenses common across all jurisdictions in the United States, though the terminology differs depending on the jurisdiction. For example, although most states use the term *rape* to define offenses involving nonconsensual oral, anal, and/or vaginal penetration, this is called *sexual imposition* or *gross sexual imposition* in North Dakota and is called *sexual assault* in Colorado. Additionally, the specific definitions of this crime differ in terms of who can be a victim or an offender (male and/or female), the class of felony or misdemeanor, and the age of the victim (some define the different degrees by age ranges, with acts committed against younger victims being more serious offenses).

Many states also label some consensual sexual acts as offenses. For instance, in 1999, 26 states still listed as an offense consensual sodomy.[1] In some of those states, sodomy is only illegal between members of the same sex, and the crimes are variously called *sodomy, crimes against nature, homosexual conduct, buggery, sexual misconduct, unnatural and lascivious acts,* and *unnatural or perverted sexual practices.* Other consensual acts that are also illegal in some states include incest (intergenerational and between siblings), adultery, bigamy, female genital mutilation, fornication, masturbation for hire, indecent dancing, prostitution, and public indecency (Leiter, 1999). In addition to these offenses, other crimes that are not necessarily sexual in nature are registerable offenses,[2] such as kidnapping.

For most sexual offenses, there must be a lack of consent on the part of the victim and some level of intent on the part of the offender. The laws in most states stipulate that consent is lacking from a sexual act when:

- The act is the result of force, threat, or duress,
- A reasonable person would understand that the victim did not consent due to a clear or implied statement that he or she would not want to engage in the sexual act, or
- The victim is incapable of consenting because he or she is below the age of consent (this ranges from age 16 to age 18 in various states); is mentally disabled; is mentally incapacitated; is physically helpless; is under the custody of correctional services; is placed within the care of children and family services (or any other organization in charge of monitoring and caring for those in care of the state).

Offenses vary by type, degree of severity, class of offense, and length of sanction. In some states, these are defined simply by class of felony or misdemeanor. In other states, they are divided into first, second, and third degree offenses, with first degree offenses being the most severe. For example, Table 1.1 shows how New York defines rape into three degrees.

PREVALENCE AND SCOPE
OF SEXUAL OFFENDING

It is impossible to accurately assess the extent of sexual offending and the characteristics of offenders. Most data on sex offenders relates either to those who are arrested or those convicted, and these represent a small portion of all sex crimes. From 1992 to 2000, only 31 percent of rapes and sexual assaults were reported to

Table 1.1 New York Penal Code Definition of Rape

Code Section	Offense	Degree	Definition
§130.25	Rape	Third	He or she engages in sexual intercourse with another person, to whom the actor is not married, who is incapable of consent and is not less than 17 years old; actor is over 21 years old and engages in sexual intercourse with someone less than 17 years old. Class E Felony.
§130.30		Second	Actor is over 18 years of age and he or she engages in sexual intercourse with someone less than 14 years of age; victim is otherwise mentally disabled or mentally incapacitated. Class D Felony.
§130.35		First	He or she engages in sexual intercourse with a person by forcible compulsion; who is incapable of consent because he or she is physically helpless; who is less than 11 years of age; who is less than 13 years old and the actor is over 18. Class B Felony.

SOURCE: New York Penal Law (2000)

the police (Hart & Rennison, 2003). Of those that are reported, not all end in arrest, and not all of those go on to indictment or conviction. This "funnel" system means that the further researchers are from the point at which the crime was committed, the further they are from knowing the true nature and scope of the problem of sexual offending. Knowledge of sex offenders and rates of victimization are based upon two primary sources: criminal justice data (including arrest and conviction data, victimization surveys, and social service data) and empirical studies. Table 1.2 shows the strengths and weaknesses of the different data sources.

Criminal Justice Data

Criminal justice statistics come from several sources, including arrest and conviction rates on a local level, the Uniform Crime Reports (UCR), National Incident-Based Reporting System (NIBRS), social service data, and victimization surveys (primarily the National Crime Victimization Survey—NCVS). The UCR is compiled annually by the Federal Bureau of Investigation (FBI) and contains information provided by nearly 17,000 local police departments (Grant & Terry, 2005). The local police agencies or state agencies give their arrest data to the FBI on a voluntary basis, and the FBI then tabulates the data on a national level. Despite its voluntary nature, there is a 97 percent compliance rate among police agencies.

Table 1.2 Comparison of Data Sources

Source of Data	Strengths	Weaknesses
Uniform Crime Reports (UCR)	■ Most common source of official criminal justice data in the United States ■ Reliable because it measures the same offenses each year ■ Makes it possible to compare the crime rate in jurisdictions of varying sizes	■ Hierarchy rule ■ Relies on official statistics, voluntary reporting by police ■ Definitions of some offenses incomplete
National Incident-Based Reporting System (NIBRS)	■ Gathers incident-based data ■ Detailed information available on offenders, victims, properties, and locations of offenses	■ Not yet widely implemented ■ Complicated, time-consuming reporting system
National Crime Victimization Survey (NCVS)	■ Provides information on the dark figure of crime ■ Gives information on why crimes are underreported ■ Most extensive bounded study	■ Self-reports not totally reliable
National Child Abuse and Neglect Data System (NCANDS)	■ Provides annual reports of child abuse ■ State-by-state information distinguished by types of child abuse	■ Information is not always reported to social services and thus may be incomplete
Empirical Studies	■ Can provide deeper analysis of issues by observing samples of the population	■ Studies use varying methodologies and definitions, and thus may not be comparable

The UCR consists of two sections: Part I and Part II offenses. Part I offenses, which are also called *index offenses*, are divided into categories of violent and property offenses, of which there are four each. The four violent offenses are murder (and non–negligent manslaughter), forcible rape, robbery, and aggravated assault, and the four property offenses are burglary, larceny-theft, motor vehicle theft, and arson. Part II offenses consist of all other offenses, including simple assaults, other sexual offenses, forgery, fraud, vandalism, embezzlement, vice crimes such as gambling and prostitution, weapons violations, alcohol and drug violations, and curfew violations.

The UCR is used to determine the crime rate in the United States and in local jurisdictions. In order to compute the crime rate, you take the number of total reported crimes, divide by the total population of the reporting area, and multiply by 100,000. The most significant strength of the UCR is its reliability; it measures crimes using the same definitions every year and across all jurisdictions. Therefore, it allows jurisdictions to understand how their crime rates change each year and how they compare to crime rates in other jurisdictions, even those with different populations (for example, rural and urban areas).

Unfortunately, the UCR has several weaknesses. Most significantly, crime is underreported, and this only measures the number of crimes that are reported and cleared by arrest or exceptional means.[3] Since sexual offenses are the least reported crimes, it is not necessarily a valid measure of sexual offense statistics. A second weakness with the UCR is that it follows the "hierarchy rule," meaning that it only compiles data on the most serious offenses if multiple offenses are committed at one time. In other words, if a person breaks into a house, rapes the occupant, murders her, and steals her car, only the murder will be counted in the UCR. A third weakness of the UCR is that it uses one definition for each crime, yet the definitions of these crimes vary by jurisdiction. This is particularly troublesome for sexual offenses, as the UCR defines forcible rape as "the carnal knowledge of a female forcibly and against her will. Rapes by force and attempts or assaults to rape regardless of the age of the victim are included. Statutory offenses (no force used—victim under age of consent) are excluded" (Uniform Crime Report, 2002). Thus, the UCR is beneficial in giving us a comparison of statistics on forcible rape of women by men but not other sexual offenses. These are complied into the broad category of "sexual offenses" in Part II crimes, defined as: "Statutory rape and offenses against chastity, common decency, morals, and the like. Attempts are included" (Uniform Crime Report, 2002).

Despite its weaknesses, the UCR remains the best source of official statistics for crimes. According to the Uniform Crime Report (2002), forcible rapes in 2002 accounted for .8 percent of all index crimes. The rate of forcible rapes has decreased 10.3 percent from 1993 to 2002, though since 1999 it has been increasing. Between 2001 and 2002, the rate of forcible rapes rose 3.6 percent. Of those rapes that were reported, 44.5 percent were cleared by arrest.

In an effort to improve the compilation and reporting of crime data, the FBI devised the National Incident-Based Reporting System (NIBRS) database in 1989. NIBRS is an incident-based reporting system, and as such allows for the calculation of multiple offenses, multiple victims, multiple offenders, and multiple arrests within a single incident. It still has flaws, however. Currently, police departments representing only 17 percent of the population submit data to NIBRS. Also, like the UCR, it relies on reported offenses. However, it does eliminate the hierarchy rule by counting all offenses in each incident. It is also beneficial in that it collects detailed data on the offenders, victims, locations, properties, and arrests on each single crime incident, thus offering insight into offenses that we do not currently have with the UCR.

Victimization Surveys Victimization surveys provide valuable information on the extent of sexual abuse. The National Crime Victimization Survey (NCVS), in particular, is the largest and most significant national survey in the United States and is central to our understanding of the "dark figure" of crime, or the extent to which crimes are underreported.

In order to better understand the magnitude of the underreporting of crime and the reasons why it is underreported, the Bureau of Justice Statistics began conducting an annual survey of approximately 49,000 households in 1972. The survey collects self-report data on all crimes against the household and individuals in the household who are over the age of 12. The NCVS finds that crime is severely underreported, with only about 37 percent of all crimes reported to the police. It has found that crime is underreported for numerous reasons, including that the offenses were personal (particularly domestic violence and sexual offenses), the victim believes that the police will not be able to do much about catching the offender, the victim does not trust the police, the victim fears that his or her own criminal behavior (for example, drug use) would be exposed, the victim fears that his or her reputation would be damaged, and the victim thinks the perpetrator will retaliate.

Like all sources of official statistical data, however, there are some drawbacks to victimization surveys. In particular, the reliability of self-reported data is questionable, and the NCVS does not provide a way to gather victimization information from young children who may be victims of abuse. Nonetheless, victimization surveys tell us the following in regard to race and ethnicity, age, and victim-offender relationship for victims aged 12 and older (Rennison, 2001; Rennison & Rand, 2003):

- *Race and Ethnicity* Though there are differences in victimization rates, there is no significant distinction between victims of sexual offenses on the basis of race and ethnicity. In 2002, Whites were victims of sexual offenses at a rate of .8 per 1000 in the population, Blacks were victimized at a rate of 2.5, and those of other races were victimized at a rate of 1.2. Additionally, Hispanics were victimized at a rate of .7 per 1000. The rate of victimization for Blacks increased from 2000, when the rate was 1.2 per 1000. At the same time, the rate of victimization for Whites decreased, from 1.1 per 1000.

- *Age* The highest rate of victimization for a sexual offense is with victims aged 16–19, whose rate of victimization in 2000 was 4.3 per 1000 and rose to 5.5 in 2002. In 2002, those at the next highest level of risk were aged 20–24 (at a rate of 2.9) and aged 12–15 (at a rate of 2.1). The NCVS does not collect data on victims under the age of 12, which would likely be a large percentage of the victim population based on arrest and conviction statistics.

- *Victim-Offender Relationship* It was more common for both male and female victims to be abused or assaulted by a nonstranger than a stranger. With male victims, 52 percent were abused by nonstrangers, all of whom were friends or acquaintances.[4] Female victims know the perpetrator in 69 percent of the cases, with the highest percentage of abusers (57 percent of all cases) being friends or acquaintances.

Another victimization survey on sexual abuse is the Minnesota Student Survey. This self-report survey was administered to 6th, 9th, and 12th grade students in Minnesota in 1989, 1992, 1995, 1998, and 2001, and more than 90 percent of students in these grades in Minnesota participated in the surveys each year. The survey contains two questions about sexual abuse, the results of which show a slight rise in abuse between 1989 and 1992, followed by a 22 percent drop from 1992 to 2001.

Social Service Data The best source of information for prevalence of child sexual abuse is the annual publication of the *Child Maltreatment Reports.* The National Child Abuse and Neglect Data System (NCANDS) of the federal Department of Health and Human Services has been collecting data on child sexual abuse based on incident-level reports from state child protective services. They summarize this information on allegations of abuse of minors under 18 in all states and have published it annually since 1992. The *Child Maltreatment Reports* define sexual abuse of a minor as any activity in which a perpetrator receives sexual gratification or financial benefit as the result of activities involving a child under the age of 18 (Child Maltreatment, 2001).

According to the annual *Child Maltreatment Reports,* there is a decline in sexual abuse of children from 1992 through 2001 in all but four reporting states. This further supports the findings from the Minnesota Student Victimization Survey, which shows a decrease in the same time period. Table 1.3 shows the state-by-state compilation of statistics for this 10-year period.

After analyzing NCANDS data from more than 40 states from 1992 to 2000, Finkelhor and Jones (2004) found that child protective services substantiated significantly fewer cases each year in this time period. While the number of substantiated cases in 1992 peaked at approximately 149,800, by the year 2000 the number of substantiated cases was approximately 89,355—a decline of 2–11 percent per year. The reason for this drop is debatable, including whether the reduction in substantiated cases is real or is simply a reflection of the changes in definitions of offenses and how the cases are handled by the states (Jones & Finkelhor, 2001; Jones, Finkelhor, & Kopiec, 2001). When taking into consideration all factors that may contribute to the reasons for the decline in substantiated cases, Finkelhor and Jones (2004) propose that the drop is at least partially attributable to a national decline in sexual abuse of children in this time period. The NCVS corroborates this information, showing that sex offenses against children aged 12–17 years declined 56 percent in the same time period.

Research Estimates

In the 1980s, there was a steep rise in the number of reports involving sexual offenses by acquaintances, whether in regard to child sexual abuse or rape. These allegations shattered the stereotyped images of sex offenders at the time, leading to further research of this population. Studies found that there was an increase in cases of date rape, rape in marriage, and incestuous relations—cases that would have largely gone unreported more than 20 years earlier for reasons of stigma, self-blame, fear of not being believed, or a desire to protect the friend or family member who committed the offense (Scully, 1990). Even today, those who are most

Table 1.3 Child Sexual Abuse Statistics (1992 and 2001)

State	Percentage Children Abused (1992)	Percentage Children Abused (2001)	Rate of Children Abused per 100,000 (1992)	Rate of Children Abused per 100,000 (2001)	Percentage Change Between 1992 and 2001
AL	0.43%	0.17%	427	174	−59.33%
AK	0.69%	0.78%	688	778	+13.19%
AZ	0.31%	0.02%	307	23	−92.40%
AR	0.31%	0.31%	307	310	+1.12%
CA	0.34%	0.11%	338	113	−66.58%
CO	0.22%	0.05%	220	48	−78.21%
CT	0.14%	0.06%	138	56	−59.16%
DE	0.12%	0.08%	116	82	−29.72%
DC	0.03%	0.10%	27	96	−252.80%
FL	0.28%	0.17%	283	171	−39.38%
GA	0.30%	0.10%	299	100	−66.61%
HI	0.10%	0.09%	101	92	−8.96%
ID	0.34%	0.08%	343	79	−77.04%
IL	0.18%	0.09%	178	85	−52.15%
IN	0.50%	0.27%	496	274	−44.76%
IA	0.19%	0.14%	193	141	−27.10%
KS	0.13%	0.14%	127	142	+11.61%
KY	0.27%	0.12%	271	116	−57.21%
LA	0.11%	0.07%	108	71	−34.28%
ME	0.21%	0.29%	209	292	+40.03%
MA	0.18%	0.07%	177	74	−58.04%
MI	0.10%	0.06%	102	64	−37.77%
MN	0.11%	0.07%	114	70	−38.51%
MS	0.25%	0.10%	246	97	−60.49%
MO	0.21%	0.16%	211	158	−25.18%

likely to serve prison sentences for sexual offenses are those who have raped strangers, used weapons, physically injured their victims, and committed other crimes in addition to the sexual offense (Grant & Terry, 2001; Scully, 1990). The majority of convicted sex offenders are not in prison or jail, as nearly two-thirds of the offenders serve their sentences in the community (Greenfeld, 1997).

Studies have found that sexual offending does not discriminate on the basis of age, race, ethnicity, socioeconomic status, educational level, or any other stable characteristics for either offenders or victims. Sex offenders, particularly those who abuse children, do not necessarily "age out" of their deviant behavior, as do many property offenders, and sex crimes are generally considered to be psychologically motivated offenses. Sexual offenders are often diagnosed with personality or mental disorders, particularly paraphilias[5] (Abel, Becker, & Cunningham-Rathner, 1984), and this makes them a unique population. Despite the heterogeneity in offenders and the etiology of their offending behavior, there are many similarities

Table 1.3 Child Sexual Abuse Statistics (1992 and 2001) (*continued*)

State	Percentage Children Abused (1992)	Percentage Children Abused (2001)	Rate of Children Abused per 100,000 (1992)	Rate of Children Abused per 100,000 (2001)	Percentage Change Between 1992 and 2001
MT	0.36%	0.13%	364	126	−65.50%
NE	0.17%	0.08%	166	85	−49.01%
NV	0.12%	0.04%	120	42	−65.25%
NH	0.10%	0.08%	104	75	−27.93%
NJ	0.09%	0.04%	87	36	−58.78%
NM	0.17%	0.09%	171	90	−47.41%
NY	0.16%	0.06%	157	64	−59.37%
NC	0.09%	0.06%	89	62	−30.26%
ND	0.13%	0.07%	127	70	−44.42%
OH	0.40%	0.27%	403	272	−32.56%
OK	0.14%	0.12%	138	117	−15.50%
OR	0.40%	0.11%	404	111	−72.53%
PA	0.15%	0.08%	153	80	−47.78%
RI	0.26%	0.08%	258	79	−69.48%
SC	0.20%	0.09%	197	89	−54.88%
SD	0.27%	0.08%	266	83	−68.67%
TN	0.23%	0.17%	229	166	−27.46%
TX	0.21%	0.11%	212	110	−48.12%
UT	0.38%	0.32%	382	317	−17.18%
VT	0.56%	0.29%	563	291	−48.41%
VA	0.15%	0.07%	152	68	−55.13%
WA	0.46%	0.03%	463	26	−94.30%
WI	0.54%	0.34%	542	335	−38.14%
WY	0.28%	0.08%	283	82	−70.92%

SOURCE: John Jay College (2004)

in the population as a whole. They tend to have poor social and relationship skills, most have had poor relationships with their parents, many abuse alcohol or drugs, and many were either physically and/or sexually abused as children.

It is difficult for researchers to ascertain a true assessment of the prevalence and incidence of sexual abuse, which refer, respectively, to the total number of cases of in a given population at a specific time and the rate of occurrence over a period of time. Individuals who are sexually abused by family members or acquaintances report the sexual abuse to the criminal justice system with the least frequency. Thus, most individuals who were sexually abused as children or were sexually abused as an adult by someone known to them do not report the abuse to criminal justice authorities.

Studies on the incidence of sexual abuse, which concentrate on estimating the number of new cases occurring over a particular period of time, gained greater urgency in the 1980s, indicating that the scope of sexual victimization is extensive.

Studies often show varying levels of prevalence of sexual abuse. Some research statistics show that:

- 1 in 4 women is likely to be raped, and 1 in 3 girls is likely to be abused by an adult (Russell, 1984).

- 15.3 percent of females and 5.9 percent of males experience some form of sexual assault in their lifetimes (Moore, Nord, & Peterson, 1989).

- 12.8 percent of females and 4.3 percent of males reported a history of sexual abuse during childhood (MacMillan et al., 1997).

- 27 percent of females and 16 percent of males disclosed a history of childhood sexual abuse; 42 percent of the males were likely to never have disclosed the experience to anyone, whereas 33 percent of the females never disclosed (Finkelhor, Hotaling, Lewis, & Smith, 1990).

- Based on a meta-analysis, the overall prevalence of sexual abuse of male children is 13 percent and female children is between 30 and 40 percent (Bolen & Scannapieco, 1999).

- The lifetime prevalence of sexual assault among 12–17-year-olds, across racial and ethnic groups, is 8.1 percent, and 74 percent of child victims know the abuser well (Snyder, 2000).

- Only 5.7 percent of the incidents of sexual abuse were reported to the police; 26 percent of the incidents were not disclosed to anyone prior to the study (Boney-McCoy & Finkelhor, 1995).

- 33 percent of all victims of sexual assault reported to law enforcement agencies were aged 12–17 when abused and 34 percent were under the age of 12. The primary types of offenses committed against them are forcible fondling (84 percent), forcible sodomy (79 percent), and sexual assault with an object (75 percent) (Langan & Harlow, 1992).

Official statistics show us that rates of sexual abuse have declined in the past decade. Research corroborates this, and indicates that there has been a simultaneous reduction in related variables: most importantly, domestic violence incidents among intimate adults, and pregnancies and births among teenagers. It is not clear what has caused this reduction in sexual abuse or related factors, though one theory is the increased sanctions for sexual abuse offenders. Finkelhor and Ormrod (2001) show that between 1991 and 1997, the number of child sexual abusers in prison increased 39 percent. Nonetheless, there are likely many factors that relate to the drop in reporting of sexual abuse.

REPORTING SEXUAL ABUSE

Crime is underreported. Sexual crime is the most underreported offense, though more individuals reported their victimization to the police in 2000 than in any year of the previous decade (Hart & Rennison, 2003). In order to understand how accurate statistics are on sexual offending, it is important to understand who reports, why, after how long, and with what accuracy.

The NCVS tells us the following about individuals over the age of 12 who reported their sexual assaults to the police from 1992 to 2000 (Hart & Rennison, 2003: 5):

- *Gender* Victims were more likely to report sexual offenses to the police if the offender was male (32 percent) than female (13 percent).

- *Race* Victims were more likely to report sexual offenses if the offender was Black (39 percent) than White (29 percent).

- *Age* Victims reported sexual offenses to the police 40 percent of the time when the perpetrator was 12–14 years of age, the highest percentage of reporting in any age category.

- *Number of Perpetrators* Victims were more likely to report the sexual abuse to police if there were two perpetrators (44 percent) rather than one perpetrator (33 percent).

- *Victim-Offender Relationship* Victims were more likely to report sexual offenses committed by strangers (41 percent) than nonstrangers (27 percent).

- *Use of Weapons* Victims were more likely to report a sexual offense if the perpetrator had a weapon present during the offense (49 percent), particularly a firearm (62 percent), than if no weapon was present (28 percent).

- *Reasons for Reporting* The most common reason for victims to report sexual offenses to the police was to prevent future violence. The most common reason for victims *not* to report sexual offenses to the police was because of privacy issues.

Empirical research supports the findings in the NCVS, though the benefit of such studies is that they can also include victims under the age of 12. Child sexual abuse is the least reported of sexual offenses. Studies that analyze reporting trends of child sexual abuse all indicate that a high percentage of victims who report their abuse to authorities do so many years after the abuse occurred, and many do not ever disclose. The most common studies conducted to analyze reporting trends on child sexual abuse are adult retrospective studies. Like the NCVS, these studies found that the process of disclosing childhood sexual abuse depends on numerous variables:

- Only one-third of the victims reported the abuse to authorities before age 18, and the average age of disclosure was 25.9 (Roesler & Weissmann-Wind, 1994, in a study of 228 adult female victims of child sexual abuse by adult—primarily male—family members).

- The average age of child sexual abuse victims was just over 8, and approximately 41 percent of victims disclosed the abuse at the time it occurred (Arata, 1998, in a study of 204 female victims of child sexual abuse).

- The average age at the time of the child sexual abuse was 10, and 64 percent of the victims disclosed the abuse as adults (Lamb & Edgar-Smith,

1994, in a study of 45 adult female and 12 adult male child sexual abuse victims).

- The majority of victims waited more than 8 years to report their child-hood sexual abuse (Smith, Letourneau, & Saunders, 2000, in a study assessing disclosure rates of females raped when they were children).

- Disclosure of child sexual abuse by minors may be spontaneous or prompted, and many children and adolescents need assistance with disclosure (DeVoe & Coulborn-Faller, 1999).

- Disclosure of childhood sexual abuse may be purposeful or accidental, with accidental disclosure more common in preschool-aged children and purposeful disclosure more common in adolescents (Sorenson & Snow, 1991).

- A significant factor in whether a child reports sexual abuse and the manner in which the abuse is reported is the potential for the person to whom they are disclosing to believe their report on the abuse (Lawson & Chaffin, 1992).

- Approximately half of the children who recant their reports of childhood sexual abuse do so under pressure from their guardians (Bradley & Wood, 1996).

The Child Sexual Abuse Accommodation Syndrome, a model of reporting outlined by Summit (1983) that consists of five components, suggests reasons why child sexual abuse victims delay disclosure. First, the abuse is usually carried out in privacy, and the abuser encourages secrecy. Second, because children are obedient to adults, they are helpless and maintain the secrecy that the adult encourages. Third, the child becomes entrenched in the abusive situation, begins to feel guilt and responsibility for the abuse, and continues to accommodate the perpetrator. Fourth, the victim delays disclosure because of the promise of secrecy and feelings of guilt and shame. Finally, after delayed disclosure, the victim often retracts the report due to disbelief about the abuse by those trusted by the victim.

In addition to a general delay in disclosure of child sexual abuse, many victims report the abuse in stages. Sorenson and Snow (1991) identified four stages of disclosure in their study of 630 victims of child sexual abuse: denial (experienced by 72 percent of the victims in their sample); disclosure (78 percent of the victims progressed from tentative to active disclosure); recantation (experienced by 22 percent of the victims); and reaffirmation (93 percent of those who recanted later confirmed their original reports).

Adult retroactive studies not only help us to understand the process of disclosure, but also explain the reasons that victims disclose. The most significant variables that seem to hinder disclosure of abuse are the age of the victim at the time the abuse occurred, the victim–perpetrator relationship, the gender and cognitive or developmental abilities of the victim, the type of sexual abuse that occurred, and the chance of negative consequences related to disclosure.

The gender of the victim has an impact on the disclosure of sexual abuse, as females are more likely both as children and as adults to report sexual abuse than are males (DeVoe & Coulborn-Faller, 1999; Gries, Goh, & Cavanaugh, 1996; Lamb & Edgar-Smith, 1994; Walrath, Ybarra, & Holden, 2003). Paine and Hanson (2002) do show, however, that although gender is an important factor in the decision to report abuse, victim-perpetrator relationship is the most important factor in determining whether a victim of child sexual abuse will eventually disclose.

Several studies indicate that a victim is less likely to report or delay the report of child sexual abuse if the perpetrator is well known to the child (Arata, 1998; DiPetro, 2003; Hanson, Saunders, Saunders, Kilpatrick, & Best, 1999; Smith et al., 2000; Wyatt & Newcomb, 1990). This relationship is most significant if the perpetrator is a relative or stepparent, as Arata (1998) showed that 73 percent of victims did not disclose the abuse in such a situation; 70 percent of the time victims did not report when the perpetrator was an acquaintance. The desire not to report familial sexual abuse is compounded if the victim feels responsible for the abuse, and in such cases the victim often waits longer to disclose the abuse (Goodman-Brown, Edelstein et al., 2003; Roesler & Weissmann-Wind, 1994).

In order to report the abuse in a timely manner, it appears that children need to feel as though they will be supported by the person to whom they disclose the abuse. Children who believe that they will not be supported when they disclose abuse will wait longer to report, often until adulthood when they can choose a person they trust to support them (Lamb & Edgar-Smith, 1994). Shame and guilt also appear to play a role in the decision about disclosure. Older children who are able to understand and anticipate social consequences of sexual abuse are less likely to report the abuse than are younger children (Campis, Hebden-Curtis, & DeMaso, 1993; Keary & Fitzpatrick, 1994).

Some researchers have found that children are less likely to report sexual abuse if the abuse is severe (Arata, 1998; DiPietro et al., 1998; Gries, Goh, & Cavanaugh, 1996) or they fear further harm as a result of their disclosure (Berliner & Conte, 1995; Roesler & Weissmann-Wind, 1994; Sorenson & Snow, 1991). Sorenson and Snow (1991) found that victims who fear further reprisals will not report the abuse if the perpetrator is present or the disclosure could lead to further abuse, and Roesler and Weissmann-Wind (1994) found that one-third of the victims they spoke to delayed reporting until adulthood because they feared for their safety. Hanson et al. (1999), on the other hand, found the inverse relationship true of severity of abuse and disclosure. They discovered that in a sample of women who were raped when they were children, the more severe the sexual abuse the more likely the victims were to report the abuse sooner.

Telescoping

When victims report their crimes or complete victimization surveys long after the crime occurred, they often remember the crime as occurring earlier or later than it actually happened (Sudman & Bradburn, 1973, as cited in Schneider & Sumi, 1981). This phenomenon is called *telescoping*, and it occurs in two forms:

forward telescoping, or recalling an event that occurred prior to the reporting period in question, and *backward telescoping*, which is recalling an event that occurred after the reporting period. Telescoping is not unique to crime victims. All individuals "telescope" events that they recall long after the events happened. However, telescoping events of victimization creates challenges for researchers trying to understand criminal statistics (Schneider & Sumi, 1981). Accurate crime statistics are deemed essential by government agencies, and as such controlling for temporal telescoping is imperative to attain analyzable, accurate data.

In the 1970s, many researchers began conducting studies on telescoping to better understand its effect on crime statistics. Not surprisingly, researchers found that memory disorientations, including telescoping, occur more often in older respondents, particularly those over age 55 (Sudman & Bradburn, 1974, as cited in Gottfredson & Hindelang, 1977). Researchers also found that forward telescoping is more common than backward telescoping (Schneider & Sumi, 1981) and that the more prominent the event, the more likely the person is to forward telescope (Neter & Waksberg, 1964, as cited in Gottfredson & Hindelang, 1977). The problem with this, in terms of crime statistics, is that individuals are going to report crime as occurring more recently than it did. Another issue is that victims of nonreported events tend to telescope more than victims who report events of victimization to the police (Schneider & Sumi, 1971), thus creating a potential flaw with chronological information attained in victimization surveys.

Researchers are also interested in the prevalence of telescoping, and have conducted many surveys to determine the scope of the problem. Skogan (1975, as cited in Levine, 1976) found in a Washington, D.C., pilot survey that 17 percent of victimizations reported by respondents actually occurred prior to the six-month period specified. Another study revealed that 22 percent of larcenies reported by respondents occurred prior to the reference period mandated by the survey (Schneider & Sumi, 1981). Murphy and Cowan (1976, as cited in Schneider & Sumi, 1981), claim that crime victimization interviews have shown that victimization can be overstated by 40–60 percent in some surveys.

One factor that influences the accuracy of interviews is whether the survey is bounded or unbounded. Studies have demonstrated that *bounded interviews*, or interviews conducted after a previous visit with the respondent has occurred, show a much higher accuracy level in data gathered. Those in *unbounded interviews*, or those where there was no previous visit with the respondent, tend to report nearly twice as much crime as respondents of bounded interviews in the same time period (Turner, 1972, as cited in Skogan, 1975: 25).

CHAPTER SUMMARY

- Sexual offenses vary by type, degree of severity, class of offense, and length of sanction. Additionally, they can be contact offenses (where touching occurs), noncontact offenses (where only viewing or talking occurs), and pornographic offenses (where movies or pictures are involved).

- Statistics on the prevalence of sexual offending are derived from three types of data: arrest and conviction rates, victimization surveys, and empirical studies. It is difficult, if not impossible, to ascertain the true prevalence of offending in the population. Many researchers and research organizations have calculated rates of victimization.

- Rates of victimization have decreased in the past decade. The best estimates of victimization rates are that 1 in 4 women and 1 in 7 men are sexually abused in their lifetimes.

- Victims of child sexual abuse often wait many years to report the abusive behavior. The length of delay depends on many factors, including victim-offender relationship, severity of the abuse, cognitive and developmental variables, fear of negative consequences, and gender of the victim.

- After a delay in reporting, many victims suffer from "telescoping," and do not report the time of the abuse correctly.

DISCUSSION QUESTIONS

1. What are the best sources of statistical information on sexual offenses and offenders? How do these sources differ?

2. What are the most significant problems in determining the true prevalence of sexual abuse?

3. For which sexual offenses are criminal justice statistics the most accurate, and for which are they the least accurate? Why?

4. How accurate are reports of sexual offending many years after the abuse occurred? What factors influence the accuracy?

5. What factors influence the likelihood of reporting sexual abuse?

NOTES

1. Alabama, Arizona, Arkansas, California, Florida, Georgia, Idaho, Kansas, Kentucky, Louisiana, Maryland, Massachusetts, Michigan, Minnesota, Mississippi, Montana, Nevada, New York, North Carolina, Oklahoma, Rhode Island, South Carolina, Tennessee, Texas, Utah, and Virginia.

2. *Registerable offenses* are those for which an offender must register his or her name and address with the police. Registration and community notification laws are discussed in Chapter 10.

3. *Cleared by arrest* means that an arrest has been made and the case is turned over to the prosecutor; the proportion of crimes cleared by arrest is the *clearance rate.*

Exceptional means refers to those cases in which the perpetrator is known but cannot be arrested (for example, he was killed during the commission of the offense).

4. This, however, was based on a sample of fewer than 10 cases, so the figure may not be generalizable.

5. *Paraphilias* are recurrent, intense, sexually arousing fantasies or urges involving either nonhuman objects, suffering or humiliation of oneself or one's partner, children or other nonconsenting persons (American Psychiatric Association, 1994: 522–523). Paraphilias are discussed at length in Chapter 5.

2

Historical Perspectives on Sexual Behavior

As explained in Chapter 1, the concept of "normal" sexual behavior is a socially constructed reality that is continually adapting (Jenkins, 1998). Actions that are defined as sexual offenses vary across religions, cultures, nations, and even states. Additionally, these definitions change over time, adapting to the prevailing social norms. There are few objective standards for acceptable sexual behavior, and sexual mores are largely culture bound (West, 1987: 2). Prohibition or tolerance of various sexual acts depends largely upon the political and social ideologies of the day. Nothing makes this clearer than an evaluation of ancient cultures, many of which promoted acts that have intermittently been considered taboo, including homosexuality, bestiality, sado-masochism, adultery, masturbation, and pederasty.

HISTORICAL, RELIGIOUS, AND CULTURAL PERSPECTIVES OF SEXUAL BEHAVIOR

The sexual activity of Greek and Mediterranean cultures has been extensively detailed in art, literature, poetry, mythology, and theater (Dover, 1978). Though there was no word equivalent to *homosexuality* until 1869,[1] same-sex conduct was displayed in visual arts as early as the sixth century B.C. One of the most prominent philosophical depictions of homosexual relationships occurs in Plato's *Symposium*, which contemplates the nature of a relationship between

Socrates and a young, attractive male. Artistic depictions of transgenerational homosexuality were not uncommon, and many vases and murals show scenes of older males touching the genitals of nude young males (Dover, 1978). Men also wrote love poems about younger boys, particularly those in late adolescence, and sexual activity between older men and younger boys was acceptable and considered beautiful (Breiner, 1990).

Though same-sex relationships occurred regularly in Greece, the men were not considered homosexual in the sense of the word today. It was acceptable for men to have relationships with both men and women, and same-sex relationships were common to supplement the sexual relationship with a wife. Women were not highly respected and were typically viewed as "mad, hysterical, and possibly dangerous and destructive to men" (Breiner, 1990: 41). Marriage was considered a necessity for procreation, though sexuality was not linked to marriage and sexual pleasure could thus be received outside the marriage (Mondimore, 1996). The ideal relationship was that of an active older male and a passive younger male (Breiner, 1990; Mondimore, 1996), evident even in Greek mythology, which depicts Zeus as attracted to a young boy of legendary beauty (Dover, 1978).

Homosexuality was institutionalized into the Greek culture, and this was apparent by the arts and practices of the people. Plays, particularly comedies, were very sexual in nature and often included overt sexual acts on stage. There were also orgies to the gods that included repeated sexual acts and often the sacrifice of a child (Breiner, 1990). It was common for young boys to be sold into slavery, and socially prominent men would have slaves for their own sexual use. Though the majority of sexual behavior revolved around males, there were also women who were involved in homosexual practices. The most famous of these is Sappho, resident of Lesbos (from which the word *lesbian* is derived), who wrote love poems to women.

The Greek culture was not the only one to promote homosexuality, pederasty, and the importance of the male figure in society. Boy brothels were also found in Rome, and the Romans believed that sexual relationships with young boys would aid their mental development (Breiner, 1990). Although the Greeks viewed man-boy relationships as beautiful, Romans often subjected boys (particularly slave boys) to violence and abuse. Sadistic activities were enjoyed for entertainment, and this included watching women and children being raped and having sex with animals.

The Egyptians were similar to the Greeks and Romans in their admiration of the male figure and their acceptance of homosexuality. Other sexual behaviors common to the Egyptians included polygamy, incest, sexual play among children, and sexual touching of children by adults (Breiner, 1990). Children participated in sexual play at an early age, and it was expected that this would teach them about sexual behavior. By A.D. 200, brother-sister marriages were common, especially among those in the middle class. Though intercourse between adults and children was considered taboo, adults commonly sucked the penises of boys in order to prepare them for sexual activity later. Sexual activity among adults was very open in Egypt, and the pharaoh in particular was expected to partake in extensive sexual activity with his wives and other women while traveling (Breiner, 1990).

Open sexual activity continued in such a fashion until the early Middle Ages, at which time homosexuality became a crime in Europe. This shift in moral thinking about sexuality was influenced by the church, and all sexual acts that were for enjoyment rather than procreation were considered to be sinful (Holmes, 1991; Mondimore, 1996). Sodomy was the catchall category of all "unnatural" sexual acts, including masturbation, bestiality, anal intercourse, fellatio, and heterosexual intercourse in anything other than the missionary position. By the 14th century, sodomy was illegal throughout Europe, and perpetrators could potentially be sentenced to death. Homosexual acts were particularly discouraged, and in 1326 King Edward II of England was brutally killed because of his relationship with another male (Mondimore, 1996: 25). Though the church continued to have an influence on sexual mores for several hundred years, transgenerational sexual acts became socially acceptable in 16th- and 17th-century Europe. It was common for adults to touch and fondle the genitals of their prepubertal children, though the touching stopped when the children developed into adolescence (Breiner, 1990; Jenkins, 1998).

In the 18th century, many children were sent to workhouses and brothels and were victims of murder, assault, or rape. With this exception, there was little danger from adult offenders outside the home. The main focus on sexual behavior continued to be within the home, and separate courts were developed for criminal and moral offenses. Although acts such as incest had been accepted in ancient cultures, the church declared incest an ecclesiastical offense, and incestuous marriages were invalidated (Thomas, 2000). Moral offenses, such as masturbation, were brought before the church courts throughout the beginning of the 20th century. Other types of behavior that were considered more serious offenses—including homosexuality, bestiality, and sexual intercourse with prepubescent children—were brought before the criminal courts and were punishable by sentences as severe as death.

Though the Catholic Church dominated regulation of sexual behavior in Europe, other religions and cultures differed in their sexual mores. Polygamy was (and in some cultures, still is) regularly practiced by Muslims, Mormons, and Hebrews. Hebrew families had strict puritan regulations on sexual behavior, and, like the Catholic church, considered homosexuality an abhorrence (Breiner, 1990). Masturbation was prohibited; for young men this was equivalent to premarital sex, and a married man who masturbated was guilty of adultery. Men were even discouraged from touching their genitals while urinating, as this was thought to encourage masturbation (Breiner, 1990).

In opposition to the puritan sexual mores of various religious sects, Native American and primitive cultures often practiced sexual activities similar to those of the ancient Greeks. There was evidence of homosexuality in both North and South American tribes, where sexual play among children was also tolerated. Many tribes believed that sexual activity between children and adults was a necessary aspect of sexual development, and that a boy would have to be sexually intimate with an older man in order to develop masculine qualities (Mondimore, 1996). African tribes had similar rituals, and female circumcision was (and is still) common to many African cultures. That such acts are regularly practiced in other cultures but are condemned in Western societies shows the influence of social ideologies on accepted sexual behavior. There is no objective standard for the types of sexual behavior that should be prohibited, and sexual mores have changed drastically even throughout the previous century.

CHANGING PERCEPTIONS OF DEVIANT SEXUAL BEHAVIOR: THE 20TH CENTURY

The beginning of the 20th century witnessed a new philosophy of sexual morality. It was at that time, during the Progressive Era, that concerns began emerging about a number of issues, including the sexual behavior of women and the abuse of children. With the Industrial Revolution causing vast urban growth, adolescent women began entering the workplace in large numbers for the first time. Subsequently, they began participating in social activities outside of their local neighborhoods, experiencing unprecedented freedom from their families (Odem, 1995). It was this change in social structure that instigated the modification of "age of consent" laws for sexual behavior, and it was at this time that the courts began to regularly monitor sexual behavior.

Researchers during the Progressive Era began focusing on serious sexual offenders, classifying their behavior as a medical problem. Many sexual deviants were labeled pathological or insane and were sent to mental hospitals, where they were treated until they regained their sanity. Shortly thereafter, researchers began to study the possible correlation between hormones and sexually deviant behavior, hypothesizing that organic treatments were necessary in order to control such behavior. Research in the 1950s began to show that sexually deviant behavior might not be simply the result of hormones or psychopathology; the underlying problems might be behavioral in nature. There continued to be a lack of understanding about the complexities of sexually deviant behavior, however, and it was only in the 1970s that researchers began to link sexually deviant behavior to social problems. Researchers at this time began to take into consideration the effects of cognitive processes on the behavior of sexual deviants, and research continues in this area today.[2]

Whether researchers looked at those who committed deviant sexual acts as having medical, psychological, or moral problems, it was clear that the population of sexual deviants was unique. Because the motivation of their behavior was not—and is still not—clearly understood, reactions to their behavior have been erratic. Despite the various therapies and legislative acts that have been imposed upon those who commit sexual offenses, the reactions to this population are distinctly cyclical. Figure 2.1 outlines the cycle of legislative proposals, showing how policies regarding sexual offenders are implemented after waves of emotionally charged, notorious sex crimes occur.

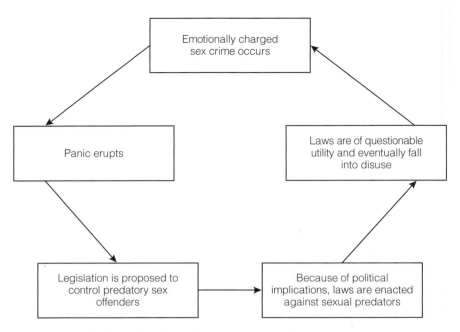

FIGURE 2.1 Cycle of moral panic and reactions to sex offenders

Though new information about sexual offenders was continually attained throughout the century, societal reaction to sexually deviant behavior has shown a repetitive pattern. At three distinct points in the 20th century, there were public outcries to control sexual "fiends," "psychopaths," and "predators." It was the highly publicized cases of sexual abuse, or, more specifically, cases involving the sexual murder of children by strangers, that largely influenced such public reactions (Jenkins, 1998). In between these peaks of interest in stranger attacks, little public attention was paid to sexual abuse. It was considered to be a problem within the family that was not shared with the public or the courts. Figure 2.2 shows the public perception of sexual abuse and abusers throughout the century.

In order to understand legislative reactions to sex offenders today, it is essential to observe the influence of research, political ideologies, and societal reactions to deviant sexual behavior throughout the 20th century.

1885–1935: The First Wave of Panic

Prior to the 1880s, little was known about those who committed "deviant" sexual acts. It was Richard von Krafft-Ebing (1886/1965) who, in his ground-breaking book *Psychopathia Sexualis*, first claimed that deviant sexual acts were the result of psychopathological problems in the individual. He attributed various sexual disorders to psychological abnormalities, stating that the sexual disorders were a permanent part of a person's character and could not be changed. His book contains case studies of individuals—both male and female—who experienced various sexual disorders and paraphilias, though a significant portion of the book focuses on homosexual activity. Krafft-Ebing said that

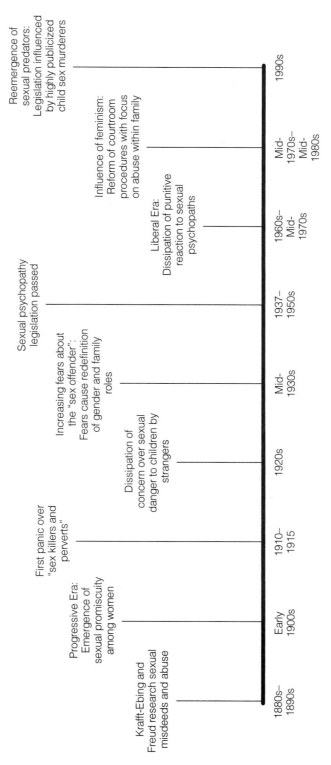

FIGURE 2.2 Changing concepts of sexuality and deviant sexual behavior in the 20th century

SOURCE: Jenkins (1998)

homosexuality could be blamed on hereditary factors, or it could be acquired from the practice of masturbation. He concluded that sexual deviants, particularly homosexuals, were mentally ill, pathological, loathsome, and a threat to social hygiene. He published 12 editions of *Psychopathia Sexualis,* and his work opened floodgates of research on sexual behavior.

Two other influential researchers at the time were Havelock Ellis and Sigmund Freud. Ellis (1899/1942) wrote a two-volume, multipart book on the psychology of sex, in which he discussed issues ranging from menstruation to marriage to sexual morality. He recognized that a changing social environment defines sexual morality, and that standards of morality are continually changing. His opinion differs from Krafft-Ebing's on the issues of homosexuality and masturbation, as he does not consider sexual deviates to be mentally ill or pathological. Though Ellis did not consider homosexuals to be "normal," he did not think there was reason to try to cure them. He did not believe that homosexuals who went through treatment for their deviation could be cured, and with this Freud agreed. Like Krafft-Ebing, Freud believed that deviant sexual behavior was rooted in psychopathology, and he attributed sexual deviation to character disorders in a 1905 essay on neuroses (Freud, 1953). He explained that "neurotic symptoms represent the patient's sexual activity," with more complex symptoms representing the patient's fantasies (Freud, 1959: 281). Much of his research focused on the sexual activity among family members; he stated that incest was a common occurrence and was consequently the root of problems for many girls.

While researchers were focusing on the causes of sexually deviant behavior, in the 1880s the public began receiving information about sexual immorality from social groups. The Women's Christian Temperance Union (WCTU)—a group primarily consisting of white, middle-class women—began lobbying vigorously in 1889 for the modification of age of consent laws in the United States (Odem, 1995: 8). They wanted to raise the age of consent from 10 to 18,[3] claiming that "male vice and exploitation were responsible for the moral ruin of young women and girls" (Odem, 1995: 16). Though it was true that some men were taking advantage of young working-class girls, many of the young women themselves were acting promiscuously. The number of women working in factories and other industrial centers nearly tripled from the 1880s to 1910, and working-class women began participating in new social activities outside the home and local neighborhoods. The purity reformers of the WCTU acknowledged the need to protect the sexual autonomy of these women, saving them from "male seducers" who would lead them into vices such as prostitution (Odem, 1995: 18). Their campaign literature highlighted the increasing frequency of sexual attacks upon women and young girls, and they called for legislative changes in the punishment for these crimes (Odem, 1995: 9).

The legislative changes they were seeking did materialize, and by 1920 the age of consent was 16 or 18 in nearly every state.[4] It was not just the religious moral reformers who were concerned about sexual activity during this era, however. While they were waging a campaign against "white slavery," a general panic was rising about sex "fiends" and "perverts" who were preying on children. It was becoming apparent in the larger cities, particularly New York, that child prostitution was rampant among both boys and girls. The number of brothels that would prostitute effeminate boys increased, and they were frequented by some of the more respectable men in the cities. The moral vicissitude was brought about in part by the spreading of venereal diseases, syphilis and gonorrhea in particular, by homosexuals and pedophiles, whose perversions were under scrutiny at this time (Jenkins, 1998: 27).

It was between the years of 1910 and 1915 that the United States reached its first retributive climax against sexual offenders. This was largely the result of a rise during this time period in sex-related child homicides, many of which were attributed to serial killers. There were series of murders in New York City, Colorado, North Dakota, Alabama, Washington, and Atlanta (Jenkins, 1998: 36). The media and the police managed to create a panic in the public by defining the "Jack the Rippers" as intelligent, manipulative criminals who were easily able to elude detection. In an effort to reduce serious sex crimes, police intervention increased for all sexual offenders who committed offenses in public—namely, homosexuals and other public "nuisances"—whereas there was a dearth of intervention for incest offenders.

During this five-year period, a number of factors influenced legislation and research on sexual offenders. Indeterminate sentences were introduced for serious offenders in most states, and these nearly always affected sex offenders. There was a move toward positivism—the belief that people are social beings who want to conform, but are compelled to commit offences for reasons beyond their control—that came simultaneously with increasing research from European academics and increasing media coverage on the problem of deviant behavior. Because the focus of criminological research at this time was primarily biological and physiological, such as with the newly translated research of Cesare Lombroso (the Italian "father of scientific criminology" who studied biological and physiological theories of crime in the 19th century), remedies for deviant sexual behavior were also physiological. The concept of eugenics, which declared that some people were genetically unfit and should therefore not procreate, was a popular one. Among those fitting this description were sex offenders, and the practice of sterilization was common. In addition to sterilization, surgical castration was a method used to reduce the sexual drive of, and therefore the number of offenses committed by, sexual criminals. At the time, the concept of eugenics was unquestioned, and the sterilization of habitual criminals was allowed until 1942, when it was declared unconstitutional in the case of *Skinner v. Oklahoma* (1942). It was only at this time that the science of hereditary criminality was seriously questioned.

The panic over sexual killers subsided in the 1920s. The reasons for this were numerous. First, the focus began to turn away from stranger assaults and toward child molestation and incest. The high amount of venereal disease among children was still questioned, though it was attributed largely to child abuse by relatives or to prostitution rather than to rape. Second, by 1917 the WCTU had essentially completed its campaign to save women and children for a life of social purity. They had, by this time, achieved their main goals: women's suffrage and an increased age of consent. Third, by the 1930s issues other than sexual offenses became more topical in the media; namely, organized crime and Prohibition. Fourth, the focus of criminologists and sociologists was shifting, and research focused largely on issues in policing (corruption, brutality), organized crime, and juvenile delinquency (Jenkins, 1998: 46). The trend of medicalizing criminal acts did not diminish in the 1920s, however. Research on incarcerated offenders to determine the levels of psychopathy in criminals increased. It was this trend that led to the hospitalization of sexual offenders in the 1930s.

1936–1976: The Rise of the Sexual Psychopath

As had happened at the beginning of the century, an awareness of stranger sex crimes during the 1930s led to new legislation for sexual offenders. Child murderers such as Albert Fish permeated the media coverage in the mid-1930s. He committed numerous assaults, sexual offenses, and murders against children, culminating in the mutilation and cannibalism of a 12-year-old boy. He was not only a sexual killer, but also a sexual deviant. He practiced infibulation, which is the practice of fastening by ring, clasp, or stitches the foreskin in boys (or the labia majora in girls) in order to prevent sexual intercourse, and upon his execution it was realized that he had more than two dozen piercings in his genital area (Holmes, 1991: 61). Though his offenses were indeed horrific, recidivist offenders such as Fish were atypical. The number of arrests for sexual offenders increased dramatically in the late 1930s, but this was due not as much to an increase in sexual offenses as it was to a change in law enforcement policies (Karpman, 1954). The police in most large cities began to crack down on minor sexual offenses, such as homosexuality and frotteurism (the sexual urge to touch or rub another person) (Tappan, 1950). Though the media fueled the idea that the nation was overrun by sex crimes, this was based more on hysteria than fact. For instance, New York City was noted as having a particularly large population of sexual criminals, yet the majority of arrests were for either consensual acts or misdemeanors. Arrests for sodomy more than doubled there from 1932 to 1938, because officers were required to pick up all those known to commit deviant acts, and the suddenly high level of homosexual activity in the subway became known as a "queer threat" (Jenkins, 1998). Despite the high number of minor offenses, the focus of political and media attention was on the relatively rare habitual sex offender. This, combined with the emerging physiological theories of criminology, created a new label for sex offenders in 1937: "sexual psychopaths."

Criminal sanctions alone were not considered sufficient to incapacitate recidivist offenders. Thus, in an effort to skirt the criminal system, sexual psychopathy legislation was initiated to civilly commit habitual sexual criminals, or Mentally Disordered Sex Offenders (MDSOs). Michigan was the first state to pass a psychopathy law in 1937, and 28 other states followed suit over the next 50 years (Schwartz, 1999: 4–3). Michigan's law, like those that followed, allowed for the commitment of sexual "degenerates" or "perverts" if they had mental disorders and posed a threat to the public. Statutes were passed on the principle that sexual psychopathy was a disorder that could be diagnosed and treated, and violent sexual predators would remain civilly committed in mental institutions until they were "cured" (Alexander, 1993). The premise of the legislation was ostensibly therapeutic, yet the result was primarily retributive. The commitment process itself was grossly subjective, and those who were committed remained in hospital for many years.

There was no consensus for the definition of sexual psychopathy, and it differed from state to state (Tappan, 1950). In California, the offender would have had an "utter lack of power to control his impulses," yet an offender in Iowa had only to have the "criminal propensities towards the commission of sex offences" (Grubin & Prentky, 1993: 383). The standard necessary to commit sexual psychopaths was twofold: there had to be proof that the individuals suffered from a mental illness and that they were a danger to themselves or others. Dangerousness was a subjective standard, and because it could not be predicted with any sense of accuracy, commitment standards were questionable (Sutherland, 1950). Civil commitment replaced criminal incarceration, and the critical factor in commitment was that it was not punishment but rather treatment. Therefore, individuals who remained dangerous but not mentally ill were no longer supposed to be confined.

That all sex offenders were a public threat was a concept promoted at this time by various persons with public influence. The media promoted the image of the serious sex fiend through newspaper articles and magazines. The police and the Federal Bureau of Investigation (FBI) were concerned with the inability of the criminal system to retain these sex fiends in the prison system, focusing specifically on two factors: the escalation of offending behavior and the use of parole. Offenses such as exhibitionism did not warrant severe sentences, yet this was seen as a gateway action into more serious deviant acts. FBI Director J. Edgar Hoover publicized his opinions during the 1930s and 1940s by describing "degenerate sex offenders" as one of the most severe problems facing children, despite the relatively low crime rate at that time (Jenkins, 1998). The FBI warned families of a looming "stranger danger"; these warnings continued through the 1960s. Parole was considered one source of recidivism, as many of the child sexual killers were repeat offenders who had been released from prison early, on parole. Politicians, too, were using the public's fears about sex crimes to promote their own campaigns. In Minnesota, for example, a young girl went missing in 1938 and was allegedly kidnapped, molested, and killed by a "sexual pervert," though her body was never found. One gubernatorial candidate claimed that he would protect the community from such "unfortunate but dangerous wretches" should he be elected, and, upon his election, sexual psychopathy laws were passed unanimously in 1939 (Robson, 1999: 2).

The use of civil commitment under sexual psychopath laws increased throughout the 1940s and early 1950s. It was not just sex offenders who were subject to adverse public reactions at this time, however. Mental hospitals had lax commitment standards for all those perceived as a social threat. The population of state hospitals increased drastically, largely with those civilly committed due to feeblemindedness or mental illnesses that deemed them a danger to society. States were vague about the types of sexual offenses that could result in the label of sexual psychopath, and some statutes included behaviors such as peeping, lewdness, and impairing morals. Both felonies and misdemeanors could result in commitment, as well as both forced and statutory offenses (for example, statutory rape, which is an offense only because of the age of the victim).

At the height of the panic over sexual psychopaths, some researchers were divided on the issue of civil commitment. For instance, Karpman (1954: 38) stated that sexual offenders were not a particularly vicious group of individuals and there was little truth to the supposition that minor offenses escalate to more serious deviant behavior. Yet he also supported indefinite commitment for sexual psychopaths to hospitals for study and treatment until such a time that they were no longer a risk to the community (Karpman, 1954: 225). Homosexual activity was still a socially unacceptable sexual alternative, and some researchers linked homosexuals and pedophiles in terms of their "perverse" sexual interests. There was said to be an inevitable connection between an attraction to one's own gender and children, both showing an "arrested psychosexual development" (Jenkins, 1998: 62). But by the late 1940s, many researchers began to oppose the "stranger danger" belief, citing exaggerated claims of sexually related homicides (Sutherland, 1950). Most researchers opposed the idea of civil commitment for sexual psychopaths, believing—correctly—that such laws would result in the overcommitment of minor offenders.

One researcher published a report on the problems of sexual psychopathy statutes, challenging the validity of the statutes due to, at the most basic level, the erroneous views about sex offenders that led to the legislation (Tappan, 1950). He points out 10 primary fallacies concerning the sex offender (pp. 13–16), strikingly applicable to the myths prevalent today:

1. Sex offenders are not usually homicidal sex fiends, and most are minor offenders. Citing Sutherland (1950), he states that there is more danger of murder by an acquaintance or relative than by an unknown sex fiend, and that a truly dangerous sex fiend is rare.

2. Sex offenders have a low rate of recidivism, and they repeat their offenses less frequently than any other property or violent offenders except those convicted of homicide.

3. There is rarely an escalation of behavior in sex offenders. Though escalation does occur in some serious offenders, most find a sexual act that gives them satisfaction (for example, exhibitionism) and persist in that behavior.

4. It is not possible to predict dangerousness in this population, a point supported by many prominent psychiatrists. He stresses the importance of this point, because sex offenders are indefinitely committed to institutions based on their perceived risks.

5. "Sex psychopathy" is not a clinical entity, and there is much disagreement on what this term means. The offenders committed exhibit a variety of psychological problems, and there is no clear definition as to what does or should constitute a sexual psychopath.

6. Sexual offenders are not oversexed individuals, but tend to be undersexed. Organic treatments such as castration are not effective remedies for deviant

sexual behavior, because sexual urges are not the driving force of the offender.

7. There is no treatment that can "cure" sex offenders, and commitment to a mental hospital does not mean that a sexual offender will be treated. Sex offenders are often confined indefinitely and offered no treatment (a problem with sexual predator legislation that is discussed in greater detail in Chapter 11).

8. Though sexual psychopathy legislation was passed in order to incapacitate the serious sexual fiend, the individuals who are most often committed are minor offenders.

9. Due process rights of the accused are disregarded because the commitment procedure is of a civil nature. Tappan asserts that there is a violation of human rights and due process in the commitment procedure, stating that "regardless of the type of court employed to attain this result, it is in effect a serious punishment in which liberty and due process are vitally involved. Reasoning to the contrary is founded in a technical legalism of the most vicious sort" (Tappan, 1950: 16).

10. The "sex problem" will not go away merely because a law was passed. The only purpose of the statute is to satisfy the public, and that experience with these laws "reveals the futility of ineffectual legislation" (Tappan, 1950: 16).

At the time the report was published, 14 states had passed psychopathy legislation. The most important point of the report is the discord between psychiatrists and lawmakers. Tappan states that "sixty-five out of sixty-six psychiatrists . . . expressed the belief that there was insufficient accord in the field to justify legislation specifically for the sexual psychopath" (1950: 37). Additionally, he outlines the dangerous precedents set by sexual psychopathy legislation, including civil adjudication of individuals without due process; indefinite commitment to hospitals for offenders who are neither insane nor seriously psychologically impaired; and that sex offenders can be indefinitely committed into hospital until "cured," though they are not necessarily being treated and the cost of commitment to taxpayers is extraordinary (p. 16).

Despite Tappan's assertions, the number of states with psychopathy legislation doubled over the next two decades. At the same time, research shifted away from sexual deviance and began focusing on "normal" sexual behavior. Alfred Kinsey (1948), in a controversial report, analyzed the prevalence of sexual acts, such as masturbation and homosexuality, that were considered by most people to be deviant. He discovered that a high percentage of individuals had, in fact, participated in such acts, therefore creating questions about the label of "deviant." Numerous reports were published shortly thereafter that pointed out flaws in Kinsey's methodology, yet these did not detract from the results of his research. Other studies on normal sexual behavior emerged throughout the next two decades (for example, Masters and Johnson and Hite) that focused on the frequency of certain sexual practices (for example, masturbation) and what acts could add pleasure to traditional relationships.

The 1960s and early 1970s brought about a social and sexual revolution, and as the Liberal Era emerged there was a dissipation of punitive reaction to sexual psychopaths. Sexual psychopathy statutes fell into disuse in many states, and the main focus on sexual behavior was the changing societal attitudes toward acts that were previously considered to be socially stigmatizing. There was a sexual liberation in the 1960s, and sexual behavior among young people was becoming openly pronounced. Additionally, homosexuality became a more socially acceptable sexual alternative as a result of the gay liberation movement, initiated in 1969 after the Stonewall Riots in New York City. The 1970s brought forth an era of social change for women, with the legalization of abortion in *Roe v. Wade* (1973). While the social and political ideologies were changing, so, too, were theories on sexual offending.

The most notable impact on research in the late 1960s came from feminist researchers. It was at this time becoming evident that male and female constructions of social reality differed (Scully, 1990: 2), and the women's movement against sexual violence arose as an attempt to combat the prevailing negative views of female victims. Police practices, courtroom procedures, and even academic research condemned the victims of sexual abuse as partially or primarily responsible for their victimization. Amir (1971), for example, studied forcible rapes in Philadelphia and claimed that 19 percent were victim-precipitated and that in many cases the victim initiated the interaction. It wasn't until the 1980s that the women's movement succeeded in changing the public perception of victims of sexual violence, and it was at this time that allegations of child sexual abuse within the family became more frequent. But by the end of the 1980s a new panic emerged about the sexual homicide of children by strangers. This panic still exists today and is the source of the backlash against sexual offenders.

1976–Present: The Emergence of a Sexually Violent Predator

Toward the end of the 1970s, a number of issues were emerging that were not previously in the public forum. Problems with mental health such as depression and eating disorders were being discussed for the first time as common problems of "normal" people, and individuals were seeking therapy at rapid rates for cures to their ills. Childhood sexual abuse was also being discussed in open forums, particularly the courts. This new discourse was beneficial in many respects: it allowed for more information about the issues to be publicized, and it modified the stereotype that the victims of abuse were to blame rather than the perpetrators. Before long, however, a new problem evolved.

In the 1980s, the courts witnessed an influx of lawsuits from adults claiming they had been sexually abused as children. These adults claimed that they had repressed the memories for years, and only after several therapy sessions was the abuse recalled. The courts were initially hesitant to accept such claims (for example, *Tyson v. Tyson*, Wash. 1986), though they gradually altered their views and began awarding damages to the plaintiffs (for example, *Hammer v.*

Hammer, Wis. Ct. App. 1987). The statutes of limitation were extended in many American states, because the alleged abuse was often recalled decades after it occurred. Repressed memories were generally retrieved during therapeutic sessions when individuals—the majority of whom were women—sought psychological therapy for problems other than the alleged abuse. Therapists suggested that the patients read self-help books (Bass & Davis, 1988; Blume, 1990; Fredrickson, 1992), many of which indicated that individuals experiencing psychological problems were likely to have been sexually abused as children. Some of these books described lists of symptoms attributable to repressed abuse; these lists included characteristics as common as eating disorders, fear of being alone in the dark, and drug or alcohol abuse (Blume, 1990).

During therapeutic sessions, various retrieval processes were used to induce recall of repressed memories, the most common being hypnosis and Amytal (Green, 1994). Hypnosis, a sleeplike condition achieved through relaxation and concentration on a particular topic, lacks scientific elucidation because it is not completely known what happens in the mind to reproduce memories. Accurate information has emerged under hypnosis by individuals who witnessed an event, as details can be recollected immediately after the event through sensory recall and mental exercise with some accuracy. Individuals attempting to recall entire events from the past, however, consistently recall information that is incorrect more often than information that is correct. This is particularly true with hypnotic age regression, where the recalled events occurred before the age of five, a time represented by "childhood amnesia" (Loftus, 1994). Amytal, the other common method used to retrieve memories, is a barbiturate that induces a hypnotic drowsiness in individuals. Although said to function as a truth serum, it has been asserted that "Amytal has no legitimate use in recovered memory cases. . . . It is worse than useless, as it encourage patients' beliefs in completely mythical events" (Piper, 1993: 447, 465). Amytal is similar to hypnosis in that it increases confidence in a subject's recollections and the quantity of such recollections; however, there is no increase in the accuracy of such memories, and without independent corroboration there is no distinction between verifiable and fantasized memories (Watkins, 1993).

The validity of repressed memories eventually surfaced as a critical issue, because many of those who were accused denied the allegations, claiming that ideas of abuse were being inadvertently planted by therapists through various memory retrieval techniques. There was a contention that during therapeutic sessions, therapists were unintentionally planting false memories through leading questions and through associations of sexual abuse to other psychological problems. As therapists probed for traumatic past experiences, they suggested on the basis of a particular symptom that sexual abuse had occurred to the patient during childhood. With the idea of such abuse planted, many of the vulnerable patients accepted the explanations as the basis of their current problems. For example, Laura Stratford consulted with a therapist to find the source of scars across her body. Though she "remembered" being abused, evidence eventually led to the conclusion that all of her physical scars were self-inflicted (Jenkins & Maier-Katkin, 1991). In another case, George Franklin was convicted of murder based solely on his daughter's retrieved memories. Eventually, it came out that not only had she revised her account of the offense to fit the facts of the case, but the facts she retrieved were originally reported in local newspapers (Loftus, 1993).

Many of the repressed memory cases included claims of childhood sexual abuse in conjunction with ritualistic satanic abuse. The first publicized account of this abuse was in *Michelle Remembers* (Smith & Pazder, 1980), and Michelle Smith's story is similar to many subsequent cases. After experiencing problems of sexual dysfunction, low self-esteem, eating disorders, and a miscarriage, she underwent therapy for a year and concluded that 22 years earlier she had been the subject of childhood satanic abuse. Extraordinary stories involving many reputable individuals surfaced about rituals of chanting, baby breeding, human and animal sacrifices, starvation, and torture. Smith's story is remarkable but not unique; almost every claim of satanic abuse concerns similar stories, implying an international satanic conspiracy if the accusations were to be confirmed (Green, 1994). However, despite the existence of a "satanic panic," evidence has yet been to be found to corroborate any of these extraordinary satanic abuse claims (La Fontaine, 1994).

Those who believe in the existence of satanic practices claim that within the past 30 years the remnants of physical evidence have deteriorated or been exhumed so as to avoid detection. While this claim cannot be discounted, it is highly unlikely that satanic rituals have been taking place for at least three decades and yet no evidence has been found regarding these rituals anywhere in the world. Therapeutic transcripts for these cases show how some psychologists ask leading questions about satanic rituals until the patients agree to the elaborate stories. In the McMartin preschool case, children were asked questions such as "Did you ever see people walking around in dark robes?" and "Did anyone touch you *here* (indicating private areas)?" (Hicks, 1991). The questions were asked repeatedly until the children answered affirmatively regarding the existence of satanic rituals in conjunction with sexual abuse. Despite children's statements, charges were dropped in all cases claiming satanic abuse due to lack of physical evidence to support the given claims.

As cases of repressed memories became more frequent, some defendants began to file countersuits against the therapists who were responsible for retrieving false memories (see, for example, *Ramona v. Isabella*, 1994). Few cases of repressed memories are brought up in the courts today, and none result in convictions without corroborating evidence. There are, however, thousands of cases brought before the courts on a daily basis involving child sexual abuse within the family. Despite the prevalence of this type of sexual abuse—which accounts for the majority of cases—another "stranger danger" panic erupted in the late 1980s. It was this panic, based upon a few highly publicized cases of child rape and murder, that initiated the current trend toward sex offenders: the emergence of the sexually violent predator.

In the late 1980s, two child molesters committed horrific acts in the state of Washington. Both offenders had a long history of sexual offending, and there was a common belief that the criminal justice system was ineffective at keeping recidivist sex offenders incapacitated. Wesley Alan Dodd sexually molested, tortured, and murdered three young boys, saying that if he were released he would do it again—and enjoy it. Earl Shriner had a long history of child molestation charges and a homicide charge from when he was a juvenile. In and out of institutions since the age of 15, he had just been released after a decade in prison when he kidnapped and tortured a seven-year-old boy. In prison he confided in a journal and to other inmates that he fantasized about killing again, and explained in great detail about how, when released, he would buy a van in which he would kidnap boys and take them into the woods to torture them. There was nothing the state could do to keep him in prison.[5] Dodd was executed, but it was the case of Earl Shriner that prompted the implementation of a legislative act for "sexually violent predators" (SVPs) who had the potential to be released from prison one day.

Washington was the first state to enact SVP legislation, though 16 states implemented legislation in the 1990s. An SVP is defined as any person who has been convicted of or charged with a sexually violent offense and who suffers from a mental abnormality or personality disorder that makes the person likely to engage in predatory acts of sexual violence. A mental abnormality was defined as "a congenital or acquired condition affecting the emotional or volitional capacity which predisposes the person to commit sexually violent offenses in a degree constituting such person a menace to the health and safety of others" (Dorsett, 1998: 125). This legislation was essentially a modification of the sexual psychopathy laws, though there were a few significant variations. Most important, civil commitment was not intended to replace incarceration, but instead to supplement it. Upon completion of a criminal sentence, sexual offenders who have a mental disorder and are deemed dangerous can be committed to some type of secure mental hospital until they are "rehabilitated."

In Washington, SVP legislation (which is discussed in greater detail in Chapter 11) also established a system of notification to the community when offenders are convicted or released from prison. It was only with the implementation of Megan's Law in 1996 that registration became a federal regulation. Megan's Law, the registration and notification scheme that originated in New Jersey, is named after seven-year-old Megan Kanka, who was sexually abused and killed by a convicted child molester living in her neighborhood. Her parents claimed that if a convicted sex offender is living in the area, the community has a right to know so that the parents can protect their children. Though registration has broader consequences (discussed in Chapter 10), this legislation focuses primarily on sexual attacks by strangers, not abuse within the home. The death of Megan Kanka, like that of Polly Klaas in 1993,[6] was an emotionally charged sex crime against a child by a recidivist offender, and politicians had little choice but to implement laws protecting the community against the "stranger danger."

Though the cases of kidnapping and child murder are horrific, these are not the norm. SVP legislation, like that of sexual psychopathy laws from the 1930s, was passed to incapacitate a small portion of the population. However, the number of offenders referred for civil commitment is growing, and there are now similar problems with the SVP population that were prevalent with those convicted as sexual psychopaths. Every one of the problems with the psychopathy population presented by Tappan (1950) are relevant in regard to the SVP population, and it is likely that the statutes will eventually fall into disuse in a similar manner.

CHAPTER SUMMARY

■   Accepted sexual behavior has changed significantly throughout history, and from the time of first writings of the ancient Greeks, "normal" sexual acts have depended on accepted social and political ideologies.

■   Sexual assaults by strangers have had a significant influence on legislation throughout the 20th century. Yet, the majority of sexual offenses are committed by an acquaintance or relative of the victim, and the legislation also engulfs these individuals.

■   There were three distinct cycles of legislative proposals regarding sex offenders in the 20th century. Each cycle is characterized by policies based on emotionally charged, notorious sex crimes.

DISCUSSION QUESTIONS

1. Why is it important to understand the historical context of the social perception of sexual behavior?

2. What is the primary cause of the "moral panic" over child sexual abuse throughout the 20th century?

3. What are the key similarities between sexual psychopathy and sexually violent predator legislation?

4. What problems may result from implementing legislation that is primarily based on "stranger" sexual abuse of children?

5. What roles did researchers, the media, and politicians play concerning public attitudes toward sexual offenders throughout the 20th century?

NOTES

1. Sexual orientation was studied at this time in Germany, when an evaluation was done to determine whether same-sex contact should constitute a crime (Mondimore, 1996).

2. Research continues today on organic treatments for sex offenders as well, discussed in detail in Chapter 8.

3. The age of consent was 7 in Delaware, 12 in Arkansas, the District of Columbia, Kentucky, Louisiana, Missouri, Nevada, Virginia, Washington, and West Virginia.

4. In Georgia, the age of consent was 14.

5. The sentencing judge in his previous case did not specify that he was to serve two 10-year terms consecutively, and he therefore was released after serving the two 10-year terms concurrently.

6. Twelve-year-old Polly Klaas was kidnapped from her bedroom during a slumber party by a child molester who had repeat convictions for kidnapping and sexual abuse. Because she was taken from her home in a suburban, middle-class neighborhood, she became known as "America's child."

3

Etiology of Sexually Deviant Behavior

There are many possible explanations as to why individuals commit sexual offenses. The theoretical literature on sexual offending provides viable biological, psychological, and sociological bases of the origins of deviant behavior. However, no one theory is capable of explaining the etiology of deviant sexual behavior for such a heterogeneous group of individuals.

Notwithstanding the complexity of the task, theorists since the beginning of the century have produced models and hypotheses to explain such behavior through biological or psychological abnormalities. By the end of the 1960s, however, theories began transforming. Few were based on abnormalities beyond the control of the individual; rather, they incorporated behavioral and cognitive-behavioral approaches. Concurrently, feminist theorists emerged with a competing school of thought, choosing to define sexually aggressive behavior through societal explanations. They voiced a global critique of men and society rather than focusing on individual causes of deviant behavior.

One deficiency that unites these traditional theories of deviant sexual behavior is their lack of empirical support. By contrast, current theories are rooted in empirical research, emphasizing developmental, interpersonal, personality, epidemiological, sociological, and situational variables, all of which have helped to develop data-driven models of offending behavior (Lanyon, 1991: 36). Yet, empirical studies on sexually deviant behavior are still in their relative infancy. Though knowledge of sexually deviant behavior has notably improved throughout the past 25 years, it is possible to further expand on the existing theories by looking at them from a combination of perspectives rather than from a single theoretical basis.

PSYCHODYNAMIC THEORIES

Austrian psychoanalyst Sigmund Freud is credited with initiating work in the field of psychoanalysis with sexual deviancy, though his theories are no longer widely supported. Freud called individuals' sexual desires "perversions"—in particular, paraphilias such as exhibitionism, voyeurism, and pedophilia—and argued that sexual deviations were the consequence of childhood deprivation, developmental fixation, or regression back to any one of the four stages of sexual development (Freud, 1953). Freud labeled the four stages of development as oral, anal, phallic, and genital; unresolved problems brought about fixations during these stages of development. These fixations were sexual in nature, and included oedipal conflicts, castration anxiety, and penis envy.

The oedipal conflict, which Freud claimed that boys could develop during the phallic stage of development, is characterized by competition between father and son for the mother's affection. Castration anxiety and penis envy result from boys and girls discovering the differences in their genitalia; boys conclude that girls are actually boys whose fathers have cut off their penises, and girls are jealous of boys. Children should eventually outgrow these stages. It is when the boys do not resolve their oedipal conflicts that they develop a permanent aversion to adult females, whose appearance brings back their anxiety about castration.

Psychodynamic theory also explains the interaction of the three elements of the human psyche: the id, the ego, and the superego. The *id*, considered to be the "pleasure principle," is the basis of desire and the division of the psyche from which instinctual human drives originate. The id seeks instant gratification of these instinctual urges. The *ego*, or the "reality principle," is the mediator between the id and superego. The *superego*, or the conscience, is responsible for decisions based on past experiences of rewards and punishments. These parts of the psyche are internalized and work together to help the individual develop a system of morals.

For more than a half century, psychoanalysts (for example, Fenichel, 1945; Hammer, 1957) expanded on Freud's explanations of sexual deviations. A common characteristic of these theories was the belief that deviant behavior was unlikely to go away. Psychoanalysts believed that the psychopathology of the offender is a deep-rooted aspect of the person's personality, and, if treatment is to occur, it must be lengthy and based on the restructuring of the character. While psychoanalysis at this time focused primarily on sexual dysfunction, paraphilias, and traits such as homosexuality, psychoanalytic theories in the 1970s began to shift toward serious sexual offenses.

In the 1980s, psychodynamic theorists proposed family-based etiological explanations for deviant sexual behavior. For instance, MacLeod and Sarago

(1987) suggested a "family dysfunction model" whereby sexual problems are characterized by an ill, absent, or sexually frigid mother who provides an unsatisfying marriage for her husband. Loneliness and the need for intimacy develop, and the husband turns to his children for the undemanding love that he seeks. All types of sex offenders show intimacy deficits and expressions of loneliness (Marshall, 1989), yet these traits are not sufficient in themselves to explain deviant sexual behavior. Nonetheless, they may be significant factors in a multicausal explanation of the etiology of sexually deviant behavior.

BIOLOGICAL THEORIES

Many researchers have attempted to explain sexually deviant behavior through biological and physiological abnormalities. Most of these explanations are based on the assumption that abnormal hormonal levels adversely affect sexual behavior. Many biological theorists (for example, Berlin and Rada) suggest that biological functions are likely to be only one component of multiple etiologies for sexual deviations—sexual behavior is multidetermined and is not likely based on hormone levels alone. Biological theories usually pertain to rape or sexual assault of adults rather than child sexual abuse, because rape is considered an act of violence and there has been a postulated correlation between aggression and high levels of testosterone (Money, 1970; Rada, Laws, & Kellner, 1976). Most acts of child sexual abuse do not result in physical violence, so biological theories are rarely linked to child sexual abuse. However, there are some biological theories of pedophilia, and these are concerned with abnormal hormonal and androgenic levels in the brain.

The primary focus of biological explanations of aggressive sexual behavior is the role of androgens and androgen-releasing hormones in males. Secretion of the androgens is controlled by the hypothalamus and the pituitary gland, and the anterior lobe of the pituitary carries the androgens to the testes. The testes control the level of hormones, particularly testosterone, that are released into the bloodstream. When testosterone circulates in the bloodstream, it may or may not be bound to proteins. If it is bound, androgens may become active if they come into contact with receptors for testosterone. This happens during puberty, at which time males experience physical changes, such as increases in body hair and muscle mass and penis enlargement, as a result of the androgenic effects (Hucker & Bain, 1990).

Because of this androgenic process, the level of testosterone in the testes increases dramatically in males when they reach puberty. Sex drive also increases at this time. As such, there is an implicit belief that testosterone is the primary biological factor responsible for sexual drive in males. Empirically, researchers have shown that increased levels of erotic activity correspond to increased levels of plasma testosterone. Pirke, Kockott, and Dittmar (1974) showed that the level of plasma testosterone for subjects watching an erotic film increased by approximately 35 percent over subjects who were not watching an erotic film. This correlation is not clear, however, as various biological studies are not able to show a clear link between these variables. Despite these inconsistent results, Bancroft (1978) states that there is a general implication that hormone levels are affected by erotic stimulus.

The underlying question posed by biological theorists about rape is whether or not there is a connection between aggression and increased levels of testosterone, and, if so, whether this hormonal imbalance leads to sexual aggression. Aggression and sex appear to be mediated by the same neural substrates involving predominantly midbrain structures (the hypothalamus, septum, hippocampus, amygdala, and preoptic area), while the same endocrines activate sex and aggression (Marshall & Barbaree, 1990a: 259). Some self-report studies have shown a correlation between aggression and high testosterone levels (Olweus, Matteson, Schalling, & Low, 1980; Scaramella & Brown, 1978), and studies of convicted prisoners have shown that those with violent histories do have higher testosterone levels than non-violent offenders (Kreutz & Rose, 1972). Although there has been some research showing a correlation between "aggressive feelings" and high testosterone levels in young men (Persky, Smith, & Basu, 1971), most studies show a tenuous correlation, if any, between paper-and-pencil tests measuring aggression and the level of plasma testosterone in males (Ehrenkranz, Bliss, & Sheard, 1974; Kreutz & Rose, 1972). Testosterone is not the only hormone important in mediating behavior (Marshall & Barbaree, 1990a). Even if aggression is linked to testosterone levels, it is unclear whether testosterone actually produces aggressiveness or simply causes an increase in muscle mass and strength, allowing individuals to manifest their aggression more effectively (Hucker & Bain, 1990: 98).

As for studies that measure levels of testosterone and *sexual* aggression, results are largely conflicting, and the correlations that do exist are slight. One study showed that rapists scored higher than controls on a hostility inventory, yet plasma testosterone levels were not related to hostility scores (Rada et al., 1976). A further study by these researchers showed no differences between hormonal levels in rapists and controls (Rada, Laws, Kellner, Stiristava, & Peake, 1983), with the lack of correlation between testosterone levels and sexual violence supported by other researchers as well (Bradford & MacLean, 1984). In some studies, only the most violent and/or sadistic offenders were found to have elevated plasma testosterone levels (Rada et al., 1976), whereas other studies did not establish this correlation (Langevin et al., 1985).

Most of the hormonal studies that have been conducted contained small samples and produced conflicting results (Hucker & Bain, 1990). Although testosterone is presumed to be the source of sexual drive in males, few researchers claim to find a link between sexually deviant acts and abnormal hormonal or androgenic levels. Most biological theorists conclude that even when a hormonal imbalance is present in a male to act as a physiological potentiator for violence, these factors must still be triggered by environmental and social learning factors in order for sexual aggression to occur (Hays, 1981; Hucker & Bain, 1990; Kreutz & Rose, 1972; Meyer-Bahlberg, 1987).

One of the most recent, and most controversial, biological theories of rape was suggested by Thornhill and Palmer (2000). They explain rape from an evolutionary biological perspective, contending that males are driven to rape in order to reproduce. They state that although rape is not a morally good or even acceptable act, it is an act of natural selection. They support this by making claims such as that most rape victims are in their prime reproductive years. They contradict most sociological research and actually promote rape myths, stating that women should not dress provocatively because those who do so are more likely to be raped. Though highly publicized because of its unique perspective, other biological and evolutionary theorists have strongly criticized their work for being unscientific and based upon anecdotal evidence (Coyne & Berry, 2000).

FEMINIST THEORIES

Feminist theories about sexually deviant behavior focus primarily on rape; specifically, they center around the motivation of men to commit acts of sexual violence against women. These theories emerged in the late 1960s, when it became evident that the female victims were persecuted as much as the male offenders in cases of sexual violence. Most researchers at this time were male, and their explanations of deviant behavior focused on the victims' actions as much as the offenders'. The feminist movement was also moderately successful at changing the perception of female victims in the criminal justice system. With the increased public support for the active prosecution of offenders, the rate of reporting and convicting these offenders rose considerably by the 1990s.

A pioneer on research regarding sexual violence in the 1970s was Susan Brownmiller, who analyzed rape in a cultural, political, and historical context and cited sexual crime as an example of men's oppression of women (Brownmiller, 1975). She and other feminists regarded sexual assault as systemic to a patriarchal society of conditioned male supremacy. Accordingly, theories surmised that the use of coercive means to achieve sexual conquest represented an exaggeration of prevailing norms rather than a departure from them (Brownmiller, 1975; Herman, 1990; Matthews, 1994). Sexual gratification is not considered by most feminists to be the primary motive for rape (Allison & Wrightsman, 1993; Brownmiller, 1975; Burt, 1980; Darke, 1990; Ellis, 1989). Rather, rape is used as just one other tool to dominate and control women, who are considered relatively powerless compared to men and, therefore, subservient to them (Allison & Wrightsman, 1993). From a theoretical level, rape is seen to be the consequence of deep-rooted social traditions of male dominance and female exploitation (Ward, 1995: 10). Men who commit sexual offenses are considered normal, rationalized through the epidemiological explanation that almost all sexual offenders are male and a notable proportion of the male population has committed a sexual offense (Herman, 1990).

Feminist theory tends to view rape as a cultural rather than as an individual problem. Sexual violence is said to represent an extension of attitudes and practices surrounding male–female relations in a male-dominated culture (Darke, 1990). Cultures that encourage gender stereotyping create "gender socialization," whereby sexually aggressive men have been socialized to feel little need for intimacy and a low capacity for empathy (Lisak & Ivan, 1995). Social violence is not unique to any one culture or historical period (Stermac, Segal, & Gillis, 1990); however, some characteristics such as interpersonal violence, male dominance, and sexual separation are common to rape-prone societies (Sanday, 1981). Long-term prevention necessitates changing the societal conditions that generate sexual violence, such as belief in rape myths and sex-role ideology favoring restricted roles toward women that lead to gender socialization and thereby encourage and sanction a generalized hostility and, subsequently, sexual abuse, toward women (Brownmiller, 1975; Darke, 1990; Medea & Thompson, 1974; Stermac et al., 1990; West, 1987).

Though feminist theories focus primarily on rape, sex-role stereotyping can also explain child sexual abuse. Whereas feminist theory describes men as having sexual entitlement over women, child molesters express sexual entitlement over children (Hanson, Gizzarelli, & Scott, 1994). Child molesters tend to be narcissistic and selfish, considering their own desires and ignoring potential harm caused by their own actions. Through their own narcissism, they exhibit "sexually specific sexist attitudes" similar to those of convicted rapists (Hanson et al., 1994: 198).

ATTACHMENT THEORIES

Attachment theory follows the premise that humans have a natural propensity to form emotional bonds to others, and that models of bonding in infancy provide a framework for understanding attachment patterns in adulthood. There are many models of attachment styles, which provide a framework for explaining how individuals react when they experience some type of loss or emotional distress. These models of attachment explain the individual's self-concept as positive or negative, depending on the degree to which they believe they deserve to be loved (Bartholomew, 1990).

Though attachment theorists study bonds between individuals from infancy to adulthood, it is the period during adolescence that is most critical in the development of sexuality and social competence (Marshall & Barbaree, 1990a). By this time, adolescents with adequate parenting should have acquired prosocial behavior, including proper inhibitions on aggression and sexual behavior. Parents should also at this time help instill in the adolescents a sense of self-confidence and the ability to form emotional attachments to others. If this is the case, adolescents should be able to transition to adulthood with both social constraints against aggression and the skills necessary to develop effective relationships with age-appropriate partners.

Individuals who have poor emotional attachments are more likely to commit a sexual offense than those with strong emotional attachments to others. Research shows that men who sexually abuse children have poor social skills and little self-confidence, and thus, they have difficulty in forming intimate relationships with agemates (Marshall, 1989). This failure creates frustration in these men that may cause them to continue to seek intimacy with underaged partners. Seidman, Marshall, Hudson, and Robertson (1994) conducted two studies that showed that sex offenders have deficiencies in social skills that restrict the possibility of developing intimate relationships. In particular, sex offenders appear to misperceive social cues and do not act appropriately as a result of these deficiencies. These deficiencies in intimacy are common across various types of sex offenders. In Seidman et al.'s study, rapists and nonfamilial child molesters in the sample had the most significant deficiencies in intimacy.

According to Bartholomew (1990), there are four categories of attachment styles: secure, preoccupied, fearful, and dismissing. An individual with a *secure* attachment style has a positive concept of himself and others, and as a result is able to make friends and have age-appropriate relationships. An individual with a *preoccupied* attachment style has poor self-esteem and low self-confidence, but does have a positive attitude toward others and often needs their assistance to deal with personal matters. An individual with a *fearful* attachment style has a poor self-concept and a poor concept of others, thus often blaming himself for his problems but being too frightened to talk to others about these problems. An individual with a *dismissing* attachment style has both a positive self-concept and a high level of self-confidence, yet he has a negative concept of others and thus does not seek out help or support. The individual who is most likely to abuse a child is the person with a preoccupied, insecure attachment style (Ward et al., 1995, as cited in Marshall & Marshall, 2002).

BEHAVIORAL AND COGNITIVE-BEHAVIORAL THEORIES

Behavioral theorists began offering explanations as to the etiology of sexually deviant behavior in the late 1970s, led by researcher Gene Abel. Behavioral theories mainly relate to the assessment and treatment of sexually deviant behavior and view the behavior itself as a disorder that can be treated. Unlike psychodynamic theories, behavioral theories are based on the assumption that there is no single underlying problem of which the deviant sexual behavior is a symptom. Abel's approach (Abel, Blanchard, & Becker, 1978) is based upon an implied model of etiology that is seen as underlying other disorders that are amenable to treatment through behavior therapy.

Langevin (1983) expanded upon Abel's theory and classified deviant sexual preferences according to their stimulus and response characteristics. As such, the deviant behavior is conditioned in the individual to the effect that "sexually indulgent behavior displays a pattern that is entrenched and perpetuated by intermittent positive rewards" (Kear-Colwell & Pollock, 1997: 21). Elaborating on the conditioning premise, Wolf (1985) developed a three-part theory as to the etiology of deviant sexual behavior. He alleged first that sexual offenders have a *disturbed developmental history,* including potentiators for later deviant attitudes; second, he stated that there is a presence of *disinhibitors* that will allow deviant behavior to occur; third, he concluded that the offender has *deviant sexual fantasies.* All three factors work together to develop and maintain deviant sexual behavior. A fourth behavioral theorist, Lanyon, states that sexual disorders are "conceptualized as an inappropriate frequency of one or more events (behavior, thoughts or feelings), and this inappropriate frequency is thought to be maintained by the pattern of antecedents and consequences for the events" (Lanyon, 1991: 38).

Cognitive-behavioral theories were developed in an effort to build on the foundation of behavioral theories by taking into account the thoughts of offenders as well as their behaviors. Abel et al. (1984) explored the content of cognitions in sex offenders and analyzed the effect of cognitions on behavior. They found that sex offenders, like most individuals, are able to legitimize their behavior and the behavior of others through cognitive distortions (CDs). There are a number of CDs common to sex offenders, discussed in Chapter 4; these allow offenders to continue committing deviant sexual acts by averting blame from themselves and projecting it onto their victims or their environment. Some researchers (Ward & Keenan, 1999) claim that CDs derive from implicit theories that sex offenders have about themselves, their victims, and the world around them. Implicit theories, which are structured from the offenders' beliefs and desires, generate CDs that in turn permit inappropriate sexual behavior. They allow offenders to exist within a socially constructed reality and behave according to their beliefs about the world and their role in it. Ward and Keenan (1999) claim that implicit theories consider the following factors in relation to child sexual abuse:

- *Offenders View Children as Sexual Objects* They assume that children, like adults, are motivated by a desire for pleasure and thus desire and enjoy sexual behavior.

- *Offenders Are Entitled to the Sexual Behavior* The desires and beliefs of the offender are more important than those of the victim, which are either ignored or viewed as only of secondary importance.

- *The World Is Dangerous* The offender views other adults as being abusive, and perceives that they will reject him in promotion of their own needs.

- *The Offender Has a Lack of Control* The offender perceives his environment as uncontrollable wherein people are not able to exert any major influence over their personal behavior and/or the world around them.

- *Sexual Behavior Is Not Harmful* The offender believes not only that there is no harm done to the victim, but that sexual activity is beneficial.

Offenders rarely modify these implicit theories, even when faced with evidence (behavior) to the contrary. Instead, the offender may simply reinterpret or reject a theory. For example, a child's friendly behavior might be evidence to the offender that the child wants to have sex with him. Though it is not clear how these implicit theories develop, it is likely from a combination of developmental, social, and psychological influences.

As for the etiology of deviant sexual behavior, cognitive-behavioral theory proposes that deviant sexual arousal is learned through classical conditioning (Hunter & Becker, 1994). As such, the effect of outcome on the offender's first deviant sexual act is important: if the act meets with no adverse consequences, an addictive pattern may be powerfully reinforced (Becker, 1990).

PSYCHOSOCIAL THEORIES

Psychosocial theories work from the viewpoint that deviant sexual behavior is a response to external factors, and that there is an interconnection between psychological and sociological variables that influence sexual behavior. Sexual behavior is a learned response to particular conditions, and deviant sexual behavior is the outcome of inappropriate socialization. This may result from personal experiences, such as childhood sexual abuse, or be influenced by general factors, such as pornography.

One trait common to rapists, child molesters, and exhibitionists is poor social skills. These individuals tend to have difficulty formulating normal adult relationships and are described as suffering from "courtship disorder," in which "the terminal phase of courtship is exaggerated and distorted, and precoital courtship is virtually absent" (Freund, 1990). Rapists see violence as the only way to secure their goals of sexual gratification (Marshall & Barbaree, 1990a), and they use as much violence as necessary to achieve a sexual relationship. Many child molesters, on the other hand, have an inability to form age-appropriate relationships. In many cases of sexual abuse, regardless of victim type and motivation for the offense, sex offenders display characteristics of low self-esteem, poor self-image, and, subsequently, poor ability to socialize and form appropriate relationships with agemates.

Many sex offenders who lack proper relationship skills tend to misread social cues, and they do so in two ways. First, they misread cues from their victims, interpreting the victims' actions as sexual in nature. For instance, child molesters often have a sexualized view of children (Hanson et al., 1994; Hartley, 1998; Ward & Keenan, 1999). They interpret children's actions as sexual in nature, and any overt symbol of affection is considered to be a sexual cue. Rapists, too, may misinterpret the actions of their victims as indicative of a sexual desire. For instance, if a woman dresses provocatively, it may be interpreted that she wants to have sex. Or if, when she is assaulted, she does not retaliate due to fear, this may be interpreted as a desire to comply with the sexual act.

Sex offenders not only misperceive cues of their individual victims, but also societal intimations. These cues can be in the form of patriarchal prerogatives of fathers for children (Hartley, 1998) or sex-role stereotyping of women (Burt, 1980). One societal condition that in Western cultures has been presumed to encourage sex-role stereotyping is pornography (Burt, 1980; Marshall, Anderson, & Fernandez, 1999). Feminist theorists recognize this as a definitive expression of male supremacy that also plays a role in masturbatory fantasy and sexual response (Herman, 1990). Some feminist researchers claim that a link exists between violent pornography and sexual violence (Allison & Wrightsman, 1993), although there has been no systematic empirical evidence to validate this statement. One study showed that some men are more likely to rape if given instructions that it is acceptable behavior (Quinsey, Chaplin, & Varney, 1981). However, another study showed that exposure to hard-core pornography enhances sexual aggression only in already angered males (Gray, 1982). In other words, pornography is the not the origin of the deviant sexual behavior, but it can promote a relapse in offenders. This later study also showed that approximately 1 in 3 convicted sex offenders said that violent pornography stimulated their desire to offend after viewing it. Gray, as well as other researchers, however, concluded that violent pornographic depictions may act as potentiators for a few sadistic individuals to commit aggressive acts against women, yet most men will not be induced by this material to commit sexual assaults (Gray, 1982; Quinsey et al., 1981).

Though negative gender socialization may be one factor that influences rape, explanations of child sexual abuse often revert to the offenders' upbringing. In addition to the familial influences mentioned previously, researchers focus on the effect of childhood sexual abuse and whether this leads to a cycle of abuse (Freund & Kuban, 1994: 560). The "cycle of abuse" theory alleges that there are statistically significant links between childhood victimization and current sexual interest in children (Bagley, Wood, & Young, 1994). Though this hypothesis has several supporters (Garland & Dougher, 1990; Groth & Burgess, 1977), there are some inconsistencies with the abused-abuser theory. To begin with, it does not account for the fact that more female than male children are sexually abused, and yet there are more male than female sexual offenders.[1] Additionally, it does not account for the fact that many offenders—approximately one-third, according to most study samples—were not sexually abused as children. Similarly, the majority of children who were sexually abused do not go on to abuse others. Most researchers therefore conclude that childhood victimization is but one of many factors that may act as a prelude to later offending behavior.

INTEGRATED THEORIES AND EMPIRICAL RESEARCH

Although the individual theories discussed lend possible explanations as to the etiology of offending behavior, they are rarely sufficient explanations of all deviant behavior. The majority of offenders do not initiate sexually deviant behavior because of one variable, such as childhood sexual abuse or exposure to pornography. Rather, there are numerous interrelated factors that, when comprehensively studied, may better explain the etiology of offending behavior through multifactor models. Various researchers (for example, Finkelhor, 1984; Marshall, 1993; Marshall et al., 1999) claim that sexually deviant behavior results from a combination of psychological, developmental, and sometimes biological factors, including (among others) deviant sexual arousal and conditioning; few or poor intimate attachments to family, friends, or partners; loneliness; cognitive distortions and lack of empathy; poor social and relationship skills.

Marshall, Anderson, and Fernandez (1999) claim that the most important factor that predisposes an individual to future deviant behavior is the strength of the bond between the child and his or her parents, for insecure children frequently lack social skills and have low self-esteem. This poor self-perception persists into adolescence and adulthood, leading to intimacy deficits and loneliness in relationships with family, friends, and partners (Bumby & Hansen, 1997). Children who have strong bonds to their parents develop a resistance to deviant behavior because of their beliefs, cognitions, skills, and emotional dispositions (Marshall et al., 1999: 28). Children from unhappy homes with poor attachments are most likely to offend, as they are most likely to accept and welcome attention and rewards from abusers. They are also the most likely to be vulnerable, lonely, and develop a fear of intimacy, particularly in adult relationships.

The integrated theories, which envelop various developmental explanations for deviant behavior, indicate that childhood experiences predict a modeling effect because experiences in childhood relationships provide a basis for the formation of adult relationships. These theories also take into consideration possible biological explanations of deviancy. For example, boys who have weak bonds with their parents may have an inability to deal with stress and bodily changes once they reach puberty. At this time, the increase in testosterone in addition to social changes related to adolescence make the transition to adulthood difficult. Those with weak familial bonds tend to be vulnerable, and these vulnerable boys seek methods of power and control. With few outlets of sexual power available, the vulnerable boys may turn toward violent relationships or relationships with children. The availability of pornography, which encourages sex-role stereotyping, and even the popular media (for example, video games, movies) may encourage deviant attitudes in those adolescents who are already vulnerable.

In regard to child sexual abuse, David Finkelhor (1984) proposed a four-factor model of the preconditions of abuse, which integrate the various theories about why individuals begin to participate in sexually deviant behavior. This organizational framework addresses the full complexity of child sexual abusers, from the etiology of the abuse through the rationalization for it. Finkelhor's model focuses on the internal communications of child sexual abusers regarding their observations and opinions about the world around them. This internal communication creates an opportunity that allows the offenders to break through barriers that, until this time, had prevented them from acting out their feelings. They are able to rationalize their actions to themselves, reducing the barriers of guilt and shame. Once these barriers are absent, they can act on the opportunities they have created, thereby reducing their negative feelings of loneliness, isolation, and other such stressors.

In order to better explain this process, Finkelhor constructed an organizational framework consisting of four underlying factors that act as preconditions to sexual abuse. He states that in order to sexually abuse, an individual must (1) have motivation to sexually abuse, (2) overcome internal inhibitions, (3) overcome external factors that may act as inhibitors to the abuse, and (4) overcome the child's resistance to the abuse.

The first precondition, *motivation,* simply means that an individual must want to abuse the child. The abuser's motivation may result from many factors, such as the idea that he or she relates better to children than adults, that there is a sexual attraction to children, or that the abuse is addictive, like a drug. Next, the offender must *overcome internal inhibitions* to abuse a child, or must be able to justify the abuse to him- or herself in order to abuse. The offender may justify the abuse by saying, for example, that he or she was abused and enjoyed the abuse as a child, that the abuse is not harmful, or that it is educational. After overcoming internal inhibitions, the individual must *overcome external factors* that may inhibit the abuse. At this stage, the abuser begins creating opportunities for the abuse to occur. Opportunities may include any situation in which trust is built up between the abuser and the family of the child (if abuser and victim are not related), such as baby-sitting, coaching the child in a sporting event, or helping the child with homework. Finally, the abuser must *overcome the child's resistance* to the abuse. This often involves emotional manipulation of the child, such as telling the child how special he or she is, or that if the child tells someone, the abuser will go to prison.

In addition to these four preconditions to abuse, Finkelhor explains that adults who sexually abuse children experience "emotional congruence" to children, sexual arousal to children, blockage to adult relationships, emotional loneliness, a belief that there is no other way of obtaining this pleasure, a failure to understand damage caused, and poor impulse control. *Emotional congruence* describes the relationship between the adult abuser's emotional needs and the child's characteristics. For example, if an abuser's emotional needs are not fully mature, he or she may relate better to children than adults. These childish emotional needs may be exacerbated if the abuser has low self-esteem and inadequate social skills, thus making the abuser more comfortable in relationships with children in which he or she is able to exert more power and control.

Finkelhor also explains that adults who abuse children must have some level of sexual arousal to the children, whether it is innate or learned. Whether explained through social learning theory (through conditioning and imprinting, the abuser begins to find children arousing later in adulthood) or poor psychosexual development, sexual arousal to children is a necessary component of the motivation to abuse. Child sexual abusers also usually experience some type of *blockage,* or lack of ability to have their sexual and/or emotional needs met in adult relationships. The abuser's blockage may be developmental or situational; with *developmental blockage,* the abuser is prevented from moving into the adult sexual stage of development (an internal blockage), while *situational blockage* is when the abuser is unable to attain or maintain an adult relationship due to external factors, such as frustration from a relationship with an adult.

Overall, this organizational framework describes who is at risk to offend. It is likely that individuals who offend have been able to cope with many of the problems mentioned (for example, developmental blockage) and opportunities (for example, access to children) at different times. However, it is the combination of these problems, in addition to some type of demand on their coping system that contributes to an attitude supportive of sexual offending, thereby establishing a risk to offend. That risk increases the likelihood that a person may act out in a sexual fashion, because his or her belief system has filtered out the normal inhibitions toward sexual offending. Unfortunately, the relief that is associated with sexual offending is reinforcing, because it provides an emotional and physical response to coping in a way in which the offenders feel they have control, unlike many of the other parts of their lives.

Traits that appear to be most strongly connected to sexually deviant behavior are *dynamic variables,* or features that are changeable, such as cognitions, feelings, and attitudes. Unfortunately, it is these variables that are least understood, though empirical research in the past two decades has focused largely on them rather than *static variables* such as age and ethnicity. Empirical research generates data-driven models that are derived from a combination of theoretical perspectives rather than a specific theoretical approach. Empirical research tends to be developmental, cognitive, and social in nature, and it has led to the development of comprehensive theories of sexual offending.

Empirical studies on rape expanded at the time of the feminist movement, following the idea that rapists were not deviant characters, but rather like "the man next door" (Medea & Thompson, 1974; Russell, 1984). Empirical research has shown correlations between offending behavior and offender psychopathology, arousal patterns, attitudes, and social skills. A variety of factors have been measured, such as rape-supportive attitudes (Scully & Marolla, 1984) and prevalence of childhood sexual abuse in offenders (Seghorn, Prentky, & Boucher, 1987), as well as cognitive factors such as emotional disturbances and loneliness (Marshall, 1989). Some researchers have constructed equations that aim to predict factors of offending behavior (Malamuth, 1986), and others have utilized traditional theories such as Cohen's psychodynamic theories of rape to build empirical typologies of offenders to aid in the assessment for their management and treatment (Prentky & Burgess, 1990).

Other researchers who have proposed integrated theories to explain child sexual abuse focus on the offender's desire for sexual pleasure. For instance, O'Connell, Leberg, and Donaldson (1990) claim that child molesters begin offending because of the attraction to the pleasure derived from the acts; they have a perception that this is the only way to obtain such pleasure; there is a lack of understanding about the damage resulting to the child from this pleasure; and there is a lack of inhibitors to prevent the offender from seeking this pleasure.

Table 3.1 Theories of Sexual Abuse

Theory	Description of Theory
Psychodynamic Theory	Sexual deviance is an expression of the unresolved problems experienced during the stages of development; the human psyche is composed of three primary elements: the id, the ego, and the superego; sexual deviancy occurs when the id (pleasure principle) is overactive
Biological Theory	Concerned with organic explanations of human behavior; physiological factors (for example, hormone levels, chromosomal makeup) have an effect of sexual behavior; androgens promote sexual arousal, orgasm, and ejaculation, as well as regulate sexuality, aggression, cognition, emotion, and personality; abnormal levels of androgens lead to aggressive sexual behavior
Feminist Theory	Analyzes rape from a cultural, political, and historical context, and feminists cite sexual crime as an example of men's oppression of women; sexual gratification is not the primary motive for rape, but instead rape is a tool to dominate and control women
Attachment Theory	Humans have a propensity to establish strong emotional bonds with others, and when individuals have some loss or emotional distress, they act out as a result of their loneliness and isolation
Behavioral Theory	Deviant sexual behavior is a learned condition, acquired through the same mechanisms by which conventional sexuality is learned; it is acquired and maintained through basic conditioning principles
Cognitive-Behavioral Theory	Addresses the way in which offenders' thoughts affect their behavior; focus on the way in which sex offenders diminish their feelings of guilt and shame by rationalizing them through excuses and justifications
Psychosocial Theory	Deviant sexual behavior is a response to external factors, and there is an interconnection between psychological and sociological variables (for example, social skills) that influence sexual behavior
Integrated Theory	There are preconditions to child sexual abuse that integrate the various theories about why individuals begin to participate in sexually deviant behavior; address the motivation to offend and the rationalization of the behavior; focus is on the inhibitions of the offenders (internal barriers) and how when these barriers are diminished, distorted thoughts can lead to deviant actions

SOURCE: John Jay College (2004)

Despite years of research, theories on sexual offending are still inconclusive. There has been a shift in theoretical focus over the past three decades, and it is now clear that no single explanation accurately encompasses the myriad factors associated with the onset of deviant behavior. While comprehensive theories are able to explain general conditions associated with sexual offending, it is not possible to predict, on an individual level, who will offend based on these general characteristics. Table 3.1 summarizes theories of sexual abuse.

CHAPTER SUMMARY

- There are many theories that set out to explain the causes and context of sexual offending. Comprehensive theories involving a multitude of variables are the most widely accepted explanations of deviant sexual behavior today.

- The most thorough explanation of deviant sexual behavior lies in integrated theories. Integrated theories consider the preconditions to sexual abuse and take into consideration other factors such as attachments, emotions, and cognitive distortions.

- Finkelhor explains that in order for sexual abuse to occur, there are four preconditions that must be met. He claims that in order for a person to abuse a child, that person must be motivated to commit the offense, overcome internal and external inhibitions, and overcome the child's inhibitions to the abuse.

- A common thread through most theories is that sex offenders tend to have poor social skills, low self-esteem, misperceive social cues, and are able to rationalize their behavior.

DISCUSSION QUESTIONS

1. Why is it important to understand the theoretical underpinnings of sexual abuse?

2. How do familial or other close relationships impact those who go on to become sexual abusers?

3. What role do social skills play in sexual offending? How is this similar or different in offenders who abuse children and adults?

4. According to feminist theorists, what societal conditions may lead to sexual abuse?

5. Can you explain how an individual may begin to abuse children based on Finkelhor's four-factor model of the preconditions to sexual abuse?

NOTE

1. One postulated reason for this is differential reactions to sexual abuse by boys and girls. Boys are likely to aggressively act out on their negative emotions about sexual abuse, whereas girls tend to internalize their feelings (American Psychiatric Association, 1999; Karmen, 2000). Rather than abuse others, girls are likely to develop symptoms such as eating disorders or depression. A more detailed discussion on the difference between male and female victims is in Chapter 7.

4

Cycle of Sexual Offending

Whereas Chapter 3 outlined theories of why individuals begin to sexually offend, this chapter discusses the offense cycle. This includes the planning that goes into the offense as well as the cognitive processes that the offender uses to be able to continue offending. When individuals commit sexual offenses, they rarely do so spontaneously. Usually, there is a high level of planning that leads up to the offense, or in the case of child sexual abuse, "grooming" behavior. Additionally, many offenders commit multiple offenses. In order to do so, they excuse or justify their behavior so that they feel little or no remorse, guilt, or shame. This rationalization, which necessarily leads to a lack of victim empathy, allows the offender to continue the abusive behavior and, thus, the cycle of offending.

The *offense cycle* describes the interaction of the offender's thoughts, feelings, and behaviors. The cycle shows how sexual abuse is not a random set of acts, but rather is the result of a series of multideterminant decisions. Once begun, this offense cycle is able to continue because sex offenders neutralize their feelings of guilt, shame, and responsibility through cognitive distortions. These altered thought processes vary in both type and intensity, and they are crucial to the maintenance of the offenders' deviant fantasies and behavior. This variation in offenders makes it difficult to assess and, ultimately, treat and manage sexual offenders in either prison or the community. Nonetheless, understanding the determinants of sexual offending is important in order to establish practical policies that are applicable to all sexual offenders.

THE OFFENDING CYCLE

When committing sexually deviant acts, offenders make a series of decisions prior to the commission of these acts. Some of the decisions in this cycle transpire after a long period of time. Other decisions may occur almost spontaneously if the offender is in a situation where an abusive opportunity presents itself. Understanding this decision process helps explain the etiology and maintenance of offending behavior, because it is necessary to understand the conditions that create a pro-offending environment and how certain antecedents to sexual abuse vary among offenders.

Sexual offenders rarely make a straightforward decision to abuse a person. Instead, they tend to make a series of seemingly insignificant decisions that, when taken together, lead to sexual abuse. This series of apparently irrelevant decisions (AIDs) (also known as seemingly unimportant decisions—SUDs—or seemingly irrelevant decisions—SIDs) creates a pro-offending environment for the offenders. For example, a rapist may decide to go to his neighborhood bar, even though his prior offense occurred against a woman he met at a bar while he was intoxicated. Another example is of a convicted child molester who goes to the corner deli at 3 P.M.—the exact time that kids in his neighborhood get out of school and stop to get snacks. Although the decisions in each example do not constitute deviant sexual behavior or even overt deviant sexual thoughts, these AIDs place the offenders in environments in which they have access to potential victims. If the process is not stopped, they may progress until the antecedent conditions create an environment in which offending is inevitable.

The offense cycle is more than just decisions, however. The offense cycle involves multiple determinants, including the interaction of thoughts, feelings, and behaviors. These determinants may be situational in nature (that is, the offender is in a situation in which offending is possible), they may involve negative affective states (in particular, depression, anger, or loneliness), they may be based on past learning (that is, the offender was abused in a similar way as a child), and the offender's actions may be reinforced (that is, from the pleasure derived from the abusive act).

There are several steps involved in the offense chain. At the outset, the offender has negative thoughts, often leading to self-pity and the idea that "nobody likes me" or "I'm no good." These self-pitying, negative thoughts lead to negative feelings, in particular anger, frustration, loneliness, and inadequacy. These negative thoughts and feelings interact and lead to negative (abusive) behavior. The thoughts and feelings lead the offender to make AIDs that, among other things, lead him or her to withdraw from others. The result is further loneliness and isolation, which results in a lack of communication that causes the original negative thoughts and feelings to go unresolved.

Once the offender is ensconced in the negative thought-feeling-behavior cycle, he or she begins to experience deviant sexual fantasies. Though the offender may not act upon the fantasies immediately, the fantasies eventually lead to masturbation, where pleasure is derived as a result of the abusive fantasy. With this positive reinforcement, the offender's negative thoughts and feelings begin to wane, further reinforcing the negative behavior. It is at this point that the offender begins to take steps toward overtly deviant behavior, targeting a victim and engaging in a fantasy rehearsal of the future abuse of that victim.

Once the offender has engaged in the fantasy rehearsal, he or she begins to plan the abusive act and "groom" the victim (see section on Grooming and Planning, following). Once adequate grooming has taken place, the offender will abuse the victim. Similarly to the masturbatory act, the abusive act itself is a tangibly positive reinforcement of the original fantasy. However, the abuse may also lead to negative feelings, particularly that of anxiety (that is, What have I done?) and fear (that is, Will I get caught?), despite the release of tension achieved through the sexual abuse. It is these negative feelings that lead to the discontinuance of the abuse cycle. Yet, the offender rarely addresses the original negative thoughts and feelings that led to the abusive behavior, and as a result the offense cycle often begins again if the offender has not been caught. Thus, the abusive behavior is cyclical.

GROOMING AND PLANNING

Throughout the offense cycle, offenders make a series of decisions that lead up to and allow the offender to commit the deviant act. Yet, many offenders do not recognize the amount of planning that occurs before a sexual offense is committed. Child molesters are more aware of the planning than are offenders who abuse adults, because they generally "groom" the child before engaging him or her in a sexual act. *Grooming* is a premeditated behavior intended to manipulate the potential victim into complying with the sexual abuse (John Jay College, 2004). Some child molesters do not recognize their grooming patterns, or they may deny that such patterns exist, whereas others carefully develop elaborate schemes that encourage children to participate in sexual activity.

Pryor (1996: 123–154) describes several methods by which child molesters approach and engage their victims in sexual behavior, including verbal and/or physical coercion, seduction, games, and enticements. He explains how child molesters are able to manipulate their victims into sexual compliance and how the offenders either continue the manipulation or adjust it in order to continue with the abuse. The first grooming tactic noted by Pryor is the seduction and testing of the child, whereby sexual activity is initiated after a common interaction such as tickling or bathing. Here, the child is seduced and sexual behavior is "tested," increasing incrementally unless the child overtly tells the offender to stop the action. The following two quotes are examples of this tactic. Both offenders were convicted of raping their daughters, though intercourse occurred only after years of touching and fondling.[*]

> [The abuse] *actually started when Christine*[1] *was three and it went on until she was eleven. I started bathing her, and I touched her while I was bathing her.*

[*] All quotes are from personal interviews with sex offenders in the English prison system.

Q: *How did you groom her?*
A: *I would ask for a kiss and a cuddle, and that is how it all started. Then I got bolder and bolder, and eventually I had intercourse with her.*

A second grooming tactic mentioned by Pryor involves catching the victim by surprise. This happens when the offender has planned for some length of time to abuse the victim, yet there was no opportunity for the abuse to occur. The offender either manipulates the situation so that he is alone with the victim or takes advantage of an opportunity that presents itself. The following offender utilized this tactic.

Q: *How did the abuse start?*
A: *Handstands. She asked me if I would hold her legs while she did handstands, and so I said yes. So she did handstands, and I asked her if she wanted to do them again. When she did them a second time I put my hand down her pants.*

A third tactic for engaging children in sexual behavior is verbal or physical coercion. Most child molesters use manipulation, but few use physical force, weapons, or threats of physical force with their victims. Yet, some serious, repeat offenders do use physical and/or verbal force to make their victims comply. For example, an offender who was convicted of abusing six victims over a period of several years made the following statement. His victims were his nieces, his grandchildren, and their friends.

I was cunning, devious, you name it. I would use every trick in the book to get them to sit on my knee. I bribed them. I threatened them as well. I threatened, but I wouldn't really do it. . . . I threatened them with violence. . . . I threatened to hit them, even though it was not my jurisdiction to hit them.

Pryor describes another tactic used by child molesters as masking sex in a game context. The offenders who use this tactic tend to be the more manipulative offenders and often have several victims. These schemes are well planned and premeditated, meant to trick the victims into participating in sexual acts. The first of the two excerpts is by an offender describing his first victim, his stepdaughter, when the abuse began at age 10. The second statement is by an offender who went to elaborate lengths to groom children and make them comfortable with the sexual nature of their games.

Q: *How did you get her to comply* [with the abuse]?
A: *I acted like it was all a game, and she went along with it. I appreciate that now, she was looking at me as an authority figure and I let her down badly. . . .*

My grooming tactics were so good that the boys never said no. I started by play-fighting and wrestling and I took them swimming. I took them to a club . . . that had a common changing room, that way I could see them undressing and they could get used to seeing me naked.

Perhaps the most common tactic used by child molesters in order to groom the victims is emotional and verbal coercion. There are many ways in which this may occur, such as bribes or lack of disciplinary action in exchange for sexual favors, or emotional blackmail if the victim does not comply. The victims are almost always given incentives in order to comply with the abuse, such as money and gifts. This is often the tactic used with incest offenders or offenders who have regular contact with their victims. Two examples of this tactic are listed following. The first offender had sexual intercourse with his biological daughter, and the second had a sexual relationship with his stepson. In both cases, the abuse went on for several years.

> **Q:** *What led up to the intercourse? Did she ever say "no" to the sexual acts?*
> **A:** *I groomed her for several weeks. The first time I tried to touch her she ran away from me.*
>
> **Q:** *Why did she eventually let you touch her?*
> **A:** *Because I am her dad, and she probably just thought it was natural.*
> *I used to bathe her, and when I would touch her I would tell her it wouldn't hurt. She used to say "no, don't do it" sometimes, but I would buy her extra sweets. . . . I told her that if she told anyone, daddy will go away for a long time.*
>
> *I don't see, I don't think I groomed them. . . . There were no treats or anything. Except with Danny. Danny was different. His treat was that he was allowed to stay up late for the simple reason so that we could masturbate each other.*

Some child molesters do not admit to initiating contact with the victim, but claim instead that the victim initiated the contact and instigated the sexual behavior. Pryor describes this as "taking over from the victim," in that the offenders carry on with the behavior once the victims initiate it. Though it is possible that such a scenario may occur, it is unlikely. A more plausible explanation is that the offenders have a distorted perception of the abuse and believe the victim to be culpable. The following excerpts are examples of this tactic:

> *From the time I first met him he was all over me. I tried to stop little Johnny from hanging around, but it didn't work.*
>
> *She used to like to go to [soccer] matches. . . . And you see, she used to come to me and say to me, "I want to go to the [soccer] match Dad, so we can do you-know-what." I didn't used to buy her presents or anything like that, just take her out to [soccer] matches.*
>
> *I know this sounds like I am minimizing, but this is the truth: it all started when I was sleeping, and I woke up and my nephew was giving me oral sex.*

Rapists, particularly those who are opportunistic, often do not recognize the level of planning that goes into their offenses. Most claim that the decision to rape was made instantaneously and believe that only child molesters plan offenses. Yet some rapists do eventually recognize that some planning went into the offenses. For instance, the following excerpt was taken from an offender who was convicted for sexual assaults against 10 prostitutes. The statement was taken after he completed a treatment program; prior to the treatment, he did not admit to planning any part of the offenses, saying they happened spontaneously.

Q: *What else about the treatment stood out to you?*
A: *Just how you plan your offense. At the time you don't think about it, you know. But it is planned, it is all sectioned. When you look at it, you think yeah, I did do that. . . . [My offense] was all planned, all planned from start to finish. I used to, I took them to a park to attack them, and I used to go out to the park beforehand to make sure no one was there. And I knew exactly what I was gonna do before it happened. It wasn't spur of the moment, it was all planned. I knew where I was gonna take them, what I was gonna do, how much time I had, and when I had to pick the wife up from Bingo.*

MAINTENANCE OF OFFENDING BEHAVIOR

Once there are motivational factors in place that create a predisposition to sexual offending, and once the offense cycle has begun, offenders must then overcome any internal or external inhibitions in order to commit an offense (Finkelhor, 1984). After the individual commits a sexually deviant act, additional factors must be present in order for the offender to maintain the deviant behavior. As with the etiology of offending behavior, there is no single variable that explains why sexual offenders continue perpetrating offenses. There are several variables, however, that have been associated with the maintenance of deviant sexual behavior. In particular, offenders almost universally exhibit distorted thought processes, or cognitive distortions (CDs), that allow for continuation of abuse without feelings of guilt or remorse for their actions (Murphy, 1990). Moreover, many sex offenders have fantasies about a victim, a particular type of victim (for example, young boys), or certain sexual practices, and the continuation of such fantasies is correlated to the maintenance of deviant behavior. The fantasies are not always sexual in nature; rather, many rapists and child molesters fantasize about issues such as power and control. Additionally, child molesters often fantasize about loving their victims, which, though not violent, is a CD and allows the offender to continue participating in the inappropriate relationship.

In addition to CDs and fantasies, sex offenders often blame their behavior on external factors, such as stress, alcohol, or strained marital relations. Though these disinhibitors are not causal, they do act as "triggers" for deviant behavior and they act as an excuse for the offender's sexually deviant act. The triggers can be either psychological (for example, use of alcohol) or sociocultural (for example, weak criminal sanctions against sexual offenders) in nature (Hartley, 1998: 26). Researchers have identified CDs, fantasies, and triggering factors as pertinent to the maintenance of offending behavior, and as such these variables are addressed at length in cognitive-behavioral treatment programs (discussed in Chapter 8).

Cognitive Distortions

When individuals commit wrongdoings, they often try to diminish their feelings of guilt and shame through "neutralizations" (Sykes & Matza, 1957). Individuals primarily neutralize feelings of wrongdoing through excuses and justifications for their behavior (Scott & Lyman, 1968; Scully, 1990). These neutralizations take the form of cognitive distortions that allow the offenders to remove from themselves any responsibility, shame, and guilt for their actions (Abel, Becker, & Cunningham-Rathner, 1984). These rationalizations of deviant behavior protect the individual from self-blame and allow the individual to validate the behavior through cognitive defenses.

Cognitive distortions are not unique to sex offenders. Rather, all individuals distort thoughts regularly. For most individuals these distorted thoughts are not necessarily harmful (for example, a student who receives a bad grade on an exam assumes the teacher doesn't like him or her), but the distorted thoughts of sex offenders generally are harmful (for example, "She didn't fight with me so she must have wanted sex"). It is not the distortions themselves that are unique to sex offenders, but rather the content of the distortions (Marshall, Anderson, & Fernandez, 1999: 60). Though sex offenders do not form a homogeneous group of individuals, they show strikingly similar CDs about their victims, their offenses, and their responsibility for the offenses.

It is unclear as to whether CDs are conscious distortions or whether offenders genuinely believe these altered perceptions of reality. Some researchers suggest that CDs are self-serving and, thus, the offender consciously distorts thoughts initially (Abel et al., 1984). However, it is also suggested that the offenders eventually believe the distortions as they become more entrenched in their behavior (Marshall et al., 1999). Regardless, CDs are considered crucial to the maintenance of offending behavior for both rapists and child molesters, because they serve the needs of the offenders to continue their behavior without feeling guilt for their actions.

There are many ways in which distortions manifest themselves in sex offenders. Sykes and Matza (1957) list five primary neutralization techniques, including the denial of responsibility, the denial of injury, the denial of the victim, the condemnation of the condemners, and the appeal to higher loyalties. Cognitive-behavioral theorists have explained these techniques in terms of CDs, the most common of which are minimization and/or denial of the offense and justification of the offense. Additionally, sex offenders often lack victim empathy and show an inability to recognize the level of planning that went into their offenses (including grooming of the victims). Some researchers also label sexual entitlement as a specific CD, resulting from the narcissistic attitudes of offenders who seek only to fulfill their own desires (Hanson, Gizzarelli, & Scott, 1998: 197). However broadly or specifically the CDs are defined, these distorted thoughts are conducive to the maintenance of deviant sexual practices.

Minimization and Denial Most sex offenders minimize or deny their offenses, including the damage caused to the victim, the violence used, their responsibility for the offense, the planning of the offense, and the lasting effects as a result of the offense. Several researchers have categorized types of minimization and denial (Haywood et al., 1994; Marshall et al., 1999); these include complete or partial denial of the offense, minimization of the offense, minimization of their own responsibility, denial or minimization of harm to the victim, denial or minimization of planning, denial or minimization of deviant fantasies, and denial of the personal problems that led to the deviant behavior.

Some sex offenders deny all or part of their offenses. They may completely deny that they committed the offense—claiming, for instance, that the victim made up the story or they cannot remember what happened—or they may not admit to aggravating factors of the offense. Partial denial, as described by Marshall et al. (1999), includes refutation of a problem (for example, "I am not a sex offender") or the refusal to accept that an act was sexual abuse (for example, "The victim consented"). Though some researchers claim that denial is not an accurate predictor variable for recidivism (Hanson & Bussiere, 1998), there is a substantial body of literature that claims the opposite (Marques, Day, Nelson, & West, 1994; Simkins, Ward, Bowman, & Rinck, 1989). Few therapists allow deniers to participate in treatment until they at least admit that they committed the offense (Marques, Day et al., 1994).

Offenders with either adult or child victims may deny the offense by claiming that they were falsely accused or that they do not remember the offense. Some blame their memory loss on the extended period of time between the commission of the offense and the arrest, whereas others blame substances such as drugs or alcohol. The following excerpts from two child molesters typify such denials.

> **Q:**   *What about the USI* [unlawful sexual intercourse with a girl under the age of 16]?
> **A:**   *The USI, the reason I am guilty is because of medication, opium-based painkillers. . . . I don't remember what happened. If anything happened I will agree to it. But I can't remember because I was on medication.*

> *This was a long time ago, 25 years ago. I have a very, very, poor memory. . . . This rape business, I have practically put it out of my mind, I never forget it but I have more or less put it out of my mind.* [He was convicted of raping his 10-year-old niece.]

If offenders do not deny that they committed the offense, it is common for them to minimize the damage resulting from their acts. They rarely acknowledge the harm they caused the victim, and this is particularly true for child molesters. Because most child molesters are not violent toward their victims, they do not recognize the damage caused by what they view as a "consensual" relationship. They tend to see the assault on the child as the product of a mutual sexual interest, and they minimize any damage that might result from a child partaking in such a relationship. The first excerpt following is a statement made by a sex offender who was convicted of raping one daughter and indecently assaulting[2] another. The second is by an offender who was convicted of raping a 13-year-old girl.

> *In court she wouldn't say she consented, that is why it came back as rape. . . . The affair started in 1978, and the first time she said no at the last minute. But after that it was consenting.*

A: *I went out on a Sunday morning and the youngest daughter of Kathy asked me if she could go for a ride. We got along, we were laughing and joking, and one thing led to another and, well, let's put it this way, I went a little farther than I should have done.*
Q: *What was going through your mind when she started screaming and crying?*
A: *I thought she was a virgin.*

While child molesters rarely acknowledge that their "consensual" relationships are harmful, offenders with adult victims tend to minimize the damage they cause in other ways. They rarely recognize the level of coercion or violence used in order to make the victim comply with the assault. This is compounded if the victim is either a partner or spouse, or if the victim is involved in an occupation such as prostitution. In such cases, the offenders express a distorted thought of sexual entitlement, believing that they have the right to sexual intercourse with this person and that the act should not be considered rape. The following excerpts are from interviews with rapists. The first was convicted of raping his girlfriend, and his CD of entitlement to sex is clear from his description of his relationship with the victim. The second offender shows severe minimization of his actions and the harm caused by them. The victim was his girlfriend, whom he severely beat, throttled, and left unconscious when she said she did not want to have intercourse with him.

Q: *Did you rape her?*
A: *We had a relationship, and there were times when we had sex and it was forceful. But she didn't leave me. . . . She ended up living with me. She didn't have to. She could have gone home.*

My offense was not against the general public, it was against my girlfriend. . . . I was brought up with ethics and so I tend to respect women. I have never committed an offense against anybody nor have I been rude to anybody in my life. This is the first time it happened. I didn't—I mean, there was no violence involved. It was just that the lady said no on this particular occasion, and I think she was more surprised than anything.

Justification   In addition to minimizing or denying their offenses, sex offenders make excuses as to why they committed the deviant acts. By justifying their actions, offenders acknowledge their guilt in the acts but they do not take responsibility for them. Commonly, they blame the victims for their offenses or justify their offenses through the victims' actions.

Justification is common in the vast majority of sex offenders, as it assists in allaying remorse and guilt for the acts committed. Scully and Marolla (1984), who interviewed 114 incarcerated rapists, explain five ways in which rapists commonly justify their behavior. Rapists claim that (1) the victim is a seductress, and she provoked the rape; (2) women mean yes when they say no, or the victim did not resist enough to really mean no; (3) most women relax and enjoy it, and the rapists are actually fulfilling the woman's desires; (4) nice girls do not get raped, and prostitutes, hitchhikers, and promiscuous women get what they deserve; and (5) the rape was only a minor wrongdoing, so the perpetrator is not really an "offender."

Child molesters also justify their actions by neutralizing their guilt. Common justifications include claims that they are helping the child to learn about sex; sexual education is good for the child; the child enjoys it; there is no harm being done to the child; the child initiated the sexual contact; and the child acts older than he or she is. Like offenders with adult victims, child molesters often assert that the child did not resist and therefore must have wanted the sexual interaction. They fail to recognize any other explanations as to why the child might not have resisted, such as fear, uncertainty about what was happening, or the idea that the perpetrator is someone they knew and trusted. The following excerpt shows an offender justifying his contact with the young daughter of his friend because she did not resist his advances:

Q: *What made you abuse her?*
A: *I don't know. The opportunity just was given to me. She came and sat in my lap and asked me how to draw something. So while she was drawing, I put my hand up her skirt. She didn't say no.*

Many children, when abused, respond to the abusers by copying their actions or by doing what they are told to do. For instance, if a man shows a young girl how to masturbate him, she may comply without fully understanding the purpose or consequence of her actions. The offenders tend to assume that this type of compliance with a sexual act is indicative of the child's enjoyment of the act, and they are able to justify their actions accordingly. Other offenders sexually touch a child but do not have the child touch them. They are aroused by the touching and usually fantasize about the act at a later time. They often believe that they are pleasuring the child, and they do not view this type of act as intrusive and harmful. Still others believe that they are teaching the child about sex, and that sexual intercourse is pleasurable and the child is enjoying the interaction. The following excerpts illustrate these points:

I was putting my thing on her private parts, mind you through her [underpants]. *At no time did I force her to do anything, nor did I ever physically force her to touch me.*

Q: *Did you know what you were doing was wrong?*
A: *At the time I was giving myself the excuse, I was doing nothing wrong. . . . I would say to myself, she likes it. She has to learn that sometime, she has to learn sooner or later. I would make myself think I wasn't doing anything wrong.*

Many children do not exert physical resistance to sexual advances. This is largely due to the grooming techniques employed by the offender leading up to the abuse, as discussed previously. Nonetheless, this lack of resistance to sexual advances signifies to most offenders that the child is enjoying the sexual interaction. Added to this are the natural biological reactions of the child to the sexual contact, such as when one offender told a researcher in an interview, "I remember touching her breasts at that point. And . . . immediately her nipples got hard" (Pryor, 1996: 127). This is particularly applicable to offenders whose victims are girls who are just reaching puberty. The following excerpt is from an offender who abused his 12-year-old niece and justified his actions through all of the listed methods of neutralization:

Q: *How did the abuse begin?*
A: *We used to kiss and cuddle, and then it progressed from there. She never really objected to any of it, only sometimes did she say she didn't like it. And only once did she say no, we can get in trouble for this. She was such a pretty little girl, so well developed for her age. . . . I suppose this must have mentally scarred her, but I know deep down that she really just loved it.*

Many child molesters seek out children who are vulnerable for abuse. This includes children who are abused physically, emotionally, or sexually, and who often desire the attention paid to them by the offender. The offender is able to neutralize guilt in such a situation by believing that he is showing the child love as no one else does. Or, the guilt is neutralized because others have already abused the child and the offender is therefore not to blame. The following excerpt illustrates this point:

I abused my nephew and two of his friends. My brother was also abusing my nephew, and I guess I thought "He's already been abused, so I can abuse him too."

All sex offenders have a tendency to misread social cues by others and are poor at identifying emotions such as anger or fear in the victims. Both rapists and child molesters often perceive their victims as initiating sexual contact, and see their victims' actions as sexually provocative. Rapists view any flirtatious actions by their victims as indicative of desiring a sexual relationship. Many do not understand prosocial limitations to sexual contact and believe that if a sexual interaction has begun, then it should continue through intercourse. Thus, if the victims later make an attempt to terminate contact (victim says "No"), the rapists do not take the desire to stop the contact seriously (offender assumes she means "Yes"). Blaming the victim for initiating sexual contact alleviates the guilt of the act from them and transposes it to the victims.

Child molesters misread cues from children in several ways, and the better they know the victim the more likely this is to happen. Children are naturally affectionate toward adults, particularly those whom they know well. Child molesters view these naturally affectionate actions—such as sitting on an adult's lap—as sexual in nature and perceive the children as initiating sexual contact. They also perceive any sexual curiosity displayed by the child as a desire to know about sex, and they want to "teach" the child through sexual experiences. These misperceptions reinforce the offenders' narcissistic beliefs and detract from the ability of an offender to feel any empathy for his victims.

Victim Empathy Research in cognitive psychology suggests that all individuals interpret situations differently, and they construct implicit theories about their worlds in order to explain the reality as it relates to them. The socially constructed reality of sex offenders revolves around two concepts: desires and beliefs (Ward & Keenan, 1999: 825). They form mental constructs about what they believe the victim wants, and because offenders exhibit narcissistic traits, they generally believe that the victim desires sexual activity with them (Hanson, Gizzarelli, & Scott, 1994). As such, they are often unaware of the damage that they cause their victims. Without understanding the impact of their actions, or feeling empathy toward the victim, offenders are not likely to cease their offending behavior.

Empathy refers to the understanding of another's feelings and emotions. There are several components of empathy, with researchers now focusing on both cognitive and emotional factors (Davis, 1983; Moore, 1990). It is believed that prosocial empathic response patterns develop primarily during childhood, with parents having a significant impact upon the development of behavior and emotional responses (Zahn-Waxler & Radke-Yarrow, 1990). Simply put, if parents show low empathic response patterns, it is likely their children will model their conduct and also be deficient in empathic behavior. This deficiency in empathy is apparent in almost all sex offenders, and this is what allows them to continue offending despite the damage they cause to the victims.

Studies measuring general empathy in sex offenders show mixed results. Williams and Finkelhor (1990) claim that incestuous fathers lack empathy; Pithers (1994) claims that rapists lack empathy more than child molesters; Hayashino, Wurtele, and Klebe (1995) claim that there is no difference in empathy between child molesters and non-sex offenders. Additionally, sadistic rapists do not lack empathy, which is the failure to understand the feelings and emotional state of others. Rather, they do understand the pain, degradation, and humiliation of the victim and seek this out for sexual arousal.

Marshall, Hudson, Jones, and Fernandez (1995) propose that sex offenders do not necessarily lack empathy as a general trait, but they lack victim-specific empathy. Sex offenders do express empathic responses toward victims of sexual offenses. There are particularly pronounced group differences for empathic responses to victim harm: child molesters are distressed about violence toward women, and rapists are sympathetic toward child victims. The following excerpt shows such a situation:

> *I was very disturbed after hearing about* [a rapist] *who stabbed his victim's eyes out and then mutilated her genital area, and then I had to go back to my cell to think about it. Me, I never hurt my victims so this is disturbing.*

The offender who made this statement was convicted of nearly 200 counts of child molestation. The victims were 11- to 14-year-old boys, and the abuse occurred over a 10-year period. Even after treatment, he failed to recognize the harm that he brought upon his victims, which is common to child molesters when the victims display no overt resistance to the abuse (Stermac & Segal, 1989). Many offenders believe that there are degrees of offending behavior and, thus, degrees of harm (Ward & Keenan, 1999), and that the "consensual" nature of their offenses makes them less culpable than those with intrusive, violent offenses. The same offender went on to describe his relationship with his victims in the following way:

> I treat my boys, I mean my victims, better than I was ever treated. I have never forced them to do anything. I loved some of the boys. Some of them will not be affected; some will be homosexual anyway. This was just an earlier experience for them.

Many child molesters feel similarly to this offender, and many believe that the victim enjoys the sexual behavior. Offenders who abuse adolescent boys most commonly feel this way, seeing the relationship as consensual rather than harmful. Two more examples of such relationships are as follows:

> **Q:**   *Did you ever think about the consequences* [of the abuse] *for the victims?*
> **A:**   *Not with Danny. With him it was a mutual thing, it was something that we both wanted, even though he was only fourteen.*

> *I met my boyfriend* [14-year-old victim] *through another man and the boy told a friend of his. That is how I got caught. All the boys consented to the intercourse, but they were underage.*

Child molesters have a narcissistic view of their power, which is derived from the offenders' implicit theories about the importance of their desires taking precedence over those of the victims. Child molesters made the following statements upon completion of a treatment program, exemplifying this type of narcissistic behavior:

> I thought I was not doing any harm, and yet it was so blatantly obvious that I was. I didn't pick up, or I didn't care, or I was so high in my ego that I didn't think about the other person.

> **Q:**   *Why did you continue to abuse her* [15-year-old victim]?
> **A:**   *Because it was easier to keep abusing her than to get a regular partner. I was being totally selfish.*
> **Q:**   *Did you think she was enjoying herself?*
> **A:**   *Yes, because she did not complain.*

Rapists, like child molesters, lack victim empathy and express feelings of sexual entitlement, assuming the victim is less important and should exist to satisfy their sexual needs (Ward & Keenan, 1999: 828). They, too, have a narcissistic view of their power and importance. Feelings of sexual entitlement often develop at a younger age, as a child observes the interaction between his or her parents or other adults. The following excerpts are examples of such scenarios:

> **Q:**   *You didn't think your first offense was rape?*
> **A:**   *No. . . . I honestly thought that men just coax women. I looked at it like, if a man buys a woman a drink in a bar, all you are doing is coaxing her at the end of the date to have a sexual relationship of some sort.*

> *I think I had a lot of wrong messages given to me growing up as well. My father, the way he treated my* [mom], *well, he sent a lot of the wrong messages. . . . It was*

that you could take what you want when you want it. It was the same kind of sce-
nario here. . . . I was like, you look all right and I wouldn't mind having you.
You've got no say in the matter.

This feeling of sexual entitlement is even more pronounced when the victim is a partner or someone viewed as promiscuous by the offender. Offenders feel they are allowed to treat such individuals either as property or as someone who should comply with their sexual requests. The following two excerpts are examples of this attitude:

Right up until I was sentenced I was saying this is ridiculous, I didn't rape my
wife. But . . . most of us [sex offenders] . . . are very selfish. We think only about
ourselves. You don't see it at the time; you just think of yourself. It's not until you
start thinking about the other side, the victim, that you start realizing there are two
sides.

I run a club . . . and the girls who were around the club were promiscuous. So I
started judging everybody else by the world I lived in. It was attitude. . . . I just
thought that all women were the same.

The Role of Fantasies

Historically, researchers assumed that sex offenders had deviant sexual fantasies, which in turn motivated them to commit deviant sexual acts. Additionally, it was believed that these deviant fantasies were conditioned through masturbation (McGuire, Carlisle, & Young, 1965) and that the fantasies could be modified through deconditioning or aversion therapy (Abel & Blanchard, 1974; Evans, 1968). Even the *Diagnostic and Statistical Manual of Mental Disorders* (American Psychiatric Association, 1994) lists sexually arousing fantasies as a condition of paraphilias, indicating that this belief continues to be prevalent (Langevin, Lang, & Curnoe, 1998).

Unfortunately, there is little empirical evidence to support the notion that sex offenders have more fantasies than non-sex offenders or that these fantasies are more deviant (Langevin et al., 1985). The prevalence and type of fantasies that the sex offenders have seem to vary by type of offender and extent of offending behavior. Pithers et al. (1989) claimed that only 17 percent of the rapists and 51 percent of the child molesters in their study had deviant sexual fantasies. Marshall, Barbaree, and Eccles (1991) reported that 53 percent of child molesters in their study had deviant sexual fantasies, and of those only 29 percent had fantasies prior to adulthood. Prentky et al. (1989) looked at a group of offenders convicted of sexual homicide and found that 86 percent of the serial sexual offenders had deviant fantasies, but only 23 percent of those convicted of only one offense had such fantasies. Additionally, it is impossible to know how many men who have never been convicted of a sexual offense have deviant sexual fantasies.

It is difficult to accurately measure fantasies in sex offenders, and it is equally difficult to know how to interpret the role of these fantasies in deviant behavior. Commonly, sex and non-sex offenders give self-reports about the type of fantasies they have, though many offenders either deny that they have fantasies or do not recognize that their fantasies are deviant. A second method of measuring arousal, and one that is more reliable than self-reports, is through the penile plethysmograph (PPG), which gauges the circumference of the penis through an elastic mechanism attached to it. Though the accuracy of PPG results is disputed because of methodological variance, the majority of results show that deviant sexual interest is a significant problem for extrafamilial child molesters (Laws, Hanson, Osborn, & Greenbaum, 2000). Results are not as consistent for other groups of sex offenders, and many rapists and incestuous offenders show the same level of deviant arousal as non-sex offenders. For these offenders, there is often arousal to depictions of consensual adult erotica as well as deviant stimuli (Marshall et al., 1999). Even when arousal exists to the deviant stimuli, it is not clear whether the sex offenders fantasized about such issues prior to the commission of their offenses or whether the act itself caused the fantasies.

For those who do have deviant sexual fantasies, the types of fantasies vary widely depending on the type of offender and the motivation of the offense. Some offenders are motivated by sexual needs, while issues such as power and control motivate others. The fantasies may center on a particular sexual behavior, violence, power, control, or a specific victim or type of victim. As Marshall et al. (1999) point out, many offenders do not admit to fantasizing about deviant sexual behavior prior to their first deviant act. However, offenders who participate in a treatment program may admit to their deviant fantasies upon completion of the program. For example, the following excerpts are from a child molester prior and subsequent to treatment, when asked about his sexual attraction to children:

Q: *Are you attracted to children?*

Pretreatment:
I am not attracted to them, no, no.

Posttreatment:
You see, next door to me there was a woman with daughters, 13 and 15 years old, and they used to go out in the backyard in skimpy bathing suits in the summer. I used to fantasize about them. About the time my wife started rejecting me, I started fantasizing about these girls . . . and I used to go down to the beach, I used to go down there to watch the kids, sort of swimming and playing and all that. I wouldn't say I used to fantasize about them, but I liked watching them.

Some offenders compare their desire to commit deviant sexual acts to a drug addiction. They say that they have to have a "fix," and though they feel guilt while committing the acts, they desire the act again soon afterward. Whether or not the fantasies are related to the etiology of offending behavior is unclear, but the fantasies do play a role in the maintenance of their behavior. The following excerpt illustrates this point:

All I had on my mind was sexual gratification. Sex is like a drug—you know that when you haven't got it the desire is always stronger than when you have some. So you need someone to give you that little kick.

Behavioral Triggers

Many sex offenders blame their deviant sexual behavior on situational and transitory factors such as drugs, alcohol, stress, and loneliness. Though these factors alone do not necessarily cause deviant behavior, they are often triggers to the commission of deviant sexual acts. These triggering factors can act either as *disinhibitors,* the most common of which is alcohol, or as *potentiators,* including negative affective states such as depression. Both disinhibitors and potentiators contribute to offending behavior, though they do so in different ways.

Disinhibitors such as alcohol allow the offender to justify the deviant behavior as being caused by an altered mental state. Many offenders are intoxicated before or at the time of their offenses, and intoxication acts as a link in the causative chain of events leading to the deviant act (Marshall et al., 1999). The offenders sometimes cite alcohol as the reason they committed their offenses, without recognizing other risk factors beyond the alcohol. For example, the following excerpt shows how one rapist used alcohol and drug use as an excuse in his offense:

Q: *Were you drinking or on drugs the night of your offense?*
A: *Oh, yes.*
Q: *If you had not been drinking or on drugs, would this have happened?*
A: *If I had not been drinking or on drugs, no, it probably wouldn't have happened.*
Q: *What happened the night of your offense?*
A: *. . . I went over to my [friend's] house and got ahold of some grass and started getting wasted. At 8:00 in the evening, I decided to go down to the shop and get some special lager, extra strength. I drank these five bottles within the space of a half-hour. Going into town, I bumped into the girl I had been going out with. I got the sense that she was not amused with me turning up at this pub. So I thought, fair enough, I'll just carry on drinking for the rest of the evening. And at each pub I went into I had a couple of bottles of Newcastle Brown Ale. In one of the pubs, I saw a dealer in there and bought some speed and some acid and I dropped them all in one go. So by this time I was quite intoxicated. By 11:00 I was a . . . mess. There were a lot of people who witnessed me sitting there smoking drugs. . . .*

It is likely that the drug-induced state of this offender was one causative link in the decision to commit the rape. However, the offender also explained during the interview that he had received divorce papers from his wife earlier that day and had argued with his girlfriend before going out that night. The negative affective states of anger, loneliness, and inadequacy were present, and these likely acted as potentiators for the offense he committed. His level of intoxication during the evening, however, acted as a disinhibitor and allowed him to justify his offense through a removal of responsibility.

Several researchers have shown a link between negative affective states and deviant sexual behavior. McKibben, Proulx, and Lusignan (1994) claim that rapists exhibit characteristics of loneliness, anger, humiliation, and inadequacy; Pithers, Kashima, Cumming, Beal, and Buell (1988) show a link between deviant sexual behavior and anxiety, depression, boredom, and resentment. When asked about their emotional state at the time of the offense, rapists and child molesters made the following comments:

> *I was getting really depressed. At times I couldn't talk to anybody. People would come over to the house and I would just go upstairs. . . . It got so bad that I wanted to kill myself.*

> *Before, I would be depressed an awful lot. I tried to get through that by artificial means at different times with the drugs, but they only work for a period of time.*

> *I felt trapped. . . . I'd get pissed off, and anxious. . . . I felt claustrophobic when I got close to people. When I get close to people, I feel like they know me and they're trying to take me over. Not that they're trying to take control of me, but like they know me and I can't get away from them. I wind myself up over it. Maybe I won't do that now, but I used to let it affect me.*

> *I was feeling frustrated. . . . I was feeling inadequate. During [the offense], I was becoming more and more frustrated, and I was taking my frustrations out on her. I was angry but I felt like I was losing control, like I was out of control on the inside but on the outside I was controlled.*

Negative affective states such as the ones above may act as catalysts for deviant sexual behavior. However, they also may play a significant role in the maintenance of deviant behavior. Several offenders explained a link between their fantasies and their feelings of anger, frustration, and inadequacy. The following excerpt is from a rapist who said he would set himself up for rejection with women, which would in turn create feelings of anger and a desire for power over women:

> *My fantasies were about rape, taking off her clothes, trapping her. I think they started through lack of self-confidence, my own inadequacies, rejection. . . . I was always setting myself up for rejection so that I would have an excuse to be angry. In my fantasy, I could do anything I wanted, I had complete control. But [during the rape] Lisa kept saying to me "I don't want to do that, why are you doing this to me?" This type of thing was not in my fantasy.*

CHAPTER SUMMARY

- Sexual offenses do not just happen spontaneously. The offense takes place over a cycle, including a series of decisions regarding the potential victims and potential actions against the victims. This cycle includes planning the offense, fantasizing about the victim, grooming the victim (if the victim is a child), making decisions to commit the offense, and rationalizing the deviant behavior.

- "Grooming" occurs when the offender participates in a premeditated behavior intended to manipulate the potential victim into complying with the sexual abuse. Not only does the offender groom the victim, but often grooms the family of the victim.

■   Sex offenders have cognitive distortions that allow them to excuse and justify their behavior. The purpose of this rationalization is to alleviate feelings of guilt, shame, and remorse, and often the offender blames the victim for the offense.

■   Sex offenders often lack victim empathy. Though they may empathize with victims generally, they lack victim-specific empathy, or empathy for their own victim.

DISCUSSION QUESTIONS

1. What is grooming? What is the most common type of grooming behavior?

2. What are the key components of the offense cycle?

3. How are sex offenders able to maintain their abusive behavior without feeling guilt or shame? What types of sexual offenders are most likely to rationalize their behaviors?

4. Describe the role of fantasies in sexual offending. Is it possible to eliminate sexual fantasies? Change sexual fantasies?

5. Give examples of behavioral triggers and how they may lead to sexual abuse. What is the difference between potentiators and disinhibitors?

NOTES

1. The names of all victims have been changed.

2. Indecent assault is a charge in England equivalent to sexual assault in the United States. It involves inappropriate sexual touching in any way, and can include manual penetration, penetration with a foreign object, or oral sex.

5

Types and Typologies of Sexual Offenders

With the increase in reporting of sexual offenses in the 1980s, it became apparent that sexual offenders do not fit into "stereotyped caricatures" (Hollin & Howells, 1991: 1). An offender is more likely to be the man (or woman) next door than the cloaked stranger jumping out of the bushes. Victims can be female or male, a fact acknowledged by modified definitions of *rape* in many states to include male victims. Children are more likely than adults to be victims, and the offender is almost always someone with whom the victim is acquainted. Additionally, many offenders suffer from paraphilias, and some researchers have showed that multiple paraphilias are common in particular types of offenders (for example, see Abel & Rouleau, 1990).

Many studies focus on the offenders' motivation for committing sexual offenses, and researchers derive typologies from these studies. These typologies classify offenders into categories based on characteristics of the offenders and their offenses, considering both stable (historical) and dynamic (changeable) characteristics. Although some offenders might have similar characteristics, there is no single typology that can account for all offenders. Some background and cognitive traits are common to most sex offenders, yet the heterogeneity of offenders rarely allows for single typologies to be an adequate characterization. As such, it is now more common to describe offenders using a cross-classification of various typologies. Although no classification of sexual offenders has universal validity, it is important to understand characteristics common to offenders and to be able to classify them accordingly for two reasons: first, to identify individuals who have been predisposed to offending behavior, and second, because it is necessary to understand the characteristics of offenders for purposes of treatment and management.

TYPOLOGIES OF RAPISTS

Rapists, like the general population of sex offenders, do not form a homogeneous group (Barbaree, Seto, Serin, Amos, & Preston, 1994; Knight & Prentky, 1990; Solicitor General of Canada, 1990; West, 1987). In order to understand why individuals begin offending, researchers have tried to identify common characteristics among sexual assaulters. Although all rapists display differing characteristics, there are some cognitive factors present in many aggressive offenders: they generally have negative views of women, endorse rape myths, condone violence, and display a hyperidentification with the masculine role (Marshall, Laws, & Barbaree, 1990b; Scully, 1990). Additionally, rapists tend to display personality deficits such as a sense of worthlessness and low self-esteem, a sense of vulnerability, impaired social relations, a dysphoric mood state (with an underlying mood state of anger, fear, and/or depression), and a mismanagement of aggression (Groth, 1983: 163).

Researchers commonly classify rapists by the primary motivation of their offenses, and classifications of rape can be most broadly categorized as sexual or nonsexual in nature (Barbaree et al., 1994). These can be broken down even further to create typologies, as indicated by several researchers (Burgess, Hartman, Ressler, Douglas, & MacCormack, 1986; Cohen, Garofolo, Boucher, & Seghorn, 1971; Groth, 1979; Knight & Prentky, 1990; Perkins, 1991; Rada, 1978; Scully & Marolla, 1985; Seghorn & Cohen, 1980). For the purpose of this book, typologies of rapists are summarized and classified into four categories: *exclusively sexual, sadistic, power/control,* and *opportunistic.*[1] Those classified as exclusively sexual and sadistic are motivated by sexual needs, whereas those classified as power/control and opportunistic rapists are motivated by nonsexual needs. Though rape is a sexual offense, many researchers believe that nonsexual needs, in particular power and control, most commonly motivate rape (Brownmiller, 1975; Stermac & Segal, 1989). Researchers have identified at least three variables that suggest some rapists are motivated by nonsexual needs. First, some assessment studies of arousal indicate that most rapists are aroused more by consensual than nonconsensual sex (Marshall & Barbaree, 1990b). They also tend to score almost equally to control groups consisting of non–rapists when exposed to violent erotic material (Barbaree et al., 1994). Second, there is a high incidence of sexual dysfunction during rapes (the offender is either unable to get an erection or ejaculate) (West, 1987). Although this could be attributed to the increased level of anxiety in such circumstances, it is unlikely that sexual dysfunction would occur if rape were based purely on the sexual needs of the offender. Finally, soldiers in nearly every war have committed mass rapes of the enemy. Research indicates that this is an expression of power over the

Table 5.1 Rape Typologies (Based on Motivation)

Sexually Motivated	**Exclusively Sexual:** Offender seeks sexual gratification and uses as much force as necessary to achieve such gratification
	Sadistic: Offender achieves sexual gratification through pain and/or fear from the victims; often psychopathic; offense may lead to sexual murder
Non-Sexually Motivated	**Power/Control:** Offender desires power and dominance over the victim; sometimes the motivation is humiliation, degradation; the offender is often angry; a pseudo-sexual act
	Opportunistic: Recreational/situational offender who leads impulsive, adventure-seeking lifestyle; assault often committed during another offense
	Mass Rape During War: Need for power and domination of another people; weapon to demoralize and destroy community honor

enemy, and, thus, a nonsexually motivated crime (Brownmiller, 1975; Lees, 1996). Table 5.1 shows a summary of these typologies.

These typologies are neither exclusive nor exhaustive and should be regarded as an outline of the most common categorical classifications of rapists. Although some rapists will fit into one of the typologies, most will be cross-classified into one or more categories. In addition to the specific typologies, some particular traits are common to all sex offenders. One example is negative affective states; emotions such as loneliness, isolation, and anger have been linked to hostility and aggression in sex offenders (Marshall, 1989; Marshall & Barbaree, 1990a; McKibben, Proulx, & Lusignan, 1994). Most rapists exhibit traits of social inadequacy, thus leading to negative emotional states and ultimately resulting in low self-esteem, stress, anxiety, and aggressive behavior. Additionally, many rapists have difficulty processing information from women and misconstrue negative cues and messages (Lipton, McDonel, & McFall, 1987; Stermac, Segal, & Gillis, 1990).

Rapists often begin committing deviant sexual acts at a young age; half of the known population of sexual assaulters have attempted or committed their first deviant sexual acts before the age of 18 (Abel & Rouleau, 1990; Benoit & Kennedy, 1992; Epps, 1993; Groth, 1983). Rape-supportive attitudes are seen to be strongest in adolescence, and as such adolescence is critical in the development of sexually aggressive behavior (Groth, Longo, & McFadin, 1982; Herman, 1990; Marshall & Barbaree, 1990a). Because sex drives surge dramatically in young boys at puberty, it is important at this time to establish proper sociosexual interactions. Animal research has shown that the development of controls over sexual behavior arises from a socialization process, and it is necessary for human males to acquire inhibitory controls over this "biologically endowed propensity for self-interest associated with the tendency to fuse sex and aggression" (Marshall & Barbaree, 1990a: 257).

Sexually Motivated Offenses

Exclusively Sexual Rarely is rape motivated purely by sexual needs; however, this type of rape is labeled here as *exclusively sexual*. These are sometimes labeled *sexual, nonsadistic* rapes (Knight & Prentky, 1990), thereby distinguishing them from rapes that occur when the offender seeks sexual gratification and uses as much force as necessary to achieve such gratification (Perkins, 1991). Like the majority of rapists, offenders who commit a rape because of sexual needs have difficulty achieving normal relationships; they see violence as the only way to secure their goals of sexual gratification (Marshall & Barbaree, 1990a). Freund (1990) describes this as "courtship disorder," or the inability to form a normal relationship with a partner of the same age. Rapists often have problems with intimate relations and feel they lack the ability to establish a satisfying love relationship with a woman (Rada, 1978). These feelings of sexual inferiority are common to rapists and can lead to exaggerated masculine behavior and eventually rape.

Sadistic Sexually motivated rapes can also be classified as *sadistic,* where offenders achieve sexual gratification from the victims' pain and/or fear (Perkins, 1991). These are the most dangerous sexual offenders, whose crimes frequently lead to sexual murder. They tend to be predatory, exhibit a high rate of recidivism (which often occurs shortly after release from institutions), be strangers to their victims, use violence in their offenses, and show little empathy for their victims (Ganzar & Sarason, 1973; Hare & Jutai, 1983; Hare & MacPherson, 1984; Pithers, 1994; Quinsey, Rice, & Harris, 1990; Quinsey, Warneford, Pruesse, & Link, 1975; Serin, 1991; Serin, Malcolm, Khanna, & Barbaree, 1994).

Sadistic rapists share many of the same characteristics as individuals with antisocial personality disorder, more commonly known as "psychopathic personality," though sadistic rapists are not all diagnosed with the disorder (Abel, Becker, & Skinner, 1980). Similar characteristics include impulsivity and aggressiveness, and both sadistic rapists and individuals with antisocial personality disorder tend to live unstable lives with no long-term plans (Hare & MacPherson, 1984; Serin, 1991). Additionally, they are often deceitful, irresponsible, and have a reckless disregard for the safety of others. Most important, both lack remorse when they cause injury or pain to another individual. The primary difference between the two is that sadistic rapists not only show little empathy for their victims, but the pain they cause sexually excites them. They seek out this pain and humiliation in order to become sexually excited, and the level of violence they use often escalates with each offense committed.

Dietz, Hazelwood, and Warren (1990) analyzed 30 sadistic offenders and described how they are different from nonsadistic offenders. Though there were only 30 offenders in their sample, their study provides insight into the sadistic criminal. They claim that the offenders showed a high degree of planning for their offenses, with most taking the victims to a preselected location, binding them, and intentionally torturing them. The types of torture varied, but included acts such as use of torture instruments, inserting foreign objects, beating, biting, whipping, and electric shock. The researchers admit that their study is not generalizable to all sexual sadists; however, it does give insight into the most serious of this type of offender.

Non-Sexually Motivated Offenses

Power/Control   All rapes are inherently motivated by an element of power and control; yet, there are some rapes in which the offender expresses power and control that are motivated by anger and/or hatred. They are usually considered to be interpersonal acts involving the need for power and aggression. Groth defines rape as a pseudo-sexual act, emphasizing the desire of offenders to achieve power and dominance rather than sexual gratification. He states that rape is "the sexual abuse of power and the sexual expression of needs, motives, and issues that are predominantly non-sexual. It is the sexual expression of aggression rather than the aggressive expression of sexuality" (Groth, 1983: 165).

The issue of power and control is also evident in rape cases where date-rape drugs, or Rohypnol (a.k.a. "roofies"), are used. This drug can cause the person ingesting it to black out, have memory loss, and lower his or her resistance to sexual abuse. These effects are increased if ingested with alcohol, and this is the likely form of ingestion when used as a date-rape drug. Victims generally report that they are drugged involuntarily when an acquaintance or date slips a dose of Rohypnol, which is odorless, tasteless, and colorless, into their drink. Though Sturman (2000) points out that drug rapes can be either planned or opportunistic, he states that in either situation the offender produces a situation in which he is in control of the victim.

Some theorists expand upon the idea of anger-motivated rapes by saying that sexual assaults are attempts to control and humiliate women (Darke, 1990; West, 1987). Darke proposes that the humiliation of women causes sexual arousal in the offenders, allowing the men to dominate and control vulnerable female victims. Although it may be argued that humiliation is a subjective term and the definition of "humiliating acts" lacks consensus, some researchers have noted an increase in "nastiness" of sexual assaults since the 1980s (Lloyd, 1991). Many victims claim that rapists use insulting and humiliating language during attacks, and force the victims to perform unusual sexual acts that they consider particularly degrading (West, 1987). Lloyd (1991) says that one interpretation of this could be that men who rape have an increasingly misogynistic attitude toward women and these acts are performed to humiliate them; however, these "humiliating" sexual acts could also be representative of consensual sexual acts that are now accepted sexual practices. It is nearly impossible to define "normal" sexual attitudes and behavior today, with society forming a "tolerantly critical acceptance of sexual acts" that would have previously been regarded with moral outrage (Saunders–Wilson, 1992).

Opportunistic   Opportunistic offenders, the other category of rapists who are motivated by nonsexual needs, are adventure-seeking individuals who lead impulsive, delinquent lifestyles. Also called "recreational" (Scully & Marolla, 1985) or "situational" (West, 1987) offenders, they usually commit sexual assaults during the course of another crime such as burglary. They commonly have a history of antisocial behavior, characterized by poor social and relationship skills. Many offenders have experienced poor socialization in childhood, which does not allow them access to appropriate sociosexual interactions. This is often facilitated by a violent parenting style, resulting in feelings of resentment, hostility, and the use of aggression (Marshall & Barbaree, 1990a). Langevin et al. (1984) found that many rapists had parents who would administer punishment frequently but inconsistently. He described the fathers as often drunken, aggressive, and in trouble with the law, and said the sons are likely to reproduce this behavior. Knight et al. (1983) further claim that if a boy is taught antisocial behavior and grows up in a hostile home, then there is a greater likelihood that he will become a rapist. A perceived social inadequacy may increase the level of stress and anxiety, which will in turn disinhibit sexual aggression and facilitate offending behavior.

Mass Rape: Sexual Violence as a Weapon of War   The typologies of rapists discussed previously indicate that nonsexual needs play an important role in the motivation of many sexual offenders. This is apparent more than ever with the extensive accounts of mass rape during wartime. Rarely, if ever, is rape during war motivated by sexual needs. Because rape is often associated with "the ideology of masculine aggressiveness" (West, 1987: 155), the motivation behind rape during wartime is the need for power and domination of another people. Usually occurring when victorious armies march through conquered territories, rape is used as a weapon to demoralize and destroy community honor (Lees, 1996: 59). Rape is often viewed as the ultimate humiliation of an enemy because it symbolizes a defiling of its people. War situations encourage an extreme type of machismo associated with a hegemonic form of masculinity (Connell, 1990). There is evidence that some soldiers have been given direct orders from superiors to rape victims both as a part of a military strategy and as a way to motivate hatred of the enemy (Lees, 1996). Although this helps to explain why some "ordinary Joes" (Brownmiller, 1975) are capable of performing sadistic acts that deviate from normal behavior, it does not explain the many victims' accounts that soldiers appeared to enjoy raping and demoralizing them (Seifert, 1993).

Rape in war has occurred throughout history, continuing in many cultures through present-day conflicts. It has been documented in wars of revolution, such as in George Washington's papers in 1780, and in wars of religion as far back as the First Crusade (Brownmiller, 1975). Nonetheless, few detailed accounts had been written about rape until World War I, and it was only with the mass rapes in Bosnia that the issue finally came into the public consciousness (Lees, 1996). Brownmiller has called the gang rape by soldiers a normal rather than abnormal aspect of war, although the extent of rape is dependent on the status of women in society. For example, the Vietcong consider women to have status equal to that of men, and as such they considered rape to be a serious crime (Brownmiller, 1975). In other societies, the women may be viewed either as objects that can be used and discarded (such as with the Jewish women in concentration and rape camps in World War II) or as objects that can be used to eradicate the enemy (such as with the "ethnic cleansing" of Bosnia). Even though international laws have been passed that make rape in wartime a serious offense, it is unlikely that the machismo role assumed by soldiers, which appears to be the primary cause of sexual assaults in wartime, will be eliminated (Cipolat, 1996).

Although these typologies look at the motivation to commit sexual assault, they do not take into consideration the relationship between the offenders and the victims. Some researchers have attempted to form typologies based on multiple axes that take into consideration all of these factors, believing that sexual assault is very different between strangers and acquaintances no matter the motivation (Knight & Prentky, 1990).

TYPOLOGIES OF CHILD MOLESTERS

Prior to the 1980s, perpetrators of child sexual abuse were viewed as "a small group of individuals with psychological abnormalities whose emotional disturbances resulted in inappropriate sexual interest in children" (La Fontaine, 1990: 99), but this group proved to be neither small nor distinct. Although the generalizations may be true of some perpetrators, they are usually incorrect (Abel & Rouleau, 1994). The majority of child sexual abusers are ordinary and do not stand out in a crowd (La Fontaine, 1990). It was the emergence of the feminist movement (Brownmiller, 1975), an extensive national survey in Canada that looked at sexual offenses against children (Canada, 1984), and empirical research with large groups of child molesters (for example, Abel et al., 1990; Finkelhor, 1986) that helped expose the true extent of child sexual abuse.

Many child molesters display characteristics similar to rapists: they tend to be socially inept in adult relations, have low self-esteem, feelings of inadequacy, and a sense of worthlessness and vulnerability. However, they usually exhibit characteristics opposite to those rapists who are overly aggressive, act on impulse, and are insensitive to victims' feelings (West, 1987). Some child molesters are violent; however, these are rare and tend to be non-incestuous offenders who abuse both girls and boys (Porter, 1984). Nonetheless, they usually seek a mutually comforting relationship with a child, and because of their poor social skills they find comfort in relationships with children that they consider to be passive, dependent, psychologically less threatening than adults, and easy to manipulate (Groth, 1983; West, 1987). Offenders who prefer relationships with agemates might regress to adult-child relationships because of a hindrance to normal adult relationships (Finkelhor, 1984; West, 1987). They frequently see themselves as physically unattractive, have problems with potency, have moral inhibitions, or have previously had frustrating experiences with adult relations.

There is often a connection between negative affective states and deviant sexual behavior for child molesters; however, unlike rapists, these tend to be states of inadequacy, humiliation, and loneliness rather than anger and hostility (McKibben et al., 1994).

Although several researchers have attempted to develop typologies of child molesters (Groth, Hobson, & Gary, 1982; Howells, 1981; Knight & Prentky, 1990), the existing literature fails to render consistent psychological profiles and characteristics that can distinguish these offenders (Conte, 1991). Some researchers explain child sexual abuse along three dimensions: age difference, specific sexual behavior, and sexual intent (Conte, 1991). Others (for example, Gebhard et al., 1965; Knight & Prentky, 1993) have classified offenders into subtypes based on an empirically derived classification system. The most common classification of child molesters, however, is based on the level of sexual attraction to children: whether an individual is primarily attracted to children or to adults (Finkelhor, 1984; Groth et al., 1982). It is this distinction that is the basis for most typologies of child molesters, even those that add factors relating for social competence and level of interaction with children.

The Fixated-Regressed Typologies

Classification of child molesters began in earnest in the 1970s, when researchers began to distinguish types of child molesters based on their motivation for committing sexually deviant behavior. By the 1980s, Groth et al. (1982) had developed a classification scheme based on the level of primary attraction to either children or agemates. As such, they devised a fixated-regressed dichotomy of sex offending.

Fixated offenders are an individual who exhibits persistent, continual, and compulsive attraction to children. They tend to be exclusively involved with children, and are usually attracted to children from adolescence (Finkelhor, 1984). Fixated offenders are most likely to choose extrafamilial victims who are either male adolescents or prepubescent girls (Abel & Rouleau, 1990; Simon, Sales, Kaskniak, & Kahn, 1992; West, 1987). Fixated offenders show psychological and emotional characteristics of children (Holmes & Holmes, 2002), and they do not develop sexually to the point of finding agemates attractive and desirable. They are often unable to attain any degree of psychosexual maturity and, during adulthood, have virtually no age-appropriate sexual relationships. The fixated offenders' desires are embedded in their psyche, and as such their actions usually do not result from the negative thoughts and feelings of the offense cycle discussed in Chapter 4.

Because of fixated offenders' sexual attraction to children or adolescents, researchers claim that they constitute both "a public health problem" (Abel, Lawry, Kalstrom, Osborn, & Gillespie, 1994) and a "criminal problem" (Freeman-Longo, 1996). They recruit, groom, and develop relationships with vulnerable children (in either an emotional or a situational sense), and these "relationships" often continue for several years (Conte, 1991). Because of their own inappropriate desires, many fixated offenders believe that their sexual relationships with children are caring and mutual, and that the child is able to derive pleasure and educational experience from the interaction (Abel & Rouleau, 1995; Marshall & Barbaree, 1990b).

Most fixated child molesters have committed more offenses than those for which they have been convicted, and for that reason they constitute a high risk to the community. The extensive grooming process often creates a close personal relationship between the offender and the victim, and as a result the victims are less likely to report the abuse, or when they do report the abuse, there is a significant delay in reporting (Abel & Rouleau, 1990; Abel et al., 1994; Elliot, Browne, & Kilcoyne, 1995). Fixated offenders who abuse boys are likely to commit more offenses than other types of offenders, and they are at the highest risk of reoffending after being convicted (Marques, Day et al., 1994; Marques, Nelson et al., 1994). In one well-cited study, Abel and Rouleau (1990) evaluated 561 male sex offenders who voluntarily sought treatment. The results showed that the non-incestuous offenders in the sample who assaulted young boys had, on average, 281 offenses and 150 victims.[2]

Unlike the fixated offenders, child molesters classified as *regressed* have a primary attraction to agemates. Their abusive behavior is not fixed, but rather is a temporary departure from their attraction to adults (Simon et al., 1992). The regressed offenders' behavior, which usually emerges in adulthood, tends to be precipitated by external stressors. These stressors, which are an important part of the offense cycle, can be situational in nature (for example, unemployment, marital problems, substance abuse), or they can be related to negative affective states (for example, loneliness, isolation). These stressors often lead to poor self-confidence, low self-esteem, and a self-pitying attitude (Schwartz, 1995), which subsequently lead to the abusive behavior.

Most regressed offenders develop normal relationships with agemates, and in fact many are married or cohabiting. They begin committing deviant sexual acts at times when they are having negative thoughts and feelings, like those represented in the offense cycle; commonly these negative thoughts and feelings develop at times of unrest with marital relations or as a result of stress, loneliness, and depression. Regressed offenders are rarely attracted to a particular type of child or adolescent in terms of age and gender. Instead, they victimize children to whom they have easy access—often their own children. Incestuous offenders tend to spend most of their time with their family and isolate the family from society in general (Miner & Dwyer, 1997). Incestuous relations are often more common and more severe in stepparent families, with the most frequent sexual relation occurring between stepfathers and stepdaughters (Redding Police Department, 1996).

Sexual abuse by a relative can be very traumatic, often more so than a stranger assault, because it is difficult for the victim to avoid contact with the perpetrator and cease such relations (West, 1987). Sexual acts among family members are also likely to be more intimate than abuse by strangers. Stranger assaults often consist of mild abuses such as exhibitionism or fondling, which are not physically intrusive in nature (La Fontaine, 1990). Though most incestuous offenders prefer heterosexual relationships, they form sexual relations with the children they have access to, regardless of the gender. Studies do not show child sexual abuse (either incestuous or non-incestuous) to be more prevalent in particular ethnic groups, and, contrary to popular perception, there is no significant difference between abuse in urban and rural areas and among various economic and social classes (La Fontaine, 1990).

Incestuous offenders almost always fit the regressed typology, since they tend to be attracted to agemates and develop relations with children for non-sexual reasons. Studies have found that incestuous offenders, like most regressed offenders, have similar arousal patterns to "normal" men (Freund, McKnight, Langevin, & Cibiri, 1972; Marshall & Eccles, 1991; Quinsey, Steinman, Bergerson, & Holmes, 1975). Sexual arousal is most commonly measured through a penile plethysmograph (PPG) as the male is shown erotic material. The control group ("normal" men) generally shows some level of arousal to photos of young children in erotic poses, and it is therefore difficult to differentiate between the groups of normal and regressed offenders. Fixated offenders, on the other hand, tend to show a strong level of attraction to the erotic material involving children. This indicates that, as with rapists, not all child molesters are motivated by sexual needs to commit their offenses.

Most studies show that, as a group, incestuous offenders have fewer victims and commit deviant sexual acts less frequently than extrafamilial child molesters (Berliner, Schram, Miller, & Milloy, 1995), and they are more disgusted with their desires than the average perpetrator of child sexual abuse (Langevin & Lang, 1985). However, it is unclear whether they actually offend less frequently or have lower rates of charges and convictions. Additionally, some incestuous offenders have also committed extrafamilial sexually deviant acts (Abel, Becker, Cunningham-Rathner, Mittlemen, & Rouleau, 1988). In Abel et al.'s study, 49 percent of stepfather-stepdaughter incestuous offenders also abused outside of the home, 18 percent of those committing rapes of adults as well as sexually abusing children. Another recent study showed that there is much more crossover than previously thought between inter- and extrafamilial child molesters (Berlin et al., 2003). This supports the notion that sex offenders constitute a heterogeneous group, and even the offenders who appear (at least superficially) to be the least dangerous to society do not always fit perceived typologies.

The fixated-regressed classification system is not only based upon the degree of sexual attraction to children, but also the degree of violence or force used in the sexually abusive act. Groth, Longo, and McFadin (1982) make a distinction between a sex-pressure offense and a sex-force offense. A *sex-pressure offense* is one where the offender either entices or entraps the victim into cooperating. Here the offender would prefer for the victim to cooperate, and if the victim resists, it is unlikely that the offender will follow through with the abuse. Alternatively, in a *sex-force offense* the offender uses either intimidation or physical aggression. These offenders attempt to intimidate victims who can easily be overpowered and present little resistance toward the sexual advance. If the victim does resist, the sex-force offender is more likely to use physical aggression to commit the act of abuse, despite the resistance.

Table 5.2 Fixated-Regressed Typologies of Child Molesters

	Motivation	Primary Victim Preference	Risk of Reoffending
Fixated Offender	■ Having never developed an attraction to age-appropriate partners, the fixated offender has a persistent, continual, and compulsive attraction to children ■ Behavior emerges in adolescence ■ Offenses are premeditated in nature and do not stem from stressors ■ Most likely to be diagnosed with pedophilia/ephebophilia	■ Extrafamilial Female (prepubescent), male (pubescent/adolescent) ■ Typically recruits vulnerable children and engages in extensive grooming in order to ensure continuation of the abuse	■ Very high risk of recidivism ■ The risk of recidivism increases according to the number of victims
Regressed Offender	■ Offending stems from stressors in the individual's environment that undermine self-esteem and confidence ■ Behavior emerges in adulthood ■ Offending is a departure from the offender's attraction to adults ■ Similar to rapists, the offender is not necessarily motivated by sexual needs alone	■ Intrafamilial, acquaintance ■ Gender varies, depending on who is accessible ■ Tend to victimize children to whom they have easy access	■ Because they are not sexually fixated on children, they are at a lower risk of reoffending if treated ■ Capable of feeling remorse for their actions

SOURCE: John Jay College (2004)

Since it was originally proposed, researchers have tested and expanded upon the fixated-regressed typology, though the concept of a motivation-based classification system has remained constant. The level of attraction to children is a common variable on which to base any classification system for child molesters, though this is not a dichotomous typology. Rather, the fixated-regressed typology is a continuum. Offenders are not simply attracted to children or agemates, but they have varying levels of attraction toward children.

Simon et al. (1992), who attempted to empirically validate the fixated-regressed typology, found support in their study for such a continuum. They

Table 5.3 FBI Typologies of Child Molesters

Type of Offender	Characteristics of Offenders
	Situational Offenders
Regressed	Offenders have poor coping skills, target victims who are easily accessible, abuse children as a substitute for adult relationships
Morally Indiscriminate	Offenders do not prefer children over adults and tend to use children (or anyone accessible) for their own interests (sexual and otherwise)
Sexually Indiscriminate	Offenders are mainly interested in sexual experimentation, and abuse children out of boredom
Inadequate	Offenders are social misfits who are insecure, have low self-esteem, and see relationships with children as their only sexual outlet
	Preferential Offenders
Seductive	Offenders "court" children and give them much affection, love, gifts, and enticements in order to carry on a "relationship"
Fixated	Offenders have poor psychosexual development, desire affection from children, and are compulsively attracted to children
Sadistic	Offenders are aggressive, sexually excited by violence, target stranger victims, and are extremely dangerous

SOURCE: Information from Holmes & Holmes (1996); table from John Jay College (2004)

reviewed the cases of 136 child molesters, looking at case history, Minnesota Multiphasic Inventory (MMPI) results, presentence reports, and police report data. They found a continuous distribution of offenders rather than the bimodal, dichotomous classification, and said that in order for the fixated–regressed typology to be correct, it must be considered on a continuum. Table 5.2 outlines the fixated–regressed typologies of child molesters discussed in this chapter.

The FBI Typologies

In constructing their classification system, the Federal Bureau of Investigation (FBI) used Groth's fixated–regressed typologies as a basis and expanded upon them, classifying child molesters into seven distinct subgroups. These seven subgroups correspond directly to the original regressed (regressed, morally indiscriminate, sexually indiscriminate, and inadequate) and fixated (seduction, introverted, and sadistic) typologies. Table 5.3 summarizes the characteristics of each of these types of offenders.

The MTC:CM3 Typologies

Like the FBI, Knight and Prentky (1990) also took into consideration issues of social competence and decision-making skills when they revised their original typologies of child molesters and arranged a model based on their degree of fixation and degree of contact. They developed multidimensional typologies of child molesters through a system known as the Massachusetts Treatment Center: Child Molester Typology, version 3 (MTC:CM3). This classification system is based on two axes: Axis I evaluates the level of fixation with children and the offender's level of social competence; Axis II evaluates the amount of contact, both interpersonal and sexual, that an offender has with children, including the amount and type of physical injury resulting from the contact. Each offender is assigned a separate Axis I and Axis II typology. Studies show that this classification system has a reasonable level of reliability and consistent ties to developmental antecedents of child sexual abuse (Knight & Prentky, 1990). This classification system also has distinctive prognostic implications, as shown in the preliminary results of a 25-year recidivism study conducted by the same researchers.

Other researchers have tried to replicate the findings by Knight and Prentky with further studies involving the MTC:CM3. Looman et al. (2001) conducted a study in Canada, whereby they classified 109 child molesters in accordance with the MTC:CM3 typology. They were able to classify all of the offenders except for the sadistic types into all subgroups with an acceptable level of reliability, thus replicating the original results. They found differences between the subgroups in phallometric assessments, with the high fixation-low social competence group showing the highest levels of sexual deviance on the Axis I assessment. The only group to show a clear fixation, or sexual preference for children, was the high fixation-low social competence group, the majority of whom preferred male victims and were more likely to have been victimized as children. The deviance indices for their sample for all four levels of Axis I indicated that child molesters fail to differentiate between appropriate and inappropriate stimuli. The preferential (high fixation) child molesters had the highest level of deviant sexual arousal and the greatest numbers of victims, but they caused the least amount of physical harm.

When analyzing the Axis II indices, Looman and colleagues found that low contact-high injury offenders were the most intrusive in their offenses and were the most likely to use physical force. This group also had a greater number of victims, were more likely to target strangers, and were the most likely to have deviant sexual arousal. Most offenders classified into Axis II groupings were equally likely to choose male and female victims except for the exploitative group, who were significantly more likely to choose female than male victims. Table 5.4 outlines the axes of the MTC:CM3 classification scheme.

Other Typologies

The level of fixation is not the only factor on which typologies of child molesters are based. Some researchers have examined the static information related to sex offenders to see if their background history is linked to their current abusive behavior, creating typologies based on this information. For example, Baxter, Marshall, Barbaree, Davidson, and Malcolm (1984) conducted a study whereby they analyzed the criminal records, personal history, social-sexual competence,

Table 5.4 MTC:CM3 Classification of Child Molesters

Axis I	■ Assesses the extent to which the offender is fixated with children (on a continuum)
	■ Measures the level of social competence of the offender
Axis II	■ Assesses the amount of contact the offender has with children (for example, exclusively involved with extrafamilial children, abuses own children)
	■ Meaning of the contact (sexual and interpersonal)
	■ Amount and type of physical injury involved in the contact (including threats and use of force)

SOURCE: John Jay College (2004)

and phallometric responses of incarcerated pedophiles, ephebophiles (individuals with recurrent, intense, sexually arousing fantasies about adolescents), and rapists. Their results showed that each of these groups had significantly different criminal and personal backgrounds, though all showed traits of social and social-sexual inadequacy, lack of assertiveness, low self-esteem, and negative attitudes. Otherwise, pedophiles were older, more poorly educated, less likely to be married, were rarely involved in nonsexual crime, and had a higher level of recidivism for sexual offenses. They also showed a higher degree of deviant sexual arousal, or, more specifically, they failed to show a sexual response or erotic preference for adults.

In another study, Simkins (1993) conducted an exploratory investigation to determine how sexually repressed and nonrepressed child molesters in therapy progress, measuring this change on a battery of personality and research instruments. He categorized 68 child molesters as repressed, nonrepressed, or exploitive based on their psychosexual histories. He found that the sexually repressed child molesters were significantly less likely to complete therapy. He also found differences between the these classifications of offenders on the MMPI, the Burt Rape Myth Scales, some of the Multiphasic Sexual Inventory Scales, and the Mosher's Sex Guilt Scale.

Yet another group of researchers analyzed 168 pedophiles, ephebophiles, and incest offenders in order to differentiate between characteristics of these types of child molesters (Danni & Hampe, 2002). They gathered data from the presentence investigation reports and found that eight independent variables—sexually victimized as a child, prepubertal victim, seduction motive, age-appropriate relationships, stress, own child as victim, social façade, and anger—significantly discriminated between these types of sex offenders in approximately 90 percent of the cases. They found that pedophiles were the most likely group to have experienced sexual victimization when they were children, were the most likely to prefer and have prepubertal sex partners, and were the most motivated to seduce their victims. Alternatively, the ephebophiles were the most likely to have experienced external stress, and incest offenders were the most likely to feel a sense of entitlement to their victims.

Laws, Hanson, Osborn, and Greenbaum (2000) conducted a study with 124 child molesters who voluntarily participated in treatment, where the aim was to determine the extent to which multiple measures of pedophilic interest improved the diagnostic accuracy of any single measure. All participants admitted that they had a sexual attraction to children or had committed a sexual act with a child. Only 72 of the child molesters completed the treatment program, and those completed a self-report card-sort measure of sexual interest and had their levels of sexual arousal measured with a penile plethysmoghraph (PPG, with both audio and visual stimuli). All three measures used to assess pedophilic interest (that is, card sort, PPG slides, PPG audio) significantly differentiated boy-object and girl-object child molesters. Though the card-sort measure showed the greatest classification accuracy, all three measures together showed a classification accuracy of 91.7 percent.

PARAPHILIAS AND OTHER
SEXUAL DISORDERS

Many sexual offenders are diagnosed with paraphilias or other sexual disorders.[3] Paraphilias are not necessarily criminal; they are sexual disorders described in the fourth edition of the *Diagnostic and Statistical Manual of Mental Disorders (DSM IV)* (American Psychiatric Association, 1994). The features of all paraphilias are recurrent, intense sexually arousing fantasies or urges involving either nonhuman objects, suffering or humiliation of oneself or one's partner, children or other nonconsenting persons (pp. 522–523). For some paraphiliacs, these fantasies or stimuli are necessary in order to achieve erotic arousal, whereas for others they are episodic and the individual can be stimulated otherwise. The behavior, urges, and fantasies cause clinically significant distress or impairment in social, occupational, or other areas of functioning. Most paraphiliacs suffer from more than one paraphilia, or have at some point in their lives experienced multiple paraphilic interests (Abel, Becker, Mittelmen, Cunningham-Rathner, Rouleau, & Murphy, 1987).

There are eight primary paraphilias listed in the *DSM IV*: exhibitionism, voyeurism, frotteurism, sadism, masochism, fetishism, transvestic fetishism, and pedophilia. Additionally, there are several others labeled "paraphilias otherwise not specified." Most paraphilic acts do not come to the attention of authorities for several reasons (American Psychiatric Association, 1999). These are often private acts that take place in the home, and they only come to the attention of authorities (or therapists) when they become habitual or when the person acts on the paraphiliac urge outside the home. For offenses that do not take place within the home, the paraphiliac and victim are generally strangers and do not have a relationship. Because many acts take place quickly (for example, exhibitionism), the victim is unlikely to get a sufficient view of the perpetrator and offer a full

Table 5.5 Eight Main Paraphilias of the *DSM IV*

Noncontact/Minimal Contact Paraphilias	**Exhibitionism**: Exposure of genitals to a stranger; may include exposure only or masturbation during the exposure
	Frotteurism: Touching or rubbing up against a nonconsenting person in a crowded area; may rub genitals against or fondle the victim
	Voyeurism: Watching a stranger who is naked, disrobing, or engaging in a sexual act; no sexual activity sought with the victim
	Fetishism: Sexual attraction to nonliving objects, such as a shoe or undergarment; individual often masturbates while holding the object or has a partner wear the object during sexual encounters
	Transvestic Fetishism: Cross-dressing; heterosexual man is sexually aroused by himself wearing the female clothing
High-Contact Paraphilias	**Sexual Masochism**: The act of being humiliated, bound, beaten, or made to suffer in some way; may occur with a partner or during masturbation
	Sexual Sadism: The act of humiliating, binding, beating, or making another person suffer in some way; sexual excitement the result of control over the victim
	Pedophilia: Sexual activity with a prepubescent child; may involve own children or nonrelated children, males or females

SOURCE: American Psychiatric Association (1994)

description to the police. Additionally, some victims do not know they are subject to this abuse (for example, voyeurism) and are unable to notify authorities.

Paraphilias differ greatly; some involve no contact with a victim (for example, fetishism), some involve minor contact (for example, frotteurism), whereas others contain much contact and even violence (for example, sadism). They can also be based on urges and fantasies that are mild (the individual may be markedly distressed by his feelings but not act upon them), moderate (the individual occasionally acts on his urges), or severe (the individual repeatedly acts on his urges). Reports show that paraphiliacs typically have more than one paraphilia, and that there is crossover between types of acts committed by paraphiliacs. For instance, one report states that "paraphilac persons tend to cross over between touching and non touching of their victims, between family and nonfamily members, between female and male victims, and to victims of various ages" (American Psychiatric Association, 1999: 47). The primary paraphilias, shown in Table 5.5, are described following.

Noncontact and Minimal Contact Paraphilias

The most common noncontact paraphilia that comes to the attention of thera-pists and authorities is *exhibitionism,* or the exposure of genitals to a stranger. Exhibitionism is almost exclusively male, though there are some females known to be exhibitionists. Sometimes the offender masturbates when he exposes him-self, and at other times the act is simply to shock the stranger. However, many exhibitionists fantasize that the stranger is aroused by their exposure, and they go home to masturbate about this fantasy after the act occurs. Those who expose themselves tend to do so frequently, and often expose themselves many times before being caught and arrested. Additionally, they have the highest known number of sexual offenses per offender (Abel et al., 1987).

Because the rate of exhibiting is so high, many studies have been devoted to this paraphilia. Researchers have found that exhibitionists, like rapists and child molesters, often experience loneliness and have intimacy deficits (Marshall, 1989), and they show higher levels of arousal to consensual adult sexual relations than exhibiting (Marshall, Anderson, & Fernandez, 1999). This indicates that sex-ual needs are not the only motivating factor for exhibitionists, and their primary motivation may be nonsexual in nature.

Another common paraphilia, though one that comes to the attention of authorities far less frequently than exhibitionism, is fetishism. *Fetishism* involves sexual fantasies and urges involving nonliving objects. Usually the fetish is required for sexual excitement, and without it there is some type of erectile dys-function. The range of fetishes is vast; though the most common fetish objects are women's underclothes and shoes, there are also extreme fetishes, such as with urine and feces (labeled *urophilia* and *coprophilia,* respectively). Some individuals even have fetishes about stuffed animals; "furries," as they are called, dress like and surround themselves by stuffed animals, and they have conventions and Internet sites associated with their fetish. Those sexually aroused by the stuffed animals (a paraphilic interest in them) are referred to as "plushies" (Gurley, 2001). Though this type of paraphilia is considered amusing by some and deviant by others, it, like all paraphilias, can be distressing to the individuals involved.

Though the most common fetish involves women's clothing, this is not the same as dressing up in women's clothing. *Transvestic fetishism* is another type of paraphilia; this involves men who keep a collection of women's clothing and intermittently use it to cross-dress. While dressed, the man will usually mastur-bate and imagine he is the object of his sexual fantasy. This occurs only in het-erosexual males, or males whose primary sexual preference is to be with women. As with all paraphilias, there are different degrees of transvestic fetishism. For some males cross-dressing creates a peace of mind, whereas others are depressed about their need to do so. One convicted rapist who cross-dresses describes his experience with transvestic fetishism in the following way:

> I was leaving the house at night, going off, dressing up, and spending the night dressed up in the stuff, which made me feel totally different. But it also put a strain on my relationship, so I turned to the drugs. Because I would get so low, my self-esteem would go so far down, that I would take drugs to bring myself back up. . . .

I want to be a normal human being, I don't want to be weird. I want to be a normal person, a father to my kids, a husband to my wife.

A fourth paraphilia is *frotteurism,* which is touching and rubbing up against a nonconsenting person. This occurs in a crowded place, such as a subway car during rush hour, and is an almost exclusively male paraphilia. He may touch his genitals against the person or "accidentally" rub the other person's genitals or breasts. He usually fantasizes about having an exclusive relationship with this person, and he will generally masturbate about the contact at a later date.

Another noncontact paraphilia is *voyeurism,* which is the observation of unsuspecting individuals in the process of either disrobing or engaging in sexual activity. No sexual activity is sought with the "victims," though the voyeur may masturbate while watching the persons or later in response to the memory. This is a noncontact offense and does not seem particularly dangerous (though, perhaps, unnerving if discovered); yet, some offenders who commit serious sexual offenses such as rape often begin their deviant sexual behavior through "peeping" (Terry, 1999). Some offenders explain that they inadvertently witnessed an individual disrobing and they became excited, thereafter seeking out more of the same type of stimulation. One offender, who attempted to rape a woman and ultimately murdered her, described his escalation of fantasies in the following way:

> *I went out and got drunk one night and walked by a clothesline and saw some women's underwear and* [stole] *them. Then I started peeping in women's windows. And then I started fantasizing about having sex. I started fantasizing about raping and, it wasn't only rape, it was about me hitting her on the head, and her unconscious and then having sex with her, because that is the only way I thought I would get sex.*

This excerpt shows an individual with more than one paraphilia—voyeurism and fetishism—and it shows how there was an escalation of paraphilias into a serious, violent fantasy. Most paraphiliacs do not become violent, though many voyeurs do eventually desire sexual contact with an individual they are watching.

In addition to the noncontact or minor contact paraphlias discussed, the *DSM IV* lists paraphilias otherwise not specified, many of which are also noncontact. For example, telephone scatologia is the urge to make obscene phone calls, and the paraphiliac repeatedly calls strangers and speaks to them sexually. These are not consensual phone calls, and the caller is sexually aroused sometimes by a conversation that ensues and sometimes by the shock that is caused (Holmes, 1991). The common element between the noncontact or minimal contact paraphilias is that the offender typically is excited by his behavior and masturbates in response to the behavior later. With exhibitionism, frotteurism, and scatologia, the offender envisions excitement by the victims. He misperceives the victims' cues of shock, anger, or fear as sexual excitement at his exposure, touch, or sexually suggestive words. Though the paraphilic act may cause some distress to the victim, the distress is not likely to be severe. Rather, the paraphilias may be more distressful to the paraphiliac than the victim. For example, he may not understand why he has desires to cross-dress and may seek therapy to "cure" this disorder. Other paraphilias, however, may be very dangerous.

High-Contact Paraphilias

Serious paraphilias are those involving violence, children, or other nonconsenting persons, and in extreme cases may lead to death. *Pedophilia* involves sexual activity with children and may cause significant harm to the victims of such offenses. For an individual to be classified as a pedophile, he must have

> recurrent, intense sexually arousing fantasies, sexual urges or behavior of at least six months duration involving sexual activity with a prepubescent child in which the fantasies, sexual urges or behavior cause significant distress or impairment and the individual is at least sixteen years of age and at least five years older than the child. (American Psychiatric Association, 1994: 528)

Not all child molesters are pedophiles because, like rapists, they are not all driven by sexual needs and therefore may not experience these intense sexual urges. Neither are all pedophiles child molesters, because they might not act on these intense sexual urges.

Pedophilic acts conducted by fixated offenders tend to occur on many instances over a long period of time. Other dangerous paraphilias involve violence or prohibited sexual acts, the most common of which are sexual sadism and sexual masochism.

Sexual masochism is the act of being humiliated, beaten, bound, or otherwise made to suffer. Some acts are conducted on the person's own, such as binding themselves, shocking themselves electrically, sticking themselves with pins, or similar such actions. Other times acts are committed with partners, such as bondage, blindfolding, and whipping. *Sexual sadism* takes place when the individual derives sexual excitement from the psychological or physical suffering of another person. This involves the same actions as in masochism, but performing instead of receiving. The acts can be minor and cause little damage, such as humiliating one's partner, or the acts may potentially cause a lot of damage, such as *hypoxia* (the deprivation of oxygen). Sexually sadistic acts often increase in severity over time, and sadists who are diagnosed with antisocial personality disorders may cause serious injury or even death to their victims (American Psychiatric Association, 1994).

Many sadists and masochists experience both of these paraphilias, and as such they are often combined into one disorder: sadomasochism. They partake in giving and receiving pain, humiliation, and degradation. Though called a paraphilia, there are many "normal" couples who participate in sadomasochistic activities. This once again illustrates how our changing societal acceptance of acts once considered deviant is modified over time, resulting in acts no longer being taboo. The only time sadomasochistic acts are brought to the attention of authorities is when the violence involved creates a negative outcome. One controversial case involving such activity occurred in England in 1987. In the case of *Brown and others* (1992), the police arrested three men who were in possession of videotapes of them performing sadomasochistic activities with 44 other men over a 10-year period. The activities included maiming of the genitalia (for example, piercing with fish hooks and needles), branding, and beatings with hands and instruments such as cat-o'-nine-tails, some of which drew blood and caused scarring.

All of the activities that occurred were consensual,[4] they took place in the privacy of the home, and they occurred for no other reason than sexual gratification. The case eventually went to the European Court of Human Rights in order to determine if the state has a right to interfere in private sexual encounters. The court stated that the state does have a right to intervene, even though the behavior constitutes a "private morality" because of the harm (potential and actual) resulting from the acts. The decision was based on the extreme nature of the acts and was deemed necessary for the protection of public health. The court compared the nature of the acts to drug abuse, declaring that the state has the obligation to intervene in activities that potentially may result in harm to an individual, even if that individual chooses to participate in that activity and it harms no one other than him- or herself.

Sexual sadism is a paraphilia that typically develops in adolescence, with interests piqued through masochistic masturbatory practices. *Autoerotic asphyxia* is a dangerous activity that constricts the oxygen during masturbation, accomplished with the use of a strangulation device (typically, a ligature with padding in order to prevent rope burns), a plastic bag, a chemical (for example, nitrous oxide), water, chest compression, or choking (Geberth, 1996; Hazelwood, Dietz, & Burgess, 1983). Both males and females participate in autoeroticism, and the purpose of it is to create a higher level of sexual excitement through the restriction of oxygen to the brain. The sexual excitement does not just occur through the restriction of oxygen, but as a combination of ritualistic behavior, oxygen deprivation, danger, and fantasy (Geberth, 1996: 319). Unfortunately, accidental deaths occur from this activity—estimated at 500 to 1,000 per year in the United States—many of which are mistaken for suicides or homicides (Hazelwood et al., 1983).

Though autoerotic asphyxiation is generally linked to sexual masochism, not all individuals who partake in autoerotic activities are diagnosed with this paraphilia, and many exhibit other paraphilias. Hazelwood et al. (1983) conducted a study on autoerotic fatalities, with a sample of 150 subjects. Cited as the most extensive study on this issue (Geberth, 1996), the authors noted that subjects evidenced the following paraphilias in addition to masochism and/or sadism: fetishism, transvestic fetishism, pedophilia, voyeurism, coprophilia, and mysophilia (sexual attraction to mud or dirt). These diagnoses were substantiated through previous actions (for example, repeated abuse of children substantiated pedophilia), material the subject possessed (for example, drawings of sadistic activity), or the state in which they were found (for example, the bodies are often found dressed in women's clothing, indicating transvestic fetishism).

Like other forms of deviant sexual behavior, autoerotic asphyxiation has been documented historically, with the earliest known origin a Mayan relic dating to A.D. 1000 (Hazelwood et al., 1983). It was also documented in

European artifacts and books from the 18th through the 20th centuries, presumably sparked by publication of papers by the Marquis de Sade (Hazelwood et al., 1983). Though it is unclear what prompts individuals to become involved with this behavior, anecdotal evidence indicates that adolescents hear through word of mouth that this activity provides intense sexual pleasure. Unfortunately, proper precautions are not always taken to ensure that oxygen intake is resumed after sexual pleasure is achieved.

Another deviant sexual act that occurs more often than previously believed is *bestiality,* or sexual activity with animals.[5] Any sexual activity with animals is prohibited, yet it is practiced in many rural areas where animals are easily accessible. One offender described his sexual intercourse with a cow as a "rite of passage. . . . All the boys did it and you had to do it so you wouldn't be a virgin." Several sexual offenders who are participating in cognitive-behavioral treatment programs today admit to participating in bestiality, though this population is hardly representative of the general population. Yet, it is clear from the popularity of Internet sites containing images of bestiality that the practice is intriguing, if not avidly practiced, among a subsection of the general population.

Bestiality was also of concern to practitioners at the beginning of the century, as Krafft-Ebing (1886/1965) recorded several cases of bestiality in *Psychopathia Sexualis* involving intercourse with rabbits, hens, goats, dogs, and other domestic animals. Some of the cases involve the paraphilia of *zoophilia,* or cases that Krafft-Ebing claimed were of a pathological nature. For instance, one man "was convicted of having committed masturbation and sodomy on dogs and rabbits. . . . A., stated that . . . if he were called upon to choose between a woman and a female rabbit, he would choose the rabbit" (p. 472). He describes other individuals who have sexual intercourse with animals because of perceived sexual inadequacy with women rather than a sexual attraction to the animal. For instance,

> a man was caught having intercourse with a hen. He was thirty years old and of high social position. The chickens had been dying one after another, and the man causing it had been wanted for a long time. When asked by the judge for the reason for such as act, the accused said that his genitals were so small that coitus with women was impossible. Medical examination showed that his genitals were, in fact, extremely small. (pp. 470–471)

Bestiality, sexual sadism, and masochism involve dangerous acts, though they do not always lead to death. Another serious paraphilia is *necrophilia,* or sexual intercourse with dead bodies. Rosman and Resnick (1989) describe three types of necrophiles, with varying degrees of severity. The first is the *pseudo necrophile,* also called a fantasy necrophile; this is an individual who either fantasizes about sex with dead bodies or has sex with dead bodies only periodically. The pseudo necrophile prefers the sexual partner to be alive but pretend to be dead, and there are many reports from prostitutes that their "clients" make them partake in this behavior. A second classification of necrophile is the *regular necrophile;* this is an individual who regularly has sexual intercourse with dead bodies. He is attracted to corpses and frequently works in an occupation where there is access to dead bodies, such as a coroner, or in a place like a morgue or graveyard.

Though the pseudo and regular necrophiles are dangerous and partake in prohibited behavior, they do not kill the victims in order to have sexual intercourse with them. This describes the third degree of necrophilic behavior, where the person is labeled a *homicidal necrophile*. This person kills in order to have intercourse with dead bodies, which is an extreme form of the paraphilia. Some serial killers are homicidal necrophiles, the most infamous being Jeffery Dahmer. Dahmer lured young men to his apartment and then proceeded to drug, strangle, dismember, and cannibalize them. He kept them alive for several days, turning them into "love slaves" by torturing them prior to killing them.[6] Once dead, he had sexual intercourse with some of the victims before dismembering them and keeping body parts (and photos of the dismembered body parts) as trophies.

The case of Jeffery Dahmer is extreme, and most offenders who commit sexual homicides do not commit necrophilic acts. Rather, most sexual murderers achieve sexual gratification by killing a person. It is common after a sexual murder (also called *lust murder*) for the individual to masturbate over the body or to insert a foreign object into the vagina or rectum as an act of sexual substitution (Ressler, Burgess, & Douglas, 1988). Ressler et al. (1988) conducted a study of sexual murderers and found several commonalities between the offenders; most important, they have an active fantasy life, and their fantasies are violent and sexual in nature. They found a link between sadistic acts and fantasies, as sadists' violent fantasies can lead to sexual murder. It therefore follows that some sexual sadists are in danger of escalating into becoming sexual murderers if they are not detected and stopped.

Though there is crossover among rapists who kill, necrophiliacs, sexual sadists, and sexual murderers, there are also differences between typologies with regard to motivation and postmortem actions with the victims. Some rapists (generally, of the sadistic rapist typology) and sexual sadists are aroused by the torture and pain of the victim, and their actions sometimes result in death. Unlike sexual murderers, these offenders do not derive satisfaction from the murder itself. All three types of offenders, however, are likely to mutilate and torture the victims, and the killer becomes more aroused as the victim is in an increasingly high level of agony. Though this is also common to some necrophiliacs, they differ in that they are likely to kill the victim earlier in order to maintain control over the situation. Some sexual murderers are like necrophiliacs in that they like to keep "trophies" of their victims. Though these can be body parts, they are more likely to be photos or an object (for example, an article of clothing) belonging to the victim. These trophies act as a catalyst for further fantasies about the act they committed. Many sexual murderers are diagnosed with antisocial personality disorders, and often they are serial killers. This is because the desire to kill for sexual gratification is similar to a paraphilia, and the individual needs to kill in order to repeatedly achieve the same level of sexual gratification.

CHAPTER SUMMARY

- Individuals who commit sexual offenses share a number of common characteristics, and as such it is possible to create typologies of offenders based on these commonalities. Although researchers have devised a variety of sophisticated typologies, very few offenders fit precisely into any one category.

- Most typologies are based on the offenders' motivation for committing the deviant acts (for example, sexual versus nonsexual needs).

- Rapists commonly commit offenses for nonsexual reasons, in particular out of a desire for power and control. This is also true of rapes that occur during wartime, as the rape leads to further humiliation of the enemy.

- The most common basic typology for child molesters is the fixated-regressed model. Fixated offenders are primarily attracted to children, whereas regressed offenders are primarily attracted to agemates; they regress to abusing children at times of upheaval in their lives (for example, ending of a marriage, loss of a job, stress at work).

- Typologies are best considered in two ways: on a continuum rather than as dichotomous, as there are various levels of the typologies (this is the case with the fixated-regressed typologies); or, typologies can be explained on multiple axes (like the MTC:CM3).

- Many sex offenders are diagnosed with paraphilias, which are medical diagnoses, not legal classifications. Some paraphilias are serious, causing significant distress for the offender and possibly leading to harm or death of the victim. Others are relatively minor, do not involve contact with the victim, and are practiced as consensual acts among "normal" adults.

DISCUSSION QUESTIONS

1. What is the benefit of creating typologies of offenders? Do all sex offenders fit into specific typologies? Why or why not?

2. What is the most common motivation of rapists? Explain through supporting evidence how we know this.

3. Typologies of child molesters are based primarily on what factor?

   How have typologies of child molesters evolved over the past 20 years?

4. What are paraphilias? Are they criminal acts? Why or why not? Why is it important to diagnose paraphilias?

NOTES

1. Many researchers have developed typologies of rapists, and all vary slightly in their categories and definitions. These four categories are a summary of the available literature. For more intricate models of rapists based on multiple axes, see Knight and Prentky (1990).

2. Some researchers cite their definitions of *offense* and *victim* as problematic, stating that the definitions may include behavior that is uncomfortable but not abusive. Additionally, these numbers refer to a single incident as an offense, thus causing the number of offenses per offender to be substantially high. Despite these reservations, their findings on sexual abuse are generally accepted as credible and sound.

3. Individuals diagnosed with paraphilias are not necessarily sex offenders. However, the paraphilias usually only come to the attention of therapists once the individual has been convicted of an offense and is required to participate in a treatment program.

4. Though consensual, one of the 44 men videotaped was under the age of 21. The age of consent for homosexual behavior was, at that time in England, 21 years of age. As such, the defendants were also charged with committing a sexual act with a minor.

5. If a person does commit a sexual act with an animal, it is not necessarily a paraphilia. In order for a person to be diagnosed with a paraphilia, the individual must have zoophilia, or a sexual attraction to animals. This is similar to how child molesters are not all pedophiles because they do not all have intense, recurring sexual urges about prepubescent children.

6. For instance, he drilled holes into the victims' skulls while they were alive and filled the holes with acid. He was trying to turn them into zombies so that they would be his love slaves (Geberth, 1996).

6

Juvenile Offenders

Much of the literature on sexual offending relates to adult male offenders, with little insight provided into the juvenile offender populations. Though smaller in numbers than the adult male population, juvenile sexual offenders are unique in their characteristics and in the way that they are managed, treated, and monitored. Knowledge of this population is limited, largely because of the lack of reporting or delays in reporting combined with the low numbers of juveniles who are convicted or adjudicated delinquent. Much of the information that does exist on juvenile sex offenders comes from self-report studies of adults who retroactively discuss their deviant adolescent behavior (Weinrott, 1996).

Juveniles who sexually offend vary significantly in age, understanding of sexual issues, development, maturity, and availability of coping mechanisms (Knight & Prentky, 1993). Like adult offenders, they form a heterogeneous group and commit a variety of offenses (Harris, 2000). Many clinicians and researchers note two distinct groups of juvenile offenders: adolescent and preadolescent offenders. Both groups offend for a variety of reasons, and there are no universally accepted theoretical models that can explain why either group begins and continues to offend (American Psychiatric Association [APA], 1999). There are, however, characteristics, pathologies, and histories common to most juvenile sex offenders.

It is pertinent to address sexually deviant behavior in juveniles, because an overview of the adult population indicates that deviant behavior and paraphilias often develop prior to adulthood (Abel, Mittleman, & Becker, 1985).

Additionally, adult sex offenders who had sexual convictions as adolescents generally commit more offenses as adults, and commit offenses that are more serious than those committed by adults who were not juvenile offenders (Abel, Rouleau, & Cunningham-Rather, 1986). As such, early intervention is essential in order to reduce the potential for future offenses (Abel, Osborn, & Twigg, 1993). The aim of this chapter is to present an overview of juvenile sexual offenders and to examine what steps must be taken in order to effectively treat and manage this group.

WHO ARE JUVENILE SEXUAL OFFENDERS?

Because the majority of literature regarding sex offenders focuses on the adult male population, it is surprising to find that juveniles commit a large number of the known sexual crimes. There are many similarities between adult and juvenile sex offenders, particularly in terms of the etiology of offending behavior, their patterns of behavior, their social characteristics, and the cognitive distortions that help them to maintain the behavior (Ryan, 1999). However, Ryan states that when compared to adults, juveniles tend to be either less aware of the harm they cause as a result of their behavior or more aware and thus more uncomfortable. Shaw, Lewis, Loeb, Rosado, and Rodriguez (2000) found that there is no significant difference between the victims of juvenile and adult sex offenders in terms of the type of abuse endured, whether there was penetration during the offense, and the amount of force used by the perpetrator. Alternatively, Allard-Dansereau, Haley, Hamane, and Bernard-Bonnin (1997) found that young sexual aggressors were more likely to engage in penetrative acts than were adult aggressors.

Epps (1999) found many traits in juvenile sex offenders that are similar to those in adult sex offenders, including low self-esteem, poor social skills, peer relationship difficulties, social isolation and loneliness, emotional problems, shyness and timidity, educational and academic problems, intellectual and neurological impairments, psychiatric problems, gender identity confusion, feelings of confused masculinity, problems arising from sexual and physical victimization, sexual deviancy and dysfunction, substance abuse, and family problems (p. 11). Though all studies on juvenile sex offenders do not support Epps's assertion that these characteristics are significantly increased in juvenile sex offenders compared to nonsexual offenders, nonoffenders, or adults, most find similar trends.

Statistics on Juvenile Sexual Offenders:
Prevalence, Delinquency, and Recidivism

One key study on juvenile sex offenders comes from the National Adolescent Perpetrator Network (NAPN) (1993), an organization that collected data on 1,600 juvenile sex offenders in 30 states. Their report showed that 90 percent of juvenile sex offenders are male, and 60 percent penetrate the victim in some way. This study also showed that the majority of juvenile sex offenders have committed nonsexual offenses, and only about 7 percent committed only sexual offenses. The age range for juvenile sex offenders in their data sample was 5 to 19, with an average age of just over 14 years. Broken down, the average age for male offenders was nearly 15 years, whereas females were younger, at just over 13 years. The literature review by Davis and Leitenberg (1987) produced slightly different results, as they found the average age of juvenile sexual offenders to be 15.

The exact amount of sexually deviant behavior perpetrated by adolescents is not clear, though official statistics, studies, and self-report surveys give an idea as to the amount of offending. Weinrott (1996) summarizes official statistics from the Uniform Crime Reports (UCR) 1984–1993, which indicate that juveniles are responsible for 15.4 percent of forcible rape and 17 percent of other sexual offenses. Weinrott also summarizes the self-reported data from the National Youth Survey, which show that approximately 3 percent of the adolescent population has committed a sexual offense—much higher than estimates given by the National Crime Victimization Survey (NCVS), which are lower than 1 percent. According to Becker et al. (1986), juveniles are responsible for approximately 20 percent of rapes and between 30 percent and 50 percent of cases of child sexual abuse. Ryan (1999) states that more than half of the male child victims and 20–30 percent of female child victims are abused by an older juvenile.

Most juvenile perpetrators are fewer than five years older than the victim, and in the NAPN sample, only 4 percent of juvenile sex offenders' victims were adults. A large amount of sexual offending by juveniles takes place in the home, and 90 percent of the perpetrators know their victims. Of those victims, 39 percent are blood relatives, 10 percent peers, 6 percent total strangers, and many others are known in an acquaintance or authoritative capacity, such as a neighbor. These statistics are similar to the results of a study by Fehrenbach, Smith, Monastersky, and Deisher (1986). They show that of the 305 11- to 17-year-olds in their study, 60 percent had victims under the age of 12. One-third of the juveniles' victims in this study were family members, 12 percent were acquaintances, and fewer than 10 percent committed a rape against a peer. The researchers found the most common abuse situation occurred when the juveniles misused a position of authority (for example, a female in a baby-sitting situation). Graves, Openshaw, Ascione, and Ericksen (1996) conducted a meta-analysis of the literature and found that nearly all juveniles adjudicated delinquent for sexual offenses came from lower and middle socioeconomic status.

Juvenile sex offenders begin their deviant behavior at a young age. Burton (2000) showed that 46 percent of the juveniles in his sample of 243 juvenile sex offenders began offending before the age of 12. Also, the offenders who began abusing prior to the age of 12 and continued abusing committed more serious offenses. The NAPN found that juvenile offenders often have multiple victims, with an average of 7.7 victims per offender.

Researchers have found numerous factors associated with an increased risk of recidivism. Miner (2002) states that juvenile sex offenders are at a higher risk of reoffense if they are young, have victims who are significantly younger than them, and show symptoms of impulsivity. Smith and Monastersky (1986) found that juveniles are more likely to recidivate if they have peer-aged, adult, or male victims, or if they commit noncontact offenses. Kahn and Chambers (1991) found that recidivism is linked to young offenders, young victims, cognitive distortions such as denial and minimization, and poor social skills. Langstrom and Grann (2000) found four factors associated with an increased risk of recidivism: commission of a previous sexual offense, poor social skills, male victim choice, and multiple victims.

Another way to analyze recidivism data is to reconstruct the sexual histories of juvenile sex offenders. In doing so, Awad and Sanders (1991) showed that approximately 40 percent of juveniles who abused children and 61 percent of the juveniles who had abused peers or adults had a history of offending behavior. They also found that the juveniles tended to show patterns of behavior, often abusing the same or similar victims. Fehrenbach et al. (1986) also showed a pattern of abusive behavior in juvenile sex offenders.

Many studies indicate that juvenile sex offenders have extensive criminal backgrounds, often for both sexual and nonsexual offenses (Awad & Sanders, 1991; Fehrenbach et al., 1986). However, some studies have shown that sexually deviant behavior in juveniles is not strongly linked to other types of aggressive delinquent behavior (Smith, 1988). Broken down by offender type, Awad and Sanders (1991) show that those who sexually abuse peers or adults are more likely to have committed previous delinquent acts than are child molesters. Similarly, Ford and Linney (1995) found that juveniles convicted of rape were three times more likely than child molesters to have prior offenses, and that more than 60 percent of juveniles who abuse children have no prior offenses. In a 10-year longitudinal study, Hagan, Gust-Brey, Cho, and Dow (2001) found that child molesters (20 percent) have a higher likelihood of recidivism than either rapists (16 percent) or other delinquent juveniles (10 percent). Though their findings did not result in a significant difference between adolescent rapists and child molesters, the authors noted that it is an important trend.

Previous Abuse

Many reports indicate that a large number of perpetrators were physically and/or sexually abused at a young age (for example, Becker & Hunter, 1997; Fagan & Wexler, 1988; Fehrenbach et al., 1986; Knight & Prentky, 1993; NAPN, 1993; Ryan, Miyoshi, Metzner, Krugman, & Fryer, 1996). NAPN (1993) shows that 42 percent of juvenile offenders have a history of physical abuse, 39 percent of known sexual abuse, and 26 percent of child neglect. Awad and Sanders (1991) found that juveniles who molested children were more likely to have been abused than those who offended against their peers. Nonetheless, many studies indicate that the prevalence of physical abuse is higher than the prevalence of sexual abuse in juvenile sexual offenders (Awad & Sanders, 1991).

Research shows children are more likely to sexually abuse if they were abused (Becker, Cunningham-Rather, & Kaplan, 1987). Not only are they more likely to abuse, but juvenile sex offenders who were abused generally begin offending at an earlier age, have more victims, are more likely to abuse both males and females, commit more intrusive offenses, and tend to show more psychopathology than those who were not abused (Cooper, Murphy, & Haynes, 1996; Hilliker, 1997). Phan and Kingree (2001) show that in a sample of 272 juvenile sex offenders, the females were more likely than the males to have experienced prior sexual abuse. Burton, Miller, and Shill (2002) found that juveniles who were sexually abused were more likely to abuse others if they had a male perpetrator (or both male and female perpetrators). Additionally, they found that they were more likely to abuse if they were abused over a long period of time and if the abuse included forceful acts or acts of penetration. Kobayashi et al. (1995) show that juveniles who were physically abused are more likely to increase sexual aggression, but those who show close bonding to their mother show less sexual aggression. Though Weinrott (1996) has criticized this report (and many other studies on adolescent sex offenders) for its methodological flaws, there is likely some credibility to their findings.

Juvenile Sex Offenders and Non-Sex Offenders: A Comparison

Many studies have compared juveniles who committed sexual offenses to either juveniles who have committed nonsexual offenses or to nonoffending juveniles in order to determine similarities and differences between the groups. Though these studies have provided important information, many have produced conflicting results. For example, Jacobs, Kennedy, and Mayer (1997) found that there are no significant differences between sexual and nonsexual offenders in terms of IQ and academic testing. Similarly, the NAPN (1993) states that the majority of juvenile sex offenders are either average or above average in their academic work, thereby not differentiating themselves from nonsexual offenders.

However, these results differ from most studies, which indicate that juvenile sex offenders perform poorly in academic settings (for example, Veneziano & Veneziano, 2002). Awad and Sanders (1991) claim that nearly half of juvenile sex offenders have diagnosable learning disabilities, and 83 percent have some difficulty in an academic setting. Ford and Linney (1995) found that the majority of juveniles in their sample had lower than average intelligence and many school suspensions. Ferrara and McDonald (1996) found that nearly one-third of juvenile sex offenders have a neurological impairment of some sort. Kahn and Chambers (1991) found that school behavioral problems are linked to an increased risk of recidivism in juvenile sex offenders.

Another difference is in terms of psychopathology and mental disorders. Many juvenile sexual offenders have diagnosable disorders, such as conduct disorder, depression, and attention deficit hyperactivity disorder (ADHD), but studies differ on whether the rate of these disorders is higher for sex offenders than other juveniles. Kraemer, Salisbury, and Spielman (1998) found that in their sample of juveniles in a residential treatment program, only 32.1 percent had no diagnostic disorders. Veneziano and Veneziano (2002) say that psychopathology is common to adolescent sex offenders, but Cooper et al. (1996) claim that it is only more common to adolescent sex offenders who were sexually abused. Frick (1998) says adolescent sex offenders are more likely than other types of adolescent offenders to show signs of psychopathy, as well as callousness and apathy. Smith, Monastersky, and Deischer (1987) found that juvenile sex offenders show a high level of impulsivity. Kavoussi, Kaplan, and Becker (1988) found that nearly half of their sample of child molesters had conduct disorder, a finding similar to that of Graves et al. (1996). Becker et al. (1991) showed that sexual offenders scored twice as high on depression scales as nonoffending junior and senior high school students, and Veneziano and Veneziano (2002) found the link between social isolation and deviant sexual behavior to be very common. Alternatively, Fagan and Wexler (1988) found that most juveniles who abuse peers or adults are very similar in terms of psychopathology to nonoffenders. They claimed that the juvenile sex offenders showed highly prosocial behavior and did not differ significantly from a nonoffending population.

Another factor with contradictory results in the literature relates to substance abuse by the offenders and their families. Whereas several studies indicate that juvenile sex offenders are likely to abuse substances, all studies do not confirm these results. Lightfoot and Barbaree (1993) summarized the literature on this topic and found that substance abuse rates range from 3 percent to 72 percent. Overall, it seems that there may be a link between substance abuse and sexual abuse of peers or adults (Lightfoot & Barbaree, 1993), but not abuse of children (Becker & Stein, 1991). In terms of alcohol and substance abuse by the parents of juvenile offenders, a study by Graves et al. (1996) shows that alcohol abuse ranges from 17 percent to 43 percent, and substance abuse ranged from 43 percent (of mothers in their sample) to 62 percent (fathers) (Graves et al., 1996).

Both juvenile sexual and nonsexual offenders show more personal distress than nonoffenders (Lindsey, Carlozzi, & Eells, 2001). This means that they tend to be emotionally reactive, self-oriented, and are unable to focus on the distress of their victims. Though not significant, Lindsey et al. (2001) found that sex offenders tend to score slightly lower on an empathic scale than both nonsexual offenders and nonoffenders.

Juvenile sex offenders and nonsexual offenders do not differ on all factors, though. Hastings, Anderson, and Hemphill (1997) found that both groups experienced similar levels of stress and there are no significant differences between the groups on most static factors. Ford and Linney (1995) found that there are no differences between juvenile sexual and nonsexual offenders in terms of assertiveness, self-concept, and family history variables.

There are also differences between types of juvenile sexual offenders. Those who abuse younger children are more likely to show traits of schizoid personality disorders as well as dependent and avoidant traits. Alternatively, juveniles who sexually abuse adults or their peers are more likely to show narcissistic traits (Carpenter, Peed, & Eastman, 1995). Many studies also show that juvenile sex offenders were likely to witness domestic violence within the home, even when they were not abused themselves (Caputo, Frick, & Brodsky, 1999). However, even though all types of juvenile sexual offenders were likely to observe or be victims of domestic violence within the home, child molesters were more likely to experience this than rapists (Ford & Linney, 1995).

WHY JUVENILES SEXUALLY OFFEND

As with adult offenders, many researchers have attempted to theorize about why juveniles commit sexually deviant behavior. Researchers do not agree as to specific theoretical models that can explain juvenile sexual offending (APA, 1999), and some claim that there is a distinct difference in the etiology of offending for adolescent and preadolescent offenders. Until the 1980s, this behavior was almost universally dismissed, and sexually aggressive behavior was considered to be normal for adolescent males, or at the very least was a behavioral rather than sexual problem (Barbaree, Hudson, & Seto, 1993; Ryan, 1999).

Experimental or Criminal Behavior?

When juveniles perpetrate sexually deviant behavior, it is commonly excused as experimentation. However, empirical research does not support this notion, and most researchers believe that when juveniles act out abusively, the behavior should not be seen as a "normal" sexual development process (Groth, Longo, & McFadin, 1982). The question of what constitutes a sex offense or sexual abuse perpetrated by a juvenile still remains a difficult one to discern (APA, 1999). Though serious cases of sexual abuse exist, most juvenile acts take place on a continuum of behavior, and the point at which they become abuse is often unclear.

Most juveniles who are convicted of sexual offenses commit their offenses against children, and the children are much younger than the child victims of adults (Russell, 1986; Shaw et al., 2000). With adults, it is easy to define "sex offender" when the offense is against a child. Most states have a statute whereby it is an offense if the person is at least five years older than the child and the behavior is generally coercive, manipulative, unwanted, or forced in some way. With juvenile sex offenders, the age and social relationships between the perpetrator and the victim must be examined (Groth & Loredo, 1981). The greater the age discrepancy, the more inappropriate the sexual behavior is and the more likely that the act is not consensual.

In order to determine whether a juvenile's behavior is abusive, a number of factors in addition to the act must be taken into consideration. Specifically, what is the sexual knowledge of the juvenile, and is there any intent to commit a sexual offense? Many adolescent sex offenders have had some consensual sexual experience prior to the commission of their offense (Becker et al., 1986). Alternatively, some offenders were abused and act reactively, whereas others have minimal sexual knowledge. Because of the vast spectrum of knowledge among juvenile offenders about sexual behavior, some researchers classify juveniles into two groups of perpetrators—adolescents and children—in order to discern differences between the two groups (Calder et al., 2001).

The amount of sexual knowledge a child has is of particular importance in determining whether he or she has committed an offense. Sexual behavior is learned, and children can learn about sex and sexuality in many ways, such as through peers, television, their parents, self-exploration, and so forth. Some children learn about sex at a very young age, and this can occur through overt or covert sexual abuse, exposure to pornography, or witnessing adult sexual behavior. Some children react to this behavior by acting out and mimicking a learned response, but with counseling may not go on to become sex offenders.

What is normal sexual behavior for children? It is normal for children to explore their own bodies and touch themselves. It is also normal for children to be curious about children of the opposite sex, and for a child to touch a sibling or another peer-aged relative. The question is then: At what point does this experimentation become an offense? The difficulty in this determination is particularly evident in the case of sibling incest. Finkelhor (1980) stated that sibling incest occurs in approximately 13 percent of the population (15 percent of females, 10 percent of males). Sibling incest generally occurs in households where the parents are either absent or inaccessible, or where there is a situation of excessive or open sexual behavior within the home and witnessed by children (Smith & Israel, 1987). The absence of the parents, either physically or emotionally, can lead to increased dependency on siblings (Smith & Israel, 1987).

Despite the apparent prevalence of sibling incest, many children and families ignore or do not report it (Araji, 1997). As with other sexual offenses, the victims of sibling incest may experience feelings of guilt, dirtiness, shame, and worthlessness. The taboo of incest may also lead to confusion and create a difficulty in establishing future sexual relationships (DiGiorgio-Miller, 1998). These feelings are often exacerbated if the family does not take the abuse seriously, press charges against the abusive sibling, and support the victim in the treatment process (DiGiorgio-Miller, 1998).

Theories and Antecedents of Offending Behavior

According to the literature, the most common antecedents of juvenile sexual offending are family dysfunction, particularly a family environment that fosters violence; lack of attachments and bonds, especially to parents; excessive use of pornography; a history of sexual abuse, physical abuse, and/or neglect; substance abuse by both the offender and the offender's family; and lack of empathy. Additionally, factors such as deviant sexual arousal and cognitive distortions may serve to facilitate this offending behavior.

Many researchers have noted a significant correlation between family dysfunction and sexually abusive behavior in juveniles. Despite the findings supporting this notion (for example, Smith 1988), there are few patterns of family dysfunction in particular subsets of juvenile sex offenders (Weinrott, 1996). Though an abusive family situation may increase the level of violence or sexual violence in a juvenile, Kobayashi et al. (1995) found that bonding to the mother reduces the amount of sexual aggression.

Linked to this is the development of empathy. Empathy is a socialized construct, and therefore it is affected by familial interaction and bonding. Juvenile sex offenders often come from households where familial interaction is minimal or nonexistent, and many of these offenders often experience neglect. Juveniles who experience familial neglect appear to have a poor understanding of empathy (Lindsey et al., 2001). Similarly, many juvenile sex offenders with low empathy scores have poor social skills with peers and experience a high level of social isolation (Veneziano & Veneziano, 2002).

Though debatable, some researchers claim that exposure to pornography enhances the likelihood of deviant sexual behavior in juveniles. In particular, they link excessive exposure to explicit sexual material, especially when young (that is, prepubertal), to deviant behavior (Harris, 2000; Zgourides, Monto, & Harris, 1997). Most sex offenders report exposure to both hard- and soft-core pornography. Becker and Stein (1991) reported that nearly 90 percent of their sample of adolescent offenders had some exposure to pornography, including magazines, videotapes, television, and books. It is likely that the percentage of adolescents viewing pornography has increased since the time of their study, with the increased use of the Internet. As such, it will be interesting to see future results of studies with juveniles who are consistently exposed to pornography on the Internet.

Deviant sexual arousal is also correlated to deviant sexual behavior in juveniles. Hunter and Becker (1994) in their summary of the literature found that individuals who abuse children often have deviant sexual arousal. Becker et al. (1989) found that there was more deviant sexual arousal in juveniles who had been sexually abused. Though this was true of the offenders despite the gender of their victims, those who had male victims scored higher on the pedophile coercion and noncoercion indices. Hunter and Becker (1994) found that there is generally early onset of pedophilia in adult males who abuse children. Additionally, Kahn and Chambers (1991) found a link between deviant sexual arousal and recidivism. As such, it is important to determine whether adolescent sex offenders have deviant sexual arousal. If they do, these arousal patterns must be addressed in the treatment goals.

Though all these factors are important to understand, they do not explain the etiology of offending behavior. Epps (1999) points out that deviant sexual behavior in juveniles can and should be explained through biological, psychodynamic, behavioral, social-cognitive, social-emotional, developmental, cognitive, trauma, family, and sociological explanations. One theory about the onset of deviant sexual behavior is the social learning theory (Burton, Miller, & Shill, 2002), which is derived from a developmental perspective. Ryan (1999) explains that this perspective supports the view that deviant sexual behavior is learned, and that juvenile offenders should be able to learn socially acceptable sexual behavior despite any developmental deficits. Some researchers do not agree with the idea that deviant sexual behavior is learned based on the concept of conditioning. Marshall and Eccles (1993) state that deviant sexual behavior may be one factor in the etiology of deviant behavior, but it is likely a predispositional rather than a causal factor.

Ryan et al. (1987) created a model of a sexual abuse cycle that follows a theoretical framework for conceptualizing abusive patterns. The cycle begins when the juvenile has a negative self-image. There are a number of factors that may create a low self-image in the child, primarily relating to his or her upbringing. Many juveniles who abuse are sexually or physically abused, and many others come from chaotic or violent households. All of these factors can lead to low self-image, low self-esteem, and situations of social isolation for the child. This low self-image can lead to poor coping strategies when negative situations arise, or it can cause the juvenile to predict negative reactions from others. This anticipation of negative reactions may lead to further social isolation, withdrawal, and fantasies stemming from lack of power and control. If the juvenile experiences a triggering event (the most common of which, according to Gray and Pithers, 1993, is boredom), these thoughts, feelings, and behaviors can lead to the commission of an offense. This offense, in turn, facilitates the low self-image in the juvenile, thus creating a sexual abuse cycle.

Once the offending cycle begins, cognitive distortions often help to facilitate the offending behavior. Common cognitive distortions in juvenile sex offenders include the minimization of responsibility, blaming the victim, and minimizing the harm to the victim (Knight & Prentky, 1993). Juveniles also may have distorted thoughts regarding social roles (that is, supporting rape myths) and sexuality. However, Weinrott (1996) states that few empirical studies have yet been conducted to determine the extent of cognitive distortions and their role in the etiology of offending behavior.

Typologies of Juvenile Sex Offenders

Juvenile sex offenders constitute as heterogeneous population as adult sex offenders, and as such, different offenders have varying characteristics and needs and create varying risks. Several researchers have attempted to categorize juvenile sex offenders into typologies in order to better understand subsets of the juvenile sex offender population. O'Brien and Bera (1986) designed one of the most sophisticated typological systems, classifying offenders into seven categories.

First, they identified the *naïve experimenters*. These offenders tend to be young, lack social skills and sexual knowledge, and participate in situational acts. Their second category of offenders is the *undersocialized child exploiters*.

Like the naïve experimenters, these juveniles generally do not have a history of delinquent behavior, but they tend to show a more severe degree of social isolation. They often come from families with a high level of dysfunction, and they have a high level of insecurity and a poor self-image. The third typology consists of *sexual aggressives*. These juveniles are the most likely to use force and violence during the commission of their offense, and they will most likely abuse peers or adults. They may have a history of delinquent behavior, substance abuse, a high level of impulsivity, and come from a household ripe with dysfunction and violence. *Sexual compulsives* make up the fourth typology; these offenders have deviant sexual fantasies that become compulsive. They may be quiet, anxious, and exhibit paraphilic behavior such as voyeurism. Unlike the sexual aggressives, they are likely to come from a rigidly strict and perhaps religious household. The fifth typology is the *disturbed impulsives,* whose actions are impulsive and may result from psychiatric disorders. The sixth typology consists of *group-influenced offenders,* who commit offenses to impress their peers. The final category is the *pseudo-socialized,* who show characteristics similar to psychopaths. They tend to exhibit psychological disorders such as narcissism, lack intimacy, have many superficial relationships with peers, and show a high level of intelligence.

O'Brien and Bera's (1986) classification system is quite thorough because it addresses major psychological and sociological issues related to the etiology and maintenance of offending behavior. Similarly, Prentky, Harris, Frizzell, and Righthand (2000) created an empirical classification of juvenile sex offenders consisting of six typologies based on their clinical work with the population. Their classification scheme is based on a more basic offending structure than O'Brien and Bera's. First, they differentiated between *child molesters* and *rapists*. The third typology is of *sexually reactive children*, or those who follow a method of socially learned behavior. Their fourth category includes less invasive offenders, labeled *fondlers*. They also distinguished *paraphiliac offenders,* or those who as juveniles committed offenses such as voyeurism and exhibitionism. Finally, recognizing that typologies cannot be mutually exclusive or exhaustive, they added a category for sex offenders who do not fit into the defined typologies.

Though O'Brien and Bera's and Prentky et al.'s typologies appear to be the most valid and well supported, several other researchers have also categorized juvenile sex offenders into typologies. Jacobs (1999) claims that there are three ways by which juveniles should be classified: by the *age differential* between offender and victim; by the *intrusiveness* of the offense committed; and by the *gender* of the victim(s). Graves (as defined by Weinrott, 1996) claims that juvenile sex offenders can fit into three typologies: *pedophilic,* or those who consistently abuse children at least three years younger than themselves; *sexual assault,* or those who abuse peers or adults; and *undifferentiated,* or those who abuse a variety of victims. Once they begin offending, Becker and Kaplan identify three paths of behavior: *continued delinquency, continued sexual offending, no further offending.* See Table 6.1 for a summary of typologies.

Table 6.1 Typologies of Juvenile Sexual Offenders

Researcher	Number of Typologies	Classifications
O'Brien and Bera (1986)	7	Naïve experimenters, undersocialized child exploiters, sexual aggressives, sexual compulsives, disturbed impulsives, group influenced, pseudo-socialized
Prentky et al. (2000)	6	Child molesters, rapists, sexually reactive children, fondlers, paraphiliac offenders, and others who do not fit into these classifications
Jacobs (1999)	3	Classifications should be based on age differential between offender and victim, the intrusiveness of offense, gender of the victim(s)
Graves (as defined by Weinrott, 1996)	3	Pedophilic, sexual assault, undifferentiated
Becker and Kaplan (1998)	3	Three paths of behavior: continued delinquency, continued sexual offending, no further offending

The purpose for categorizing sex offenders, both adult and juvenile, into classification schemes is to better assess and treat them. By breaking up heterogeneous groups into identifiable and relatively homogeneous categories, treatment providers can better assess the risks and needs of offenders.

ASSESSMENT AND TREATMENT
OF JUVENILE OFFENDERS

According to mental health professionals, all communities should strive to offer treatment for the juvenile offender. The literature shows that the recidivism rates for adolescent sex offenders tend to be relatively low with treatment, measuring approximately 10 percent after treatment (Davis & Leitenberg, 1987; Sipe, Jensen, & Everett, 1998; Smith & Monastersky, 1986). Those who reoffended were most likely to commit property crimes (Brannon & Troyer, 1995). The rate of recidivism is higher for violent juvenile sex offenders, who are more likely to commit further sexual offenses than are nonviolent sexual offenders (Sipe et al., 1998). Many researchers have found that rates of recidivism are lower for juveniles who are offered treatment early on in their offending careers (Freeman-Longo & McFaddin, 1981; Groth, 1979). Currently, it is estimated there are 800 treatment programs in the United States for juvenile offenders, and more than half of those are community based. Repeated references to the importance of family involvement in treatment are found in the available literature.

The treatment schemes commonly used for juvenile sex offenders include family therapies, cognitive-behavioral therapies, relapse prevention, and psychoeducational interventions. In order for treatment to be effective, the juvenile must be accurately assessed so that the therapist fully understands his or her treatment needs (Lane, 1997). Brannon and Troyer (1995: 324) claim that "successful" treatment emphasizes high levels of community involvement, stress–challenge education, student interpersonal problem-solving activities, energetic administrative leadership, and extensive staff training.

Studies have shown that inappropriate matching of risks and needs can actually increase recidivism among offenders (Andrews, Bonta, & Hoge, 1990). This is especially true of adolescent offenders when their behavior is misdiagnosed or considered to be "normal" (Longo, 1983). Additionally, many juveniles who participate in treatment programs do not complete them. This is particularly true of residential treatment programs, as one group of researchers consistently found that just over half of the participants completed the program (Kraemer et al., 1998). Kraemer et al. found two factors significantly associated with failure to complete a residential treatment program: impulsivity and age. They found that older adolescent offenders and those who showed generally impulsive behavior were the least likely to complete the program successfully. This supports other research that indicates younger children are more amenable to treatment. They found that treatment completion did not depend on the juvenile's IQ, ethnicity, or grade level. Hagan, King, and Patros (1994) looked at the number of adolescent rapists in a residential treatment program who were able to successfully complete the program (that is, they were not convicted of a future sexual offense in the following two years). Though 58 percent of their sample committed another delinquent act in this time, only 10 percent were convicted of another sexual offense.

Treatment should focus on offense-specific interventions to address the realities of the developmental needs and deficits of the juveniles. Treatment should also address offense-related issues such as substance abuse, eating disorders, childhood abuse, domestic violence that the juvenile may have witnessed, other crimes such as property offenses and arson, self-abusive behavior such as eating disorders and suicidal tendencies, and any behavior that harms others (Ryan, 1999). Because their sample showed a high level of generally delinquent behavior, Hagan et al. (1994) stated that treatment should also focus on antisocial criminal behavior. They found that antisocial behavior is likely to continue posttreatment if it is not specifically addressed in the program.

The Assessment Process

The assessment process for adolescent sex offenders is very detailed and time consuming, because these assessments require multiple interviews with the adolescents and their parents (APA, 1999). Though the process varies from institution to institution, the National Task Force on Juvenile Sexual Offending promotes six stages of evaluations: the *pretrial investigative assessment;* the *presentence risk assessment* to determine placement and prognosis; the *post-adjudication clinical assessment* to address treatment issues and modes; a *needs assessment* for treatment planning and progress in treatment; an *assessment for release or the termination from treatment program,* which aims to determine community safety and successful application of treatment tools; and a *follow-up assessment* to monitor the juvenile in the community.

The primary goal of the assessment process is to accurately identify the risks and needs of the offenders, and to make sure that the juvenile understands the dynamics of his or her offense (DiGiorgio-Miller, 1994). This means that the treatment provider must find out detailed information about the deviant act, including the degree of damage inflicted on the victim and whether the goal of the act was to control, degrade, or embarrass the victim, as these are factors that alert experts to juveniles suffering from paraphilias. Additionally, it is important to establish the sophistication of the deviant sexual act and to assess whether the knowledge demonstrated is beyond the average knowledge of children in the particular age group (APA, 1999). If so, this likely means that the child was abused or has been exposed to deviant sexual behavior previously.

Treatment providers also must aim to find out the true rate of abuse caused by the juvenile. In their research of three treatment programs, Baker, Tabacoff, Tornusciolo, and Eisenstad (2001) found that more than half of the juveniles in the sample disclosed more offenses and/or victims than those for which they were convicted. Throughout the treatment, the juveniles also revealed more information about previous sexual and physical abuse, and information about the abusive household they live in (often with the father subjecting the mother to domestic violence incidents).

In order to accurately identify the risks and needs of the juveniles, the treatment provider should use various assessment tools including official documents (that is, police records, victim statements), interviews, phallometric testing, polygraphs, and psychometric testing (Righthand & Welch, 2001). The official documents are necessary to understand the specifics of the crime committed, including the amount of harm caused to the victim. The interviews allow the treatment provider to assess the offender's sexual knowledge, family history, abuse history, and cognitive distortions, including the amount of denial, minimization, justification, and whether the offender feels any empathy toward his or her victim. Phallometric testing should be used to determine the level of deviant sexual arousal in the offender. Though this is ethically questionable and should not be considered an entirely accurate method by which deviant sexual arousal can be measured, it can give the treatment provider some basic understanding of the offender's arousal patterns. Polygraphs should be used throughout both the assessment and treatment processes to ensure that the offender is being truthful about his or her offense and offense history. Finally, psychometric tests are pertinent in understanding factors such as the offender's IQ, whether he or she has any diagnosable disorders, whether he or she shows traits of psychopathy, and his or her opinions about sexual issues (that is, supporting rape myths).

The Treatment Process

Once the offender is fully assessed, the treatment provider must determine what type of program is appropriate for the juvenile. Most researchers promote a cognitive-behavioral approach to treating juvenile offenders (for example, Charles & McDonald, 1996; O'Reilly, Morrison, Sheerin, & Carr, 2001), though there is no consensus that this approach is best for all juveniles. For instance, Brannon and Troyer (1995) suggest that specialized programs are equivalent to general treatment programs that work to improve social skills, self-esteem, and other general problems that the juvenile may be experiencing. Also, juveniles diagnosed as psychopathic should be considered high-risk offenders who need extensive treatment beyond the core cognitive-behavioral program (Reiss, Grubin, & Meux, 1996).

O'Reilly et al. (2001) claim group-based cognitive-behavioral approaches are the most beneficial for the majority of juvenile offenders. The group-based approach, specifically in terms of relapse prevention (discussed at length in Chapter 8), helps to motivate juvenile sex offenders to change their behavior. The cognitive-behavioral group treatment process aims to help juvenile offenders address problems with their interpersonal relationship skills, which are often an antecedent to deviant sexual behavior. This process also helps the offender learn to take responsibility for his or her actions, reduce and restructure cognitive distortions, and learn about sex education (Grant & MacDonald, 1996).

There are several goals of a juvenile treatment program. According to Righthand and Welch (2001: 43), the target areas of treatment are impaired social skills; empathy deficits; cognitive distortions; deviant sexual arousal; problematic management of emotions; impulsive, antisocial behavior; and consequences of personal history of child maltreatment. Though all of these factors must be addressed in treatment, Ryan (1999) states that the key to treatment for juveniles is victim empathy and empathic accountability. She states that "the absence of empathic accountability is the most obvious deficit in abusers" (p. 428). This is particularly important for offenders who have experienced neglect, which may be linked to a lack of empathy. Early interventions (for example, treatment early on in the juvenile's offending career) may help to increase empathic accountability (Hagan et al., 1994).

MANAGEMENT OF JUVENILE OFFENDERS

A key to reducing recidivism in juvenile sex offenders is proper management of the offenders. Unlike with the adult system, there are numerous systems involved in the supervision process for juveniles, such as child protection services, child and family services, and social services. The key to effective treatment, supervision, and management of juvenile sex offenders is a multi-agency approach in which the agencies work together to reduce the chance of recidivism (Erooga & Masson, 1999). Some of these agencies work together, support the treatment process, and assist in the supervision of the offender. However, others do not, and rather than support the treatment of the offender, some agencies may support the denial by the offender and his or her family. This complicated nature of the multi-agency system requires that complex treatment plans be established (Ryan, 1999).

The supervision of juvenile sex offenders begins during the court process. As with any type of criminal activity, juvenile offenders deserve legal counsel when dealing with the legal system. Adolescents often benefit from the presence of guardians *ad litem* (GADs), who are appointed by the court to protect the interests of the adolescents during the proceedings; however, societal pressures now mandate that community protection must override all other concerns. In many states, this means that juvenile offenders are treated like adults.

In more than half the states, juvenile sex offenders now must register with the police (registration and notification procedures are discussed at greater length in Chapter 10). In some of these states, the juveniles must register for the rest of their lives, and the community is notified about high-risk offenders. Becker (1998) states that there should be caution in applying such supervision and management techniques to the juvenile population, because there need to be further longitudinal studies on juvenile sex offenders to determine what their true long-term risks are.

CHAPTER SUMMARY

- Like adults, juveniles who commit sexual offenses make up a heterogeneous group of individuals. They have various family histories, offend for a number of different reasons, and require different methods of treatment and supervision.

- Though historically, juveniles who committed offenses were considered to be "experimenting," it is true that juvenile offenders are responsible for many serious sexual offenses.

- As with adults, researchers classify juvenile sex offenders into typologies. However, unlike with adults, the juvenile typologies tend to be based on levels of psychosocial development and/or attachment and bonds to family.

- Juveniles are often dismissed out of the criminal justice system prior to conviction. However, when their cases do go to court and the juveniles are found delinquent, they receive an extensive assessment process and treatment regime.

- Treating juveniles in a cognitive-behavioral treatment program early on in their offending careers can help to reduce the risk of recidivism. However, some researchers (for example, Weinrott, 1996) claim that there are no empirical studies to prove that point, and such treatment programs may actually harm some of those who participate.

DISCUSSION QUESTIONS

1. What are some of the similarities and differences between adult and juvenile sexual offenders?

2. Can criminal justice officials or psychologists distinguish between juveniles who are "experimenting" with sexual behavior and those who are committing criminal acts? If so, how?

3. Explain the benefits and the problems with juveniles going through the juvenile justice or criminal justice system after being accused of a sexual offense. Is it better to divert juveniles out of the system, or to have them go through the system? Why?

4. What are the assessment and treatment processes like for juvenile sexual offenders? What are some of the key obstacles to juveniles receiving treatment?

7

Victims

S exual assault is one of the most severe and intrusive violations that can be
committed against a person, and it may have lasting effects on the victim
physically, psychologically, and emotionally. Though less so now than in
previous decades, there is a stigma attached to victims of sexual offenses.[1]
Whether real or perceived, it is this stigma that often keeps victims from
reporting the offense to authorities. Because of feelings such as fear, embarrassment, or shame, sexual assault is consistently the most underreported of all violent crimes. When reported, the victim must endure a lengthy legal process in
which he or she is "revictimized" by the system. Through rape reform laws,
victim advocacy groups, and improved knowledge about sexual offending, the
system has attempted to reduce the level of revictimization, though it remains
fraught with problems.

It has only been since the mid-1970s that talk of sexual offending has come
to the forefront. For the next two decades, rates of reporting increased significantly, though they have since stabilized (Rennison, 2001). In this time, the
definitions of sexual offending also changed considerably. For example, statutes
are no longer gender specific, spouses are no longer exempt from the sexual
assault statutes, and rape reform laws require more of a focus on the offender
instead of allowing for a demoralization of the victim. It is also since that time
that the effects of victimization have begun to be understood. This chapter
aims to identify the effects of sexual victimization, the difficulties encountered
by victims throughout the criminal justice process, and the support groups that
assist them in the restorative process.

WHO IS A VICTIM?

Just as anyone can be a sexual offender, anyone—an adult or a child, male or female—can be a victim of a sexual assault. The person who is assaulted, however, is not the only victim. The family, friends, coworkers, and acquaintances of the victims, referred to as *secondary victims* (Holmes, 2002), are also affected. It is the people close to the person victimized who must help him or her to deal with the trauma and recover, though it is often just as traumatic for the secondary victims. The fact that most victims know their attackers aggravates the recovery process. For instance, if a woman discovers that her husband is abusing her daughter, she must help her daughter to recover. Yet, she must also cope with the fact that her daughter was being abused in the home, and that she knew the perpetrator of the crime. Also, she must deal with the potential deterioration of the family unit as a result of the offense.

Rates of sexual victimization are higher than official statistics show, though there is no way to gain an accurate picture of the true extent of sexual victimization. The previous chapters have shown that sexual offenders are not of a common age, socioeconomic status, marital status, or educational background. However, most victims of sexual offenses are young. When looking at the victims of imprisoned rapists, the average age of their victims is 22 years (Bureau of Justice Statistics [BJS], 1999), and it is estimated that 16 percent of rape victims are under the age of 12 (Langan & Harlow, 1994).[2] The average victim age of all other sexual assaulters is 13 years, and 8 out of 10 prisoners who were convicted of sexual assault had victimized children under the age of 12 (BJS, 1998). Overall, one-third of all known sexual assault victims are under the age of 12 (National Report Series, 1999).[3] The studies by Langan and Harlow (1994) and the National Report Series (1999) reveal that children under age 12 are particularly likely to be raped or sexually assaulted by a family member or acquaintance, at 96 percent and 91 percent, respectively.

Accurate rates of sexual abuse by gender are difficult to measure, because male victimization seems to be acutely underreported (Brochman, 1991; McMullen, 1992). Quotes of victimization rates vary, though victim service agencies estimate that approximately 1 out of every 3 or 4 girls and 1 out of every 7 boys is victimized in their lifetimes (see National Institute of Justice, 1992: 3, for a summary of victimization rates in the literature). The rate of victimization varies by age, however. National Incident-Based Reporting System (NIBRS) data show that whereas male victims account for only 4 percent of adult sexual assault victims and 8 percent of victims aged 12–17 years, they account for one-quarter of sexual assault victims under age 12 (National Report Series, 2000). It is unclear whether males are victimized more at a young age than as adults or if this difference is the result of reporting variance, though it is likely a combination of both factors.

Most sex offenders do not seem to single out a particular type of victim in static terms—for example, socioeconomic status, physical attributes—but rather they assault whomever is accessible. They may have preferences for age, though not all do. Some regressed child molesters (those whose primary sexual attraction is to agemates) claim that they only abuse children because they have easy access to them.[4] Some fixated child molesters (individuals who exhibit persistent, continual, and compulsive attraction to children) have a preference for gender, particularly those who abuse adolescent boys. However, many child molesters and even some rapists may abuse any victim to whom they have access regardless of gender (Groth & Burgess, 1980). In families with interfamilial child abuse, it is not uncommon for the parent to abuse children of both sexes if available.

Sex offenders do target particular victims on dynamic terms. Above all, they seek out victims who are vulnerable in either a situational or emotional sense. Child molesters target such children and subsequently employ a number of grooming techniques (as described in Chapter 4) to ensure compliance with the abuse (Conte, 1991; Conte et al., 1989; Groth & Burgess, 1977; Pryor, 1996). Rapists also tend to target vulnerable victims; in particular, prostitutes, hitchhikers, individuals who are intoxicated, or those over whom they believe they can assert control. The methods by which they approach the potential victims depend on their confidence in obtaining power over the individuals, and so they may employ tactics such as a *con* (the offender uses a ploy for accessibility, such as posing as a serviceman), a *blitz* (direct physical assault), or a *surprise approach* (waits in hiding for the victim) (Hazelwood, 1983: 3). It is primarily the stranger rapists who use these tactics, though acquaintance rapists use similar tactics, such as encouraging or taking advantage of intoxication.

As with many crimes, the most common thread among victims of sexual offenses is vulnerability. Just as a small percentage of the offender population commits the majority of offenses, small percentages of the victim population suffer a large percentage of victimization (Farrell, 1995: 469). As was explored in earlier chapters, sexual offenders often seek out emotionally vulnerable victims, many of whom were abused previously. Other than this common thread of vulnerability, victims of sexual offenses are rarely chosen based on a particular set of static characteristics. In addition to heterogeneous physical attributes, victims respond differently to sexual assaults, which vary in type, length, and severity. When combined with a variety of personality characteristics and avenues of support, this produces varying effects of victimization on the victim population.

EFFECTS OF VICTIMIZATION

Sexual assault victims are likely to experience a range of physical and psychological reactions to sexual abuse. The literature on effects of victimization is immense; the following sections provide an overview of the reactions and phases of victimization.

Physical Harm

Types of sexual assault vary, and the more minor offenses (for example, touching above the clothing) are not likely to yield physical injuries. However, violent offenses that include intercourse may well lead to serious injury (beyond the injury of the intercourse itself). When a victim is sexually assaulted, he or she may react in many different ways and thereby suffer varying degrees of physical harm. Some victims scream, some fight back, some are too shocked and afraid to react, and still others remain compliant so as to avoid possible additional violence (Rape Crisis Federation, 2002).

Victims of rape and sexual assault are not likely to face armed offenders. They are less likely to do so than victims of any other violent offense; approximately 6 percent of sex offenders threaten their victims with weapons (Rennison, 2001). The National Crime Victimization Survey (NCVS) shows that approximately one-quarter of all rape victims between 1992 and 1998 were physically injured during the attack in some way, however (other than the direct injuries resulting from the rape) (Simon, Mercy, & Perkins, 2001: 2). Although only a small percentage of those injuries involved wounds from weapons, broken bones, and severe bodily harm, they did include bruises, black eyes, cuts, or other such consequences. Some victims do not show any signs of physical violence, yet this does not mean that the experience is any less traumatic (Rape Crisis Federation, 2002).

It is also common for victims of sexual abuse, particularly those abused over a period of time when they were children, to experience medically unexplained symptoms. Called *somatization,* it is hypothesized that this allows the victim to express emotional pain through physical symptoms (Nelson, 2001). Common physical symptoms for which there is no obvious cause include back pain, pelvic pain, and headaches, and the victims tend to have negative perceptions of their health (Calhoun & Atkeson, 1991; Walker et al., 1992). Without an obvious organic cause to their pain, doctors may dismiss them as hypochondriacs. In fact, women who were sexually abused as children score higher on the hypochondriasis scale of the Minnesota Multiphasic Personality Inventory (MMPI) than women who have no history of abuse (Lundberg-Love, 1999). It is debatable whether the physical symptoms that victims experience are, in fact, somatic or whether they may be the result of physical trauma that occurred during childhood victimization.[5]

In addition to the physical injuries, other medical problems, such as sexually transmitted diseases and pregnancy, may occur as the result of rape. Though medical in nature, these are also likely to produce psychological harm. Sexually transmitted diseases occur in up to 30 percent of rape cases, with HIV being transmitted in approximately 0.2 percent of the cases (Resnick, Acierno, & Kilpatrick, 1997). Pregnancy also occurs in some cases, with an estimated 4.7 percent of raped women becoming impregnated (Homes, Resnick, Kilpatrick, & Best, 1992). Women who become pregnant must decide whether to carry the child through to term, and if so whether to raise it. This decision may have a significant impact on the victim, as even in a consensual relationship this choice is often stressful (see Strahan, 1991, for a review of psychological and socioeconomic effects of abortion on women). Whatever action is taken, the women are likely to experience some psychological symptoms such as depression, anxiety, insomnia, or even mental illness (Frank et al., 1985).

Rape Trauma Syndrome and the Stages of Victimization

It is the psychological effects of sexual abuse on the victim that are perhaps most detrimental because of their long-term nature. Victims are likely to feel guilt, shame, fear, anxiety, stress, and fatigue as emotional reactions to the assault (Burgess, 1995; Isley, 1991). Additionally, they may develop eating disorders, depression, dissociation, and suicidal feelings (Bass & Davis, 1988; Eby, Campbell, Sullivan, & Davidson, 1995; Resnick et al., 1997; Thompson, Wonderlich, Crosby, & Mitchell, 2001). Burgess and Holstrom (1974) conducted research on rape victims and found that men, women, and children experience distinct reactions to the offense. Today, rape trauma syndrome (RTS) is clinically recognized as the "stress response pattern of the victim following forced, non-consenting sexual activity" (Burgess, 1995: 239). This is similar to posttraumatic stress disorder (PTSD) in that it is based on a particular event in the victim's life that produces similar responses in nearly all who experience it, though RTS relates specifically to the psychological effects resulting from a sexual assault. Responses to sexual assault are often long term and include recurrent recollection of the event, reduced involvement in the environment, and hyperalertness, disturbed sleep patterns, guilt about the incident, or avoidance of activities that arouse recollection.

Much of the victimization research details stages that victims experience as a result of RTS. Burgess and Holstrom (1974) explain two phases of RTS as the acute and the reorganization phases. The *acute phase* lasts a short period of time immediately after the assault and includes a variety of emotional responses from the victim (for example, crying, swearing, laughing). The *reorganization phase* involves learning how to accept and cope with life after the sexual assault. Some have since expanded on the two-phase model, such as the Rape and Rape Prevention researchers (1999), who list six stages as *denial, anger, grief, depression, taking action,* and *acceptance.* Drawing on four sources of rape research, Koss and Harvey (1991: 48–55) explain four stages of reactions, including the *anticipatory* phase (behavior before and during the assault, use of defense mechanisms to preserve a feeling of invulnerability); the *impact* phase (intense fear, anxiety, and guilt immediately after the assault); the *reconstitution* phase (an outward appearance of adjustment though a psychologically tumultuous phase); and the *resolution* phase (like the reorganization phase, learning to accept and cope with the abuse).

Holmes (2002: 215) provides a basic yet thorough analysis of three stages of sexual victimization, which are shock, denial, and integration. When the victim is in *shock,* he or she experiences feelings of anxiety, guilt, and fear. Similar to the acute phase of RTS, this stage occurs for a short period after the victimization ends and is followed by a stage of denial. *Denial* occurs in most victims of sexual assault, and is when the victim tries to forget about the abuse. This could include complete or partial denial of the event, as well as suppression of any feelings of guilt and anxiety. Generally, the victim tries to forget about the event and return to a normal routine, which is also seen in Koss and Harvey's (1991) reconstitution phase. Before victims move past this stage, they may begin to experience emotional problems such as grief and depression before they subsequently attempt to integrate the experience into their lives. As in the reorganization phase of RTS, they learn to cope with the trauma of what happened, and many of the initial psychological or physiological symptoms begin to subside (though not disappear). During this period of *integration*, the impact of the abuse is fully absorbed. The victim may have nightmares in which the experience is relived or there are resulting feelings of fear, stress, and anxiety. Personal and work relationships may also be affected, and there may be difficulties concentrating on work or professional duties. This stage is important, however, because it is the point at which victims begin to accept the abuse and try to adjust.

Though most sexual offense victims exhibit characteristics from these stages, the stages are by no means mutually exclusive or exhaustive. Victims clearly experience a distinct set of reactions to a traumatic event of this nature, but adjustment to sexual victimization is a long-term process and is affected by a complex interaction of variables that include level of social support, coping mechanisms, and demographic characteristics (Calhoun & Atkeson, 1991: 8). Other factors that influence the rate of recovery include the type of person who is a victim, the type and severity of the sexual assault, the environment in which they recover, and the type and timing of interventions (Koss & Harvey, 1991; Ward & Inserto, 1990).

Psychological Reactions

The most prevalent psychological reactions to sexual victimization are fear and anxiety, beginning with the fear created during the act itself. At this time, victims may fear for their lives, and this fear then leads to nervousness, specific anxiety about future sexual assaults, and ultimately a generalized anxiety (Calhoun & Atkeson, 1991: 9–10). Many of those abused as children develop anxiety-related disorders, such as phobias, panic disorders, obsessive-compulsive disorder (OCD), and sleep disturbances (Lundberg-Love, 1999: 6). OCD is particularly prevalent as a washing ritual (Calhoun & Atkeson, 1991), symbolizing the cleansing of the victim from the abuse. Similarly, many women, particularly adolescents who were abused, resort to dangerous eating disorders and weight regulation practices. In particular, women practice bulimia, where they binge and purge repeatedly (Bass & Davis, 1988). Alcohol and substance abuse is also common, again with excessive binging.

Another frequent consequence of sexual abuse is depression, particularly if the abuse was ongoing and the perpetrator was someone close to the victim (Lundberg-Love, 1999). Calhoun and Atkeson (1991: 11) describe how victims are likely to experience a number of depressive symptoms immediately following the sexual assault, including crying spells, fatigue, feelings of guilt and worthlessness, a sense of hopelessness, and suicidal thoughts. They also tend to experience low self-esteem and self-blame, and they are likely to withdraw from social interaction. This withdrawal can further perpetuate the cycle of depression, because when victims most need social support, they are instead avoiding those close to them. Victims generally show fewer of these symptoms after three or four months (Calhoun & Atkeson, 1991), though many victims do experience long-term depression or other disorders that help them cope with the trauma.

One such coping mechanism is the development of dissociative disorders, which are common in victims who were abused at a very young age. Described by Lundberg-Love (1999: 7) as "a disruption of the integrated functions of consciousness, memory, identity, or perception of the environment," dissociative disorders allow the victims to depersonalize traumatic events and/or remove the event from their memory. Extreme cases of sexual abuse can lead to severe mental problems such as mental breakdowns, psychological disorders such as schizophrenia (Rape Victim Advocates, 2001), or personality disorders such as multiple personality (Calhoun & Atkeson, 1991).

Sexual abuse also affects how victims develop and maintain relationships. Both male and female victims may experience sexual dysfunction as a result of the rape (Golding, 1996), particularly if they are experiencing long-term anxiety about the assault (Calhoun & Atkeson, 1991). Even if there is no physical dysfunction, victimization may result in altered sexual practices such as avoidance of sex, increased sexual activity, or loss of satisfaction with sex (Ellis, Atkeson, & Calhoun, 1981). Many victims go through a period of social adjustment immediately after the assault (Calhoun & Atkeson, 1991), and women in particular are likely to go through periods in which they feel very angry with everyone close to them. While childhood sexual abuse may lead to sexual dysfunction for some women, it leads to sexual promiscuity for others (Thompson et al., 2001). For most victims, these effects are short-term rather than long-term consequences of abuse (Calhoun & Atkeson, 1991), though healing once again depends on the support systems for the individual.

Women and men experience many of the same physical, emotional, and psychological reactions to sexual abuse; however, there are some differences between the genders. Women are more likely to internalize their reactions, meaning they are more likely to suffer from psychological and emotional problems or physically harm themselves rather than others. Whereas some women need to talk about the experience of sexual assault in detail, many remain in the denial stage of abuse for a long time and do not talk about the abuse. Women are more likely than men to experience behavioral responses such as crying, pulling out hair, hitting or burning themselves, substance abuse, and adverse sexual behavior (Lundberg-Love, 1999: 7).

Some women do act out and abuse others or partake in other criminal acts. Harlow (1999: 2) examined the prior abuse of those serving correctional sentences and found that abuse was more common for women in the correctional than in the general population. She showed that 57.2 percent of females in state institutions, 39.9 percent in federal institutions, 47.6 percent in jail, and 40.4 percent of probationers had been abused prior to their sentences (with 39 percent, 22.8 percent, 37.2 percent, and 25.2 percent sexually abused while serving in each of the institutions, respectively). Although many men who were incarcerated were also abused,[6] women tended to be abused as both adults and juveniles, and by family members, acquaintances, and spouses. Additionally, three-quarters of the incarcerated women who were abused had parents who abused alcohol or drugs, and nearly two-thirds have at some point had a family member incarcerated. Women who were abused are more likely to act out and harm others if they do not have the support of a secure family unit.

Though they experience much of the same psychological trauma, men who are victims of sexual offenses are more likely to externalize their feelings than women. Male rape is most common in male-dominated institutions such as prison, military institutions, fraternities, and athletic organizations. As a reaction to the assault, some male victims attempt to reassert their masculinity through the stigmatization of others (Rogers & Terry, 1984; Watkins & Bentovin, 2000). This externalization comes from feelings of anger and a need to retain the socially constructed feelings of power and control that are associated with masculinity in today's society (McMullen, 1990). Because of the inclination to act out, some boys who were abused (though by no means all) go on to physically or sexually abuse others.

Socially, male rape is stigmatizing. Because of the shame associated with men who have been raped,[7] many victims are not likely to report the offense (Isley, 1991; Scarce, 1997). Men who rape and the male rape victims may be heterosexual or homosexual, yet male victims commonly experience confusion over their sexual identity as a reaction to the assault (National Center for Victims of Crime, 1997). Male rape, like female rape, is often wedded to feelings of power and dominance, and male victims are likely to experience feelings of self-blame and embarrassment that they could not prevent the victimization (Scarce, 1997). This is compounded if throughout the rape they experience an erection and then ejaculate. Though a common and reflexive reaction to the physical pain of the rape, many victims associate these actions with pleasure and consent (McMullen, 1990). Groth and Burgess (1980) explain how rapists try to get the victim to ejaculate, thereby reinforcing the feelings of power and control and the myth that the victim "wanted it."

Children who are victims of sexual abuse also experience many psychological problems and atypical behavior. Summarizing the literature, a National Institute of Justice (1992: 18–19) report describes several common reactions by children who are sexually abused. Some are similar to adult reactions, including affective problems such as guilt, shame, anxiety, and fear, and physical reactions such as sexually transmitted diseases and somatic injuries. They also show poor self-esteem, self-blame, and a need to please others, which could result in long-term depression, destructive behavior, and suicidal thoughts. Like adults, children can experience serious psychological disorders such as multiple personalities, neuroses, and character disorders. Children also experience age-related problems such as poor concentration in school, which often leads to failing grades. Additionally, they act out both physically and sexually, such as with antisocial or delinquent behavior and overt sexual behavior such as masturbation. Though researchers have recognized similar characteristics in abused children as a group, a single diagnosis of "sexually abused child syndrome" has been all but discarded due to variance in victim and type and length of abuse (National Institute of Justice, 1992: 20).

Secondary Victims

Secondary victims, or people close to the person who has been sexually abused, are also significantly affected by the sexual abuse. Additionally, these individuals must help the primary victim to cope with the abuse and work through any psychological reactions that emerge. Secondary victims include parents, siblings, partners, peers, colleagues, and employers (Ward & Inserto, 1990). Though all play different roles in the victim's life, many of these individuals may need counseling themselves in order to understand the offense and help the victim overcome the trauma.

When considering issues of child sexual assault, the most important role is that of the parents, particularly the mother.[8] Parents of abused children have varying levels of knowledge of the abuse and, as a result, have varying feelings of guilt, negligence, and responsibility once the abuse is known. Johnson (1992: 2–3) describes three models of mothers of incest survivors based on their knowledge of the abuse and reactions to it. The first model is the *collusive* mother, who knows the abuse is occurring and ignores it. Johnson explains that this mother not only is lacking guilt and anxiety about the abuse, but also may herself be psychologically impaired and has pushed the daughter into the abusive situation. The second model is that of the *powerless* mother, who may want to help her child but cannot because she is weak and defenseless compared with the father. This mother is often a victim herself and is either physically or emotionally helpless in preventing the child abuse from occurring. The third model Johnson describes is that of the *protective* mother. She is able to assist the child once she becomes aware of the abuse because she has alternative resources available outside of the marriage. This mother is generally surprised to find out about the abuse and is likely to feel guilt that it happened and empathy toward her child.

Both parents and siblings of the victim are likely to experience emotional reactions to the abuse, including denial, disbelief, remorse, regret, and even trauma. When the abuse is interfamilial, the family is likely to go through significant changes, because in most cases either the victim or perpetrator will be removed from the home (Ward & Inserto, 1990). This uprooting will cause disruption for the entire family, and disruption may create emotional trauma for all involved—particularly the victim, who may feel responsible for the upheaval. The reaction toward the offender also varies: whereas some see the perpetrator as hateful and repugnant, others see him or her as sick and in need of help (Johnson, 1992).

The spouse or partner of a rape victim also plays a significant role in the recovery process. Whereas some partners are fully supportive, sympathetic, and helpful to the victim, others become withdrawn or blame the victim partially for the offense (Baker, Skolnik, Davis, & Brickman, 1991; Ward & Inserto, 1990). Rape elicits a stronger negative reaction from partners than other violent crimes (Baker et al., 1991), which in some cases leads to feelings of vengefulness or a lack of support for the victim. Though many of the partners are supportive, problems may emerge in the relationship due to feelings of uncleanliness or unfaithfulness (Ward & Inserto, 1990: 82). The study by Baker et al. (1991) showed that female peers of sexual assault victims show the most positive and supportive attitudes toward the victims, and as such this relationship is important for the victim who is recovering from the trauma.

If the victim does decide to report the sexual abuse to the authorities, he or she will become involved in a criminal justice process that may, ultimately, "revictimize" the victim. Victims often find this process to be as or more traumatic than the sexual assault itself.

SEXUAL ABUSE AND THE CRIMINAL JUSTICE SYSTEM

Once the victim reports a case of sexual abuse, a series of agencies become involved in the investigation and the prosecution of the case. The hospital must conduct a medical examination to collect evidence and test for any signs of sexual assault, while the police begin collecting evidence from the crime scene, victim, and offender (if known). Once a suspect is arrested, the prosecutor takes over the case and assesses whether charges should be made and, if so, what they should be. The prosecutor also has the option of offering the defendant a plea bargain. Unfortunately, victims of crime have little or no input into whether plea negotiations are offered or accepted. If the case goes to trial, the prosecution must show beyond a reasonable doubt that the sexual offense occurred, and the defense counsel will generally embark on severe questioning of the victim in order to break down the case. Whatever the outcome—and few cases result in convictions[9]—the legal process is trying for the victim.

There have been many institutional changes in the criminal justice system over the past two decades in the response to victims of sexual assault. For instance, some police departments have implemented sex crime units, prosecutors' offices have implemented victim specialists and specialist prosecutors, there has been an increase in the numbers of rape crisis centers and victim advocates at those centers, and there are victim counselors at many hospitals (Burgess, 1995: 239). Nonetheless, the criminal justice process is a psychologically taxing experience for most victims of sexual offenses. In fact, many experience a condition of *critogenesis,* which is the exacerbation or genesis of a condition by legal processes (Gutheil, 2000). In other words, the criminal justice system causes more victimization when it should be addressing, helping, or reducing victimization.[10] As long as the criminal justice system is offender rather than victim centered, critogenesis is likely to occur.

The Hospital

The hospital is a key institution in rape investigation because it is often the first place that victims go to be treated after an assault. It is the goal of the hospital to examine the victim and take evidence relating to the offense. Because the medical exam must be thorough, it is generally quite long and intrusive. A victim spends several hours at the hospital while the staff treats him or her both medically and psychologically (New York City Alliance Against Sexual Assault [NYCAASA], 2001). The procedures that the victim endures are lengthy, uncomfortable, and may cause the victim to feel further degraded and humiliated. As such, it is important to have specially trained hospital staff to work with the victims and victim advocates on call at the hospital.

The hospital has three duties in terms of helping victims of sexual abuse: the examination, the treatment, and postexamination (Ward & Inserto, 1990: 96). The examination includes a physical exam, a pelvic exam, and a collection of laboratory samples, as well as questions about the offense and perpetrators. The primary purpose of the examination is to determine if there are physical indications that a crime was committed and, if so, to preserve the evidence. However, there are many difficulties in doing this. In cases of both rape and child molestation, many victims do not go to the hospital immediately after the offense occurs. Even some who do go to the hospital shortly after the assault shower or bathe first, thereby eradicating any forensic evidence from their bodies. In cases where forensic evidence is available, the perpetrator may claim that sexual intercourse took place but was consensual. This is particularly prevalent in cases where an acquaintance, date, or spouse assaults the victim.

Another purpose of the hospital examination is to determine whether the victim has contracted any sexually transmitted diseases or has become pregnant. If the victim has been infected, the hospital must then offer treatment and/or counseling. Many hospitals now offer rape victims "morning after" pills in order to avoid pregnancy. If taken within 48 hours of intercourse, these work similarly to birth control pills and do not allow the egg to be fertilized. If the victim goes to the hospital more than 48 hours after the assault and is pregnant, she must make the decision as to whether she will continue or abort the pregnancy. The duty of the hospital in this situation is to counsel her about the options she has and arrange for a pregnancy termination, if so desired (Ward & Inserto, 1990).

Cases of child abuse present another set of difficulties in obtaining forensic evidence. To begin with, some doctors will not do vaginal examinations on children (Ward & Inserto, 1990), though guidelines exist for doctors to follow when performing exams on children suspected of being sexually abused (American Academy of Pediatrics Committee on Child Abuse and Neglect, 1991). When an examination is done, the purpose is to check for evidence of sexual abuse, usually penetration, and this is done through examination of the hymen. Unfortunately, this evidence is often inconclusive because the hymen can be stretched or broken in several ways, and the medical examination does not necessarily prove penetration (Prior, 2001). There is rarely any forensic evidence collected from children during the examination, because the abuse does not usually take the form of intercourse. Sexual intercourse is more prevalent in incestuous relations than extrafamilial relations (West, 1987), and because such abuse is likely to go on for a long time, it is unlikely that a child will go to the hospital directly after the intercourse takes place so that forensic evidence can be collected.

Studies show mixed results as to the effects of a hospital examination on children. Some researchers claim that hospital exams produce similar results to the sexual abuse—namely, fear, anxiety, pain, and anger, though rarely long-term anxiety or distress (Berson, Herman-Giddens, & Frothingham, 1993; Lazabnik, Zimet, Ebert et al., 1994). Other researchers, however, show that the hospital experience is not that traumatic for most children. In one study, more than two-thirds of the parents of sexually abused children said that the hospital did not have a negative impact on the child (Allard-Dansereau, Hebert, Tremblay, & Bernard-Bonnin, 2001). In fact, the hospital had a positive impact in that it reassured the children about the physical integrity of their bodies after the traumatic experience of abuse. Though it is unclear exactly what factors about the examination may have a negative impact on children, the study by Allard-Dansereau et al. indicates that one important factor is the demeanor of the doctor and the extent to which he or she explains the examination process.

In order to reduce the level of emotional trauma for adult and child victims, the hospital should offer support throughout the exam and the subsequent treatment. Additionally, all hospitals should have rape-designated facilities in order to ensure proper collection of evidence and medical and psychological treatment for the victims. Some states have such facilities available in designated hospitals, whereas others have gone further and established hospital-based sexual assault nurse examiners (SANEs). SANEs are forensically trained nurses who are specifically taught how to conduct evidentiary exams on sexual assault victims (Littel, 2001). They are involved in cases from the initial collection of evidence through the prosecution and can testify as experts in court as to the meaning of evidence. This is true even in cases where the victim has no physical injuries or there is no sperm (and therefore no forensic evidence) available (Littel, 2001). In many communities they create a link between the evidence collection in a hospital and the criminal justice process, thereby increasing the likelihood of conviction for the sexual offender (NYCAASA, 2001). The victim is never required to report the assault to the police, but when he or she does, the police face an arduous task of responding sensitively to the complainant while collecting evidence and finding the perpetrator of the crime.

The Police

Sexual assault differs from other criminal offenses in many ways, one being that it is a private offense that generally takes place in the home of the perpetrator and/or the victim. Sexual assault is a difficult crime to prevent, and the police response is almost always one of control after the crime has been committed. In this vein, the police have three primary duties in cases of sexual assault: to interview the victim, investigate the crime, and collect evidence (Office for Victims of Crime, 2001).

In most cases of sexual assault, whether the victims are children or adults, there are no witnesses to the offense. As such, it is pertinent for the police to interview the victim, who is likely the only witness to the crime. Adult victims are often reluctant to speak to the police, because sexual assault is such an intrusive and personal offense. The police should therefore be trained in interviewing victims of sexual assault so as not to appear patronizing or overprotective, and to be aware of the victims' desire for privacy about the situation (Office for Victims of Crime, 2001). In order to get the most accurate and thorough statement, the police may come across as interrogating the victim. The victim may interpret this as lacking in sensitivity or that the police do not believe his or her story. Additionally, when relaying the account of the offense, the victim might forget details of the crime. The police should not consider this, or any emotional outbursts, the result of a false allegation but rather the effect of a severe trauma (Office for Victims of Crime, 2001).

Child witnesses present a different set of difficulties. Though the majority of children's cases are handled through social services or family courts, the police may have to interview children who are victims of sexual abuse. The interviewer must be trained in interviewing children and have special skills in order to elicit truthful information from the child. Though the interviewer must establish rapport with any victim of sexual assault, it is particularly important with children. If the child is uncomfortable talking to the interviewer, he or she may not be willing to speak to the interviewer without the presence of a parent, if at all. Interviews are also more effective if the child is comfortable, which is more likely to occur if the child is in a familiar place like the home or a child advocacy center (Office for Victims of Crime, 2001; Ward & Inserto, 1990).

The National Institute of Justice (1992: 33–42) describes three main techniques used in questioning. First, the interviewer may use anatomically correct dolls. Benefits to this approach include reducing stress for the child; reducing vocabulary differences between children and adults; and reducing embarrassment for the child. However, the dolls may have an adverse effect by provoking negative emotions related to the abuse or contaminating the child's memories at the sight of the genitalia. A second way in which children can be questioned is through normal interview techniques but with leading questions. This is risky though often necessary in order to elicit information. Children often do not report sexual behavior unless asked leading questions; however, presentation of inaccurate information may lead to a false memory being remembered (Loftus & Davies, 1984). A third method of questioning is to use videotapes, which are beneficial because they reduce the number of interviews, show the child's body language in response to questions, and can be used as evidence in court cases.

During the interview, the maturity and competency of the child must be established. The interview should begin with personal questions to establish rapport, with questions asking about the victim's name, address, pets, or siblings (Ward & Inserto, 1990). The interviewer can establish the level of development and maturity through personal questions such as religious affiliation, and establish the concept of time through asking about days of the week or month (Ward & Inserto, 1990: 69). Vocabulary must be age appropriate; it should not be too scientific or childish. Finally, the interviewer should provide reassurance and compassion to the child throughout the interview as well as praise, assuring the child that he or she is not in trouble.

Because children are considered the ultimate innocent victims, they are usually treated with sympathy and respect and their word is taken as truth despite the difficulties that arise from the interviews. Rape victims, however, are treated variably. If an offender attacks a stranger, the victim of the sexual assault is usually treated with respect and sympathy because this is seen as a "real rape." If the police see the victim as having any culpability in the assault, such as by drinking or hitchhiking, or because he or she is a prostitute, the police may treat the victim with less respect than they would a "real" rape victim. Many male rape victims also experience difficulties with the police (Pelka, 1995), though gender role stereotyping is less overt now than in previous years (Turner, 2000). To effectively elicit information and at the same time be supportive of all victims of sexual assault, the interviewer should show acceptance of the victim's statement, resourcefulness, empathy, sensitivity, persuasiveness, persistency, patience, and tolerance (Ward & Inserto, 1990: 54–55).

The police response to victims is critical, and the ability of the victim to cope with the assault is largely dependent on the police reaction (Office for Victims of Crime, 2001). In order to reduce the disparity in the ways in which victims are treated, almost all police departments have employed training for interviewing victims of sexual assault or have established specialized sex crime units. Others have established specialized programs within the police department, such as Austin's Victim Assistance Program. The purpose of this program is to assist both the victim and the victim's family in the recovery process by providing them with emotional and psychological support (Parker, 2001). At the same time, the coordinator of this program ensures that the police are educated about the realities of sexual assault and the needs of the victims. Victim service agencies at the law enforcement level are particularly important, as very few crimes go on to prosecution, and those that do rarely end in conviction.

The Adversarial Process

Once the police have investigated the crime and arrested the perpetrator, the adjudication process begins. There are several stages to this process, and the case can be dropped or settled through plea negotiations at any stage. After the perpetrator is arrested, taken into custody, and booked, he or she goes before the court for an initial appearance. At this time, the judge or magistrate makes a decision about pretrial release. Unless the case is very serious, such as rape of a stranger using excessive violence, it is likely that the defendant will be released either on his or her own recognizance or on bail. The pretrial release decision is based on several factors, including the nature of the crime, the safety of releasing the person into the community, and the best interest of the accused. Because many sex offenders are employed, have strong community ties, and show little likelihood of escape, they are usually released at this stage.

After the initial appearance, formal charges are filed against the defendant. At this time, the case is given to the prosecutor, who has the discretion to determine whether there is evidence to indicate that the defendant committed the offense and, if so, what the charges are going to be. If the prosecutor decides to proceed, the case will be brought before either the grand jury or the bench (in a preliminary hearing) to determine if there is probable cause to continue on to a trial. Once there is a formal charge, the defendant is arraigned and enters a plea. Most defendants plead guilty at this stage with the offer of a plea bargain, discussed following. For those who plead not guilty, the case goes on to trial. Many cases do not make it to trial, however, and are dismissed at various stages throughout the adjudication process. When trials take place, they generally take place many months or even years after the offense occurred due to factors such as legal maneuvering and overcrowding in the system. Because there are rarely witnesses to the offense, most victims have to testify against the offender and be cross-examined by the defense. Because of the high standard for conviction in criminal cases—proof beyond a reasonable doubt—sex offenders are rarely convicted if the case is based on the word of the victim, which contradicts the word of the only other witness: the defendant.

The adjudication process is often traumatic for victims, whether the case is dropped, the defendant pleads guilty, or the case goes to court. This begins with the decision made by the prosecutor about whether to charge the defendant at all. If the case goes to trial, the victim is usually revictimized in the courtroom. Though rape reform laws have emerged in the past decade to avert such abuses and victim advocates will assist the victims throughout the trial, many victims continue to feel a critogenic effect from the system.

Despite the offender-centered system, there are some fundamental changes that can be made in the way that victims are treated. An example of victim-centered legislation comes from the United Kingdom. In 1990, the Home Office created the Victims' Charter, a document outlining the rights of victims and what they can expect from the criminal justice agencies, which set out uniform standards of service for victim support. This nationally mandated code of practice ensures consistency throughout the country and is constantly developing in accordance with victim research. The general purpose of the charter is to set standards so that victims are treated with dignity, provided with information, protection, and support, and given information about their case. For victims of rape and sexual abuse, the charter also requires provision of specialized police officers to rape victims. Additionally, the charter establishes collaboration between agencies, primarily the police, probation, and Victim Support (the national charity for people affected by crime).

Role of the Prosecution: Dismissal, Plea Bargain, or Trial Once a perpetrator is arrested and the case of sexual assault is passed on to the prosecutor, he or she must determine whether to prosecute and, if so, on what charges. There are many factors that go into the decision of whether to file charges; most important is the strength of the evidence. Beyond these factors, the prosecutor must also look at the credibility of the victim, who will inevitably take the stand as a witness. Though rape crisis counselors and rape advocates are available to support the victim throughout the criminal justice process, the duty of the prosecutor is simply to secure conviction. For this, the prosecutor may look for ways in which the victim displays rape-relevant behavior (for example, promiscuity) or has participated in criminal behavior in the past, behavior that the defense attorney will likely exploit at a trial. As one prosecutor states, "There is a difference between believing a woman was assaulted and being able to get a conviction in court" (Frohmann, 1995: 214). Some communities have established specialist lawyers to prosecute at rape trials in order to reduce the insensitivity of the approach and the amount of revictimization from the prosecution.

If the case goes to trial, it is the burden of the prosecutor to prove beyond a reasonable doubt that the defendant committed the crime in question. Unfortunately, there are low conviction rates with sexual offenses that do go to trial because of the lack of witnesses, the lack of forensic evidence, and clever defense tactics used to undermine the victim's testimony. Unless there are visible bruises, cuts, or other injuries, it is difficult to show physical coercion (a sexual act compelled by force). It is also difficult to prove emotional or mental coercion (a sexual act compelled by threats) when there is a prior relationship between the victim and offender, the victim is lacking in "moral turpitude" (for example, the rape of a prostitute), or there are "contributory factors" (for example, the victim was drinking). Those cases most likely to end in conviction are those committed by strangers where there is forensic evidence or cases of child abuse where there is clearly physical intrusion. As such, a prosecutor is only likely to take a sexual assault case to court if there is evidence corroborating the victim's story (Taslitz, 1999).

Because convictions are so difficult to obtain in court, the majority of cases do not ever go to trial. Approximately 90 percent of cases in the criminal justice system are settled through plea bargains, yet this number is even higher for sexual offense cases. Plea bargains, which are arranged among the prosecutor, the defense attorney, the defendant, and the judge, are negotiations of guilty pleas in exchange for reduced charges or lenient sentences. There are many benefits to plea bargaining for the prosecutor; most important, guilty pleas avoid the time, expense, and work of proving guilt at a trial, and they assure a conviction. It is beneficial to defendants as well, because they may receive a charge reduction, a dismissal of some charges, a softer label, or a lenient sentence. Plea bargains are beneficial to the correctional system, as lenient sentences result in shorter sentences or fewer prison sentences, thus reducing overcrowding. Plea bargains even benefit victims in the sense that the victim does not have to testify at a trial when the offender pleads guilty.

Another reason that prosecutors offer plea bargains is that there is a high rate of attrition at each stage of the criminal justice process. The primary reason for this is the increase in acquaintance and intimate rapes and child abuse within the family. These are the most difficult cases to support with evidence, and as a result they are often dismissed (Harris & Grace, 1999). The first point that cases can be dismissed is by the police after the investigation. If the case is lacking evidence, police will not pursue the allegation. The second place at which the case can be dismissed is at the initial appearance in court. At this time, approximately 24 hours after the perpetrator was arrested, it is not uncommon for the victim to recant his or her statement. Other reasons for dismissal are a voided arrest due to lack of probable cause, or lack of evidence even if probable cause does exist. A third point at which dismissal occurs is at the formal charge. If the grand jury or the judge during the preliminary hearing finds a lack of probable cause, there will be no true bill, or formal charge. The case can again be dismissed during the pretrial phase. When this happens, it is usually due to loss of evidence or confession[11] or because the witness-victim is incompetent or mentally disabled and cannot testify.

Despite the benefits of plea bargaining, there are many problems with it as well.[12] Though victims do not have to testify at trial when a plea bargain is offered, they are often dissatisfied with the lenient sentences given to offenders, and they rarely have a say in whether a plea is offered. The rationale behind this is that the adjudication process must look at facts rather than emotion, but the lack of inclusion of victims in the negotiation process may leave them feeling as though their plight is less important than that of the offenders'. Though the adjudication system in any state in the United States does not seem to be nearing change in this area, legislation in the United Kingdom was recently modified to become more victim centered. Under the Victims' Charter, the prosecutor is required to take into consideration the victim's views before a negotiation is offered.

It is difficult to obtain a conviction for rape or sexual assault against adults, though problems also arise in court trials when the children are victims. There are four main issues of concern in regard to child witnesses, which are competence, credibility, children's rights, and defendant's rights (Perry & Wrightsman, 1991). The National Institute of Justice (1992: 56) explains four competencies that the court has established for child witnesses. The first is *capacity for truthfulness,* or the basic understanding between truth and fantasy as well as an understanding of the necessity to speak the truth. The second competency is *mental capacity,* or the ability to accurately understand the act that took place. A third competency is *memory,* or the ability to recall correctly the specifics of the act. The fourth is *communication,* which is the ability for the child to explain in court what occurred and answer questions about the act. Though all states have different provisions relating to child competency,[13] these four requirements must be present in order for a child to be a viable witness.

Once the child is declared competent, the prosecutor must determine the strength of the child's credibility, or how believable the child is (Mapes, 1995). Some children have difficulty in interpreting and explaining acts of sexual abuse, which detracts from their credibility (Loftus & Davies, 1984). Even when the child gives an accurate depiction of events, mock jury studies indicate that evidence in the case is of more concern than the testimony of the child (Ross, Miller, & Moran, 1987). Both children's and defendants' rights also present dilemmas. The child abuser may not be convicted if a child does not testify; yet, testifying may be a frightening experience for a child (Perry & Wrightman, 1991). At the same time, the defendant has the Sixth

Amendment right to face his or her accuser and confront the witness in court, though such a confrontation may be harmful to the child. The child should not have to relive the trauma of a frightening event unless it is absolutely necessary, and the prosecutor should consider whether this testimony is sufficiently likely to improve the chances of conviction.

Rape Reform Laws and Defense Tactics If a sexual assault case does go to trial, the victim is likely to face an emotionally trying ordeal while testifying. The adjudication process, however, has changed considerably since the 1970s due to significant rape reform laws. At that time, the trial of a rape victim was likened to a "second rape," because the defense was allowed to bring up the victim's sexual history, her chastity (or lack of), and any motive she had to claim that a sexual encounter was rape (Estrich, 1987). The victim rather than the offender was blamed for the offense, as it was either suggested that she was lying about the offense, that she consented, or that she prompted the sexual encounter and it therefore was not rape (Cuklanz, 1996). It was not a crime for a man to rape his wife, following the traditional belief that she was his property. The laws were gender biased, so that a man could not be a rape victim and a woman could not be a rapist. A stranger who was raped was said to be "asking for it" if dressed provocatively, and if the victim lacked sexual experience it was suggested that she was repressed and "wanted it" (Taslitz, 1999). In order to convict, there had to be evidence corroborating the victim's account, and a woman had to show physical resistance to the offender in order for the act to be considered rape (Berger, Searles, & Neuman, 1995).

Rape law reforms were led by feminist researchers (for example, Brownmiller, 1975; Estrich, 1987; Griffin, 1979; Russell, 1975) who attempted to change not only the existing laws but also the public perception of both offenders and victims. The four legal areas of change represented by the reform agenda were definitions of sexual offenses, evidentiary rules, statutory offenses, and penalties for sexual offenses (Berger et al., 1995: 225). Socially, reformers felt that by reducing the prevalence of rape myths they could change public perception of victims and, ultimately, increase the number of sexual offense convictions. They believed that public perception and the law were interlinked, as the law promoted rape myths and represented male authority and female subversion in society (Berger et al., 1995). They were successful in many of their aims; legal definitions have changed and the gender bias has been all but eliminated. Physical resistance is no longer the only factor used to prove coercion, and lack of evidentiary corroboration of the victim's testimony does not imply that the victim is lying about the rape. Socially, the prevalence of rape myths has been reduced. The resultant increase in reporting of acquaintance and intimate rapes, as well as child abuse within the family, is testament to the success of their efforts. Unfortunately, sexual offenses are still difficult to prove, and defense tactics still create emotional stress for many of the victims.

Rape shield laws prohibit the defense from bringing up the promiscuity or character of the victim, and they limit the amount of information that can be introduced regarding the personal or sexual history of the victim. This includes information such as the victim's previous sexual partners, preferred type of clothing, occupation (for example, if the victim is a prostitute), or other such issues that may influence the victim's credibility. However, the defense can skirt the laws by asking questions that are indirectly correlated to the victim's character and may produce bias against the victim (Taslitz, 1999: 84). The defense lawyer may try to get the victim to offer statements about his or her personal or sexual life, after which the lawyer can ask any questions relating to the information offered. The language used by the lawyer might also introduce bias, such as asking about previous partners (plural), her "child's father" (as opposed to her husband), questions about regular use of drugs or alcohol (low moral turpitude), or comment on the victim's low social status (though completely unrelated to sexual behavior). Therefore, even though rape shield laws prohibit direct questions about the victim's character, the defense can either ask questions that are ultimately overruled (yet the jury hears the leading questions and may make assumptions about the victim's character) or ask questions irrelevant to the case whose only purpose is to paint a negative view of the victim.

Because the duty of defense attorneys is to get their clients acquitted, they use various strategies that aim to exculpate their clients. Some of these introduce bias against the victim, whereas others are simply intended to introduce reasonable doubt in the minds of the jurors; yet most put pressure and emotional stress on the victim. Ward and Inserto (1990: 108–109) explain three defense ploys, the first of which is admitting that the victim was raped, but claiming that the defendant is not guilty and it is a case of mistaken identity. This is only possible if the rapist did not leave behind semen and therefore DNA, in which case the second ploy is to admit that sexual intercourse occurred but that it was consensual. This is a very common claim and is used often to introduce doubt in the mind of the jurors. If the victim did not go to the doctor immediately or the forensic evidence is ambiguous, the defense may employ a third tactic by admitting that a sexual encounter occurred but deny that intercourse took place.

Taslitz (1999: 22–23) explains four other common defense strategies, most of which are meant to upset the victim while he or she is on the stand. First, the defense attorney may repeatedly ask questions about the rape. This serves two purposes: to unnerve the victim and to find any inconsistencies in the victim's version of events. A second tactic is to emphasize a delay in reporting the crime, if there was one. Here the defense is implying that if the victim really was raped, he or she would have been distressed enough to report it immediately. A third tactic is to reveal prior relationships, often indirectly, particularly if the relationship was with the defendant. Finally, the defense must try to undermine the general character of the victim and appeal to gender bias, if possible.

Though defense attorneys appear ethically void in their tactics of questioning sexual assault victims, it is their duty to defend their clients to the best of their ability. Some lawyers argue that to not introduce information that leads to bias against the victim would "thereby undermine the lawyers' duty of zealous representation" (Taslitz, 1999: 106). Even the most conscientious of defense attorneys makes a distinction between victims of "real" rapes and rapes of women who may, in the eyes of some jurors, have some culpability in their victimization. By playing up the rape myths to juries, the defense attorney is able to "assault" the victim without even talking about her past or actions. He or she can talk about how men are brought up in a sexist society and when the woman went back to the defendant's apartment and was flirting with him, he took this to mean that she wanted something sexual. By directly talking about the defendant, the defense attorney indirectly talks about the victim and puts her in a negative view to the jury. In some areas, the rapist is even allowed to represent himself in court and cross-examine the victim[14] (Beneke, 1995).

VICTIM TREATMENT AND COUNSELING

The researchers who focused on rape law reforms not only succeeded in changing legal and social perceptions of victims, they also unveiled the need for victim support. Prior to the 1970s and consistent with social beliefs that rape was rare and victims played a role in their abuse, there were no government-sponsored agencies specifically devoted to assisting sexual assault victims (Koss & Harvey, 1991). At this time rape crisis advocates began challenging the long-held perceptions of rape victims while informing the community about the realities of rape. They began forming individual rape crisis centers across North America, Europe, and Australia, and eventually gained the assistance of established groups such as the National Organization for Women (NOW) (Koss & Harvey, 1991). Today, there are rape crisis centers or victim advocate centers in nearly every major city in the United States.

Rape crisis centers have several purposes, the first of which is to supply the victim with information about medical issues such as pregnancy, abortion, and sexually transmitted diseases. Advocates from the centers can accompany victims to the police station, court, and hospital. Though they talk to the victims about their options in regard to medical and psychological treatment, they do not tell the victims what to do. They do not even persuade the victims to contact the police and report the assault; rather, they give them information about the criminal justice system and encourage them to do that with which they are comfortable. They provide the victim with assertiveness training through empowerment groups, as well as self-defense training for future protection. Most important, the centers provide counseling for victims by telephone or in person, on a short- or long-term basis, and on an individual or group basis.

Counseling is confidential and can assist victims in understanding the offense, their reactions to the offense, and how to protect themselves from future offenses (Largen, 1991). When counseling at a rape crisis clinic or hospital is sought, it is generally in the immediate postrape period (within two to three months after the assault) and is a short-term form of support. In fact, most victims attend a single intervention session, the reason for which is that shortly after this point they enter the denial stage of victimization (discussed earlier in the chapter). A primary purpose of this initial counseling session is to establish social support for the victim, accepting his or her story and building an empathic (though not dependent) relationship (Koss & Harvey, 1991). It is important for the victim to seek help during this immediate postrape period, because the counselors can help him or her cope through adaptive (rather than maladaptive) behavior (Minden, 1991).

Few rape victims seek extensive support immediately post-rape. Instead, they are more likely to seek group treatment or individual clinical treatment with a trained psychologist several months later, when they move out of the denial stage of victimization. The role of the clinician is similar to that of the counselor, though the clinician is more likely to focus on the long-term needs of the victim. Both counselor and clinician encourage the victim to express emotions resulting from the assault and provide the victim with factual information about medical and psychological symptoms they may experience (Calhoun & Atkeson, 1991; Koss & Harvey, 1991). The most important role for the clinician is to address any psychological problems that materialize as a result of the assault, such as depression, eating disorders, and suicidal thoughts. Victims who experience serious psychological disorders are encouraged to continue therapy for an extended period of time. Victims who experience fear, anxiety, stress, and other common feelings of vulnerability are encouraged to participate in a group treatment process.

Koss and Harvey (1991: 208–210) explain nine benefits of the group treatment process for victims. First, it *reduces isolation* and helps the victim to see that others have shared a similar experience. Second, group treatment provides the victim with *positive support* that is adaptive and empowering. Third, it provides *validation* of the victim's feelings by helping him or her to understand that such reactions (for example, anger, rage, fear) are normal. Fourth, it provides *confirmation* of experience in that the victims can share their experiences and coping mechanisms with each other. This leads to the next benefit, which is that group treatment helps to *counteract self-blame* and *promote self-esteem* by removing blame from the victim and placing it on the offender. A sixth benefit to group treatment is the *egalitarian* rather than hierarchical mode of the session, where the victims not only seek support but also have a voice in the healing process of others. Group treatment also offers opportunities for *safe attachment,* with a safe context in which to meet, share similar feelings, and develop bonds with similar individuals. This links to the next benefit—groups provide a forum through which victims can *share grief* with others who understand their plight. Finally, the group experience allows victims to *contemplate and assign meaning to their experiences,* while committing themselves to recovering and moving on to the future.

Like their female counterparts, male victims of sexual assault also need counseling and treatment. Despite this, they are often presented with barriers when seeking support. Rape crisis centers were developed around a feminist philosophy, and several male victims have reported that the centers have negative attitudes toward men. The reason for this is that traditionally women have been the reported victims and males have been the aggressors (Mezey & King, 2000). As such, male victims are not necessarily comfortable in a setting that appears to be gender biased and at times hostile (Turner, 2000). Men are less likely to seek out treatment than women, and for those who do, there is a high attrition rate from the counseling. Male victims who receive a negative initial response when reporting the abuse (whether from the police, hospital, or acquaintances) are not likely to seek further support. Of those who do seek support, most have the same treatment needs as female victims (Mezey & King, 2000).

Perhaps most in need of treatment are children who have been abused. Because of the secretive nature of child sexual abuse and the grooming tactics used by perpetrators, the victims are highly likely to assign self-blame to the abuse. Child molesters frequently use emotional coercion to get the child to comply with the abuse, and use emotional blackmail to keep the child from telling others (Pryor, 1996). The child molester will also frequently tell the child that the abuse occurred because he or she wanted it, thereby creating feelings of guilt, blame, fear, and anxiety in the child at a young age. Though children experience many of the same symptoms as adults, these symptoms may manifest themselves differently in the child. The child victim is far more likely than the adult victim to experience psychological disorders such as dissociation in order to cope with the trauma (Cairns, 1999). This helps the victim to separate the negative identity of abused child from the positive sense of being desired. Finkelhor (1986) explains four common responses to childhood sexual abuse as *traumatic sexualization* (confusion and distress resulting from inappropriate sexual behavior, which may lead to sexual dysfunction as an adult), *stigmatization* (applying self-blame once the child realizes the sexual contact is inappropriate), *betrayal* (due to the trusting relationship built up with the abuser, who is often a relative of the child), and *powerlessness* (they are unable to control the situation). If the abuse is revealed when the victim is a child, extensive therapy should begin immediately.

Unfortunately, most children do not report abuse immediately but only report it in adulthood. At this time there is a high prevalence rate of psychological disorders such as mood disturbances, sexual dysfunction, and interpersonal and relationship problems (Jehu, 1988). Because of the severity of the reactions, adult victims of childhood abuse are likely to receive individual rather than group therapy as a primary mode of treatment. Because childhood victimization often comes to attention in light of other problems (for example, marital or sexual problems), the victim may also participate in additional forms of treatment such as family or marital therapy. Whatever form the treatment takes, it is generally extensive and long term.

If the child reports the sexual abuse when it happens, he or she will go through a similar criminal justice process to that of adult victims of abuse. Unlike with adult victims, research on the effect of the criminal justice process on abused children is varied. Children who testify in juvenile court are seemingly helped by the process, as it purportedly restores a sense of power and control to the child. In most states, children are appointed a guardian *ad litem* (GAD) in juvenile court to act as a legal assistant and help them with the court process (National Institute of Justice, 1992). On the other hand, the criminal justice process is damaging to children who appear in criminal court, have to testify many times, are lacking maternal support through the process, are involved in the adjudication process for a long period of time, and whose cases are lacking corroborative evidence (National Institute of Justice, 1992). Whatever the effect of the system, children do need treatment to help them cope with the effects of sexual abuse, and the earlier this treatment takes place, the better the outcome.

CHAPTER SUMMARY

- Sexual abuse, whether of adults or children, may be a highly traumatic event for victims. They are likely to experience physical and psychological problems, some of which may be chronic and lifelong.

- The psychological trauma experienced by sexual abuse victims seems to be even greater if the abuse continues for a long period of time or is committed by someone close to the victim.

- Friends and relatives of the sexual abuse victim also experience trauma, particularly parents of abused children and partners of rape victims. These individuals are called secondary victims.

- The criminal justice process exacerbates the feelings of critogenesis for the victim, or revictimization as a result of legal processes. This revictimization is a result of the hospital exam (which is intrusive and long), the police interviews (the officer asks the same questions multiple times, appearing as though he or she does not believe the victim), and the adjudication process (during which the victim must explain the event and then be cross-examined by the defense attorney). If the defendant is famous, such as Kobe Bryant or Mike Tyson, then the case may be tried in the media to the detriment of the victim.

- The level of revictimization has decreased in the past two decades because of rape shield laws. Prior to the enactment of these laws, blame for the sexual offense was placed primarily on the victim. Despite the rape shield laws, the victim still has little say in the criminal justice process. Despite the difficulties in alleviating victim anxiety resulting from the system, some communities have implemented schemes that reduce trauma and assist in the restorative justice process.

- Despite the assistance of laws that support victim rights, sexual offenses are still the most underreported of all offenses. This is particularly true for cases of childhood sexual abuse.

DISCUSSION QUESTIONS

1. Explain the most common physical effects of sexual abuse victimization.

2. What are the characteristics of rape trauma syndrome?

3. What are the most common psychological or emotional consequences of sexual victimization of adults? What effect may this have on familial and acquaintance relations?

4. How do the psychological consequences of sexual victimization differ between males and females?

5. What are the most common effects of child sexual abuse at the time of the abuse? When the child becomes an adult?

6. How have victim rights evolved? What rights are victims afforded today? What improvements can be made with these laws while still upholding the rights of defendants?

NOTES

1. In much of the current literature, primarily that of victim support agencies, the term *victim* is substituted by the term *survivor*. This book utilizes the term *victim* to denote a person who has been sexually victimized at any age but recognizes that these individuals are, in fact, survivors.

2. This is a difficult statistic to accurately predict for two reasons. First, rape statistics in the Uniform Crime Report (UCR) are seriously underreported, and this is the main source of information on official statistics. Second, the National Crime Victimization Survey (NCVS), which aims to determine the "dark figure" of crime, does not collect information from household residents under the age of 12. Therefore, this information was collected from a Bureau of Justice Statistics state survey on victim ages, with 12 states responding with this information about the ages of rape victims.

3. The data in this survey are from the National Incident-Based Reporting System (NIBRS) and are also derived from 12 states (though different states from the ones in the study cited in note 2).

4. For instance, one offender who abused his seven-year-old daughter explained that he lived and worked on a farm and his wife took the car out during the day and the night. He said he wasn't particularly attracted to children, but his daughter was there, and he regressed to abusing her.

5. Nelson (2002) illustrates the possible link between childhood abuse and actual rather than somatic pain through the example of children who were forced to give oral sex as children. The adult women in her sample complained of back pain, neck aches, and throat aches years after the abuse stopped. She explained how as children they had their hair pulled back during the abuse, thereby straining their necks and backs. Additionally, the abusers forced their penises down the victims' throats. She explores the possibility that such actions may have caused long-term physical damage, and that the physical symptoms may represent more than just a tangible outlet for emotional trauma.

6. 16.1 percent of men in state facilities, 7.2 percent in federal facilities, 12.9 percent in jail, and 9.3 percent of probationers were abused either physically and/or sexually. Most of these were abused when they were juveniles (Harlow, 1999: 2).

7. Men who rape men are more commonly heterosexual than homosexual, yet homosexual men are raped at a higher rate than heterosexual men (Scarce, 1997: 17).

8. In child abuse cases, this assumes that the child has a positive relationship with one or both parents (Ward & Inserto, 1990). For women who are raped, the mother also plays an important role in the recovery process.

9. A recent study in England—with similar conviction rates to those in the United States—produced statistics that only 1 in 13 reported rape cases ends in conviction.

10. This is similar to *iatrogenesis,* the condition caused unintentionally by medical treatment. With iatrogenesis, a medical treatment is offered to treat an illness, but the treatment makes worse the original condition rather than eliminates it.

11. Loss of evidence or loss of confession may be a physical loss, but it is more likely due to the suppression of evidence. The defense can file a motion to suppress if there has been a violation of the defendant's Fourth Amendment rights during the investigation process and evidence was obtained illegally. Confessions obtained illegally are also subject to scrutiny under the Fourth Amendment.

12. There are many concerns about plea bargaining for the defendant as well as the victim. This chapter does not explore such problems, but it should be noted that prosecutors have the discretion to offer plea bargains to whomever they want. As a result, two individuals who committed the same crime may be treated quite differently in the system. Another problem is that some individuals who have not committed a sexual offense plead guilty if there is no evidence to show they did not commit the crime. In such a case, they are likely to choose a lenient sentence rather than choose trial and a potential conviction with a long sentence.

13. See the National Institute of Justice (1992: 57) for an explanation of all state competency requirements.

14. Though allowed in the United States, this is no longer allowed in the United Kingdom as a result of the Victims' Charter. If the defendant represents himself, he is not allowed to cross-examine the witness.

❖

PART II

The Response
to Sexual Offending

8

Assessment
and Treatment
of Sexual Offenders

The results of sex offender treatment programs are conflicting, and researchers are largely divided as to the benefits of treatment. Because the heterogeneity of offenders is immense, treatment will not help everyone who participates. There is a general consensus that not all sex offenders can be rehabilitated (Holmes, 1991; Prison Reform Trust, 1990; Rizzo, 1981; West, 1985), and some researchers even claim that recidivism rates might increase for offenders who have undergone treatment (Quinsey, Khanna, & Malcolm, 1998). However, studies that summarize treatment literature indicate that the majority of cognitive-behavioral programs are effective at reducing recidivism if properly administered (for example, Polizzi, MacKenzie, & Hickman, 1999; Solicitor General of Canada, 1990).

The aims and types of treatment have changed significantly throughout the past century. From the late 19th century through the 1930s, treatment for sex offenders was mainly psychodynamic in nature, whereas the 1940s gave rise to organic (that is, hormonal) treatment methods. Behavioral methods of treatment began appearing in the 1950s and 1960s, though organic treatment continued for serious sexual offenders. Cognitive-behavioral treatment programs began developing in the 1970s, and these were the first multimodal treatment programs to address sex offenders' various cognitive, social, and behavioral problems. Although it is clear that there is no "cure" for sex offenders, certain treatment regimes appear to be successful at reducing rates of recidivism in this population as a whole. Unfortunately, it is not possible to present definitive statistics on the reduction of recidivism due to the numerous problems associated with sex offender treatment studies.

The first problem with these studies is that researchers do not use common definitions for the term *recidivism*. A *recidivist* is variously defined as an individual who commits another sexual offense (only), an individual who commits another violent offense or sexual offense, or an individual who commits any other offense (including a violent or sexual offense). Depending on which definition is used, studies produce distinctly different rates of efficacy. Specifically, the question "Does treatment work?" must be broken down into smaller questions, such as for whom does a particular treatment regime work, in what settings, and with what intensity the treatment should be delivered (Marques, 1999).

A second problem with these studies is that they often are not based on a representative sample of offenders (Marshall & Barbaree, 1990b). Many studies are based on incarcerated sex offenders, who represent only about 1 percent of the total sex offender population. Studies that are based on community samples involve either individuals who have voluntarily chosen to participate in treatment and who have enough money to pay for private treatment, or those mandated to participate in treatment while on probation or parole. These individuals tend to be older, better educated, and from a higher socioeconomic background than the general population of sex offenders. It is rare for researchers studying either of these populations of sex offenders to use control or comparison groups in their studies, as it is unethical to deny treatment to those offenders who want to be treated; and those who do not want treatment are not likely to be a representative control group. As a result, it is not always possible to determine whether the lack of recidivism is a direct result of the treatment. They might not have reoffended without treatment, or it is possible that they did recidivate and were not caught for these offenses.

A third problem with these studies is the short follow-up periods used by most researchers in assessing recidivism. Although a few studies have used extensive follow-up periods (Christiensen, Elers-Neilson, LeMaire, & Sturup, 1965; Rice, Quinsey, & Harris, 1991; Soothill, Jack, & Gibbons, 1976), most are based on follow-up periods of two to five years. Such short follow-up periods do not allow for sufficient time to measure recidivism levels. Despite these problems with sex offender treatment studies, the majority of researchers agree that some methods of treatment effectively reduce recidivism in some individuals. This chapter explains how treatment programs have developed, what treatment is available today, and for whom this treatment appears to be most effective.

HISTORY OF TREATMENT

Because psychologists originally thought sexual offending was the result of individual psychopathology, many of the first treatments were either organic or psychoanalytic in nature. They were based on a medical model, which implied that offending was a disease that was out of the control of the individual. At the beginning of the 20th century, Freud claimed that deviant behavior was not likely to change; if treatment through psychoanalysis was to work, it would have to be lengthy, because the deviant behavior was a deep-rooted aspect of the person (Freud, 1953). Organic treatments for sex offenders surfaced in the 1940s, when researchers began linking hormonal reactions to sexual behavior. The first hormonal treatment used was an estrogen called stilboestrol, in an experiment by Dunn (1940) on one incarcerated sex offender. Estrogen proved to be fairly successful at reducing deviant sexual behavior when tested on a larger sample (Foote, 1944); however, it was not widely used because of its side effects, which included vomiting, nausea, and feminization (Bowden, 1991; Bradford, 1990).

The idea that sexual offending was a medical problem continued through the 1950s, when the Fauteaux Committee in Canada stated that research should be carried out on sex offenders once they are removed from the population. In the 1960s, a number of new medical treatments were developed to control sexual behavior. Some of the first studies were conducted using the major tranquilizers thioridazine (Sanderson, 1960) and fluphenazine (Bartholomew, 1968), both of which caused the reduction of sexual interest in some offenders. The two most common medical treatments for deviant sexual behavior— cyproterone acetate (CPA) and medroxyprogesterone acetate (MPA)—were synthesized in 1961 and 1968 respectively, and despite their many side effects, they are still used by some practitioners today. Other agents such as benperidol and progestogens were also developed in the 1960s, but were not as widely circulated as CPA and MPA. Finally, there was surgical castration, which is rarely used now for ethical reasons as well as the fact that it is not the panacea it was originally assumed to be (Bowden, 1991).

In the 1950s, psychological methods of treatment for sexual offenders began to change. It was German-born psychologist Hans Eysenck's criticism of traditional psychotherapy that facilitated the move toward behavioral therapy as the preferred form of psychological treatment (Marshall, Anderson, & Fernandez, 1999). Many researchers at this time believed that deviant sexual practices resulted from deviant sexual arousal; therapeutic practices were therefore developed to modify deviant fantasies. They took various forms, such as operant conditioning (Skinner, 1953), aversion therapy (McGuire & Vallance, 1964), orgasmic reconditioning (Marquis, 1970), and shaping (Bancroft, 1971). The focus was not only on modifying serious sexual fantasies, such as those about children, but also on eliminating homosexual desires.

The first behavioral treatment programs were limited in their scope and concentrated on single elements of deviant behavior. Two groups of researchers in the early 1970s—Gene Abel and his colleagues and William Marshall and his colleagues—expanded on these and made the programs multimodal in nature by adding components such as social skills training. Abel, upon recognizing the prevalence of cognitive distortions (CDs) in sex offenders, modified behavioral treatment programs so that they were cognitive-behavioral in nature to address these distortions. In the 1980s, Pithers and colleagues adapted the therapeutic technique of relapse prevention (RP) to help sex offenders; this was said to be the most important development for sex offender research of that decade, as offenders were finally trained to recognize and manage their fantasies and behavior that could not be cured (Marshall, 1996). Other developments in the 1980s involved cognitive restructuring, victim empathy training, the refinement of sexual arousal monitoring, and an increased validity of phallometric testing (a measure of arousal assessment) (Prentky, 1994). The most significant addition to treatment in the 1990s was the use of the polygraph. Though it is not valid for legal purposes, the polygraph gives treatment providers insight into the acts of offenders and shows whether they are being truthful during the treatment programs (Ahlmeyer, Heil, McKee, & English, 2000).

Though treatment is available today for many offenders under the care of correctional authorities, either in prison or in the community, there are few standardized programs. Most are a conglomeration of various treatment regimes without a coordinated approach from the agencies concerned on a federal or a state level. Approximately 60 to 70 percent of sex offenders are given probation sentences (or a combination sentence of jail and probation), and nearly 90 percent of those are required to participate in treatment programs as a condition of their sentences (for example, Office of the Legislative Auditor, 1994). There are simply not enough treatment providers, particularly in large cities, to treat all those with community sentences. This is compounded by the problem of language; not all sex offenders are native or fluent English speakers, and yet there are few bilingual treatment programs (Cullen, 2001, personal communication).

There are even fewer sex offender-specific treatment programs in prison. This is true not only in the United States, but in most countries; in Canada in the early 1990s there were only about 200 treatment places for the 1,400 incarcerated sex offenders. This is not much higher than the percentage of offenders treated there in the 1970s, when only 10 percent of the sex offender population in Canadian federal penitentiaries had received specialized treatment (Solicitor General of Canada, 1990). Statistics were similar in England until 1991, when the passing of the Criminal Justice Act (CJA) caused the percentage of sex offenders being treated in prison to increase dramatically. This act authorized the establishment of a multisite, uniform treatment program at 25 prisons throughout England and Wales, and extended obligations of the prison and probation services for supervising sex offenders (Grubin & Thornton, 1994; Guy, 1992).

Many researchers now agree that treatment for sex offenders should be a necessary aspect of the correctional regime; however, this was not always the case. In the 1960s, the idea that sex offenders could be treated in prison was novel, and treatment programs were established too quickly and without adequate planning. Although these initial programs worked somewhat, they were not as effective as it was originally hoped they would be (Ross & McKay, 1980). The 1970s brought about a decline in the "rehabilitative ideal" for all correctional treatment programs (Andrews, Zinger et al., 1990), and the declining faith in sex offender treatment programs was consistent with these beliefs. Politicians of all parties were turning against the notion of rehabilitation; liberals felt that offenders were being coerced into treatment, and conservatives wanted retribution rather than rehabilitation for hardened criminals (Andrews, Zinger et al., 1990). Some researchers at this time were proclaiming that correctional treatment does not work (Lipton, Martinson, & Wilks, 1975; Martinson, 1974; Wilks & Martinson, 1976). Other researchers (Chaneles, 1976; Hallack & White, 1977; Serrill, 1975; Smith & Berlin, 1977), led by Palmer (1975), analyzed the treatment regimes and rash judgments made by those dubbed as the "Nothing works" theorists and claimed that treatment *does* work for some individuals. Many agreed that "the effectiveness of correctional rehabilitation is dependent upon what is delivered to whom in particular settings" (Andrews, Zinger et al., 1990: 372). Gendreau and Ross (1979) considered the biggest problem with the efficacy debate to be the lack of objectivity from the researchers who were arguing their points, describing those from the differing disciplines as "strangers trying to communicate in different languages by raising their voices." In defending the notion that rehabilitation can work, he said that "the 'nothing works' belief reduced to its most elementary level suggests that criminal offenders are incapable of relearning or acquiring new behavior. Why should this strange learning block be restricted to this population?" (Gendreau, 1979: 465).

In the 1980s there was an increased acceptance of rehabilitative beliefs, yet criticism still existed. Several researchers (Furby, Weinrott, & Blackshaw, 1989; Walker, 1989; Whitehead & Lab, 1989) produced critical evaluations of treatment efficacy, concluding that no data existed to show that treatment could be effective. These researchers failed to take into consideration the methodological problems of the studies they were evaluating (Marques, Day, Nelson, & West, 1994). Other researchers who did take these problems into consideration proclaimed that positive results have been produced through multimodal cognitive-behavioral programs (Andrews, Zinger et al., 1990; Marques, Day et al., 1994; Marshall & Barbaree, 1990b).

VARIABLES IN TREATMENT EFFICACY

Cognitive-behavioral treatment programs for sex offenders will be effective only if certain variables are addressed before the treatment begins. The two most important factors include *accurately assessing offenders for the correct treatment programs* (Andrews, Zinger et al., 1990; Glaser, 1974; Gleuck & Gleuck, 1950; O'Connell, Leberg, & Donaldson, 1990; Perkins, 1991; Ross & Gendreau, 1980), and *selecting staff who are well trained and capable of conducting these programs* (Andrews & Kiessling, 1980; Epps, 1993; Groth, 1983; Hogue, 1995; Marshall & Pithers, 1994; Sampson, 1992; Saunders-Wilson, 1992). Other variables will also affect the operation of the treatment programs, particularly social and financial factors of the institutions where they are being conducted (Holmes, 1991). Summed up by the Working Party in Canada,

Offender rehabilitation requires intensive programs that are based on sound theories, trained and motivated staff to deliver the programs, proper classification to allow matching of the programs to offenders, and research to guide the development and optimal delivery of the programs. Institutional programs need a supportive climate, and there must be a continuity of treatment from the institution to the community. (Guy, 1992: 2)

Who Should Participate: The Assessment Process

The most important factor in assessing offenders for treatment is predicting and matching the risks and needs of the offenders (referring to the offenders' levels of "treatability" and characteristics that are to be treated, respectively) with the appropriate treatment programs (Andrews, Zinger et al., 1990; Nicholaichuk, 1996). Offenders who are at a high risk to reoffend should be matched to high-intensity treatment programs; those who are considered low-risk cases will not benefit from such intensive therapy. Studies have shown that inappropriate matching of risks and needs can actually increase recidivism among offenders (Andrews, Bonta, & Hoge, 1990); this is especially true of adolescent offenders, who are sometimes misdiagnosed or whose behavior is considered to be normal (Longo, 1983).

In matching offenders with programs, offenders must be differentiated by their offenses, criminal history, and lifestyles before the time of intervention (creating a behavioral analysis of the offender) (Glaser, 1974; Perkins, 1991). Treatment can only be effective if the therapists know the full nature of sexual deviancy in the offenders, and as such they should do extensive background checks of the offenders' histories (O'Connell et al., 1990). Speaking to the offenders directly is helpful but in itself not sufficient, as most offenders either distort their histories or attempt to manipulate and "con" the therapists (Scully, 1990; Solicitor General of Canada, 1990; West, 1987). In checking records to validate the offender's history, therapists should ideally review police reports, victim statements, and presentence investigation (PSI) reports (Longo, 1983). The most important variable in risk assessment is the offender's past criminal history, particularly if the crimes are of a violent or a sexual nature (Hanson & Bussiere, 1996; Mair & Stevens, 1994; Marshall & Eccles, 1991; Nicholaichuk, 1996; Scully, 1990), and many researchers have found that offenders who have at least two past violent offenses are at the highest risk of reoffense. Also at a high risk of reoffense are offenders diagnosed with an antisocial personality disorder, and as such it is important to include psychopathy as a predictor variable in treatment assessment (Quinsey, Rice, & Harris, 1990; Serin, Malcolm, Khanna, & Barbaree, 1994).

Other factors associated with risk assessment include the offenders' behaviors, feelings, cognitions, and personalities (Andrews, Bonta, & Hoge, 1990: 28). Although some manifestations of these concepts can be observed from background checks, they are more likely to be assessed through various psychological inventories. Most programs require offenders to undergo a battery of psychometric tests to assess these variables, measuring factors such as psychopathology, personality, social attitudes, morality, respect for others, the presence of negative emotional states, and responses to normal and deviant sexual interactions (West, 1987).

Psychologists use a variety of inventories to assess sex offenders. Some are common, large-scale personality inventories, such as the Minnesota Multiphasic Personality Inventory (MMPI). Psychologists and researchers have developed numerous evaluative instruments in recent years that are specifically devoted to measuring traits specific to sexual offending, such as the Multiphasic Sex Inventory (MSI), which measures sexual cognitions. The Sex Offender Risk Appraisal Guide (SORAG), Rapid Risk Assessment of Sexual Offense Recidivism (RRASOR), Static-99, and the Minnesota Sex Offender Screening Tool-Revised (MnSOSTR) were designed to measure sex offender recidivism, but researchers also use general recidivism instruments such as the Violence Risk Appraisal Guide (VRAG) and the Psychopathy Checklist-Revised (PCL-R) with sex offenders. Some researchers (for example, Barbaree et al., 2001) have found that the VRAG, SORAG, RRASOR, and Static-99 are capable of predicting general, violent, and sexual recidivism, whereas the MNSOST-R scores may be able to offer predictions on general recidivism. Out of all of these measures, the PCL-R, when used alone, was sensitive in predicting general and serious recidivism but was unable to predict sexual recidivism.

Other assessment tools distinguish types of offenders. For example, Knight, Prentky, and Cerce (1994) constructed the Multidimensional Assessment of Sex and Aggression (MASA), which they felt adequately differentiated the various types of rapists. Such an assessment is successful in distinguishing among rapist subtypes; however, it is not much use for treatment programs that are offered to all types of sex offenders. Another example comes from Hillbrand and Waite (1994), who developed the Experience Sampling Method (ESM) to measure thoughts and their relations to mood states. They constructed the ESM because they claimed that most psychometric tests were inadequate at addressing psychological determinants (for example, fantasies, defenses, and mood states) and how they interact with environmental determinants (for example, precipitating stressors, victim availability, and disinhibitors).

In addition to the psychological tests, assessments are also done to measure the level of deviant sexual arousal in offenders. A common method of measurement is through the Abel Screening Tool (Abel, Lawry, Karlstrom, Osborn, & Gillespie, 1994), where offenders must answer a questionnaire and rank slides depicting children, adolescents, and adults based on how arousing the offenders find these images. Their physiological responses are measured through a psychophysiological hand monitor, a volumetric phallometer, and a circumferential plethysmograph (also known as a PPG, or a penile plethysmograph), all of which show respectable to high levels of specificity, efficiency, and sensitivity in their measurements.[1]

It is important for a therapist to know if an offender is having deviant sexual fantasies (Saunders-Wilson, 1992), and for this reason any device that measures the physiological responses of sexual offenders is important, but alone these measurements are inadequate. When offenders are assessed with a PPG, they are exposed to erotic stimuli, and it is difficult to identify deviant sexual attraction through reaction to erotic images alone. Rapists often show equal arousal to consenting and nonconsenting sex, and many "normal" individuals show some level of arousal to deviant stimuli (Marshall & Eccles, 1991). Unless the offender is sadistic or has a high level of fixation with children, it is often difficult to differentiate between "normal" and "deviant" arousal patterns. Second, not all sexual offenders are driven by sexual needs, and the arousal patterns will not explain much about why the offender commits deviant sexual acts. As Marshall states, the most important element in a rape is not the deviant sexual arousal but rather the frame of mind of the offender at the time of the act (Marshall & Eccles, 1991: 256). This is particularly true for incest offenders, who are usually attracted to agemates but have abused children; they rarely show arousal patterns that are different from the general population of males.

Participation in a Treatment Program

One debate concerning sex offender treatment programs is which offenders should be excluded from participating in treatment. Most programs assess offenders through the various tests and eliminate from participating those who do not meet particular requirements. An example of one study, conducted by Marques and her colleagues at the Atascadero State Hospital in California,[2] used the following guidelines for their treatment program: subjects consisted of all child molesters 18–30 months from their dates of release; they were 18–60 years of age; they had no more than two prior felony convictions; they admitted to committing their offenses; they had no pending warrants or arrests; their IQ was estimated to be at least 80; they spoke English; they had no psychotic or organic disorders; they did not require nursing care; and they had not exhibited any severe management problems in prison (Marques, Nelson et al., 1994: 579). Many of these factors are typical of program requirements, and offenders who do not fit the assessment criteria will not be able to participate in programs. Exclusionary requirements eliminate many offenders, and those who participate may be the least likely to offend again anyway (Marshall, Laws, & Barbaree, 1990c). Some researchers have argued that it would be better to adapt treatment programs to individual needs of the offenders rather than to exclude those who need the treatment most. Unfortunately, this is not usually possible where group treatment sessions are offered, namely for those offenders under correctional control either in the community or in prison.

In addition to the assessment procedures discussed, there is also a requirement in most programs for treatment to be offered to offenders on a voluntary basis. The reasoning behind this is that treatment will only be effective for offenders who are willing to cooperate and are willing to change their behavior (Perkins, 1991; West, 1987). The offenders' attitudes are vital, as negative attitudes toward the treatment program may negatively affect them as well as the others in the program (Sampson, 1992). This causes a predicament for convicted offenders, most of whom do not *want* to participate in treatment. In one study (Terry & Mitchell, 2001), approximately half of the offenders participating in a prison treatment program said they were doing so either for incentives within the prison or because they had to in order to be eligible for parole. In another study, 73 percent of the rapists interviewed stated either that they did not want or need treatment, though 41 percent of those said that they would participate if they were expected to do so while in prison (Grubin & Gunn, 1990).

Offenders in the community and in prison may be offered incentives to participate in treatment. Not all prisons will use early parole dates to entice offenders to participate in treatment programs. However, many will not allow an offender to be released on parole without the treatment. Treatment participation is perceived to be a no-win situation by many offenders: on one hand, they are aware that they are not likely to gain early release without participating; but on the other hand, they are aware that genuine disclosures of their deviant acts and fantasies during treatment may reduce their chances of parole. Other offenders will agree to take hormonal treatments or participate in a psychological treatment program while serving a community sentence, therefore avoiding a prison sentence altogether. The result of this trade-off—a lesser sentence for treatment participation—may cause the sex offenders to be "involuntary clients" (Groth, 1983). Many of these offenders who do not want to participate in the treatment programs do not do so honestly (Sampson, 1992); there is a question, therefore, about the effectiveness of treating offenders who feel they have been "coerced" into treatment participation.

Not all researchers believe that voluntariness is an absolute variable. Bowden (1991), for example, describes voluntariness as a matter of degree, saying that prisoners are not in a position to choose freely. He states, "We should be treating those accused of criminal acts, despite the commonly held view that the voluntariness of their consent is compromised by their position" (p. 133). Other researchers claim that motivation is not always necessary in order for treatment to be effective. One study showed that there is no difference in the reduction of cognitive distortions for offenders with adult victims who were and were not motivated to participate in a treatment program (Terry & Mitchell, 2001). This implies that some offenders who do not want to participate in treatment may still benefit by participating.

Staff Selection and Training

Researchers agree that treatment will only be effective if it is delivered by adequately trained staff whose attitudes toward offenders are positive and supportive. A successful therapist will be one who is carefully selected to work with sex offenders, has the ability to deal with sexual issues, is able to understand the difficulties in working with these offenders, and understands their need for treatment (Perkins, 1991: 227). The staff who work with sex offenders in prison are not always qualified to do so. They often lack the multidisciplinary knowledge that is necessary to properly treat sex offenders, and as a result the offenders sometimes end up recycled into the community without the proper knowledge of how to stop offending (Groth, 1983; O'Connell et al., 1990). As recently as 1990, some Canadian therapists admitted that they did not always have highly trained staff despite the fact that a key need for effective treatment is staff training and motivation. Training should cover a broad range of subjects, including communication skills, human relations, and the ability to control negative situations such as depression, suicidal thoughts, and inappropriate behavior (Longo, 1983).

In addition to their training, the personal qualities of the staff are important if treatment is to be effective (Saunders-Wilson, 1992). In order for offenders to respond to the treatment, those delivering the treatment must be

> interpersonally warm, flexible, yet sensitive to conventional rules and procedures. These workers make use of authority inherent in their position without engaging in interpersonal domination; demonstrate in vivid ways their own anti-criminal/pro-social attitudes, values and beliefs; and enthusiastically engage the offender in the process of increasing rewards for non-criminal activity. (Andrews, Bonta, & Hoge, 1990: 36–37)

Treatment staff must be able to develop a rapport with the offenders, although it is not enough for them to always be "friendly" (Glaser, 1974). Therapists are required to be somewhat confrontational by demanding that offenders acknowledge their inappropriate behavior and attitudes; however, they must not do so in a hostile fashion (Groth, 1983). They should be persuasive in their strategies to help offenders overcome the denial and minimization of their offenses, yet not pushy or negative. Rather, they must be appreciative of the offenders' low self-esteem and lack of confidence and treat the offenders with respect (Marshall & Pithers, 1994).

Research has shown that positive staff attitudes are critical in facilitating change in offenders (Glaser, 1969), and as such it is important for sex offenders to perceive the treatment staff as having positive attitudes toward them and the treatment programs. Staff should be "direct, open, truthful, and consistent in their attitudes" (Groth, 1983: 168). They should not be uncomfortable around sex offenders or when dealing with sexual issues, and training should increase their confidence in working with these offenders (Hogue, 1995). One factor that may influence the offenders' honesty about their behavior is the gender of the therapists. Most offenders feel more comfortable opening up to either a male or female, and for that reason it is a good idea to have staff of both genders working together (Longo, 1983). Though it is always best for staff to work together as a team to help maintain positive attitudes toward the offenders and the programs, there does not appear to be a decrease in treatment efficacy when only one therapist is assigned the treatment program (Marshall et al., 1999).

There are three problems that commonly occur with therapists who are treating sex offenders: *countertransference, negative emotional reactions to the offenders, and burnout.* Countertransference refers to the emotional responses that therapists experience in relation to the offenders (Houston, Wrench, & Hosking, 1995). Although this may be positive in that it assists the therapists in understanding the offenders' beliefs, it does not allow for objective treatment (Greer & Stuart, 1983). Secondly, therapists are likely to experience negative emotional reactions to sex offenders, as they are not immune to the contempt felt toward sex offenders by most individuals in society (Greer & Stuart, 1983). Problems arise when this contempt becomes destructive to the rehabilitative efforts of the treatment programs. As Glaser states, people "view themselves on the basis of their perception and interpretations of how others view them" (Glaser, 1974: 146). If offenders perceive staff to have negative feelings toward them, they are likely to develop low self-esteem and self-confidence, even viewing themselves as victims. The third problem is that staff are likely to experience burnout as a result of an excessive, highly intensive workload (Longo, 1983; Marshall et al., 1999). This is magnified by programs that have few resources and therefore limited staff and low salaries for the staff, resulting in a high turnover rate for those involved with the treatment programs (Holmes, 1991). All of these factors assist in creating a negative atmosphere for the treatment programs and, thus, may lead to a negative treatment outcome. Although some of these emotional responses will be present in many therapists working with sex offenders, they can be diminished through proper staff selection and training.

Length and Timing of Treatment

There has been a debate about how long treatment programs should last in order for them to be effective and at what point in their sentences incarcerated sex offenders should be treated. As of yet, there is no definitive answer for either of these questions. When considering how long a treatment program should last, either in prison or in the community, the answer will depend largely on the group being treated and the type of treatment program being implemented. Some programs last 12 weeks and are said by the therapists to be sufficient (Marshall & Pithers, 1994), whereas other community treatment programs last up to five years. The length of the program should depend on the individuals being treated, matching their levels of risk to their needs (Longo, 1983). Those who are at a high risk to reoffend should have a more intensive program with added components of treatment that are not necessary for all sex offenders. For example, those offenders who have been labeled as psychopathic should be considered high-risk offenders who need extensive treatment. In one study of young psychopathic offenders, treatment averaged 4.6 years (Reiss, Grubin, & Meux, 1996). Those at a low risk to reoffend do not need such lengthy or intensive programs. Another factor that must be considered is the point at which intervention takes place in the offender's career. Those with a long history of offending behavior will need more intensive treatment regimes, whereas those who are receiving treatment at an early stage of the offending career will be considered at a lower risk to reoffend (Marshall & Eccles, 1991). If offenders are properly assessed into the correct treatment groups, then program lengths will match the needs of the offenders.

Another question is, If an offender is incarcerated, at what point during the offender's sentence will treatment be most effective? Some say that treatment should be administered at the end of the offender's sentence, just before their release into the community (Longo, 1983). Others say that treatment is most effective at the beginning of the sentence with a "refresher" course at the end, as offenders will otherwise spend the beginning of their sentences pondering over their deviant fantasies, which will become a normal process of thought (Hagan, King, & Patros, 1994). Thus far, there has been no conclusive evidence to imply that treatment occurring at either the beginning or the end of the offenders' sentences is more likely to reduce recidivism (Grubin & Thornton, 1994). One factor that must be taken into consideration with regard to timing of treatment is that if treatment occurs at the beginning of the offender's sentence, there should be a booster course for the offender before release. This is because a delay between treatment and release may negatively affect recidivism rates (Marshall, Barbaree, & Eccles, 1993).

MEASURING TREATMENT EFFECTIVENESS

The biggest problem with sex offender treatment programs is producing objective evaluations of the programs. Varying methodologies are used for treatment and for program evaluations, and these do not utilize common definitions of efficacy or recidivism. "Successful" treatment is an ambiguous term, often defined by researchers to be made applicable to their studies. The success rate of programs depends on the time frame of follow-up, the type of offense, and the definition of reoffense (Holmes, 1991). Unless strict definitions and measures are used for evaluations, it is difficult to determine how successful sex offender treatment programs actually are.

The majority of program evaluations are based on offender recidivism, and as such it is important to establish criteria that accurately measure reoffending. Researchers define *recidivism* in a variety of ways (Marshall & Barbaree, 1990b), depending on the aim of the study. The varying definitions are likely valid, but they must be explained clearly in order to avoid any misinterpretations of the findings. In addition to disparate definitions, the various studies use differing follow-up lengths to assess recidivism (Marshall & Barbaree, 1990b). Most researchers consider a two- to five-year follow-up period to be adequate; however, studies that use long-term follow-up periods show that much of the recidivism occurs after five years (Guy, 1992; Soothill et al., 1976). Soothill et al. (1976: 169) claimed that recidivism is most apt to occur soon after the offender is released from prison; however, one-quarter of the recidivists in their study were reconvicted after 10 years. Some researchers also claim that measuring recidivism through official statistics is not sufficient for program evaluations, as the recorded levels underestimate the true rate of reoffense (Marques, Day et al., 1994; Saunders-Wilson, 1992; Tracy, Donnelly, Morgenbesser, & MacDonald, 1983). For a true measure of treatment efficacy, it would be necessary to measure the amount of denial and minimization displayed by the offenders, the frequency of deviant fantasies, and any lapses the offenders have experienced (Marshall, 1994). These factors can be measured through self-report studies or paper-and-pencil tests; however, they will be subjective and, like official statistics, may inaccurately portray the rate of offending behavior (Marques, Day et al., 1994).

In addition to the factors already listed, there are a number of variables that must be taken into consideration when statistically measuring the effects of treatment. Treatment cannot be accurately measured without a control or comparison group. Ideally, offenders who want to participate in a treatment program would be randomly allocated to either a treatment or a control group; however, this is not usually ethical and therefore is rarely possible (Marshall, 1994). More commonly, researchers either do comparisons between two types of treatment, or else they compare the rate of pre- and posttreatment offending behavior within one group of offenders. The latter type of assessment allows for a measurement of self-improvement, which does not require a control group (Tracy et al., 1983; West, 1987). When studies do include control groups, the types of offenders, their ages, type of employment, marital statuses, criminal histories, levels of arousal, and presence of mental disorders must be established so that the comparisons are accurate (Marques, Day et al., 1994). All treatment studies must use comprehensive designs, have a sufficient base rate, account for attrition, use proper assessment procedures, use statistical methods that account for a cumulative survival or failure rate of the offenders, and therapists must adhere to treatment protocol (Marques, Day et al., 1994; Marshall, 1994). The treatment outcome will depend on these factors as well as types of offenders, types of treatment, the nature of the treatment setting, the intensity of the treatment, and the nature of the posttreatment environment (Ross & Gendreau, 1980). In addition, evaluations must be objective, and it is best for those evaluating the offenders not to be directly involved with the program. If therapists do the evaluations, the offenders are likely to manipulate and con them so that they can be released for parole; if program directors do the evaluations, they will likely be biased in their results in order to make the treatment appear effective. For this reason, it is best for evaluations to be done through those in contact with the offenders but who are not involved with the treatment program. Offenders may be able to con or manipulate anyone doing their evaluations, however, and it will always be difficult to have an absolutely neutral evaluation.

In addition to the variables mentioned, there are certain factors that can positively influence treatment outcomes. Multicomponent cognitive-behavioral treatment programs have shown the most promising results (Marques, Day et al., 1994; Marshall, 1994; Marshal et al., 1999), and the most effective aspect of these programs is said to be relapse prevention. For certain high-risk offenders, these programs have worked well in conjunction with hormonal treatments; however, organic treatments tend to be effective only in the short term unless they are continued for an indefinite period of time (Solicitor General of Canada, 1990). For younger sex offenders, particularly adolescents, some authors claim that successful treatment emphasizes high levels of community involvement, stress-challenge education, student interpersonal problem-solving activities, energetic administrative leadership, and extensive staff training (Brannon & Troyer, 1995: 324).

To summarize the literature on treatment results, the offenders *least* likely to recidivate are incest offenders, those over age 40, and those with no past offenses. The offenders *most* likely to recidivate are those who are young, have a sexual preference for violence, and have committed one or more previous sexual offenses (Hanson & Bussiere, 1996; Williams, 1996). Offenders who have molested young boys or both boys and girls are at a greater risk to commit another sex offense; however, those who raped adult females are at a greater risk to commit a nonsexual violent offense (Hanson & Bussiere, 1996). Some researchers believe that a low IQ is correlated to offending behavior (Marques, Day et al., 1994; Reiss et al., 1996), whereas others feel that intelligence and educational level are weak predictor variables (Marshall & Barbaree, 1990b). Some researchers have also found that offenders who are unemployed, had older or multiple victims, and who did not admit their offenses are at a high risk to reoffend (Berliner, Schram, Miller, & Milloy, 1995). Although all of these factors may be relevant to recidivism, because of offender heterogeneity it is difficult to predict future offending behavior for any sex offenders.

No treatment approach can guarantee success to all offenders (Solicitor General of Canada, 1990), and no sex offenders will be "cured" by a treatment program (Guy, 1992). Most important, there should be coordination within the community and among all agencies involved with sex offenders. The research literature shows that comprehensive cognitive-behavioral treatment programs have reduced recidivism for the majority of offenders who participate (Marshall et al., 1999; Polizzi et al., 1999; Solicitor General of Canada, 1990). The literature also shows that the recidivism rates for adolescent sex offenders tend to be relatively low with treatment, measuring approximately 10 percent after treatment (Davis & Leitenberg, 1987; Smith & Monastersky, 1986). Those who reoffended were most likely to commit property crimes (Brannon & Troyer, 1995). One factor that must be considered is whether the analysis of offenders occurs while the offenders are in a custodial setting; if so, the analyses may be inaccurate. It is only in the community that real-life settings of high-risk coping responses can be tested (Kear-Colwell & Pollock, 1997). Therefore, even if treatment is beneficial in a custodial setting, it will be even more so if it is followed up with community treatment programs where behavior may be influenced by environmental triggers.

MEDICAL TREATMENTS

Some serious sex offenders are offered organic (hormonal) treatment in order to reduce their sexual drive and, thus, their deviant sexual behavior. As stated previously, the first hormonal treatment used to control deviant sexual behavior was estrogen. Although not in use for long, it was beneficial in showing researchers that hormonal treatments were capable of decreasing levels of sexual drive. It also became clear to the researchers who used estrogen that side effects may occur with some individuals using hormonal treatments. One hormonal treatment used today is CPA, which works as an antiandrogen and antigonadotrophin to reduce sexual drive (Bowden, 1991). Several studies have shown positive effects from the use of CPA, both in Europe and North America (Marshall & Eccles, 1991), including reductions in ejaculate, erections, and sexual fantasies. Despite its apparent successes in these areas, CPA, as well as a similar hormonal treatment called ethinyl estradiol (EE), does not seem to have any effect on sexual fantasy or erectile responses outside of experimental situations, and it does not necessarily reduce sexual aggression (Bowden, 1991; Bradford, 1990). As for side effects, CPA can cause depression, breast enlargement, increased weight, and osteoporosis; however, these effects are limited and usually occur after years of treatment.

The most common hormonal agent used to control sexual deviancy is MPA, which is administered in weekly doses to reduce serum testosterone levels. Also referred to as Depo-Provera,[3] this hormonal agent causes a temporary "chemical" castration for the length of time it is used (Solicitor General of Canada, 1990). Although it causes reversible testicular atrophy, there are ethical considerations with its use as well as questions about the long-term benefits for those who cease taking the weekly doses. Studies have produced conflicting results as to the effects of Depo-Provera years after treatment ends. Two early studies reported that it has many beneficial effects, including decreased frequency of erections, reduced sexual drive, and reduced orgasm rates, which continued for several years upon cessation of treatment in some patients (Blumer & Migeon, 1975; Money, Wiedeking, Walker, & Gain, 1976). Another study, however, showed that almost all of those who terminated the doses of Depo-Provera against medical advice relapsed, as did a small number of patients who were still taking doses of the hormonal agent (Berlin & Meinecke, 1981). Research has shown that it does have positive effects for most offenders who comply with the treatment protocol, and because it is administered through weekly injections, its compliance can be documented (Berlin, 1989). Still, some offenders will prematurely end treatment, saying they are "cured," thus potentially bringing about adverse consequences. Though sexual drive can be measured during treatment through blood tests (measuring serum testosterone levels), self-ratings, or with penile plethysmographs, when treatment has ended, the benefits are often only measurable through reconviction rates (Bowden, 1991).

Medical treatments are generally offered to paraphiliacs, particularly pedophiles, rather than rapists or child molesters such as incest offenders who do not experience intense sexual urges. The function of medical treatments is to reduce sexual drive, and as such they are generally helpful for pedophiles who have difficulty resisting their urges without medical treatment. The use of these drugs, however, is limited without additional psychological treatments. For example, antiandrogens and antigonadotrophins can reduce sexual drive but not nonsexual violence, nor can they change the direction of sexual urges (Bowden, 1991). Additionally, there are difficulties to administering medical treatments to incarcerated offenders. There is a requirement for the indefinite continuation of treatment, and it is unclear whether there will be any benefits for offenders who terminate usage prematurely. Also, informed consent is necessary for medical treatments, and because they are likely to be offered only in exchange for parole or reduced sentences, it is assumed that consent will not always be entirely voluntary (Bradford, 1990).

Another medical treatment offered to sex offenders is physical castration, though it is now rare for this to be offered even when offenders request the procedure. Despite the fact that castration dramatically reduces the circulating testosterone (the hormonal effect that induces sexual drive), the effects of castration are not complete. Many offenders who have been castrated stayed sexually active for a while after the surgical procedure (Heim, 1981). Because of the numerous ethical problems associated with physical castration, it is more common for chemical castration to be offered through the use of Depo-Provera. Some researchers encourage the use of hormonal castration, saying that it effectively reduces sexual drive and that compliance can be monitored (Bowden, 1991). There are, however, problems with hormonal treatments; it is suggested that even though testosterone is the *main* contributor to sexual arousability and functioning, it is not the *only* contributor (Bradford, 1990; Perkins, 1991). Therefore, chemical castration, which affects serum testosterone levels, may reduce but not eliminate the problem of sexual aggression.

Medical treatment is controversial; sex offenders under the care of correctional authorities in some states are denied this treatment, whereas other states make it mandatory in order for offenders to be released. Deviant sexual behavior may be the result of a biological drive in some individuals, and as such medical treatment may be required to suppress intense urges. Nonetheless, there are ethical considerations with its use as well as questions about the long-term benefits for those who cease taking the weekly doses. As such, the mandated use of this chemical is highly questionable. California is the first state to require mandatory chemical castration for offenders convicted of two or more predatory sexual offenses.[4] After one sexual offense, this is an optional treatment that will allow the offender to serve his sentence in the community rather than in prison. Five other states allow for the discretionary, rather than mandatory, use of Depo-Provera, whereas New York and Vermont require supplementary mental health treatment components when offenders are treated with Depo-Provera (Bund, 1997). Because of its many potential side effects, chemical castration is unlikely to become a mandatory treatment for sex offenders in most states. However, organic treatments may be effective in some individuals if administered in conjunction with psychological treatments (Marshall & Eccles, 1991).

COGNITIVE-BEHAVIORAL TREATMENTS

Cognitive-behavioral programs are the most common form of treatment for sex offenders today. Many treatment programs in the community are ATSA-certified, meaning that they follow a specific cognitive-behavioral regime developed by researchers at the Association for the Treatment of Sexual Abusers. (For

Table 8.1 Goals of a Cognitive-Behavioral Treatment Program

Aim of Treatment for Sexual Offenders

1. Offenders should recognize their problems and behaviors.
2. Offenders should understand the feelings that led to their deviant behavior.
3. Offenders should be able to identify and eventually eliminate their cognitive distortions.
4. Offenders should accept responsibility for their behavior.
5. Offenders should reevaluate their attitudes and behaviors.
6. Offenders should acquire prosocial expressions of sexuality.
7. Offenders should gain a higher level of social competence.
8. Offenders should be able to identify their high-risk situations.
9. Offenders should understand the repetitive nature of their behavior and be able to break the sequence of offending.

more information on ATSA, including standards, guidelines, and publications, see http://www.atsa.com.) Though cognitive-behavioral treatment programs may vary in their specific processes, Table 8.1 describes the common goals of a typical cognitive-behavioral sex offender treatment program.

All treatment programs differ in their processes, though there are some commonalities between them, particularly for those in the community. Before treatment begins, it is necessary to accurately assess the risks and needs of the offenders. To do so, the treatment provider should conduct a background check, give the offender a battery of psychometric tests, conduct an interview, test levels of sexual arousal through a PPG, and, when possible, use a polygraph. The polygraph is best used prior to treatment to determine if the offender is telling the truth about his or her offenses, and then after treatment to determine if the offender has been truthful throughout the treatment process. The offenders are asked few questions—usually about four—during this process, as too many questions negatively impact the results of the polygraph exam. The polygraph results are used only for treatment purposes, and the results are not valid in a courtroom. The primary benefit of the polygraph is that offenders tend to be truthful to the therapists when they know they are going to be tested on a polygraph. One study showed a significant increase in truthful admissions for both inmates and parolees by the second administration of a polygraph, though the most important result from their study is the high level of deception practiced by sex offenders (Ahlmeyer et al., 2000). The researchers found that 80 percent of the inmates and 74 percent of the parolees were deceptive in their responses about the number of victims, type of victims, or number of previous offenses. Because the polygraph allows the therapist to see when the offenders are misleading them about the true extent of their offending behavior, the polygraph is considered by many therapists as the most significant improvement to treatment in the 1990s (Cullen, 2001, personal communication).

After the assessments are complete, the treatment program can begin. Most cognitive-behavioral programs are conducted through group processes, called by some the "cornerstone of therapy" (Hagan et al., 1994). There are two main reasons for this: namely, that peer confrontation tends to be the most effective way to overcome CDs (Marshall et al., 1999), and it is the most cost-effective form of treatment when resources are limited (Houston et al., 1995). Group therapeutic sessions generally address both *offense-specific targets,* for example, denial and minimization, victim harm and empathy, deviant sexual fantasies, distorted attitudes, beliefs, and perceptions that have led to the offenses, and relapse prevention (Marshall, 1996: 181) and *offense-related targets,* or factors that are correlated to deviant sexual behavior such as anger management, social skills, assertiveness training, life management skills, marital therapy, and substance abuse therapy (Marshall, 1996).

Group treatment processes are effective in many areas of psychotherapy, and sex offender treatment is no exception. Peer confrontation is helpful in making sex offenders admit their offenses and acknowledge responsibility for their offenses, two main goals of treatment. According to Yalom's (1985) general psychotherapeutic framework for group processes, all group therapy sessions develop in stages. Houston et al. (1995) have described the three stages of group treatment programs for sex offenders, utilizing Yalom's framework, as the initial stage, the stage of conflict, and the cohesive stage. In the initial stage, the offenders search for similarities—between themselves and their problems—and establish a hierarchy within the group. There is a struggle at this time to establish roles, and there is a search for approval with each other and with the therapists. The second stage consists of a competition for dominance among the group members, as well as feelings of hostility toward the therapists and attempts to sidetrack from the actual topic of treatment. The third stage is one of cohesion, the point at which the group will finally be able to achieve work without distraction. Although they have noted other issues involved with group processes, it is these stages that have appeared consistently in various types of group therapy.

Though sexually deviant behavior is not necessarily addictive (Kear-Colwell & Pollock, 1997), the acquisition of this behavior is often compared to addictive processes (for example, alcoholism). For this reason, many of the therapeutic techniques to overcome such behavior are similar to those for overcoming addictive behavior. In addition to the stages of treatment that take place in group processes, each individual offender also experiences distinct stages of change. Prochaska and DiClemente (1982) described five stages of change that the offender may encounter, although all stages are not necessarily experienced by all individuals. The first stage is *precontemplation,* where the offender can be classified as a "denier." He does not yet acknowledge that he has a problem, and he is defensive and unmotivated to change. The second stage is one of *contemplation,* where the offender acknowledges that a problem does exist yet minimizes the problem or the extent of damage that has resulted from the problem. The third stage is *preparation,* where the offender recognizes the significance of his problem and is finally motivated to change his behavior. The fourth stage is one of *action,* where he participates in the treatment program in an effort to change his behavior. The fifth stage is one of *maintenance,* where change is consistently sustained upon termination of the program. In applying these stages of change to the sex offender, Kear–Colwell and Pollock (1997) have also added a sixth stage to this process: *relapse.* When the offender is unable to sustain change and "slips" into deviant fantasies and subsequently deviant action, he relapses and returns to either the precontemplation or contemplation stage of change.

Group processes are particularly important for offenders in these first two stages of change. Most sex offenders at first deny or minimize their offenses to some extent, and studies have shown that offenders do exhibit a gradual change throughout the treatment process in the amount of information that they are willing to reveal about themselves (Perkins, 1991). Marshal (1994) examined a treatment program for offenders who deny or minimize their offenses, showing how denial can be overcome in a group treatment context. In this study, the offenders had to disclose the nature and extent of their offenses in detail to the group, including thoughts, feelings, and emotional states. The role of the therapist was only to explain what the disclosures revealed, while it was the group's task to encourage and/or challenge the offender who was speaking. In addition, the therapist had to distinguish for the group the difference between the crime and the offender—the offender himself is not heinous even though he committed heinous crimes. It was found that when the offenders were encouraged and treated with respect, their self-confidence increased and they were more likely to admit their offenses.

There are two ways in which group treatment processes can be conducted: through confrontational or motivational approaches (Miller & Rollnick, 1991). The *confrontational approach* aggressively challenges offenders about their behavior in an effort to overcome denial, rationalizations, and deceit, and it does so by disempowering the offender and putting the responsibility of change with the therapist. It encourages self-labeling and attacks the self-image and self-esteem of the offenders, which can cause some to take up a position of "psychological reactance"—they argue for their position of not having a problem rather than taking the responsibility to change the problem (Brehm & Brehm, 1981; Kear-Colwell & Pollock, 1997; Miller & Rollnick, 1991). In opposition to the confrontational approach, the *motivational approach* leaves the responsibility to change with the offender. The therapist does so by creating "cognitive dissonance," or a psychological discomfort that acts as a motivator for the offender to change (Miller & Rollnick, 1991). Some researchers believe that the motivational approach is best when working with deniers, as it encourages them to consider changing their behavior rather than staying in the precontemplation stage of denial (Garland & Dougher, 1991; Kear-Colwell & Pollock, 1997). Nonetheless, most group processes use a combination of these approaches, as all individuals respond differently to the two techniques.

Whichever approach is used, group processes are important for combating CDs. Although denial and minimization are two of the main distortions exhibited by offenders, there are also other attitudes, beliefs, and perceptions that must be modified. Whether they are negative attitudes toward women (by rapists) or the perception that sex is educational for children (by child molesters), it is these distortions that help to maintain the deviant sexual behavior (Marshall & Barbaree, 1990b). The group process assists offenders in understanding the distortion of their beliefs, as they are able to hear the other offenders' attitudes toward sexuality and sexual acts. The effect is greater when the groups are mixed with rapists and child molesters, as the distortions then appear more pronounced. These mixed groups are also beneficial because offenders who have committed similar offenses are not allowed to confer with each other and reinforce their deviant beliefs. Rather, the group helps the offenders to overcome their deviant thoughts by offering alternative beliefs and perceptions that are considered prosocial in nature.

Another CD found in many offenders is the lack of victim empathy, with *empathy* described as "the capacity to perceive another's perspective, to recognize affective arousal within oneself and to base compassionate behavioral responses on the motivation induced by these precepts" (Pithers, 1994: 565). In her study, Scully (1988) found that 54 percent of rapists felt nothing toward their victims at the time of the offense, and Langevin, Wright, and Handy (1988) found a positive correlation between denial and empathy scores. One goal of sex offender treatment programs is therefore to make offenders understand the consequences of sexual abuse for their victims (Abel & Rouleau, 1995; Marshall, 1996). Researchers have learned that most sex offenders function on a concrete rather than an abstract level, and as such it is more productive to act out rather than talk out problems (Groth, 1983). Many cognitive-behavioral programs utilize a system of role playing to induce empathy in offenders, which has shown to be very effective in a group process. In this method of therapy the offender acts out the role of his victim(s) while the therapist or other members of the group take the role of the offender. Through the physical act of playing the role of the victim, the offender is often able to understand for the first time the amount of fear that he instilled in the victim at the time of the attack and the subsequent harm that was caused.

Group processes can also be used to teach offenders about proper sexual behavior, from general sex education to arousal reconditioning. Many sex offenders are raised in sexually dysfunctional homes and thus lack an understanding of normal sexual behavior. As one researcher stated, it is surprising to find out how little sex offenders know about sex (Saunders-Wilson, 1992). Many offenders suffer from sexual dysfunctions (for example, premature ejaculation) that, when in conjunction with other predisposing and triggering factors, may induce them into committing deviant sexual acts (West, 1987). When these sexual dysfunctions are discussed, the offenders are often relieved to find that others in the group suffer from similar dysfunctions. For those offenders who fantasize about deviant sexual stimuli—whether children, violence, or situations of power and control—the group process helps to recondition their arousal patterns. The therapist teaches the offenders how to retrain their sexual fantasies, usually through classical conditioning, with negative consequences occurring when the offender experiences deviant thoughts. The therapist may use smelling salts (Marshall, 1996) or other devices such as rubber bands (the offenders put the bands around their wrists and snap them when a deviant thought occurs). Arousal reconditioning requires the cooperation of the offender, because unless the offender is aroused by known stimuli and arousal rates are recorded on a PPG, only the offender knows if he is having deviant fantasies. If the motivational approach to therapy is accurate and offenders are more willing to change when the therapists exhibit trust and understanding toward them, then the reconditioning should be successful.

Although it is necessary for sex offenders to redirect their deviant sexual interests toward appropriate adult channels, they are not able to maintain proper social relationships without also improving their social skills. Social incompetence increases the likelihood of offending behavior by blocking legal sexual outlets. Until offenders acquire appropriate conversational skills, living skills, and use of leisure time, they are likely to experience anxiety in adult relationships (Marshall & Barbaree, 1990b). The three sets of social skills in which sex offenders are generally deficient include *decoding skills,* or the interpretation of situations and other people's behavior; *decision skills,* or considering possible responses to situations and choosing the best option; and *enactment skills,* where the decided response is carried out (Marshall & Eccles, 1991: 250). Without prosocial attitudes and expressions of sexuality, it is probable that offenders will experience negative emotional states such as stress, anger, and loneliness. Strategies for controlling negative emotional states are included in most group processes in addition to the social skills training, as these states may act as triggering factors for deviant sexual behavior and offenders must learn how to effectively deal with such emotions. Negative emotional states are also commonly experienced prior to relapse, and as such are targeted in the treatment process.

There are several stages to the cognitive-behavioral treatment process, and though they differ in each individual program, most follow a similar progression (Cullen, 2001, personal communication). The first step is *engagement,* where the therapist helps the offenders get used to speaking in front of a group. In this stage, the offenders begin speaking about their family, childhood, adolescence, and the facts of their current offenses. The next step is *covert sensitization,* where the offenders continue giving active accounts of their cases. In this stage, the therapist spends a significant amount of time with each individual until he or she fully discloses the facts of the case. This is where it is important for the therapist to have the victim statements and police reports in order to challenge the account of the offender if there is denial and minimization (Marshall et al., 1999).

Once all the offenders in the group have fully disclosed the facts of their offenses, the group begins *social skills training* and *assertiveness training.* During this stage, the therapist teaches them how to have normal social relationships with adults and tries to get the offenders involved with social groups (for example, church groups). The therapist should also include a stage about human sexuality, because most sex offenders have an insufficient understanding about sexual issues such as pregnancy, sexually transmitted diseases, and sexual dysfunction. At this stage of the treatment process, the therapist begins *cognitive restructuring.* Most offenders have by now reduced their primary CDs and are no longer denying their offenses or blaming their victims for the offenses. However, the therapist spends time going over general CDs, such as the importance of victim empathy and how the offender must take responsibility for his or her actions.

The final stage of the treatment process is *relapse prevention* (RP). RP is defined as a "maintenance-oriented self-control program that teaches sex offenders how to determine if they are entering into high-risk situations, self-destructive behavior, deviant cycle patterns, and potential reoffenses" (Alaska Department of Corrections Offender Programs, 1996: 5). This strategy for maintaining treatment-induced changes was originally developed as a model for controlling substance abuse, and was later adapted by Pithers, Marques, Gibat, and Marlatt (1983) to address deviant sexual behavior. RP teaches offenders how to interrupt the succession of events that lead to the commission of deviant sexual acts over time and across situations, and requires offenders to analyze the factors that have previously led them to commit deviant acts. Upon determining what constitutes a high-risk situation for the offenders, they are then taught coping strategies and given general instructions on problem-solving procedures so that they can devise their own avoidance strategies upon termination of treatment.

The job of the therapist is to help develop realistic expectations for the offenders, as it must be understood that deviant sexual interests may not be eliminated and therefore must instead be managed (Alaska Department of Corrections Offender Programs, 1996). Offenders should be made to realize that if they experience a *lapse* (fantasy or initial occurrence of sexually deviant behavior), it will not necessarily lead to a *relapse* (performance of and complete return to pattern of sexually deviant behavior) (Pithers et al., 1983). Pithers explains that a relapse usually occurs after the offender makes a series of "apparently irrelevant decisions" (AIDs). An AID is a minor decision that is relatively harmless on its own, but several AIDs can lead to an offense. For example, a child molester will not necessarily commit an offense if he drives past a school; however, this is an AID because it is the first in a series of decisions that may put the offender at risk of committing an offense.

There are a number of factors that can trigger a relapse, and these are similar to the factors that help cause the original instance of offending behavior. Most commonly, relapses are triggered by negative emotional states—in Pither's study, 75 percent of relapses were precipitated by negative moods and feelings such as anger and depression (Pithers et al., 1983). These emotional states can lead to fantasies or cause an offender to act upon fantasies that he has already been having. If RP strategies are successful, then the offender's perception of self-control should be maintained until a high-risk situation occurs. Upon reaching such a situation, the offender will increase his self-confidence if he copes successfully with the situation and will similarly feel a sense of failure and helplessness if he is unsuccessful. RP should help offenders to maintain the changes that have been induced by other components of the treatment programs, providing offenders with "cognitive and behavioral skills that will reduce the probability of another offense" (Pithers et al., 1983: 239).

PRISON TREATMENT PROGRAMS

Once convicted, a sex offender is more likely to serve a sentence in the community than in prison. The courts often require the offender to participate in a treatment program as a condition of his or her community sentence. As such, there are more treatment programs for offenders in the community than in prison in the United States. Nonetheless, those sentenced to prison are more likely to have used violence in their offense, committed an offense against a young child, or be a recidivist offender. It is important for these individuals to participate in treatment while incarcerated, and some prisons have thus established sex offender-specific cognitive-behavioral treatment programs.

Prison treatment programs establish the same goals for offenders as community treatment programs. However, therapists face practical problems in prison that are not present in the community. Examples of such problems include difficulties in securing treatment rooms, getting prisoners unlocked at a particular time, continual interruption, and fitting the treatment program into the prison regime (Houston et al., 1995). Some researchers say that treatment works best in the community, for the reasons listed and also because offenders in prison are not subject to the environmental triggers that are present in the community (Kear-Colwell & Pollock, 1997; West, 1985). Others say that all treatment programs vary, whether they are outpatient or institutional (Marshall & Barbaree, 1990b), and that, overall, treatment programs in prison are as effective as those in the community (Marshall & Eccles, 1991). It is important to offer offenders the option of treatment in prison, as one researcher states that "if one enters prison because of an inability to cope successfully with a sexual orientation directed towards children, in most cases there is little reason to believe that prison alone will alter that situation" (Berlin, 1989: 234).

One problem with institutional treatment programs is that the offenders are rarely followed up with long-term supervision and maintenance upon release from prison. There tends to be little communication among the various organizations about what treatment has occurred, and what is still needed for each offender. The lack of communication extends to the prisons themselves, as the institutions rarely communicate with each other about what aspects of treatment are most effective and upon whom, and what programs are being run where. There are no uniform prison treatment programs run federally or on a statewide basis in the United States. In Canada, there are some excellent prison treatment programs offered in Ontario, and there is now a multisite, uniform treatment program at a number of prisons across England and Wales. The Sex Offender Treatment Programme (SOTP) in England has been very beneficial in that it is the first attempt at a uniform program run through the country's prison headquarters, and it is continually being refined and improved. It is not a panacea for the problem of sexual offending; however, it is a unique treatment regime with several beneficial qualities that can be utilized in other countries.

In 1990, one of the most serious riots in the history of British prisons occurred at HMP Strangeways, which houses numerous sex offenders. The riot provoked an inquiry into prison conditions, and as a result Lord Woolf, a prominent British judge, offered recommendations on the reevaluation of sex offenders' situations in prison. At this time, sex offenders were segregated from the general prison population for their own protection and, though some incarcerated sex offenders were offered treatment, the treatment was erratic and there was no continuity or consistency in the programs (Programme Development Section, 1997a). Lord Woolf recognized sex offenders as constituting "a group with special needs," believing that it is the responsibility of the prison to provide regimes that are not damaging for the prisoners (Prison Reform Trust, 1990: 24). As a result of his report, the Criminal Justice Act, passed in 1991, increased the demands on the prison and the probation services to better provide for sex offenders, stating that "without treatment, they are likely to leave prison as dangerous, if not more dangerous, than when they entered and highly likely to reoffend" (Guy, 1992: 2). The number of sex offenders in British prisons increased nearly 300 percent from 1980 to 1990 (Grubin & Thornton, 1994), a rate similar to that of the United States. This increase led to heightened interventions and expectations that prisons should be capable of treating sex offenders before they are released into society (Guy, 1992).

The Prison Service developed its national initiative based on evidence of effective treatment programs that were running in North America, with particular help from Dr. William Marshall from Ontario, Canada. He helped them to establish a cognitive-behavioral treatment program for sex offenders who would likely be a high risk to the community upon their release. Priority risk factors include having four or more convictions of any kind, any previous conviction for a sex offense, a current conviction of a sex offense against three or more victims, a current or previous conviction for a nonsexual assault, and a current sentence of at least four years.[5] Three or more of these factors constitutes a high-risk offender (Grubin & Thornton, 1994). The SOTP follows exclusionary guidelines similar to those used by Marques and her colleagues at the Atascadero State Hospital (Marques, Nelson et al., 1994), discussed earlier in the chapter, including that offenders who suffer from an acute mental illness, have an IQ below 80, risk self-injury, suffer from severe paranoia or personality disorder, have chronic brain damage, or are for some other reason unsuitable medically are not eligible to participate in SOTP (Clarke, 1997).

At the time of this publication, there are 25 prisons running the SOTP, and all prisons follow a strictly structured program. The main, or Core, program addresses offense-specific targets, or the primary issues common to most sex offenders, whereas an Extended Program addresses offense-related targets, such as intimacy, marital, and relationship problems. There is also a Booster Program, which acts as a refresher course for those offenders who are serving long sentences. Its main function is to reinforce the understanding of RP strategies for offenders who participated in treatment well before their release dates. A fourth supplementary program has been introduced for those who completely deny their offenses, based on the belief that treatment is capable of undermining denial in some offenders (Schlank & Shaw, 1996). A fifth supplementary program is an adapted version of the Core Program, and has been established for those who are learning disabled and require different communication methods from the verbal and written communications utilized in the Core Program. The tutors, or those who deliver the treatment, are drawn from all disciplines within the prison system. Though there is a general assumption that effective therapists will be drawn from psychiatrists or psychologists familiar with the etiology and maintenance of offending behavior, the SOTP employs multidisciplinary teams comprised mainly of lay therapists (for example, corrections officers). These multidisciplinary teams have shown to be as effective in group-work as those with all professionals, as the importance lies in the personal qualities of the tutors rather than their education (Mann & Thornton, 1997). There are three tutors assigned to work with each treatment group, with at least one being male and one being female. Those who have recently completed the training course are teamed with more experienced tutors, and, when possible, there is at least one tutor with a professional background on each group.

The effectiveness of the SOTP will be evaluated in several long-term projects. Short-term evaluation projects have all shown that treatment is effective for some individuals, yet change was greatest with high-risk offenders to whom treatment risks and needs were matched. In one study that measured change in rapists only, 11 of the 22 variables analyzed showed significant change; however, all but one of the variables changed at least slightly in a positive direction (Bowers, 1996). Many of the offenders not only showed change through the psychometric tests that were administered, but also through their actions in the prison as observed by the prison officers (Clark, 1996). Although the majority of offenders showed improvement, some did not show any changes in behavior, and others deteriorated.

There are currently no multisite programs like the SOTP in the United States. The SOTP, in short-term evaluations, has proved to be cost effective and reduce rates of recidivism in various sex offenders. Not only has the use of lay therapists proved to be successful, but the offenders claim to prefer them to psychiatrists. As such, it may be beneficial to consider implementing such a program on a statewide level.

CHAPTER SUMMARY

■   There are a number of treatment regimes available to sex offenders in prison and in the community. Researchers have found that that multi-modal cognitive-behavioral treatment programs have the greatest potential of all treatment regimes to reduce recidivism. The combination of treatment components helps offenders to understand why they committed the deviant acts, a precursor to changing their behavior.

■   Most treatment programs consist of group therapy, where the offenders are encouraged to take responsibility for their offenses, modify their cognitive distortions, acquire an understanding of prosocial sexual fantasies and behavior, learn social skills to help them achieve normal adult relationships, gain an understanding of the harm they have caused to their victims, and control their negative emotional states.

- Relapse prevention is one of the most important aspects of current cognitive-behavioral treatment programs, because during this component offenders learn strategies on how to recognize high-risk situations and employ avoidance strategies in order to successfully manage their deviant sexual behavior.

- Cognitive-behavioral programs are relatively short term, and many offenders need lifelong supervision and maintenance to control their behavior. Nonetheless, studies show that these programs, particularly when employed with relapse prevention strategies, can reduce the rate of reoffense for some offenders.

- For offenders who have high levels of deviant sexual arousal, hormonal treatments can be used concurrently with psychological treatment programs to alter the serum testosterone levels and reduce arousal.

- For any treatment program to be effective, the offenders' risks and needs must be matched. Though most thorough cognitive-behavioral programs follow an ATSA-approved regime, these programs must still be tailored to the specific individuals in order to adequately treat them.

- Although well-staffed, well-run treatment regimes are likely to be effective for some sex offenders, there is no treatment program that is applicable to everyone.

DISCUSSION QUESTIONS

1. What are the key components of a standard cognitive-behavioral treatment program today? Can you explain the importance of each of these components?

2. Why is it important to offer sex offenders who are receiving hormonal treatments (for example, Depo-Provera) cognitive-behavioral treatment as well? What problems might arise if the cognitive-behavioral treatment is not offered?

3. How can you determine whether or not treatment is effective? What are some common methodological problems with studies on treatment efficacy?

4. Why is relapse prevention such an important part of a treatment program?

5. What are problems with treatment in prison? Treatment in the community? How can these problems be overcome?

6. What type of sex offender is most likely to be excluded from a treatment program? Discuss the obstacles in treating high-risk sex offenders. Is there a way to overcome these obstacles?

NOTES

1. The Abel Screen displays a specificity of 77 percent to 98 percent, sensitivity of 76 percent to 91 percent, and efficiency of 77.5 percent to 96.9 percent; the volumetric phallometer shows sensitivity of 86.7 percent, specificity of 95 percent, and efficiency of 94.6 percent; and the circumferential plethysmograph displays a sensitivity of 47.5 percent, specificity of 100 percent, and efficiency of 97.4 percent.

2. This is cited by many authors as one of the best methodological studies on sex offenders because, unlike most research in this area, it was conducted with a control group. The use of a control group was considered ethical here only because there were more volunteers for the treatment program than places available, and as such a control group was available for evaluation studies.

3. Another common agent is Lupron, similar to Depo-Provera but administered in doses every other week or monthly.

4. There are currently several cases in the California court system opposing the use of mandatory organic treatment for offenders. Groups such as the American Civil Liberties Union (ACLU) are comparing chemical castration to mandatory sterilization, which the courts declared unconstitutional in *Skinner v. Oklahoma* (1942).

5. Priority is given to those serving four years or more because it is assumed that the length of sentence reflects the seriousness of the offense, and also because offenders will still have time to complete the program if they are allowed parole. Other prisoners serving fewer than four years may be allowed to participate if they are identified as high-risk offenders (Guy, 1992).

9

Management and Supervision of Sex Offenders in the Community

D espite the legislative popularity of incapacitating sexual offenders in either prison or hospital, the majority of known sex offenders are living in the community. Sex offenders who are living in the community fall into two broad groups: those who are under the care of correctional services and those who have completed their sentences and are no longer under direct supervision. Approximately 60 percent of sex offenders under care of correctional services are serving their sentences in the community at any given time. Most of these are either on probation or parole, though a few also serve sentences in halfway houses or under house arrest and electronic monitoring. Once an offender completes his sentence, he must register his name and address with the police. The only supervision these offenders receive is from the registration agency; such supervision, in most states and for most offenders, occurs for a finite period of time (registration and community notification is discussed at length in Chapter 10). The question is, How can we effectively manage this population to ensure community safety and public protection?

Effective policies for management and supervision are required now more than ever, with a nearly 400 percent increase in convicted sex offenders in the past decade. This increase strains resources and makes the supervision of sex offenders in the community one of the most challenging issues in the criminal justice system today. The many difficulties associated with the task of sex offender supervision include (but are not limited to) the lack of communication between supervising agencies; the lack of training for those who work with offenders; the lack of specialized units for supervising sex offenders; the lack of funding and resources for specialized treatment programs; the inherently secretive nature of sexual crimes; and the need for more resources for agencies in charge of registering sex offenders.

What makes supervision most difficult is that sex offenders do not fit the profile of other offenders in the criminal justice system. As a group, sex offenders tend to be older, better educated, and from higher socioeconomic backgrounds than the general population of offenders. As a result, they present few case management problems to those in charge of supervising them because they tend to follow the conditions of their supervision (Orlando, 1998). Despite the apparent adherence to requirements, a sexual offender must receive intensive, specialized supervision by a field agent who is familiar with the offender's high-risk situations to help him or her avoid a relapse. To compound the problem, the media often presents hostile broadcasts about sex offenders in the community, thereby enhancing public intolerance of their offenses (McGuicken & Brown, 2001). The politicians, community, and media alike tend to focus only on the risk management failures of this group of offenders, thereby presenting the supervision agencies as largely ineffective (Kemshall, 2001).

Because sex offenders represent such a heterogeneous group of individuals, there is no one-size-fits-all policy for effective management, and management will never be 100 percent successful at reducing recidivism. Some organizations, such as the Center for Sex Offender Management (see http://www.csom.org), work to improve the management of sex offenders who are in the community by establishing training programs for supervisors and sponsoring research on best practices for supervision. This chapter explores the most pertinent issues relating to supervision and management.

MANAGEMENT OF SEXUAL OFFENDERS: ACTORS IN THE SUPERVISION ROLE

There are three areas of concern for agencies that manage the potential risk of sex offenders: providing protection against offenders in the home; providing protection against risk in the workplace; and providing protection of the community at large (Thomas, 2000). No single agency can accomplish these three goals; rather it must be a collaborative effort by many agencies. The primary agencies in charge of supervising sex offenders include the police, probation and parole officers, treatment providers, and victim service agencies, though other agencies such as prosecutors, social services, family and child care services, health care providers, housing authorities, and employers are also involved. Ideally, these agencies can work together to help offenders and keep them from relapsing, though rarely does this happen. Instead, most agencies focus on their own roles in the supervision of sex offenders, which are as follows:

- *Police* The police have a dual role when it comes to sex offenders: they must respond to and investigate sexual offenses, and they must proactively work with the community in order to deter such offenses from occurring. Since the implementation of Megan's Law, officers are now aware of the whereabouts of sex offenders in the community. Though this information should be helpful if a sex crime occurs, police must be mindful of the rights of sex offenders and balance their individual rights with community protection.

- *Probation* A city- or county-run agency, probation is in charge of the majority of sex offenders under care of correctional services. In large cities, probation officers have high caseloads (between 100 and 250 clients per field agent), making it difficult to appropriate extra attention to any individual or class of offenders. Some cities have intensive supervision probation (ISP), allowing for smaller caseloads for the most serious offenders. However, the majority of sex offenders fall under regular probation schemes.

- *Parole* A state-run agency, parole faces many of the same problems as probation. However, because parolees tend to be more serious offenders, the caseloads in parole tend to be much smaller than those of probation. The reduction in caseload size often translates to more effective management of clients.

- *Treatment Providers* Most states now mandate treatment as a condition of probation and/or parole. The treatment providers must find out the high-risk situations of sex offenders and communicate these risks to parole or probation and the police. Another critical issue at this time for the treatment provider is the development of relapse prevention (RP) strategies for the offender (see Chapter 8 for details). Supervision of the offender by external agencies will only be effective if combined with internal controls and the offender's own understanding of how to manage his or her high-risk situations.

- *Victim Service Agencies* The criminal justice system tends to be almost entirely offender rather than victim centered. As such, victims are not always provided with information about their cases, their perpetrators, or the resources available to them. Victim service agencies need to work with offender supervisory agencies in order to speak about the relationship between victim safety needs and offender supervision.

- *Prosecutors* Prosecutors play a key role in sex offender issues, beginning with the charges made against the offender. Additionally, because sexual offenses are very difficult to prove in a court of law, prosecutors often strike plea deals with offenders. This may result in a lesser charge that is still a sexual offense (for example, original charge of Rape I reduced to Rape III in exchange for a guilty plea) or a non-sexual offense (for example, assault). The reduction in charge has critical implications for management and supervision.[1]

- *Social Services and Local Child Protection Agencies* Social services, along with the local child protection agencies, are in charge of the well-being of child victims or children living with sex offenders. Whereas the police focus on criminal matters of child sexual abuse, social workers have a duty to ensure protection of the child against abuse and neglect in the home, and, if necessary, they must remove a child who is in danger of becoming a victim.

- *Employers* The onus of protection in the workplace is on employers. There are certain jobs that are unsuitable for known sex offenders, particularly those who have abused children. Employers must ensure they do not hire convicted child molesters in or around schools, parks, or recreation centers, for example. Other areas of concern should be facilities near beaches, sporting facilities such as ice rinks or gymnasiums, children's clothing stores, or photography studios, to name but a few. Equally, convicted rapists should not be employed as bartenders or security guards, or in other places where they may have easy access to victims.

Effective supervision of sex offenders requires an in-depth knowledge of each individual sex offender's high-risk situations and an ability to understand when the offender is nearing relapse. This can only be accomplished through collaboration between supervision agencies and treatment providers, who can coordinate surveillance, control, and treatment (Orlando, 1998). Before they can participate in effective collaborative management schemes, however, each agency—particularly the police, probation and parole, and treatment providers—must improve its own understanding of and duties toward this unique population.

The Police: Investigation, Prevention, and Control

In the past decade, the role of the police has changed in regard to sex offenders. Prior to this, their duties consisted almost solely of investigating sex crimes when they occurred. However, now that there is a sex offender registry in every state, the police must also monitor known sex offenders. This includes duties specific to registration and community notification laws (RCNL)—for example, taking the offender's name and address, notifying the community of high-risk offenders—as well as being aware of the high-risk offenders who are living in the community and controlling any community disorder (see Chapter 10 for more information on RCNL).

Sexual offenses, unlike most other criminal offenses, usually occur within the home or another intimate setting. They are crimes of secrecy, not public crimes, and as such they are difficult to prevent. Some public attacks are committed by strangers, yet these are not nearly as common as offenses committed by acquaintances or intimates.

The primary duty of the police in sex crimes is to investigate any allegations made. The role of the police with the victim is discussed at length in Chapter 7, but in relation to the offenders, the police must conduct investigations and determine if there is probable cause to believe that a sexual offense did occur and, if so, who the perpetrator of the crime is. They must collect evidence and liaise with the prosecution to determine whether the evidence is sufficient to continue with a prosecution on the case.

Evidence in a sex crime comes from three main sources: the victim, the suspect, and the crime scene. Many police departments have formed sex crime units that are specially trained to investigate these offenses, as they are unique and often require specialized investigative skills. The victim is the most important source of information in a sex crime, yet this is often not a sufficient source of information in itself. The information collected from the victim includes the identity of the offender (if known) and details about the offense. The police must also collect any evidence such as hair and semen samples, though it is usually trained forensic examiners in hospital who assist in this collection. Many victims either wait to report the offense until such a time that this trace evidence is no longer valid, or they shower or change clothes so that this evidence is gone. If the victim does not know the offender or does not offer a sufficient description, the police must depend on other sources for their information, namely the crime scene and any witnesses to the offense.

Once the police identify a suspect, evidence on him or her can be compared to that on the victim or at the crime scene. Unfortunately, although there may be fingerprints, bodily fluids, or trace evidence at the crime scene, on the suspect, or on the victim, this does not indicate whether an individual consented to a sexual act. Ultimately, many cases of sexual assault on adults depend on the testimony of the accused and the victim rather than evidence if the suspect says the sexual act was consensual. Nonetheless, all evidence collected and the manner in which it is collected is important and can have an effect on the outcome of the case, which is why specialized training is necessary. The police report is particularly important, as it will be used in court, in the development of the presentence investigation (PSI), and in treatment for the offender.[2] Once the offender is arrested and the case is passed on to the prosecution, the police work at the investigative stage is essentially complete.

The other duty of the police in regard to sex offenders is to monitor those on the sex offender registry. In regard to this responsibility, the police can be divided into specialists and generalists: the specialist officer deals specifically with known sex offenders, whereas the generalist deals with any disorder that results from the offender living in the community (McGuicken & Brown, 2001). Some cities form specialist teams to handle the registration and monitoring of offenders. For example, the New York City Police Department has formed the Sex Offender Monitoring Unit (SOMU) for this task, because the police are in charge of handling such a large number of offenders. The generalist officers, however, must be able to work with the community to educate them on the sex offender population so as to avoid any potential disturbances or vigilante acts.

Treatment Providers

Treatment providers are important in the collaborative approach for two reasons: they teach the offenders how to manage their deviant behavior through internal controls, and they provide information to supervisory agencies about the offenders' high-risk situations. This second task is particularly important; in order for probation and parole officers to effectively manage offenders in the community, they must look at each case on an individual basis, and they must understand each offender's high-risk situations. It is only through this knowledge that parole and probation officers will be able to recognize if and when the offender is nearing relapse. This external form of supervision is necessary to supplement the offender's internal system of control, though the internal form of control is also a necessary form of prevention.

Internal control comes primarily from the offender's ability to manage his or her own behavior through relapse prevention techniques, as discussed in Chapter 8. RP teaches offenders how to interrupt the succession of events that leads to the commission of deviant sexual acts. It makes offenders learn about the factors that have previously led them to commit deviant acts, so that they can prevent future lapses and relapses. Upon determining what factors are considered high risk, the offenders are taught how to cope by avoiding the high-risk situations. If they are not able to avoid the situation, they are taught to "escape" the situation or, if that also fails, to control their urges through general problem-solving techniques. The therapist must help the offender to develop realistic expectations and understand that lapses may occur. Because sex offenders cannot be "cured," it is important that both the offenders and the supervisory agencies understand that their behavior must be managed in order to avoid relapse.

Probation and Parole

The agencies with the most supervision duties over sex offenders in the community are probation and parole. Probation officers (POs), in particular, are key stakeholders in the management of sex offenders. Most convicted sex offenders at some point will be under the supervision of either probation or parole, with approximately 60 percent of sex offenders receiving probation sentences. The many duties of POs include general supervision, development of the presentence investigation, classification through risk assessment (in some jurisdictions), house calls for intensive supervision cases, and liaison among victim service agencies, treatment providers, and offenders.[3] As a supervisor, the PO must coordinate a strategy for management, ensure the appropriate level of supervision, and enforce the conditions imposed upon the offenders (Kemshall, 2001).

Sex offenders are a unique population to manage, and POs face two significant challenges: large caseloads and lack of training regarding sex offenders. Some POs have caseloads of more than 200 clients, which allows for only a limited amount of time with each client and limited understanding of each particular case. As noted by the Center for Sex Offender Management (CSOM) (2000, January), regular probation practices are insufficient when managing sex offenders who may become lost among the other offenders. The primary reason for this is that sex offenders rarely present case management problems, and they usually appear to abide by their supervision conditions. It is not enough for the PO to have periodic contact with the sex offender and assume that all conditions are being followed; rather, there must be constant monitoring in order to ensure compliance with the probationary conditions. To this end, it would be better to have smaller, specialized caseloads for POs who manage sex offenders.

Several reports indicate that specialized caseloads are necessary in order to achieve effective management with sex offenders (CSOM, 2000, January; Scott, 1997). With specialized units, the PO is able to play a more intimate role in the offender's supervision by increased involvement in the offender's daily life. The PO can meet with the sex offenders regularly to ensure that they are employed, living at verified (and approved) addresses, participating in treatment, and abiding by any special conditions that have been imposed. With regular caseloads, it is rare for the POs to make house calls and oversee these conditions, which are an important supervision component for sex offenders. Unfortunately, lack of resources often prevents cities and counties from implementing a specialized caseload system.

The other challenge that POs face also stems from a deficiency of resources. Rarely are POs trained to fully understand and effectively deal with the sex offender population. Many POs are not comfortable working with sex offenders, and this discomfort largely stems from lack of knowledge and understanding of the population. They often do not know what questions they should ask the offenders when they meet with them to find out if they are nearing relapse. Every sex offender is different, and questions should be specifically geared toward each individual offender based on the offender's high-risk situations. When the PO discovers that the offender is in a high-risk situation but has not committed a deviant act, he or she often does not know what type of preventive technique to employ.

Despite the necessity for POs to know their particular client's high-risk situations, this knowledge is not enough. It is also necessary to have training regarding the sex offender population as a whole, because certain characteristics that sex offenders exhibit are correlated to offending behavior. For instance, many sex offenders have substance abuse problems, and many sex offenders who relapse do so while they are intoxicated. This is a common triggering factor to deviant sexual behavior (Vallerie, 1997), and as such the PO must be aware if the offender is drinking or using drugs. If so, there are a number of treatment programs designed to help the offender combat both substance abuse and deviant sexual behavior.

Another triggering factor that POs must recognize is the onset of negative affective states, including loneliness, stress, and depression. Many sex offenders exhibit a deficit in the ability to form intimate relationships (Ward, Hudson, & McCormack, 1997), and the treatment provider should help the offender learn how to develop social relationships and, thus, reintegrate into the community. Sex offenders also tend to be very self-pitying and often see themselves as victims, and these feelings are likely to bring the offender closer to relapse. The PO must be aware if the offender adopts a self-pitying attitude or lacks social acquaintances and intimate relationships, and should work with the treatment providers to help the offender overcome social inhibitions.

Another matter that is extremely important is the ability of the PO to talk openly to sex offenders about sexual issues, including their sexual practices (CSOM, 2000, January). This includes the offender's sexuality, sexual thoughts, masturbatory fantasies, sexual urges, and behaviors. Most sex offenders do not volunteer information about their sexual activity, so POs must be comfortable and able to ask sexually charged questions in a way that is least intrusive. In order to ask personal questions, the officer must build some rapport with the client. Rather than condemn the offender for his or her sexual practices, the officer should try to understand the offender and try to help the offender, even if it is through the treatment provider. At this point the PO should have an in-depth understanding of the individual's high-risk situations and be able to ask case-specific questions regarding lapses. However, the PO must remember that even if the offender lapses (for example, has sexual fantasies about a child), this does not necessarily indicate that a relapse will occur.

Speaking to an offender about his or her sexual practices is important, but insufficient in itself as a supervisory practice. The PO must also be able to visit the offender at his or her residence. House calls, particularly those that are unscheduled and at different times throughout the day and night, are a way to see whether offenders are being truthful about avoiding high-risk situations. Resources again play a pertinent role here, as only POs with small, specialized caseloads will have the ability to do house calls regularly. Training is also important here, as POs must be aware of what items in the home may be of high risk to the offenders.

Sex offenders, and especially child molesters, can be a particularly manipulative group of individuals. As such, the offenders' residences are not likely to have items out of the ordinary lying around the room, and the PO must be trained as to what might indicate that the client is participating in deviant sexual activity. The PO should look first to see whether there is anything in the room that obviously would appeal to children, such as toys, games, and stuffed animals. However, there are several things to look at beyond these obvious articles, including:

- *Children's Food* Children like certain types of food and drinks that adults are unlikely to have in the house otherwise, such as juice boxes, fruit roll-ups, bubble gum, and the like.

- *Animals* Many offenders try to lure children into the residence with animals such as puppies, kittens, and bunnies. Additionally, if the offender has an animal that must be walked, he or she is likely to do so at a park, the beach, or another area where children congregate.

- *Video Games* Any type of game such as Nintendo or Sony Playstation, as well as computer games, can be used to lure children in to play.

- *Magazines and Catalogs* Most child molesters do not have child pornography lying around their residences. Rather, they tend to keep collections of clothing catalogs or general interest magazines, both of which feature children in ads. They use these catalogs for masturbatory fantasies, which may help them to sustain their deviant sexual behavior.

- *Videos* Again, child molesters rarely have pornographic movies openly in the apartment. Rather, they are likely to keep them in legitimate movie boxes so that they will not be recognized easily. Some offenders go so far as to begin taping pornographic features in the middle of a legitimate tape, in case the police or PO begins watching the tape.[4]

- *Cable or Digital Television* If the offender has cable television, does he or she subscribe to children's channels, such as the cartoon network or the Disney channel?

- *Cameras* If the offender has either a regular or a video camera, he or she should have some photos of friends, family, places, and so on. If there are no legitimate photos, there is a need to worry that the camera is used for pornographic purposes. This is compounded if the offender has either a digital or a Polaroid camera, neither of which requires film development in a traditional sense.

- *Sporting Equipment* The offender should not have any sporting equipment—such as ice skates, soccer balls, baseball gloves, and so on—that can be taken to a place where there are children. Additionally, items such as tokens for an arcade should not be in the offender's possession.

None of these things in and of themselves states that the client has relapsed, but they do indicate a lapse. Sex offenders must be given strict special conditions so that they are aware of all rules that they must follow. The offender should be included in the case management plan (CSOM, 2000, January; English, Pullen, & Jones, 1997), and the PO must ensure that the offender understands and abides by the special conditions imposed. In summarizing the best practices of supervisors in various states, CSOM (2000, January: 11–12) suggests the following as conditions appropriate for sex offenders on probation:

- *Disclosure* The offender must agree to have his or her information disclosed to all agencies involved in the management process.

- *Treatment* The offender must participate in treatment. If insurance does not cover the cost of treatment, then the offender must personally pay for the treatment and evaluation.[5]

- *Victim Restitution* The offender should have no contact with the victim and should help to pay for victim restitution.

- *No Contact with Children* The offender should have no intentional contact with children.

- *Travel* The times that an offender travels throughout the day and night should be restricted. He or she should not travel in the morning and afternoon when children are going to school or returning home. The offender should also avoid any unauthorized travel and should inform the PO of any travel plans to different jurisdictions, and there should be no unsupervised visits with family. The PO should be able to view a driving log maintained by the offender, who must be able to account for all the miles traveled in the car.

- *Residence* The offender's residence should be in an approved community.

- *Social and Sexual Behavior* The offender should socialize with adults only, and with no known sex offenders. All sexual relationships should be with adults, and there should be no purchasing or viewing of pornographic material.

- *Work* The offender should not work in an occupation where he or she is likely to have contact with anyone under the age of 18. He or she should also not be in a position to supervise women or children (depending on the offender's specific case).

- *Alcohol* The offender should be restricted from buying or consuming alcohol or drugs. The offender should also avoid going to bars or other establishments where alcohol is sold.

- *Physiological Tests* The offender should submit to any polygraph, penile plethysmograph (PPG), or drug tests when asked.

- *Computer* The offender should be restricted from using the Internet without permission from the PO. If asked, the offender should agree to a search of the computer to verify that he or she has not been viewing any pornographic material or contacted any children via the Internet.

- *Cameras* The offender should not have possession of a still or video camera without the permission of the PO.

- *Frequent Contact between Family and PO* The PO should be in contact with the offender's family members, who should assist the PO in the monitoring process. The family may alert the PO to actions by the offender that are likely to lead him or her into a high-risk situation.

An effective PO is one who will spend much time with the clients and be thoroughly familiar with all cases. To be so intimately involved with sex offenders' cases will probably lead to personal problems, and as such it is imperative that the PO receive therapeutic support. If this is not provided, the PO is likely to experience burnout, which ultimately leads to a high turnover rate in the agency. In this respect, POs are similar to therapists who treat sex offenders, and they experience many of the same problems. These problems include countertransference, negative emotional reactions to the offenders, and burnout, all exacerbated by a lack of in-house support.

Countertransference, as discussed in Chapter 8, is the emotional response the PO experiences toward the client. Negative emotional responses to offenders are particularly common, and this is amplified when proper training specific to the population is not provided. If the PO has a negative emotional reaction to the offender, it will likely trigger low self-esteem and eventually feelings of self-pity in the offender, creating a setback with the offender's treatment. Although specialized caseloads are necessary in order to ensure adequate supervision for sex offenders, POs who work only with the population are likely to experience burnout from such a highly intensive workload. Without in-house support, these problems are aggravated, and the agency should therefore have some therapeutic system in place for POs who work with sex offenders. It is difficult to talk to offenders about their sexual behaviors and fantasies, and it is particularly difficult to hear offenders talk about the offenses they have committed. A process through which POs can regularly discuss their feelings is important for their mental and emotional health and, ultimately, for the agency, as they are less likely to suffer from burnout.

POs who work with sex offenders should be carefully selected. They should have the ability to deal with sexual issues, understand the difficulties in working with sex offenders, understand their specific needs, and be able to develop rapport with the offenders. They should have the multidisciplinary knowledge that is necessary to properly communicate with the offenders, which will help the POs to recognize when the offenders are in high-risk situations or nearing relapse. Probation and parole agencies should provide training for the officers, and the training should cover a broad range of subjects, such as communication skills and the ability to recognize conditions such as depression, suicidal thoughts, and inappropriate behavior. They must be appreciative of the offenders' low self-esteem and lack of confidence and treat the offenders with respect. It is important for sex offenders to perceive the POs as having positive attitudes toward them. POs should be open, direct, truthful, and consistent in their attitudes. Effective monitoring requires training and motivation to work with this population. They should not be uncomfortable around sex offenders, and training should increase their confidence in working with these offenders.

THE CONTAINMENT APPROACH: INCREASED COLLABORATION FOR EFFECTIVE MANAGEMENT

Sexual offenses generally occur within the home, which means that they occur in secrecy. There is a continuum of deviant behavior, however, that goes from the home to the workplace to the community (Thomas, 2000). In order to combat this continuum and the secrecy, manipulation, and deception that are involved in sex crimes, agencies must work interdependently rather than independently (CSOM, 2000, October).

Some communities have implemented a "containment approach," or a collaborative strategy among the agencies involved. All of the agencies mentioned are incorporated, and the purpose is to hold the offender accountable through internal and external controls (English, Pullen, & Jones, 1997). As described by Kim English and colleagues, proponents of the containment approach, this strategy consists of five tenets that work together to secure the highest degree of management and care of sex offenders:

1. *Overall Philosophy and Goal: Community and Victim Safety* Protection and recovery of the victim and the well-being of the community are the main concerns that guide policy development. The sex offender is able to live in the community and receive appropriate care and treatment, while supervisors ensure that the offender has no contact with the victim and is blocked from high-risk situations where contact could be made with potential future victims. For example, the supervisors should ensure that the offender's employment is proper and does not establish conditions that

could lead to relapse. Housing is also important, and supervisors must also ensure that the offender is not living within close range of potential victims or, if the victim is in the household, the offender should be removed from the household (rather than the victim being removed).

2. *Sex Offender-Specific Containment: Individualized Case Management System* Each case is different, and the supervision and management of each offender should be tailored to the specific case. Three elements must be present in order to effectively manage the sex offender. First, the offender must participate in treatment, and the treatment must be sex offender specific. Many sex offenders have behavioral problems that require additional treatment, such as substance abuse, though they must also participate in a treatment program designed to highlight their potential for relapse of sexually deviant behavior. Second, specially trained monitors who understand the individual high-risk needs of sex offenders must supervise them. If the offender does not comply with the supervisors (for example, probation or parole officers), the offender should be sanctioned accordingly. Third, the offender should be subjected to polygraph examinations periodically to ensure that he or she is complying with the supervision requirements that have been imposed.

3. *Collaboration: A Multidisciplinary Approach* This is the most important category in the containment approach process, without which the overall philosophy cannot be applied. Though each agency must employ its own procedures, the supervising teams must collaborate on management strategies. Collaboration must occur at both the case management and policy levels (CSOM, 2000, January). Without collaboration, the effort of each agency would be fragmented and lacking in necessary resources and skills.

4. *Consistent Public Policies* Public policies must be "informed, clear, and consistent." It is particularly pertinent for prosecutors to develop consistent strategies in the courtroom by disallowing plea bargains (either to a lesser sexual offense or a nonsexual offense). Additionally, sex offenders should not be allowed to plead "No contest" to their charges, as to do so would permit them to deny guilt in the act and therefore prolong acceptance of responsibility. Deferred judgments and referrals to diversion programs also may reduce the seriousness of the crime and accentuate the denial of responsibility. Other agencies must also establish consistent practices. To name a few examples, treatment providers should make consistent use of external measures (for example, the polygraph and the PPG); probation and parole should establish consistent policies on revocation if conditions are violated; child and family services or social services should create consistent policy on family reunification).

5. *Quality Control* There must be an evaluation of the system that is in place to see if the policy implemented results in effective management. Because the primary purpose of a containment approach is community protection and restorative justice for the victim, any assessment process must acknowledge these facts.

Despite the obvious benefits to the containment approach, it may be somewhat idealistic in its philosophy. Several states have applied this philosophy effectively (for example, Colorado, Vermont), though other states would have a difficult time implementing such a strategy. For example, if New York City were to implement a containment model of management, there would be 23 agencies and several thousand offenders involved in the process. Probation officers (who monitor approximately 200 offenders each) would be required to collaborate with treatment providers (some of whom treat 200 offenders per week) and the sex offender monitoring unit (which registers the more than 4,000 offenders in the city). All the while, there would be communication among these offender-centered agencies and the victim service agencies. It is unlikely that such a paradigmatic shift will take place in a city like New York, or that it would be effective if it did take place.

BALANCING THE RIGHTS OF SEX OFFENDERS AND THE COMMUNITY

The aim of sex offender management is community protection, but at what expense? How limited should the rights be of sex offenders who are living in the community? Should sex offenders have the same civil liberties as nonsexual offenders, or should they be restricted in terms of employment, housing, education, and recreation? Whatever the limitations are, sex offenders who are living in the community must be able to fulfill three basic necessities: they must have a place to live, a means of earning a living, and the ability to participate in recreational activities. However, because of the sex offender's status, all of these basic necessities are challenging to acquire.

Housing

A basic necessity for sex offenders living in the community is acceptable housing. The issue of community notification of the offender's address (discussed further in Chapter 10) complicates this, as many communities do not want sex offenders to move into their neighborhoods. Because the community is notified when a high-risk sex offender is going to move into the neighborhood, there are sometimes protests or even riots to keep the offender out. Similarly, if a community plans to build a halfway house for sex offenders or house sex offenders in a violent offenders' home, protests arise. This leaves the sex offender nowhere to go, and many offenders end up living in shelters. Ideally, an offender would be able to live in a halfway house once released from prison so that a transitional authority can both supervise the offender and assist in reintegrating him or her back into the community.

One example of community intolerance comes from Jefferson County, Colorado, where the state proposed a 60-bed treatment home for juvenile sex offenders in 2002. There was a vigorous protest against the facility, and

200 members of the community attended a two-day hearing regarding the development plans. Though the county claimed the facility would be safe, secure, and more than adequately staffed, community leaders claimed that it would be inappropriately located in a residential area and would not have strict enough security. The purpose of the house was to allow juveniles in need of treatment outside the home to live in a facility that was not a prison-type environment. Nonetheless, the prevailing attitude toward sex offenders in Jefferson County, as in most communities, is NIMBY: Not In My Back Yard.

What rights do members of the community have? Should they be able to ban a sex offender from living in their neighborhood? Should they have the right to deny a sex offender a job, even if that job does not put the offender into a high-risk situation? These are ethical dilemmas that are not easily answered. If supervision is adequate and there is a balance between internal and external forms of control, the offender should be able to live safely in the community. Nonetheless, no one wants a sex offender living in his or her neighborhood.

Employment

It is not easy for convicted felons to secure jobs, and it is even more difficult for convicted sex offenders.[6] Like the general public, most employers have negative feelings toward sex offenders and do not want the responsibility for them should they recidivate. However, employment is generally a condition of a community sentence. Additionally, several studies (Hanson & Harris, 1998; Kruttschnitt, Uggen, & Shelton, 2000) have indicated that employment is one dynamic factor correlated to recidivism rates, in that offenders who are employed are less likely to reoffend.

The type of employment that is acceptable for convicted sex offenders is limited. Clearly, they should be banned from holding jobs that put them in high-risk situations, such as a convicted child molester teaching at an elementary school. Yet, there are many positions that would give the offender access to potential victims, such as that of a security guard, doctor, mental health therapist, hospital employee, homeless shelter employee, taxi driver, and manager of a residential building (CSOM, 2002: 3). One primary purpose of the registry is for potential employers to view it when hiring employees. Yet, although a school inevitably will check out the background of a potential teacher, it may not validate the background of a janitor. If the offender is living in the community and under no form of supervision, these problems are exacerbated because there is no probation or parole officer to ensure employment standards. If the offender is under some form of supervision, these problems are reduced.

In most communities, there are strict guidelines for sex offenders on probation or parole who are seeking employment. First, probation and parole officers should discuss the offenders' high-risk situations with treatment providers to determine what type of employment is acceptable for the offender. Four factors should be considered when approving employment for sex offenders (CSOM, 2002: 7–8): community needs, supervision program needs, employer needs, and offender needs. The number one concern should be community safety, and the only jobs offered should be those that do not expose the offender to high-risk situations. The jobs must also be flexible in allowing the offender to attend any meetings that are a necessary part of the supervision program, such as treatment groups. The offender and the employer must also have input into the job selection process; the employer must ensure that the offender is able to integrate into the workplace and perform the necessary duties of the job, whereas the offender should be satisfied with the job. If the employer and the supervising agency remain in contact regarding the offender's progress, there will almost certainly be a reduction in workplace risk.

Once a sex offender is employed, there are other issues to consider, such as the rights of offenders in the workplace. This is a difficult predicament because it relates largely to privacy rights, which are not clearly defined. The right to privacy is not specifically denoted in the Constitution; however, the U.S. Supreme Court has decided many cases on the issue of privacy and has essentially identified it as the ability of an individual to control information publicized about oneself (Rich, 1995). In other words, an individual has a right to a private life, or the right to be left alone (American Civil Liberties Union, 1998). Despite this broad definition, the right to privacy has changed considerably with the increase in the use of technology. The right to privacy is limited in the workplace, with employers given access to information on office computers (including e-mail). Notification of sex offenders via the Internet has also challenged the traditional concept of the right to privacy, with the offenders' photos and addresses posted on the Internet.[7] How much should the privacy rights of a sex offender be limited at work? Should other employees be told about the offender, even if they are not at risk of becoming victims?

Nondisclosure can present many problems, exemplified best by the cases of sexual abuse in the Catholic Church (discussed at greater length in Chapter 12). Despite the recent spate of scandals in the media, sexual abuse in the church has occurred for years. It came to a head, however, with one case involving a Catholic priest in Boston that was concealed by the Boston archdiocese. As a result of the nondisclosure to the public, the priest allegedly sexually abused more than 130 children over a period of 30 years.[8]

Another difficult issue concerns juvenile sex offenders who are attending school. Juveniles who commit sexual offenses, even if the offense is against a fellow classmate, might not be removed from the school. And if the child is removed, he or she will most likely be sent to another school where the student body and parents may not be informed about the juvenile's record. This quandary is particularly difficult for school officials, who must protect the other students in the school but also protect the identity of the juvenile offender and allow him or her to receive an education. In some cases, the school officials may not even know that a juvenile sex offender is in the school, as police in some jurisdictions are not allowed to disclose such information until there is a conviction in an adult court. This was the case in Augusta, Georgia, where a 12-year-old accused of raping a 5-year-old was allowed to attend the same school as his victim and confronted the victim in the shared lunchroom (Rhodes, January 9, 2002).

Recreation and Social Relationships

The boundaries between community protection and individual rights become even less clear if the sex offender is not employed but is at an establishment, such as a church, recreationally. Should sex offenders be allowed to attend church where children congregate? To ban church attendance would certainly pose constitutional challenges, yet it is a forum through which sex offenders can socially, and legally, spend time with children. In fact, sex offender treatment providers encourage offenders to join social groups in order to assist them in developing age-appropriate and socially appropriate relationships. Institutions such as churches create ideal opportunities for sex offenders to reintegrate into society and provide social opportunities for them.

But what about other recreational activities? Though some sex offenders who are on probation will be required to abide by rules restricting their whereabouts, many are not given such restrictions. Should a sex offender be allowed to attend any sporting events where children may participate or watch the event? This would include nearly every publicized sport, such as baseball, basketball, football, and so forth. Should the sex offender be able to participate in recreational activities such as shopping at a mall or going to a movie? And what if an offender travels? If an offender lives in southern California, should he or she be able to travel to Las Vegas for the evening? Or if an offender lives in New Hampshire, can he travel to work in Massachusetts? As we move toward more legal restrictions on sex offenders, as discussed in the next two chapters, these questions about basic rights and liberties are in question.

CHAPTER SUMMARY

- Management and care for sex offenders in the community requires an in-depth understanding of the offenders by anyone in a supervisory role, as well as communication among criminal justice agencies.

- Many of those in charge of monitoring sex offenders in the community are not properly trained for their supervisory roles. This is largely due to a lack of resources for proper management and training, as well as poor communication. Effective management of sex offenders in the community requires interdependence among agencies and collaboration on both case management and policy levels.

- Supervisors of sex offenders need to help them reintegrate into the community. Sex offenders need housing, employment, and the possibility of forming social and sexual relationships with agemates. With the internal controls learned during treatment, as well as effective external management by a collaborative supervisory team, most sex offenders should be able to reintegrate safely into the community.

DISCUSSION QUESTIONS

1. What agencies have duties to manage sex offenders in the community? What are their primary duties? Is this level of supervision satisfactory? Why or why not?

2. What special knowledge must someone have who is in charge of the management and supervision of sex offenders in the community?

3. What is the aim of the containment approach? What agencies must work together in order for this to be an effective supervision system for sex offenders?

4. What are the rights of sex offenders living in the community? What should the rights be of community members so that they can be protected from sex offenders?

NOTES

1. This is a good example of how each agency is focused on its own needs rather than on the collaborative needs of all criminal justice agencies. To reduce a charge on a sexual offense allows for a guaranteed conviction for the prosecution, but often at the expense of the victim—who has no say in the final charge—and the community as a whole. In the states where registration level is based on degree of offense (for example, Delaware), plea bargains result in a shorter period of registration and a different notification status.

2. Treatment providers have access to the police reports and victim statements so that they can fully understand all elements of the offense. This helps them to reduce the denial and minimization that most offenders express at the onset of treatment.

3. This section provides only a brief overview of probation and parole practices in regard to sex offenders. For a more thorough evaluation of the role of probation and parole in the supervision of sex offenders, see Cumming and Buell (1997).

4. This information is derived from a personal interview with a police officer who has worked in the sex crime unit of a police department.

5. Treatment in some states is subsidized if it is a substance abuse program, and some sex offender treatment providers provide a dual program for offenders with substance and sexual abuse problems.

6. The most common jobs for parolees or previously convicted felons to have are those in the food industry, manufacturing, warehousing, retail, and janitorial positions. Retention rarely lasts for more than six months for these jobs, however (Terry, 2000).

7. Recently, the U.S. Supreme Court ruled in two cases that posting offender information on the Internet does not violate the constitutional rights of sex offenders (*Smith v. Doe*, 2003; *Connecticut Department of Public Safety v. Doe,* 2003).

8. The former Catholic priest, John Geoghan, was eventually tried and convicted for indecent sexual battery on a 10-year-old boy in 1991. However, at least 84 civil suits have been filed against him, and Cardinal Bernard Law—the highest Catholic Church leader in the United States at the time—has been named as a codefendant, because he knew of the abuse. Cardinal Law removed Geoghan from various parishes when complaints of abuse were put forth, helping the priest to seek out treatment for his pedophilia. However, Law simply moved Geoghan to different parishes, where the abuse allegedly continued (Claiborne, 2002; Sealy, 2002).

10

Registration and Community Notification Laws

As was discussed in preceding chapters, legislation regarding sex offenders is often enacted after an emotionally charged sex crime occurs, particularly when the crime involves a stranger attack on a child. Though this "feel good" legislation tends to reflect extreme rather than more common sex crimes such as date rape and incest, it allows for a blanket application of the laws to all persons labeled as "sex offenders." In the 1980s and 1990s, a number of child murders occurred, thrusting sex offenders into the public spotlight. These involved recidivist offenders who were released from the criminal justice system despite the knowledge by professionals that they were a high risk to the community and were likely to reoffend.

One such case occurred in the state of Washington. Earl Shriner (also discussed in Chapters 2 and 11), who had a 24-year history of sexual violence and murder, kidnapped a 7-year-old boy, cut off his penis, and left him for dead. In and out of institutions since the age of 15, Shriner had just been released after a decade in prison, during which he bragged to inmates and confided in a journal that he fantasized about killing again. He explained in great detail how, once released, he would buy a van in which he would kidnap boys and take them into the woods to torture them. There was nothing the state could do to keep him in prison or notify the community upon his release, though officials did warn an elementary school four blocks from his residence. As a result of Earl Shriner's crime of sexual mutilation, Washington State passed the Community Protection Act of 1990, which contained 14 separate provisions for ensuring community safety against such predators.

Two other cases of importance to federal laws occurred in the early 1990s. The first is that of Richard Allan Davis, who in 1993 kidnapped 12-year-old Polly Klaas out of her home in Petaluma, California, during a slumber party. She has since been labeled "America's child," because the nation sympathized with her family and recognized that it could have happened anywhere. Also in 1993, 12-year-old Jacob Wetterling was kidnapped while riding a bike with his friends near his home, and he has not been seen since. Shortly after Davis's arrest and Jacob's disappearance, the federal Violent Crime Control and Enforcement Act of 1994 was passed. Within this is a provision for sex offender registration, the Jacob Wetterling Crimes against Children and Sexually Violent Offender Registration Program, which requires sexual offenders to register their whereabouts with the police.

Arguably the most notorious of the child murder cases in the 1990s was that of Megan Kanka, a 7-year-old girl from New Jersey who was raped and killed by a recidivist pedophile living across the street from her. Jesse Timmendequas, who had been convicted of two previous sexual offenses against children, lured Megan into his house with his puppy and then raped and killed her. Her parents proposed that registration alone was an insufficient form of prevention and requested that the community also be notified of serious sexual offenders who are living in the neighborhood. They claimed that if a convicted sex offender is living in the area, the community has a right to know so that parents can better protect their children. It was this act that prompted the registration and notification system that is known today as "Megan's Law."

MEGAN'S LAW:
REQUIREMENTS AND GUIDELINES

Though simple in its aim—to protect the community—Megan's Law consists of complicated guidelines and procedures that vary from state to state.[1] President Bill Clinton enacted the federal Megan's Law statute on May 17, 1996, which set guidelines for the individual states to follow. This worked in conjunction with the Jacob Wetterling Act of 1994, which required all states to enact a sex offender registry by the end of 1997 or risk losing federal funding for state and local law enforcement. Megan's Law then encouraged the states to set up a notification system to alert the communities of those listed on the registry.

The primary ways in which states vary in their registration and notification requirements are as follows (Terry & Furlong, 2003). Table 10.1 shows some of these differences among states.

- *Conviction/Type of Offense* Some require registration only for individuals convicted of a sexual offense, whereas others allow registration when there is a finding of not guilty by reason of insanity (NGRI), of another offense that is sexually motivated or linked (for example, public exposure, murder with sexual intent, kidnapping of a minor), or of an attempted but not

Table 10.1 Differences in Registration and Community Notification Laws (RCNL) by State

Federal/ State	Number of Years to Remain on Registry	DNA	Both Adult and Juvenile Registration	Number of Days to Register after Conviction/ Release	Number of Days to Change Address after Move	Quarterly Verification for High-Risk/Home-less Registrants	Petition for Relief from Registry	Internet Notification	Sexually Violent Predators (SVP)
Federal[a]	10–life	*	*	*	*	*	*	*	
AL	Life	✓	✓	30 prior[b]	30 prior			✓	
AK	15–life	✓	✓	24 hours[c]	24 hours			✓	✓
AZ	10–life		✓d	10	3	✓	✓	✓	✓
AR	15–Life	✓	✓	10	10 prior	✓e		✓	
CA	Life	✓	✓f	5	5	✓g	✓	✓	✓
CO	10–life		✓	7	7	✓	✓	✓	
CT	10–life		✓	5	10	✓		✓	
DE	15–life	✓	✓	ASAP[h]	7	✓	✓	✓	
DC	10–life			3	3			✓	
FL	Life	✓	✓	48 hours	48 hours	✓		✓	✓
GA	10–life		✓	10	10	✓		✓	
HI	Life			3	3	✓		✓i	

a There are no specific provisions in the federal statute for the boxes that are starred (*); rather, the issues are dependent on the state in which the offender resides
b If no incarceration, 24 hours after sentencing
c 30 hours prior if incarcerated, 24 hours after sentencing to a community sentence
d Juveniles terminate registration at age 25
e Quarterly for SVPs, every 6 months for all other sex offenders
f Juveniles may petition to have records sealed
g Quarterly for SVPs, every 60 days for those with no fixed address
h Prior to release, if incarcerated
i Only if they abscond

Table 10.1 Differences in Registration and Community Notification Laws (RCNL) by State (continued)

Federal/ State	Number of Years to Remain on Registry	DNA	Both Adult and Juvenile Registration	Number of Days to Register after Conviction/ Release	Number of Days to Change Address after Move	Quarterly Verification for High-Risk/Home-less Registrants	Petition for Relief from Registry	Internet Notification	Sexually Violent Predators (SVP)
ID[j]	Life		✓	10	5	✓	✓	✓[k]	
IL	10–life	✓	✓	10	10	✓	✓	✓	✓
IN	10–life		✓	7	7	✓		✓	✓
IA	10–life		✓	5	5	✓		✓	✓
KS	10–life		✓	10	10	✓		✓	
KY	10–life		✓	48 hours	5	✓		✓	
LA	10–life		✓	21[l]	10	✓		✓	
ME	10–life			10	ASAP	✓		✓	
MD	10–life			7	7	✓		✓	
MA	20–life		✓	2	10 prior	✓	✓	✓	✓
MI	25–life[m]		✓	ASAP[n]	10	✓		✓	✓
MN	10–life		✓	ASAP[o]	5 prior	✓	✓	✓	✓
MS	Life		✓	3	10 prior	✓[p]			

j Prior to release, if incarcerated

k Residents not able to do a random search, but must have identifying information about the offender

l 10 days if the person is an SVP

m 10 years after release from prison or up to 25 years including the time of incarceration, whichever is longer

n Prior to sentencing; updated upon release, if incarcerated

o Immediately upon sentencing or release

p Quarterly verification for all sex offenders

MO	Life	10	10
MT	10–life	10 prior[q]	10
NE	10–life	ASAP[r]	5
NV	15–life	48 hours	48 hours
NH	10–life	30	10
NJ	15–life	ASAP[s]	10 prior
NM	10–20	10	10
NY	10–life	10[t]	10
NC	10–life	10[u]	10
ND	10–life	10	10
OH	10–life	7	7 prior
OK	10–life	7[w]	3
OR	10–life	10	10
PA	10–life	ASAP	10
RI	10–life	24 hours	10
SC	Life	24 hours[y]	10
SD	10–life	10	10

q 10 days prior to release from a correctional institution, or immediately upon sentencing

r Immediately upon conviction or release

s Upon sentencing or prior to release from a correctional institution

t Within 10 days of sentencing or prior to release from a correctional institution

u 10 days if released from prison or immediately upon conviction if not incarcerated

v 180 days for all others

w 3 days if released from an institution

x No general search available; person must make a specific electronic request

y Within 24 hours of release from a correctional institution or within 10 days of sentencing if given a community sentence

Table 10.1 Differences in Registration and Community Notification Laws (RCNL) by State (*continued*)

Federal/State	Number of Years to Remain on Registry	DNA	Both Adult and Juvenile Registration	Number of Days to Register after Conviction/Release	Number of Days to Change Address after Move	Quarterly Verification for High-Risk/Home-less Registrants	Petition for Relief from Registry	Internet Notification	Sexually Violent Predators (SVP)
TN	10–life			10	10	✓[z]	✓	✓	✓
TX	10–life		✓	7	7 prior	✓[aa]	✓	✓	
UT	10–life		✓	ASAP	10	✓[ab]		✓	
VT	10–life			10	3	✓	✓		
VA	10–life		✓	10	10	✓	✓	✓	
WA	10–life		✓	24 hours[ac]	14 prior	✓	✓	✓	✓
WV	10–life			ASAP[ad]	10	✓		✓	✓
WI	15–life	✓		10	10	✓		✓	✓
WY	10–life			ASAP[ae]	10	✓		✓	✓

[z] All sex offenders must verify their addresses every 90 days

[aa] Civil commitment offenders every 30 days

[ab] Lifetime parolees must verify their addresses every 60 days pursuant to a parole agreement

[ac] Depending on the date of conviction and type of offense, some offenders must register within 10 days of sentencing or release from a correctional facility; see statute for specific dates

[ad] No specific time period is given; however, the offender must sign a paper in court at the time of sentencing acknowledging that he or she understands the duty to register immediately upon release

[ae] Prior to release from a correctional institution or immediately following sentencing

completed offense. Others, still, require registration only for offenders with child victims.

- *Registration of Juveniles* Some states require juveniles to register, whereas others prohibit registration for anyone under age 18. Some that require registration do not notify the community about the juvenile.

- *Retroactive Application of the Law* Some states apply registration retroactively; offenders must register even if they committed the offense prior to enactment of the statute. This is a controversial aspect of the law, as will be discussed following in regard to constitutionality of applying laws ex post facto.

- *Length of Registration* Offenders must register for different lengths of time depending on the state and the type of offender. Currently, the registration period varies from 10 years to life, depending on the type or level of offender.

- *Removal from the Registry* Some states that require lifetime registration allow the offender to apply for expungement from the registry after a certain period of time, generally 10 or 15 years. In such a case, the offender must petition the court to have his or her name removed from the registry, which is likely to be granted if the offender has committed no further offenses since the time of registration.

- *Registration Agency* Different agencies are in charge of maintaining the registry in each state. For example, the registration agency may be the local police department, the sheriff's department, the Department of Public Safety, the Department of Corrections, the Division of Youth, Division of Criminal Justice Services, or other such agencies.

- *Time Period in Which to Register/Reregister* Each state gives the offender a certain amount of time to register with the given agency. The time period ranges from 48 hours to 10 days upon conviction or release into the community, and the offender must reregister any time he or she changes address. Additionally, the offender must register either annually or every 90 days— depending upon level of risk—with the police to confirm the address of residence.

- *Risk Assessment* Every state varies in its risk assessment of sex offenders, which determines the level of notification allowed to the community. Some make this distinction based on a felony or misdemeanor distinction, whereas others base it on the offense committed and history of offending behavior. Some states use specific guidelines to classify offenders, and others use actuarial assessments to place the offenders into risk tiers. These risk assessment guidelines are discussed later in the chapter.

- *Method of Notification* The method by which the registration agency notifies the community varies in each state. The agencies may send flyers to homes in the community or post flyers in town; there may be an 800- or a 900-number to call to find out information about a particular individual; the police departments may keep a registry that community members can look through; and most states now have Internet sites with the offenders' names, photos, and addresses.

- *Sanction for Failing to Register* If an offender fails to register with the given agency within the time period allotted, he or she is subject to sanction. The type of sanction varies among states and is often increasingly harsh with subsequent failures to register.

Offenders are responsible for registering with the police if they commit any type of sexual offense or, in some states, if they commit an offense against a minor. These offenses may include kidnapping (if the child is not related to the offender), lewdness or lascivious behavior (some states require this to be in the presence of a child), assault on a child, juvenile pimping or patronizing a juvenile prostitute, ritualized abuse of a child, and unlawful restraint of a child. An individual who commits such an offense must register for 10 years to life, depending on the jurisdiction and risk level of the offender, and must check in with the registration agency annually or every 90 days (if at the highest level of risk).

The general process by which registration occurs is that the offender is required, upon conviction or release from a correctional institution, to inform a law enforcement agency of his or her whereabouts within a specified time period. Most offenders are required to provide the agency with a photograph, fingerprints, name, address, and place of employment. Some agencies also require the offender to give a DNA sample for comparison against past and future offenses. The agency then stores this information in a central registry for informational purposes for law enforcement and/or the community. To verify the address that the offender submits, a letter is mailed to the offender's residence, and the offender is required to return the letter within a specified time period. If the letter is not returned or the offender does not register within the given amount of time, he or she has violated the registration statute and is subject to sanction. If the offender moves to a different address, he or she is required to reregister with the local agency in the new community.[2]

The number of offenders registered in each state is significantly different; this depends largely on the offenses that require registration and the date at which registration began. Also, in many states the statute is applied retroactively, and offenders who were convicted before the enactment of the statute must also register. For instance, there are more than 87,000 sex offenders registered in California, because all sex offenders convicted on or after January 1981 are subject to registration. A state such as New York, which is similar to California in many demographic and legal procedures, has only about 10,000 registered offenders, because only those convicted on or after July 1996 must register.

Another distinct and controversial difference in state registries is whether juveniles are required to register and, if so, whether the community is notified about them. Currently, 35 states (and the District of Columbia) require juveniles to register,[3] and 26 states require only adults to register. In some states, the court can make an exemption so that the juvenile does not have to register, or so that the juvenile can have his or her name expunged from the registry at a certain age. In other states, the juvenile must be over a certain age in order to register (for example, in South Dakota, the juvenile must be over the age of 15). Though juveniles are responsible for approximately 20 percent of sexual offense convictions, and some of these sexual offenses are quite serious (for example, rape), many of the juveniles would benefit from treatment rather than stigmatization. For this reason, some states vehemently protest adding juveniles to the register.

Though the states vary in their statutes and processes for registering offenders, they all have the same goal: to protect the community. The aim is to prevent future acts through knowledge, and in the process deter offenders from committing future acts. Knowledge of offenders' whereabouts allows parents to warn their children about known offenders, and it also alerts adults about rapists in the area. As is explained throughout this text, sex offenders constitute a heterogeneous group of individuals and pose varying risks to the community. Some states go to lengths to distinguish among these offenders by categorizing them into tiers (levels) of dangerousness, yet risk assessments are controversial and have resulted in many court proceedings to challenge the process of assessments.

ASSESSING RISK LEVELS
FOR SEX OFFENDERS

Though some states register offenders based on the offense committed, 20 states, including the District of Columbia, assess sex offenders using specific registration guidelines.[4] Several of these states use guidelines to classify offenders into two or three tiers based on level of risk.[5] By doing so, the states are classifying offenders based on factors such as type of offense, age and number of victims, level of force used, victim–offender relationship, and degree of contact with victim. In distinguishing offenders by tiers, the state is better able to establish who might pose a high risk to the community and about whom the community should be notified.[6] There are no specific offenses that are labeled Tier 1, 2, or 3; rather, offense and offender characteristics are taken into consideration. Some states, such as New York and New Jersey, use an actuarial assessment guide to assess offenders into risk level. Other states, such as Nevada, use an assessment procedure without specifically enumerated guidelines for classification. Texas utilizes a complicated system of classification based on the type of offense and the level of supervision in the community. Yet other states, such as Florida, use the date of conviction as a major factor of determination as to the level of a sexual predator, whereas states such as Delaware simply assign an offender a risk level based on the degree of offense committed. Whatever the guidelines, offenders are classified into tiers with varying levels of risk to the community.

Tier 1 offenders are the least serious and are considered a low risk to the community. Tier 1 offenders may have abused someone without using physical force, have touched someone only on the outside of the clothing, have only one victim, have no serious psychological disorders (such as antisocial personality disorder), are not recidivist offenders, have no history of substance abuse or domestic violence, have abused someone within the family (for example, a sibling), or have strong community ties that render him or her unlikely to reoffend. Notification for Tier 1 offenders is usually limited to law enforcement agencies, and information is not distributed to the community. However, in some states individuals are allowed to call the registry hotline and enquire about whether a particular offender is on the registry list. The agency may answer the question, but cannot give out any additional information about the offender, such as address or photo. Tier 1 offenders generally register for 10 to 15 years, or may apply for expungement in states with lifetime registration after 10 years. They must check in with the registry agency annually to verify their address, or a letter is sent to the offender's residence annually that must be returned for verification.

Tier 2 offenders pose a moderate risk to the community. They are not considered violent predators, but vulnerable members of the community should be notified of their presence. Examples of Tier 2 offenders are those who have verbally but not physically threatened the victim, have had a previous relationship with the victim, have more than one victim, have touched the victim under the clothing but have not penetrated the victim, have a history of substance abuse, or have no steady employment or strong community ties. For offenders classified in this category, notification is limited to law enforcement and any entity that may be at risk from this offender. For instance, if a child molester moves into the neighborhood, the registration agency would likely notify the schools, youth groups, community groups, church groups, day care facilities, and organizations such as the Boy Scouts or Girl Scouts. Also, some states look at Tier 2 offenders on a case-by-case basis to determine whether the general community should be notified about the offender. Some states, such as Florida and Massachusetts, release limited information to the public about Tier 2 offenders, such as name, a description of the offender, the county in which he or she resides (in Massachusetts, the work address and home address), the offense committed, and the age of the victim.

Tier 3 offenders pose a high risk to the community. In some states, they are labeled "sexual predators" or "sexually violent persons" (not to be confused with those by the same designation who are civilly committed, discussed in Chapter 11). Tier 3 offenders might have several victims, have assaulted a stranger, have abused a prepubescent child, have penetrated the victim, have a history of psychological or mental disorders, have a substance abuse problem, have few community ties or no employment, or they might not be participating in any treatment program. Whereas Tier 1 and 2 offenders usually only have to check in with the registration agency annually, Tier 3 offenders usually check in every 90 days. Tier 3 offenders are generally prohibited from living within a certain distance of schools, parks, or other recreational services, and the types of jobs they are allowed to maintain is limited. Additionally, it is these offenders about whom the community is notified.

Notification can take place in several ways. The community can be notified by police officers going around to the various residences in the community, through flyers, through community meetings, through an 800- or 900-number, through a website, or by a CD-ROM. Information given to the community is the offender's photograph, address, type of offense, and class of offense, or level of severity. Because of the restrictions on civil liberties afforded this classification of offender, designation as a Tier 3 offender is a controversial issue.

The most common classification for sexual offenders is Tier 2, or of moderate risk to the community. California provides a good example of this, as 73,000 of its 87,000 registered sex offenders were categorized Tier 2 at the end of 2001. Restriction of civil liberties for these offenders is more severe than for Tier 1 offenders, and as such this classification is also sometimes controversial. However, it is the Tier 3 offenders for whom civil liberties are most often or most severely suppressed. Therefore, the assessment guidelines used in the states have been subject to scrutiny and litigation.

The states that use general guidelines and suggestions for classification of offenders are under the most scrutiny, because much discretion is used in determining risk level. Some states, such as New Jersey, used to have a general guideline but now use an actuarial assessment to determine risk. New York also uses an actuarial assessment guide to determine risk level, which is shown in Table 10.2. The Sex Offender Registration Act, which was established in New York in January 1996, created a board of examiners to classify offenders into tier levels. They use an actuarial risk assessment instrument to calculate a numeric risk level for offenders living in the community. This consists of various questions about the offender's current offense, criminal history, postoffense behavior, and release environment. Each of the four categories is subdivided, points are given based on factors within these categories, and points are given for offender and offense characteristics (for example, whether violence was used in the offense, how many victims were involved in the offense, and so on). The more points attributed to an offender, the higher risk the offender is to the community. If the points range from 0 to 70, the offender is classified as Tier 1. If the points add up to 75–105, the offender is classified as Tier 2. If the points add up to 110–300, the offender is classified as Tier 3. Additionally, there are four override factors that classify an offender automatically as Tier 3. These include a prior felony conviction for a sexual offense, infliction of serious physical injury or death to the victim, recent threats to commit another sexual or violent offense, and a mental abnormality that renders the offender unable to control his or her actions (Canestrini, 1999: 61.)

Issues relating to the current offense, such as level of force used, number and age of victims, and intrusiveness of contact are most important, and the maximum number of points assigned in this category alone can add up to 155. Up to 55 points can be assigned in the criminal history category, with another 35 available in postoffense behavior and 15 for release environment. Though this assessment is meant to determine the level of risk an offender poses to the community, it focuses mainly on static variables, or those that cannot change. Dynamic variables, such as those relating to effectiveness of treatment or management, account for a small percentage of the risk assessment guideline. What this means is that an offender who committed a violent offense against a child with whom he was not acquainted may be classified as a Level 3 offender even if he is attending treatment programs regularly and is assessed by a psychiatrist

Table 10.2 Risk Assessment Guide for the State of New York

Scoring System Categories	Category Items	Possible Points	Actions for Which Points Are Received
Current Offense	Violence	0–30	10 = Forcible compulsion 15 = Physical injury 30 = Armed with weapon
	Intrusiveness of contact	0–25	5 = Contact over clothes 10 = Contact under clothes 25 = Anal/vaginal intercourse
	Multiple victims	0–30	0 = One victim 20 = Two victims 30 = Three or more victims
	Frequency	0–20	20 = Abuse happened on more than one occasion
	Victim age	0–30	20 = Victim 11–16 30 = Victim 10 or under, 62 or over
	Victim helplessness	0–20	20 = Victim physically or mentally helpless
	Relationship	0–20	20 = Stranger to victim
Criminal History	Age at first offense	0–10	10 = First conviction or adjudicated for sex offense before age 21
	Prior criminal history	0–30	30 = Prior violent felony/prior misdemeanor sex crime conviction/prior charge of endangerment of a child 15 = Nonviolent felony 5 = Nonsexual misdemeanor
	Substance abuse history	0–15	15 = Substance abuse history/under influence at time of offense

as benefiting from the treatment program. This is the problem posed by actuarial risk assessment guidelines, and some contend that clinical assessments and the use of discretion are sometimes more accurate.

In addition to notification and registration, some communities have implemented a system of community supervision for life (CSL). At the present time, many offenders—approximately one-quarter of those on the registries—are under no form of community supervision other than registration while in the community. Some states have asserted that registration and annual or 90-day notification are not enough, and there should be continuing supervision for sex offenders. As such, it is now a requirement in three states that sex offenders remain supervised for the rest of their lives while in the community. CSL functions similarly to parole, where the offender is required to abide by guidelines and meet with a field agent. Also like parole, the CSL can be

Table 10.2 Risk Assessment Guide for the State of New York (*continued*)

Scoring System Categories	Category Items	Possible Points	Actions for Which Points Are Received
Postoffense Behavior	Acceptance of responsibility	0–15	15 = Deny/minimize offense 10 = Expelled from treatment
	Conduct while confined or supervised	0–20	20 = Disciplinary infraction 10 = Sexual misconduct
Release Environment[a]	Supervision offender will receive	0–15	15 = No supervision after release 5 = Release with no supervised parole caseload 0 = Released to supervised parole caseload
Override Factors	Prior felony conviction for a sex offense	N/A	Automatic Tier 3
	Injury or death to the victim	N/A	Automatic Tier 3
	Recent threats (to commit another offense)	N/A	Automatic Tier 3
	Offender abnormality	N/A	Automatic Tier 3
TOTAL		0–300	0–70 = Tier 1 75–105 = Tier 2 110–300 = Tier 3

[a] The offender's employment and living information is also taken into consideration if it is known, and this accounts for another potential 20 points.

SOURCE: Canestrini, K. (1999)

revoked. If this happens, the offender is subject to a revocation hearing and may be returned to prison.

There are several potential problems with CSL, though the courts are only now beginning to hear cases in this arena. To begin with, sex offenders under CSL must remain in the state for the duration of their lives. They can petition the court for removal from CSL after a specified period of time—usually 15 years—though prior to that time period they are subject to conditions like those of parolees. This has questionable constitutional infringements, as the offenders have already completed their criminal sentences. Also, if the offenders commit an offense in a state that has CSL, they are subject to those conditions even if they reside in a different state. For instance, New Jersey has implemented CSL and New York has not. If an individual lives in New York and travels to New Jersey for the evening, commits a sexual offense, and is subsequently convicted, that individual must reside in New Jersey for at least the next 15 years. The litigable issues relating to CSL are similar to some of those relating to registration and notification—specifically, ex post facto application, due process, and cruel and unusual punishment. The remainder of this chapter is devoted to such issues.

PROBLEMS WITH REGISTRATION
AND NOTIFICATION

The purpose of registration and notification is twofold: it alerts the police to where the offender is living and also lets the community know if serious, repeat sex offenders are living in the neighborhood. Registration aids the police in managing sex offenders who are living in the community, as well as in their investigation when a sex crime occurs. Because all sex offenders are required to register, the names of all those living in the community appear on a central list, and the police can match the modus operandi of a current offense to those of offenders on the list. Whereas registration aims to help the police, notification aims to assist the community by protecting society from known sex offenders. After the death of their daughter Megan, the Kankas proposed that registration alone is an insufficient form of prevention. They believed that if they had known that a recidivist child molester was living across the street, they could have prevented Megan's rape and murder. The purpose of registration and notification is community protection, not retribution, though there have been many legal challenges as to whether the scope of registration goes past the realm of civil legislation and is therefore unconstitutional.

The aim of registration and notification is well intentioned, yet it has created a national debate about the constitutionality of such acts in relation to privacy, double jeopardy, cruel and unusual punishment, retroactive application of a state action, and many other issues. In addition to the constitutional challenges that face the statutes, some argue that registration creates problems such as vigilantism and lower real estate values, as well as a false sense of security for the public. Because the community is only notified about Tier 3 offenders, the list of offenders specified to the public is not representative of all sexual offenders. Also, the ostracism from the public that results from notification tends to counteract the benefits of treatment, such as improved social skills. This ostracism may, in some instances, create further offending behavior rather than keep the offender from acting out if he or she has no legal social or sexual outlets.

Because of all the constitutional challenges and varying decisions across states, registration procedures differ everywhere. Dissimilar legal statutes create problems in equal application of the law. For instance, a Tier 1 sex offender in Illinois, Connecticut, or Louisiana need only register for 10 years, whereas a Tier 1 sex offender in Maine or Alaska registers for 15, Massachusetts for 20, and Idaho or California for life. In the many states that have lifetime registration, an offender can petition to have his or her name expunged from the registry after a particular amount of time, which also varies; in Florida, the offender can peti-tion after 20 years; Nevada, 15 years; and Washington, D.C., 10 years. The court hears cases on a daily basis relating to many arguments, and what follows is a list of some of the more important issues debated.

Constitutional Arguments
against Registration and Notification Laws

Megan's Law has been challenged constitutionally on many fronts, most important whether registration and community notification laws (RCNL) constitute punishment. If registration and notification are forms of punish-ment, then Megan's Law could be deemed unconstitutional on four bases: dou-ble jeopardy, ex post facto application of the law, bill of attainder, and cruel and unusual punishment. *Double jeopardy,* which is prohibited by the Fifth Amendment, protects an individual from being tried twice for the same crime. Protection against *ex post facto application* of a law means that an individual is not subject to punishment for a law that was enacted after the crime was com-mitted. In other words, a law cannot be applied retroactively if punishment can result from such an application. The *bill of attainder* clause prohibits infliction of punishment upon members of a group without judicial process. Finally, if registration and notification is punishment, then it must be proportionate to the offense committed; otherwise it is unconstitutional under the Eighth Amendment's *cruel and unusual punishment* clause.

Because all four of these issues are related to punishment, the courts have regarded them together in several cases. No court has yet determined registra-tion to be unconstitutional on the basis that it is punishment, though the courts have varied in their analysis of notification requirements. Most states have not prohibited notification,[7] but the courts have put stringent requirements on the notification process and process of risk assessment. Hundreds of cases have gone through the courts; however, it is the New Jersey case of *Doe v. Poritz* (1995) that set precedents for other registration and notification cases to follow.

In *Doe* the court upheld RCNL, stating that they do not violate the consti-tutional rights of sex offenders subject to them. The court did state, however, that in order for the laws to be valid there must be some modification to the judicial review process for Tier 2 and 3 offenders. The court said that the pur-pose of RCNL is to protect society from convicted sex offenders, and that the Constitution does not prevent society from employing such preventative mea-sures. The court also stated that the community is allowed to employ these pre-ventative measures for offenders who were convicted prior to enactment of the law, so long as the means of protection are reasonably designed only for the purpose of prevention and are not designed to punish.[8] The court claimed, based on much case law, that this statute is not punitive but rather is remedial, despite the fact that it may have a deterrent effect. Because of its standing as remedial, RCNL do not violate the bill of attainder clause, and they do not constitute cruel and unusual punishment. Additionally, the court stated that retroactive application of the laws is acceptable in order to achieve the goal of the statute: community protection. If the laws were not applied ex post facto, it would take years to offer the protection they were designed to afford.

There is another problem, however, with ex post facto application of RCNL, and that is the issue of plea bargaining. Many offenders who were charged with a sexual offense prior to enactment of RCNL pled guilty to either the offense with which they were charged or to a lesser sexual offense. Once RCNL were enacted and applied retroactively, these offenders were subject to the requirements of the statute. Several offenders have appealed their decision and requested the withdrawal of a guilty plea once they were told they had to register. However, the court has largely upheld the duty to register even when a guilty plea was made prior to enactment of RCNL. For instance, in the *Opinion of the Justices to the Senate* (1996), the Massachusetts court stated that there is no constitutional requirement to notify the defendant of the duty to register prior to when the defendant enters a plea, and the failure to notify the defendant of this duty does not negate a plea negotiation. The court in other states has supported this decision,[9] though it is likely that plea agreements will be questioned again with the implementation of CSL.

Despite the declaration that notification does not violate substantive constitutional rights, the court stated that there is "sufficient impingement on protected liberty interests in privacy and reputation" so that there must be procedural safeguards in place where notification statutes are applied. The court in *Doe* determined that the state should establish specific guidelines by which the degree of risk of a further offense can be determined, focusing specifically on Tier 2 and 3 offenders because it is those offenders about whom the public is notified. It stated that notification is only allowed to members of the community who are "likely to encounter" the offender, and that this determination should be based on geographic location. Additionally, the court said it is necessary to construct a forum by which an offender designated into Tier 2 or 3 can object to such a classification. The court was careful to recognize that the individual rights of sex offenders must be protected[10]; yet, the court also said "care should be exercised not to convert them into obstacles that prevent the enactment of honestly-motivated remedial legislation." Notification statutes are constantly being challenged, but thus far the courts are continuously upholding the law based on the idea that it is remedial rather than punitive.[11]

One other punishment-based issue that is being debated in court, though to a far less extent than the issues discussed previously, is that of the Fourth Amendment rights of a sex offender. Because many of the sex offenders who are required to register are no longer under the care of correctional services, there is a question as to whether the state has a right to take DNA evidence or other bodily fluids, fingerprints, or photographs. Though some courts (for example, *Rise v. Oregon*, 1995) have stated that there must be probable cause because this would constitute a seizure, others (for example, *Rowe v. Burton*, 1994) have stated that seizure of DNA, fingerprints, and photographic evidence is constitutional. Because most offenders are under the care of correctional services at the time their information is submitted to the registry, most states apply Fourth Amendment standards of parolees or probationers to the sex offenders. Nonetheless, these are some issues for debate.

There are also arguments against RCNL in terms of due process rights of those to whom they are applied. The question in these cases has been twofold: Does RCNL trigger a due process analysis, and, if so, how much due process is necessary? The courts have been split on the issue, often on a case-by-case basis, and varying restrictions are put on the individual as a result of RCNL. Some cases, such as *Russell and Sterns v. Gregoire* (1997), have claimed that there is no protected interest involved, and as a result the statute does not trigger a due process analysis. Other cases, such as *Artway v. Attorney General of New Jersey* (1996), have stated that registration does not trigger a protected interest, yet notification does. Still others, such as *Doe v. Poritz* (1995), have recognized differential due process rights for offenders classified into varying tiers. In these cases, offenders in Tier 1 have few, if any, due process rights, whereas Tier 3 offenders are entitled to due process because of the privacy restrictions that result from notification.

In terms of the constitutional right to privacy for sex offenders, the court has often quoted *Paul v. Davis* (1976). This case decided that the government could publicize records of official convictions as long as this does not impede a person's freedom. This case is not related to registration, but it contains a thorough analysis of reputation as a result of publication of an arrest record. The defendant in this case was arrested for shoplifting, after which his name and photo were included in a police flyer distributed to store owners warning them of "active shoplifters" in the area. The Court in *Paul* stated, "Reputation alone . . . was neither 'liberty' nor 'property' by itself sufficient to invoke the procedural protection of the due process clause." As such, the flyers were not unconstitutional under the Fourteenth Amendment because of the charge of defamation. Additionally, distribution of the flyers

> could not be based on an alleged violation of the constitutional right to privacy, since the plaintiff's claim of constitutional protection against the disclosure of the fact of his arrest for shoplifting was based not upon any challenge to the state's ability to restrict his freedom of action in a sphere contended to be "private," but instead was based on a claim that the state could not publicize a record of an official act such as an arrest.

Quoting *Paul*, the court has rendered similar decisions in cases involving community notification of sex offenders. In *Doe v. Pataki* (1996), the court said that RCNL do not deprive a convicted sex offender of the right to equal protection, specifically in regard to the constitutional right to privacy. The court in *Doe v. Poritz* (1995) did recognize that RCNL would have an inevitable impact on sex offenders in terms of loss of anonymity, yet this loss of anonymity "is no constitutional bar to society's attempt at self-defense." The court recognized the difficulty in balancing the rights of offenders versus those of the community, and said that so long as the extent of notification is based on the likelihood of reoffense, it is okay to protect potential victims from these offenders through notification. The court has claimed that the state has a strong interest in public disclosure, which substantially outweighs the sex offenders' interest in privacy. Therefore, the court concluded in *Doe v. Poritz* (1995) that because the registration and notification requirements of the statutes are rationally related to a legitimate state interest, the requirements of equal protection under the Fourteenth Amendment and the state constitution have been satisfied. Essentially, there is no reasonable expectation of privacy to any information contained in public records. Therefore, the state has a right to disclose the information (though the state's interest in disclosure outweighs the individual's interest in privacy, regardless).

In March 2003, the U.S. Supreme Court made decisions on two cases related to the constitutionality of registration and notification statutes. In *Connecticut Department of Public Safety v. Doe* (2003), the Court addressed the issue of whether Connecticut was acting unconstitutionally by posting offender information on the Internet. Citing *Paul v. Davis* (1976), the Court said that this did not violate the offender's due process rights because injury to reputation alone is not a deprivation of liberty. Similarly, in the case *Smith v. Doe* (2003), the Court declared that registration and notification are constitutional even if applied ex post facto, because the law is nonpunitive.

Nonconstitutional Issues Related to RCNL

RCNL have not just come under scrutiny for constitutional reasons; there are also practical problems that result from the statutes. These problems include:

Vigilantism Despite its legality, notification has created some problems in the community, the most serious of which is increased violence through vigilantism. The court's response to vigilantism was made clear in *Doe v. Poritz* (1995), by stating that the court should not assume that the public will be punitive, and it should assume that the media will act responsibly with information that is disseminated about sex offenders. The court also stated that all community leaders and the media should emphasize the repercussions if the information released about offenders is used to punish rather than protect, as intended. Many states have issued warnings that vigilantism will not be tolerated. On websites designed to notify the community about sex offenders, there are warnings that the information contained within must be used responsibly (for example, see http://criminaljustice.state.ny.us/ for New York State's website).

Despite the warnings, acts of vigilantism have occurred and have had some serious consequences. For example, in Washington State, a sex offender's house was burned down; in New Jersey, an innocent man was beaten after being mistaken for a sex offender; also in New Jersey, a sex offender registered with a false name and address and labeled an innocent man as a sex offender (Freeman-Longo, 1996). Notification shocks those in the community, as they discover suddenly that there are sex offenders living within their midst. The individuals in the community then lash out violently, either appalled by the offenses committed by the offenders or because they assume that all sex offenders are going to reoffend and must be stopped before doing so.

Despite the problems, the court has repeatedly stated that notification will not be withheld from the community on the basis that vigilantism might occur. The court in *Doe v. Poritz* (1995) stated that a determination on the legality of notification should not be based on a "prediction of destructive and punitive community reaction," and that the court "does not perceive in this case a society seeking vengeance, demanding the names of previously-convicted sex offenders in order to further punish them." Rather, the court focused again on the issue of prevention, saying that the information can and should be used to protect the family from potential sexual offenders. The court even went as far as to say that some citizens may misuse the information and harass the known sex offenders but that these individuals will (presumably) be prosecuted. In other words, just because some citizens may act irresponsibly does not negate the benefits of preventive measures that can be taken as a result of the notification.

Absconding Many sex offenders abscond, or fail to register. Others initially register their information with the police but fail to inform them if they change addresses. Because of the vigilantism that occurs, some sex offenders are not complying with the registration requirements for fear of retaliation from the community. Others simply do not want the stigmatization that occurs as a result of notification. Thus, the community does not know where many sex offenders are living, but they have a false sense of security because the registry does exist. In large cities, the police take the offenders' names and addresses, but rarely do they check on the accuracy of the address or the proximity of the offender to schools, parks, or recreational facilities. News sources reported, for instance, that one-third of the sex offenders in Massachusetts have provided false information about their addresses, and that the state of California realized in 2003 that they did not know the whereabouts of approximately 30,000 of their high-risk sex offenders (Mullvihill, Wisniewski, Meyers, & Wells, 2003).

If an offender fails to register, it is a punishable offense, though each state varies in the type of sanction for the failure. Sanctions may be misdemeanors or felonies, or there may be a given number of days or years in jail or prison. Because offenders need to reregister annually or every 90 days, some states increase the sanction each time the offender fails to register. If the offender fails to register a specific number of times, a warrant is issued for the offender's arrest. Unfortunately, not all registration agencies have the resources to follow up on all offenders who abscond from the registration process.

Ineffective Monitoring Though monitoring offenders in small towns may not require additional resources in order to be effective, large cities often do not have the resources to effectively monitor the sex offender population. As such, information is taken, but rarely can the officers follow up to check on the offenders or dedicate resources to finding those who abscond. Though a warrant is issued for the absconding sex offender's arrest, this allows only for a reactive approach if the offender comes to the attention of officials for some other purpose.

Another issue that is of concern also relates to sex offenders in large cities. In an area like New York City, sex offenders are forced to live within a small geographical area. Because the city is built up rather than out, it is difficult for offenders to live more than 1,000 yards from a school, no matter where they live within the city. Also, it is likely that sex offenders will live within a close proximity to each other. Though the agencies that monitor sex offenders take their names and addresses, it is difficult for them to efficiently monitor the area where they are living and the distance between the sex offender and the parks, schools, youth centers, and other such organizations.

Real Estate   In many neighborhoods, the value of real estate goes down if there is a registered offender living in the community. Whereas some states allow realtors to disclose if a sex offender lives in the community, other states, such as New Jersey and Wisconsin, require this disclosure to be made. In Connecticut, however, legislation was recently signed stating that real estate brokers and homeowners are no longer required to disclose to potential buyers whether there is a sex offender living in the community. The rationale behind this is that they do not have the most updated information about the offenders, and that updated information can be obtained from either the police or the Internet. As opposed to informing potential buyers about sex offenders in the community, some housing complexes (generally, apartment buildings, townhouses, or condominiums) do background checks and do not allow registered sex offenders to move into the buildings.

Homeless Offenders   When offenders are released from prison, they often do not have a place to live. There are few establishments that house sex offenders; even correctional programs such as halfway houses are often reluctant to take in sex offenders, which leaves the offender with few choices of where to live once released. In some cities, public housing estates do not allow felons to live there, so no affordable housing is available for sex offenders. As a result of the lack of housing, many offenders are homeless or live in shelters. When a sex offender lives in a shelter, one of two problems emerges with the sex offender registry: either the offender is not listed as having a permanent residence, or he or she is listed as having a permanent residence but moves often, and therefore has an incorrect address listed with the registry. Either way, the registry is flawed.

Counteracting the Treatment Process   One of the primary problems with notification is that it goes against the philosophy of treatment. In treatment, sex offenders learn social and relationship skills, as researchers have found that lack of these skills is related to deviant sexual behavior. However, once the community is notified that the individual is a sex offender, that individual is often ostracized from others because of his or her label. Rather than keep them from offending, notification may actually promote such behavior by creating barriers to normal social behavior.

False Security The registry gives communities a false sense of security. As a result of the lack of reporting and conviction of sex offenders, there are likely to be far more sex offenders living in the community than are listed in the registry. The second problem is that sex offenders on the register are often strangers to their victims, though the literature has consistently shown that sexual offenders tend to know their victims. Because the offenders who pose the most serious threat to the community and are labeled as a high risk to reoffend are those who are strangers to their victims, it is these offenders about whom the community is notified. Though the assessment of these offenders as higher risk than incest offenders is perhaps accurate, it creates a false sense of security for the communities who are notified about the strangers. The communities learn about the stranger offenders in the area and often warn their children about the particular stranger; yet, these parents would be better suited to educate their children about the general dangers of sexual offending rather than about specific individuals.

One way to improve this is through community education. The community is rarely educated about sex offenders and is often unaware that the majority of offenders know their victims. The media promulgates the image of "stranger danger," publishing articles about "predators," "fiends," and "monsters." One possibility is to include information along with the notification about specific offenders. Some agencies and groups are trying to do this; for instance, Parents for Megan's Law is a nonprofit group with a website set up to educate and notify parents about sex offenders. On their website, they give prevention tips that include accurate information about victim-offender relationships as well as general information about various types of child molesters.

CHAPTER SUMMARY

- The aim of Megan's Law is to inform the public about known sex offenders who pose a high risk to the community with the aim of preventing recidivism. Megan's Law was first enacted in New Jersey after the death of Megan Kanka, but now every state has a version of registration and community notification laws.

- Megan's Law requirements differ by state. However, most have a three-tiered system whereby offenders are assessed as low, moderate, or high risk, and the community is notified about high-risk offenders. The method of risk assessment varies, though many states use actuarial risk assessment guidelines.

- The courts have addressed many constitutional issues related to Megan's Law, including ex post facto, due process, privacy, double jeopardy, cruel and unusual punishment, bill of attainder, and equal protection. Despite these claims, the U.S. Supreme Court decided in 2003 that both registration and community notification statutes are not punishment and do not violate the civil liberties of offenders.

■ The courts have also addressed nonconstitutional issues, such as whether juveniles should register, how homeless offenders should register, how to ensure protection from vigilantism, and others. Some opponents of Megan's Law suggest that educating the community about sex offenders would be more beneficial than notifying the community about known offenders.

DISCUSSION QUESTIONS

1. What led to the implementation of registration and community notification statutes?

2. What are the primary benefits to registration and community notification laws? Do you think that Megan's Law is successful in achieving these benefits? Why or why not?

3. What are the key constitutional issues with Megan's Law that have been addressed by the courts? Do

you think the law is constitutional? Why or why not?

4. Should juveniles register under Megan's Law? If so, under what circumstances?

5. What would be the ideal type of community notification and why? Are there any problems with this type of notification?

6. Should there be a standard system of registration and notification in all states? Why or why not?

NOTES

1. For a detailed explanation of all state and federal statutes and guidelines, see Terry and Furlong (2003).

2. Currently, offenders are allowed to move to different states as long as they reregister in the state where they reside. However, in Florida and New Jersey, all registered sex offenders are under community supervision for life (CSL) and are not allowed to move to a different state. Although this is controversial, offenders can apply for expungement from this requirement after a certain amount of time.

3. However, one state requires juveniles to register only if they are tried as an adult, and another state has a separate juvenile registry.

4. Alaska, Arizona, Arkansas, District of Columbia, Illinois, Maryland, Massachusetts, Minnesota, Mississippi, Montana, Nebraska, Nevada, New Jersey, New York, Ohio, Pennsylvania, Rhode Island, Vermont, Virginia, Washington.

5. District of Columbia, Florida, Massachusetts, Montana, Nevada, New Jersey, New York, Rhode Island, Washington.

6. The only state that does not use the tier system as a method of notification is Nebraska, which does not actively notify the community about any sex offenders.

7. The only state thus far to render registration and notification unconstitutional was Hawaii in November 2001, though it has since re-enacted RCNL.

8. Legislative intent has been another key source of legal contention. See *Doe v. Pataki* (1996).

9. For example, *People v. McClellan* (1994); *State v. Skroch* (1994); *State v. Ward* (1987).

10. For example, the court in *Doe v. Poritz* (1995) stated that New Jersey will name one judge in each vicinage to handle any hearings that involve RCNL so as to avoid any disparity in decisions.

11. For example, *Artway v. Attorney General of New Jersey* (1996); *Doe v. Pataki* (1997); *E. B. and W. P. v. Verniero* (1997); *Opinion of the Justices to the Senate* (1996); *Russell and Stearns v. Gregoire* (1997); *Snyder v. State* (1996); *State v. Cameron* (1996).

11

Controlling the Sexually
Violent Predator

Registration and community notification laws are not the only type of "knee-jerk" legislation spawned during the 1990s. Several states have passed legislation allowing for sexual offenders to be committed to secure facilities if they are assessed as having a mental abnormality or personality disorder and are dangerous. Labeling such an offender a "sexually violent predator" (SVP), the purpose of this legislation is to incapacitate recidivist sexual offenders who are "more likely than not to reoffend" until they are rehabilitated (Seling, 2000). This legislation assumes a relationship among mental disorder, risk, and sexual violence, yet the medicalization of sexually deviant behavior is not grounded in "empirically demonstrated empiricism or articulated legal standard" (Janus, 1997: 350).

SVP legislation is controversial in terms of its aim, effectiveness, and constitutionality. This legislation is largely based on the ability of clinicians to accurately predict the risk an offender may present to the public in the future. Risk assessments, or predictions of dangerousness, are controversial; most experts agree that they produce high rates of false positives for sex offenders except in extreme circumstances (for example, with psychopathic, violent sex offenders who have at least two previous offenses). Though the Supreme Court has declared SVP legislation constitutional, legal challenges against it are continuing. Alternative methods of controlling dangerous sexual predators, such as mandatory chemical castration of recidivist offenders or mandatory cognitive-behavioral treatment programs, are also being implemented in some states. All of these reactions—particularly the hospitalization of a sexual offender for treatment—serve to medicalize the problem of sexual offending. The presence in a hospital setting allows moral problems (such as sexual offending) to be recast (by the offenders themselves as well as society) as medical problems, and thus offenders do not take responsibility for their actions.

SVP legislation is, simply put, recycled Mentally Disordered Sex Offender (MDSO) laws from the 1930s. As discussed in Chapter 2, during the 1930s states began implementing sexual psychopathy legislation for recidivist sexual offenders. Psychopathy statutes were passed on the principle that sexually deviant behavior results from a diagnosable disorder and is treatable. If an individual were diagnosed a sexual psychopath, he or she would be civilly committed to a mental institution until rehabilitated (Alexander, 1993). Sexual psychopathy laws, like many of the modern laws concerning sex offenders, were constructed through reactive decision making and passed after emotionally charged sex crimes occurred. The legislation was problematic for several reasons, most obviously the subjective process for commitment. All states differed in their definitions of "sexual psychopathy," though most states required that the individuals suffered from a mental illness and were dangerous. Dangerousness predictions at this time were subjective and could not be predicted with much accuracy, and as such commitment standards were disputed (Sutherland, 1950). Several psychiatric and mental health organizations suggested that these laws should be repealed, and by 1990, sexual psychopathy laws existed in only 13 states (American Psychiatric Association, 1999). At this time, however, there was another wave of highly publicized cases of sexual assaults on children.

SVP LEGISLATION:
THE COMMITMENT PROCESS

Shortly after legislators determined that current legislation was ineffective at incapacitating dangerous sexual predators such as Earl Shriner (discussed in Chapter 10), Washington enacted the Community Protection Act (CPA) in 1990, allowing for the civil commitment of such individuals. Since that time, 16 states[1] have implemented and 20 further states have proposed similar legislation. An SVP is defined, in most states, as any person who has been convicted of or charged with a sexually violent offense and who suffers from a mental abnormality or personality disorder that makes the person likely to engage in predatory acts of sexual violence. Sexually Violent Predator Acts (SVPA) were enacted by states specifically to target "a small but extremely dangerous group of SVPs who do not have a mental disease or defect that renders them appropriate for involuntary treatment . . . " (Kansas SVPA §59-29a). The statute requires more proof than a "mere predisposition" to violence; rather, it requires proof of past sexually violent behavior and a present mental condition that is likely to cause similar violent behavior in the future.

Thus far, the U.S. Supreme Court has heard SVP cases from the states of Kansas and Washington and has rendered this legislation constitutional. As a result, many states have modeled their SVP statutes on the statutes of these states. The commitment process in Washington is as follows: First, the sex offender is referred to the court within three months of his or her release from prison.[2] The prosecuting attorney files the petition, which is followed by a hearing to determine whether there is probable cause to believe that the sex offender is, in fact, an SVP. At this hearing, the sex offender has due process rights similar to those in a criminal trial, including the right to notice of the hearing, an opportunity to be heard, right to counsel, right to present evidence, right to cross-examine witnesses, and the right to view and copy all petitions and documents in his or her file. If the court establishes that probable cause does exist, the sex offender is then transferred to a facility for evaluation.

Once the offender is in a facility, a psychiatrist does a risk assessment of the offender. If a sex offender is assessed as dangerous, the next step in the commitment process is a trial. The trial must be held within 45 days, and the offender has a right to counsel, a jury trial, and an examination by an expert of his or her choice. Again, this is similar to a criminal trial. In Washington, the prosecuting attorney must prove the case beyond a reasonable doubt; however, because it is a civil trial, some states use a standard of only clear and convincing evidence. Because this is a jury trial, the verdict must be unanimous. If the jury does not meet a unanimous verdict, the court must declare a mistrial and set a retrial date within 45 days. If the jury does return a unanimous verdict that the offender is an SVP, he or she is transferred to a Special Commitment Center (SCC), located in a prison facility, for "control, care, and treatment" until rehabilitated. In order to be rehabilitated, the SVP's condition must change so that he or she is no longer a danger to others and can be safely released into the community or to a less restrictive alternative (LRA) than the SCC (to a facility with conditions similar to those of a minimum-security prison or a halfway house, for example). As a result of an injunction in 1994, Washington State was required to construct an LRA that would be available to offenders nearing discharge.

A petition for conditional release to an LRA may be made once the offender's condition has changed so that he or she no longer fits the definition of an SVP. Once the offender has petitioned the court, a hearing is set. The offender is not present at this hearing, though he or she has a right to counsel at this time. In order to release the offender to an LRA, the offender must agree to abide by conditions stated in the judgment. This includes, among other conditions, participation in a treatment program with a qualified provider in the facility. The treatment provider must take responsibility for treating the offender and must report to the court regularly on the patient's progress. The LRA must also agree to accept the offender, and the facility must be secure enough to ensure community protection. Once the offender is situated in the LRA, he or she is not allowed to leave the facility without authorization. It is the authority of the facility to ensure the protection of the community by strict supervision of the offender, with a report to the court if the offender disobeys the regulations of the facility. The offender who is in the LRA facility will be reviewed annually until he or she is "rehabilitated" and there is an unconditional discharge. Once an offender is completely discharged from the facility, he or she is subject to the registration and community notification laws (RCNL) of the county to which he or she moves.

The most important step of this process is the risk assessment, which is, inherently, a subjective evaluation of an individual to determine what he or she might do in the future. The type of assessment conducted differs in each state, though actuarial-based assessments, such as the commonly used Static-99,[3] are often used in conjunction with the clinical assessments in order to improve on the rate of accuracy for risk predictions. Actuarial-based instruments attempt to predict future offending behavior based on past offenses or personal (static) characteristics. If the offender displays characteristics similar to a class of offenders who have shown a high degree of recidivism, it is postulated that the offender will follow the same pattern of reoffense. By measuring the base rate of reoffense for a particular cohort of sexual offenders, it is supposedly possible to determine whether an individual will reoffend. Not all experts are convinced, however. Janus and Meehl (1997) showed that unless there is a high base rate and a high accuracy rate for a particular cohort, there is less than a 50 percent probability of correctly predicting future behavior—a contention supported by many researchers (Grubin & Wingate, 1996; Heyman, 1997).

Whether or not dangerousness predictions are ethical is debatable (Grisso & Appelbaum, 1992, 1993). Some researchers say that predictions of dangerousness may be ethical if based on the expert assessments of clinicians, even in the absence of empirical evidence that they are valid (Litwack, 1993). This argument assumes that there is not likely to be much empirical data on the most dangerous offenders, as such individuals are rarely released from institutions and therefore there is no accurate base rate for comparisons (Kemshall, 2001; Litwack, 1993). Such an argument is certainly true for sex offenders who are civilly committed, because few sex offenders are released from commitment facilities.

Though risk assessment is a necessary step in the commitment process, there are problems in combining medical and legal processes (Gutheil, 1984). Risk assessments are fallible, and many researchers claim that predicting human behavior is a nearly impossible task (Hood & Shute, 1996). One key issue is that assessment is not a uniform phenomenon, and the ability to predict a person's actions depends largely on who is being assessed and the quality of the assessment (Lidz & Mulvey, 1995). Predictions of violence tend to be most accurate for certain types of cases, such as when there is a history of repeated violence (Litwack, 1993), there is evidence of psychopathy (Hemphill, Hare, & Wong, 1998; Quinsey, Lalumiere, Rice, & Harris, 1995), or there is a previous conviction for a sexual offense (McGrath, 1994). Predictions are least accurate when they are made about specific, serious offenses (Quinsey et al., 1995), and there is no single instrument or combination of techniques that can accurately predict an individual's risk (Schwartz, 1999). Historically, clinicians have been prone to overpredict future violent behavior, and several studies have shown the rate of false positives to be high in dangerousness assessments (Brody & Tarling, 1980; Dickens, 1985; Ewing, 1985; Floud & Young, 1981; Greenland, 1984; Megargee, 1981; Monahan, 1981; Pallone, 1990; Quinsey et al., 1995; Steadman, 1972; Stone, 1985; von Hirsch and Ashworth, 1996; Wormith & Ruhl, 1986).

Because future violence is difficult to predict, most clinicians admit that if they are going to err in their judgments, they will do so on the side of society (Alexander, 1993). If a psychologist approves an offender's release, he or she is deemed responsible for any actions the offender takes once in the community. One example of this is the release of Raymond Alves, a rapist, from a New Jersey prison in March 2000. Psychologists Judith Frankel and Jack Gibbons assessed him and approved his release into the community, though he was discharged before anyone could impose registration requirements upon him. When the Commissioner of Corrections realized the mistake, Alves was declared a fugitive. For the next 11 days he traveled by bus through 17 cities and eventually came back to New Jersey (Hanley, March 23, 2000). In order to point blame at an individual rather than the system for this lapse in communication, the commissioner fired the two psychologists (Hanley, March 17, 2000).

Despite the problems associated with risk predictions, they are necessary with SVP legislation. Even those who are not proponents of risk assessments say that risk to the community should not be completely ignored because of the potential inaccuracy of assessments. For instance, Gabor (1990) says, "While I agree that the prediction of future criminality is precarious, blanket dismissals of prediction grossly oversimplify the subject" (p. 544). The question must be, Is it ethical to confine someone indefinitely who we predict, with less than 50 percent accuracy, may offend in the future?

STATE VARIATION IN SVP STATUTES

Most states follow a commitment procedure similar to the one in Washington. Due to its many legal precedents, all states must abide by certain standards, such as due process rights during the commitment process, availability of treatment, and LRA facilities. Nonetheless, there are variations in each state.

- *Definition of "Sexually Violent Predator"* Most states, such as Washington and Kansas, use the three-pronged criteria of mental abnormality, dangerousness, and no availability of an LRA to declare an individual an SVP. Some states use the criteria of personality disorder or mental disorder rather than mental abnormality, whereas others still use the criteria of mental illness. Though on its face this does not seem significantly different, the tenet "personality disorder" increases the chance that an individual may be committed through a diagnosis such as antisocial personality disorder.

- *Standards of Commitment* States use different standards of dangerousness in order to commit an offender. Schwartz (1999: 4–12) notes that sex offenders in Minnesota must be "highly likely" to recidivate in order to be committed, yet in Washington they must have an "extremely high" rating of dangerousness for confinement. In Wisconsin, however, they are incapacitated if they are "most likely to reoffend" and "are distinctively dangerous." This is similar to the difference in standards with psychopathy commitment statutes, and the result is a differential in numbers of those committed.

- *Standards of Proof for Commitment* Another difference worth noting is that standards of proof vary from state to state. Most states require the same standard for commitment as with a criminal trial: proof beyond a reasonable doubt. Other states, such as Florida and New Jersey, require the lesser standard of "clear and convincing evidence" that is generally required in civil trials. Though the commitment process is civil in nature, it resembles a criminal trial in several regards (for example, due process rights allotted, removal of civil liberties, and so forth). As such, most states require a standard equal to that of criminal trials.

- *Length of Commitment* In most states, a sex offender, once committed, will remain incapacitated indefinitely until rehabilitated. However, in some states, such as California, the standard is that an offender must be reevaluated every two years in order to determine if he or she should remain committed. The offender goes through a similar (though less involved) trial process as with the original commitment process.

- *Facility* The facilities in which offenders are incapacitated vary greatly, from prisons to hospitals to special secure facilities. For instance, in Washington, the offenders are housed in a prison facility on McNeil Island called the Special Commitment Center. In California, most SVPs are housed in Atascadero State Hospital, a mental hospital that is now dedicated to the incapacitation of sex offenders. In Kansas, offenders are committed to the Larned State Security Hospital, and in Iowa, a state-of-the-art facility was built specifically for SVPs and is the most expensive facility among all states with hospital facilities. Additionally, all facilities are required to construct some type of LRA as a transitional facility for the offenders, though these vary greatly across the states.

- *Cost* The cost of the facilities differs greatly. Taking into consideration housing and treatment cost as well as legal fees, Washington has the cheapest facility at approximately $130,000 per offender per year. Iowa has the most expensive, at approximately $238,000 per offender per year by the sixth year of incapacitation (Lieb, 1998). All facilities are required to staff treatment providers, who must be available to all offenders who desire to participate in a treatment program. Additionally, the cost of legal fees is high in every state because of the many appeals, but a state such as California, which repetitions the court for commitment every two years, has higher legal fees than other states.

- *Psychopathy Statutes* Some states, such as Minnesota and New Jersey, use more that one commitment statute. Minnesota still applies the sexual psychopathy statutes as well as an SVP statute. For its psychopathy statute, called the Psychiatric Personality Act, Minnesota follows the "utter inability test"; to be committed, the offender must exhibit an "utter lack of power to control [his or her] sexual impulses" (*State ex rel. Pearson v. Probate Court of Ramsey County,* 1939). The Sexually Dangerous Persons (SDP) Act was implemented in 1994 as a result of Dennis Linehan, who could not be committed under the Psychiatric Personality Act upon completion of his criminal sentence because there was no "clear and convincing evidence that appellant has an utter lack of power to control his sexual impulses" (*In re Linehan,* 1994). After his release, the Minnesota legislature passed the SDP Act, allowing for the civil commitment of persons who suffer from "certain disorders and dysfunctions and are dangerous to the public."

THE COURTS AND SVP LEGISLATION

SVP legislation involves involuntary civil commitment, a concept that is not new and exists in every state for the mentally ill. Involuntary civil commitment originated as a last resort in which the state could assist people with mental disorders or illnesses who were unable to recognize their problems or help themselves. These statutes require proof of a mental disability that gives rise to a substantial threat of serious harm to oneself or others. Involuntary civil commitment statutes have continuously withstood constitutional challenges, despite the infraction on civil liberties to those confined.

Almost immediately after its inception, claimants challenged the SVPA in the courts on several grounds, including ex post facto application, double jeopardy, due process, equal application, vagueness of the statute, and definition of an SVP. The statute itself has been challenged, as well as its application to individuals. In addition to being the first state to enact legislation, Washington was also the first state to test the constitutionality of the law in a state court in *In re Young* (1993). However, it was the Kansas statute, implemented in 1994, that first reached the U.S. Supreme Court. In 1997, the Court upheld the civil commitment of Leroy Hendricks, a recidivist pedophile, under Kansas's SVP Act. Prior to SVP legislation reaching the U.S. Supreme Court, several cases were heard in state courts that influenced the legislation and commitment procedures.

The first two cases of importance in regard to civil commitment did not even concern sexual offenders, though both cases are cited often in SVP decisions. The case of *O'Connor v. Donaldson* (1975) is the first to analyze the constitutionality of civil commitment and the limitations thereof. Kenneth Donaldson, who suffered from paranoid schizophrenia, remained civilly committed in Florida for approximately 15 years despite several petitions for release. Though the Court found that he was mentally ill, they stated that this finding alone does not justify confinement. He was not deemed to be a danger to himself or others, and the Court therefore ordered that he be released.

The second case looked at the other tenet of commitment statutes, that of dangerousness. Until 1992, civil commitment was tolerated without firmly establishing the presence of a serious mental disorder. At this time, however, the Court passed down a decision in *Foucha v. Louisiana* (1992) that offenders can only be detained involuntarily if they have a "mental illness" or "mental abnormality," even if they remain a danger to themselves or others. Terry Foucha was an armed burglar who was found insane and committed to hospital. When he sought to be released, two psychiatrists diagnosed him as having an untreatable antisocial personality and declared that he was dangerous and should therefore be detained. The Court ruled that as long as he could not be treated, his confinement was no longer justifiable. To confine someone in hospital who is dangerous but does not have a mental disability would merely be substituting hospital for prison. The importance of this case lies in its emphasis on the necessity of treatment in order for a hospital order to be upheld, and has been cited in many SVP cases that followed.

The first critical case regarding an SVP in Washington was that of Terry Young (*In re Young,* 1993). When the court heard his case in 1993, it declared that the SVP clause of the Community Protection Act is, indeed, civil rather than criminal in nature. As such, it is not unconstitutional on grounds of double jeopardy and ex post facto application of the statute, and it does not violate any substantive due process rights. It did, however, affirm that an individual who is not incarcerated at the time of referral must have committed a recent, overt act to indicate that he or she may require incapacitation. Though the court stated that less restrictive alternatives must be considered for the individual referred for commitment, it also said that the statute is not "void for vagueness." The court in *Young* followed the *Foucha* decision, claiming that dangerousness alone is not enough to warrant confinement; there must be evidence of a mental disability as well, whether it is mental illness or abnormality.

Similarly to Washington, the Minnesota court declared civil commitment of sexual offenders constitutional in the case of *In re Linehan* (1994). Dennis Linehan, like most sexual offenders whose cases have come before the appellate courts, had an extensive history of sexual offending. He not only had several convictions, but his offenses escalated in intensity over time, involved children as victims, and ranged from window peeping to murder. In *Linehan,* the state court declared Minnesota's SDP Act a civil rather than criminal law, confirming the decision in *Young.* Linehan petitioned for a *writ of certiorari* (a request for review of a case) from the U.S. Supreme Court, though shortly before granting the writ the Court decided *Kansas v. Hendricks* (1997).

In 1997, the first real test of the SVPA occurred in the case of *Kansas v. Hendricks.* Leroy Hendricks had a long history of sexual deviancy, and he was convicted of molesting several young boys and girls, beginning in 1955. He was diagnosed as a pedophile, and although he attempted several treatment programs, he was never able to complete them. He explained to psychologists that he harbored strong sexual desires for young children, and he says that when he is "stressed out" he cannot control his urges to molest. As a result, he was registered as a sexually violent predator and incapacitated. This is the first time the court stated that pedophilia could be considered a mental abnormality, and that the purpose of the commitment was to hold Hendricks until his mental abnormality no longer caused a threat to others. Prior to this, the court did not consider paraphillas, an antisocial personality or personality disorder to be a mental illness, and individuals diagnosed with these were therefore not confined.

Hendricks challenged his civil commitment under the Kansas SVPA on substantive due process grounds, and claimed that the act established criminal proceedings in violation of the ban on double jeopardy and ex post facto laws. Though it rendered its decision in a 5–4 split, the Supreme Court upheld Hendricks's civil commitment and declared the Kansas SVPA constitutional on all grounds. The Court supported the former state court decisions in *Young* (1993) and *Linehan* (1994), stating that the SVPA is a civil rather than a criminal statute. As such, it does not violate double jeopardy clauses by adding additional punishment, because the purpose of civil commitment is neither retribution nor deterrence. The Court stated that

> a state statute providing for the involuntary civil commitment of sexually violent predators . . . does not violate the double jeopardy clause of the Federal Constitution's Fifth Amendment where, because the state did not enact the statute with punitive intent, the statute does not establish criminal proceedings, and involuntary commitment pursuant to the statute is not punitive; thus, for purposes of analysis under the double jeopardy clause, (1) initiation of commitment proceedings under the statute against a person upon his imminent release from prison after serving a sentence for the offenses which led to his being declared a violent sexual predator does not constitute a second prosecution, and (2) the person's involuntary detention under the statute does not violate the double jeopardy clause, even though that confinement follows a prison term.

Similarly, the Court stated in regard to ex post facto application of the law,

> A state's provision for the civil commitment of sexually violent predators does not violate the Federal Constitution's prohibition of ex post facto laws . . . where the provision does not (1) impose punishment, in that because the state did not enact the statute with punitive intent, the statute does not establish criminal proceedings, and involuntary commitment pursuant to the statute is not punitive, (2) criminalize conduct which was legal before the provision's enactment, nor (3) deprive a person subject to the provision of any defense that was available to him at the time of his crimes.

The Court dismissed the notion that the term "mental abnormality" was vague or too lax a standard for commitment, thereby violating due process rights. The Court claimed that "legal definitions which must take into account such issues as individual responsibility and competency need not mirror those advanced by the medical profession." It further stated that "this Court has never required States to adopt any particular nomenclature in drafting civil commitment statutes and leaves to the States the task of defining terms of a medical nature that have legal significance." To illustrate varying psychiatric definitions from previous cases, the Court used as examples the cases of *Addington v. Texas* (1979) (interchanging the terms "emotionally disturbed" and "mentally ill") and *Jackson v. Indiana* (1972) (interchanging the terms "incompetency" and "insanity"). In regard to the wording of the SVPA, the Court said,

A state's definition of "mental abnormality," in a statute providing for the involuntary civil commitment of sexually violent predators—which statute requires as a prerequisite to commitment a finding that a person has been convicted of or charged with a sexually violent offense and suffers from a mental abnormality or personality disorder which makes the person likely to engage in the predatory acts of sexual violence—as a congenital or acquired condition affecting the emotional or volitional capacity which predisposes the person to commit sexually violent offenses in a degree constituting such person a menace to the health and safety of others satisfies substantive due process under the Federal Constitution's Fourteenth Amendment, in that such definition requires a finding of both dangerousness and an inability to control that dangerousness; while a finding that a person is dangerous, standing alone, is ordinarily not a sufficient ground upon which to justify indefinite involuntary commitment of that person, a civil commitment statute may be upheld where it couples proof of dangerousness with proof of some additional factor, such as mental illness or mental abnormality, which serves to limit involuntary civil confinement to those who suffer from a volitional impairment rendering them dangerous beyond their control; and the diagnosis of a person as a pedophile, which qualifies as a mental abnormality under the statute, suffices for due process purposes.

Though the Court here attempts to distance itself from the field of psychiatry, the two are inextricably linked in cases of civil commitment. Without the use of psychiatry, there would be no risk predictions of dangerousness. The Court depends on these predictions to incapacitate offenders under the SVPA, stating that "the Act unambiguously requires a precommitment finding of dangerousness either to one's self or to others, and links that finding to a determination that the person suffers from a 'mental abnormality' or 'personality disorder.'" Additionally, it is the psychiatric professional who eventually determines if an offender is "rehabilitated" and therefore eligible for release.

Perhaps the most startling point made in the Hendricks case was the acceptance of lack of treatment once incapacitated. Hendricks argues that treatment was not offered to him once he was detained, and the Court ruled that the SVPA is not punitive even if it fails to offer treatment for the mental abnormality. Quoting *Jacobson v. Massachusetts* (1905), the Court stated,

The liberty secured by the Constitution of the United States to every person within its jurisdiction does not import an absolute right in each person to be, at all times and in all circumstances, wholly free from restraint. There are manifold restraints to which every person is necessarily subject for the common good. On any other basis organized society could not exist with safety to its members.

Basing his opinion on this, Justice Clarence Thomas claimed that preventive detention was an acceptable means of incapacitation for dangerous sexual offenders. This is true despite the fact that the Court called treatment "at best" an "incidental" objective. Even the program director at the hospital testified that Hendricks had not participated in any "meaningful treatment," nor had many other SVPs. The doctor further testified that the hospital does not have adequate staffing for this population and that the SVPs were receiving "essentially no treatment." Prior to this case, the Court had allowed preventive detention in the *United States v. Salerno* (1987) but only that which was "strictly limited in duration." Civil commitment statutes are not limited, but are rather indefinite. Despite this constriction on civil liberties, the conservative milieu of the Court prevailed.

The case of *Kansas v. Hendricks* (1997) set a precedent for civil legislation, indicating that incapacitation in hospital is acceptable for the worst, most loathed criminals. The politicians in other states jumped on the preventive detention bandwagon, as incapacitating sex offenders became not only constitutional but also politically popular. Although some researchers and civil libertarians thought that the legislation would eventually be ruled unconstitutional, it has not been yet. Several cases in Washington State went through the courts after *Hendricks*, addressing the issue of whether confinement is punitive at the SCC. These included *Young v. Weston* (1999) (holding that the statute is not punitive), *In re Turay* (1999) (holding that commitment is constitutional),[4] and *In re Campbell* (1999) (holding that the statute is constitutional in its application), and *Seling v. Young* (2001).

The primary issue addressed in *Seling v. Young* (2001) was not whether the statute itself was constitutional on its face but rather as applied to him. Young argued that it is unconstitutional because there is an absence of adequate treatment. Because his confinement is indefinite, the Washington statute imposed a punitive measure because there was a lack of quality treatment to help him get better. The Court disagreed with this "as applied" analysis, and in an 8–1 decision affirmed the constitutionality of the SVPA. It is unlikely that the U.S. Supreme Court will decide other SVPA matters in the near future, as they will likely leave such issues to the state courts to decide. Therefore, civil commitment is, for the time being, a constitutionally sound method of preventive detention for serious sexual offenders.

RETRIBUTION OR REHABILITATION: EXAMINING THE GOALS OF SVP LEGISLATION

According to the decision in *Seling v. Young* (2001), proponents of SVP legislation claim that it fulfills two public policy rationales: police power and the theory of *parens patriae*. The police power rationale follows that the state has a right to protect the community. The SVPA is clearly effective in its goal of community protection, as confinement eliminates the possibility of reoffense. Proponents justify civil commitment through the second rationale, *parens patriae*, by claiming that the SVPA allows the state, in taking on the role of a parent, to act in the best interest of the individual being confined, and confinement is for his or her own good. It is this point that is argued by the opponents of civil commitment. If the individual committed is offered the appropriate treatment to overcome the mental abnormality, then commitment is in the individual's best interest. However, history shows that this is rarely the case. Opponents of commitment put forth several arguments against the civil commitment of sex offenders, four of which are discussed here. These include the pretext for commitment, the facilities in which the offenders are housed, the treatment offered, and the release environment.

Pretexuality

The first argument relates to the purpose of confinement. Though the primary purpose of commitment is ostensibly rehabilitative, some—including Supreme Court Justices and mental health professionals—have suggested that treatment is only a pretext to punishment. *Pretextuality* refers to the uninformed, biased decisions that are made based on preconceptions of a particular individual or offense. The preconceived notion of sex offenders is that they are morally reprehensible individuals who need to be incapacitated for the good of society. The importance of pretextual decisions is their lack of faith in empirical evidence, which may prove contrary to the preconceived biases.

The purpose of SVP legislation is presumably therapeutic; the purpose is to incapacitate sex offenders until they are rehabilitated and can be safely released into the community. However, to say that confinement in a hospital is not punishment is a fallacy. Potas (1982) states,

> To assume a hospital order is not punitive is to misconceive the object of this sanction. It shares with imprisonment the consequences of depriving an individual of his or her liberty. Like imprisonment, it offers protection to the community by separating inmates from normal societal intercourse. Unlike imprisonment, however, the aim . . . is to provide . . . medical or psychiatric treatment. . . . Unfortunately, it is also here that the rights and liberties of individuals are at greatest risk. (pp. 13–14)

Commitment of sex offenders into a secure facility may actually serve to retard treatment efforts by removing responsibility for criminal conduct from the offenders. This medicalization of behavior forestalls any personal attributions of autonomy or responsibility for that condition and may indeed be antitherapeutic. Problems put down to a putative disease process (an attribution that can only be facilitated by a hospital setting) may actually increase recidivism through implanting the idea that it is not the offender but rather his or her putative medical problems that control the offender's response to a situation, in which, for example, he or she is faced with the opportunity to reoffend. As such, SVP legislation may profoundly impede the treatment effort, making worse the problem that we ostensibly seek to "cure" (yet covertly seek to punish).

Similarly, the civil commitment of sex offenders can be explained through the theory of therapeutic jurisprudence (TJ), which analyzes how the law may act as a therapeutic agent by having a positive or negative effect on those going through the legislative process (La Fond, 1999; Wexler, 1999). SVP legislation tends to have a profoundly negative (antitherapeutic) impact on the SVPs by discouraging them from taking responsibility for their conduct (La Fond, 1999). To make any social problem into a medical one diminishes the possibility that a person can be cured of that problem, and it goes directly against the concept of relapse prevention (discussed in Chapter 8). Relapse prevention (RP) requires the offender to take control of his or her own thoughts, fantasies, ideas, and actions, thereby encouraging the offender to manage his or her own behavior. The larger the focus on civil commitment, the further we become from the most effective treatment philosophy found to date for sex offenders.

Facility

A second argument against civil commitment relates to the confinement facilities, which vary from state to state. Some confinement centers are within prisons, some within hospitals, and some are individual secure facilities, though all confinement centers are required to have an LRA for clients nearing release (per the injunction against Washington in 1994, discussed earlier in the chapter). Washington State provides a good example of this problem. SVPs are incapacitated in the Special Commitment Center on McNeil Island, located on the premises of a prison facility. Though the SCC is housed within a prison facility, the SVPs are separated from the prisoners. They are given keys to their cells—prison cells—and they are free to walk throughout the facility. They are contained within the confines of the prison facility, however, in that they cannot go beyond the locked gates and razor wire that surrounds the island. Working at this facility are security guards (correctional officers), psychologists, and psychiatrists, as well as a number of managerial staff members. Because the law stipulates that the facility is required to offer treatment to the SVPs, medical and psychological staff must be available to all offenders if requested. Once released, the offenders participate in the Community Transition Program (CTP), which means that although their treatment in SCC is complete, their treatment must continue indefinitely in the community.

Not only is the facility an issue, but so is cost of the facility. Civil commitment costs nearly three and a half times the amount of incarceration in a maximum-security prison,[5] and the SCC in Washington provides a good example of why this is so. The SCC, which is one of the least expensive commitment centers, is like a prison in that it is a total institution. The offenders must be fed, clothed (though they have the option of buying their own clothes), housed, offered necessary medical treatment, provided with services (for example, religious services), offered recreation and education, and they must be offered employment. Employment is a particularly costly issue; because their criminal sentence is complete, they are no longer "offenders" under the care of the correctional services and therefore they must be offered minimum wage for their services. The most expensive cost to the facility is treatment, as the SCC provides cognitive-behavioral group treatment as well as individualized counseling to the SVPs. Additionally, civilly committed sexual offenders are a particularly litigious group, and as such their legal fees run, on average, at $70,000 per offender per year.

Treatment

A third problem with civil commitment is the treatment itself. As shown previously, SVP laws are being legally contested on the basis of constitutionality, yet the courts have systematically ignored the fact that there is a dearth of research on the effectiveness of commitment based on its main premise: rehabilitation. Not all offenders can be rehabilitated; the question is whether the treatment offered is effective for SVPs. As discussed in Chapter 8, much of the current literature on sexual offenders indicates that well-established treatment programs are effective at reducing recidivism for some sex offenders. The rate of efficacy depends on the particular type of program, how it is delivered and to whom, and in what settings (Andrews, Bonta, & Hoge, 1990; Cullen & Gendreau, 1989; Gendreau & Ross, 1987; Marshall & Barbaree, 1990b). Cognitive-behavioral programs are the most common method of treatment for sex offenders today, both institutionally and in the community (Marshall, Anderson, & Fernandez, 1999). The goals of this treatment are for offenders to learn to recognize their problems and deviant behavior, understand the feelings and events that led to this behavior, identify and eliminate their cognitive distortions (CDs), accept responsibility for their behavior, reevaluate their attitudes, address issues of social incompetence, acquire new prosocial expressions of sexuality, understand the repetitive nature of their behavior, and learn how to identify and manage high-risk situations (Groth, 1983; Knopp, 1984; Marshall & Barbaree, 1990b; Williams, 1996).

SVP legislation in most states requires the indefinite commitment of sex offenders in hospital until they are rehabilitated; yet, the treatment that is currently offered to the SVPs is not adequate for several reasons. First, offenders who are civilly committed have generally been incarcerated for years without being offered treatment in prison. Most are offered treatment for the first time once civilly committed, at which point their problems have likely been exacerbated by years of disregard.

Second, treatment for SVPs follows the format of a typical cognitive-behavioral treatment program. Though this is generally considered the most effective type of treatment, SVPs are, by definition, very dangerous sex offenders who have a mental abnormality or personality disorder. They are often labeled "untreatable," or they require long-term, specialized treatment. In other words, they are the offenders for whom a typical cognitive-behavioral approach may not be effective at reducing the risk of recidivism. SVPs are the offenders who would be eliminated from participating in most standard cognitive-behavioral treatment programs.[6] In Washington, approximately 25 percent of the SVP population is described as having "special needs"—meaning, in addition to being dangerous sex offenders with mental abnormalities, they have developmental disabilities, neurological impairments, or mental illnesses (Washington State, 2000).

In order for rehabilitation to be successful, offenders must partake in a treatment regime that addresses their offending behavior as well as the potential causes of that behavior, and suggests prevention techniques that can help them to manage their behavior. The question then arises as to what, if any, methods of treatment are successful at accomplishing these tasks for SVPs. To add to these problems, not all offenders participate in treatment once committed. Leroy Hendricks claimed that although he was civilly committed on the basis of rehabilitation, no treatment was offered to him in the hospital. SVPs remain committed indefinitely until rehabilitated and, thus, it is important to discern whether SVPs are being treated effectively.

Another problem with treating sex offenders who have been civilly committed is the paradox presented by their treatment disclosures. In order to be rehabilitated, they must fully address their offending behavior, including CDs, fantasies, and (lack of) victim empathy. However, most are aware that genuine disclosures of their deviant acts and fantasies during treatment may reduce their chances of release. The result is that many sex offenders do not want to participate in treatment and are "involuntary clients" (Groth, 1983), and when they do participate, they do not do so honestly (Sampson, 1992). It is questionable whether individuals who are indirectly coerced into treatment can be effectively treated. Some studies (Hoge et al., 1993; Terry & Mitchell, 2001) showed that treatment may be effective even without motivation to participate, but the subject needs further research.

At most, two-thirds of the sex offenders who are civilly committed actually participate in treatment, and it is unclear whether cognitive-behavioral treatment is effective for those SVPs who do participate in a program. Numerous legal cases in 1994 sparked the modification of treatment procedures, though despite the improved efforts at treating SVPs they are not being "rehabilitated." By the year 2000, five offenders had been released in Washington—one decade after the introduction of the legislation—and most states at this time had not yet released any SVPs. More problematic is the rate at which they are being committed—approximately two per month in Washington—which results in an ever-increasing SVP population.

The strategic plan for modifying treatment (in Washington and elsewhere) is twofold: it aims to expand relapse prevention (the treatment component that teaches offenders about their high-risk situations and how to manage their behavior) and treatment in the community once released. The development of the LRA will assist in this goal, as the offenders can be treated in the facility, which is in the community, while still under the direction of the SCC. Finally, one of the most crucial plans for the facility is to retain qualified staff to work with the SVPs. There is a high attrition rate at all SVP facilities, which does not promote adequate treatment opportunities for the offenders. Few treatment professionals remain at these facilities for more than two years, yet some offenders have been incapacitated for 10 years. Treatment progress is hindered for offenders because the psychiatrists and counselors who are familiar with their specific cases are frequently replaced.

Release from Commitment

Those who are treated then face a fourth problem: release into a community that does not want them there. RCNL requirements stipulate that the community be notified when an offender is released in the area. In addition to the minimal number of offenders being rehabilitated, those who are rehabilitated have a difficult time adapting back into the community. The primary reason for this difficulty is the community notification statute, which requires that the neighborhood be notified when an offender is to move into the area. The SVPs must remain in the center until their safety is assured and living conditions are secured. Then, agencies must determine the best form of management and care of offenders in the community in order to reduce the likelihood of future offending.

MANAGEMENT AND SUPERVISION OF SEX OFFENDERS: WHAT WORKS

Though different in application, the philosophy behind the containment approach, registration and notification laws, SVP laws, and community supervision for life (CSL)—are the same: community protection and safety. As discussed in Chapter 9, the containment approach, in language and practice, requires the offenders to take responsibility for their actions. The second tenet of this approach stresses that sex offenders are responsible for their actions, and they must be held accountable for those actions. Without this main premise, the sex offender-specific containment would be ineffective. The SVP laws take a different approach to this philosophy; they medicalize the problems of the offenders and remove responsibility from them. The SVP, by definition, is dangerous as a result of a mental disorder or personality disorder that must be treated, and incapacitation results until the offender is rehabilitated.

It is the containment approach—not the SVP laws—that is most congruent with treatment objectives. The most common and effective component of cognitive-behavioral treatment programs is relapse prevention, which teaches the offender to recognize high-risk situations and manage his or her behavior so as to avoid relapse. It is this internal system of control that makes RP effective. However, RCNL can also be utilized with the containment approach, serving as an external form of supervision for the sex offender. In order for RCNL to be effective, however, they must not work against the cognitive-behavioral treatment objectives by stigmatizing the offender who already exhibits poor self-esteem and social skills. Though there is no empirical evidence as of yet to prove that this makes the offender's behavior deteriorate, it contradicts a core component of the treatment process that aims to improve the offender's social and relationship skills with agemates. Overall, the best policy for management and supervision of sex offenders is one that does not alleviate blame from the offenders, as do the SVP laws, and does not stigmatize the offenders, as do the RCNL, in their current applications. Offenders must take responsibility for their actions and combine internal and external forms of control in order to adequately manage their offending behavior, and this appears to best be achieved through the containment approach.

CHAPTER SUMMARY

- Sexually violent predator legislation is similar to the sexual psychopathy legislation enacted in the 1930s. Both allow for the indefinite civil commitment of sexual offenders into a secure facility instead of (psychopathy) or after (SVP) a criminal sentence, with the possibility of release once the person is no longer a danger as a result of a mental illness (psychopathy) or mental or personality disorder (SVP).

- SVP legislation follows a utilitarian principle: The protection of society from sex offenders who may reoffend is the most important goal. Civil commitment is based on the prediction of clinical experts that an individual is at risk to reoffend. The courts established a medical justification for commitment in *Foucha v. Louisiana* (1992) and supported this justification in *Kansas v. Hendricks* (1997). The accuracy of risk assessment is questionable, however, and there is likely to be a high rate of false positives (committing individuals who would not have reoffended).

- Civil commitment is expensive, at approximately three and a half times the cost of prison. In addition to cost, there are four concerns regarding civil commitment of sexually violent predators: pretext for commitment (it is ostensibly for treatment, though it is arguably retributive); facility (commitment facilities vary from prison wings to mental hospitals); treatment (not required and often not completed, treatment programs are often ineffective for SVPs); and release (there must be a release system, including a less restrictive facility prior to reentry into the community).

DISCUSSION QUESTIONS

1. What is the aim of sexually violent predator legislation? In its current state, does it fulfill this purpose?

2. How is sexually violent predator legislation similar to sexual psychopathy legislation? How does it differ?

3. What are the incapacitation facilities like? How do they differ in each state?

4. How did the case of *Kansas v. Hendricks* (1997) modify previous decisions guiding civil commitment of offenders?

5. At what point does a sex offender qualify to be released from civil commitment? Who makes the release decision? To what type of facility must offenders be released? What problems might the offender face upon release into the community?

NOTES

1. Arizona, California, Florida, Illinois, Iowa, Kansas, Massachusetts, Minnesota, Missouri, New Jersey, North Dakota, South Carolina, Texas, Virginia, Washington, and Wisconsin.

2. A petition may also be filed for juveniles who are about to be released, persons who were charged but found not competent to stand trial, and those found not guilty by reason of insanity. Most sex offenders who are committed are being referred from prison prior to the completion of their sentence. If the individual was living in the community at the time of referral, however, then he or she must commit an overt act in order to be referred for commitment.

3. The Static-99 is one of many assessment tools (too many to go into detail here) used to predict risk, and is considered (in Canada, the United States, and England) to be one of the most accurate actuarial prediction tools at this time (Hanson & Thornton, 1999). These tools, however, are constantly evolving in an attempt to predict risk more accurately.

4. Prior to this, however, the court ordered an injunction in June 1994 and told the SCC that it must reform its treatment in order to make it "constitutionally adequate" (*Turay v. Weston*, 2000). The SCC settled a suit in 1998 and paid $150,000 to the defendants and $250,000 for their legal fees. By November 1998, the court found that the standards were still unmet, and in May 1999 the court found that they made progress but had still failed. It was only in April 2000 that the court found significant improvement in the treatment provided to the SVPs.

5. This includes cost of confinement, treatment, and legal fees.

6. See exclusionary rules for treatment at Atascadero State Hospital in California in Marques, Nelson, West, and Day (1994).

PART III

The Future of Research on Sexual Offenses and Offenders

12

Sexual Offending: Future Directions of Research

There are a number of issues related to sexual offending that have not been discussed in this book, yet they are focal issues today. The public is often shocked when there is news about female sexual offenders, such as Beth Friedman, a 42-year-old middle school teacher from Broward County, Florida, who had a sexual relationship with one of her students. She is not alone; though the majority of sex offenders are adult males, almost 3 percent of known sex offenders are female. Additionally, some of these are considered high-risk offenders, and the community is notified about them. Though prior to the 1980s women were convicted mainly for assisting male sex offenders in their crimes, this profile is changing, and women are being convicted for a multitude of sex crimes. Only in the past few years have sex crime laws become gender neutral, though relatively few victims report abuse by females even to this date.

Perhaps less shocking but equally disturbing is the recent focus of sexual offending in the church. Though not a new phenomenon, it was only the case of John Geoghan that brought the extent of abuse by the clergy into the public forum.[1] Not only was it shocking to learn that he was accused of abusing more than 130 children throughout his career, but more so that church authorities knew he had a history of abusive behavior and did not remove him from his position of authority in the church. Since that time, there have been reports nearly daily about other abusive relationships within the church, and the pope has evaluated the situation in order to establish guidelines by which to deal with such abuses and curb them in the future.

Perhaps the most predominant issue today is that of distribution and possession of child pornography. With the globalization and anonymity provided by the Internet, the past five years have witnessed a proliferation of such material. It is estimated that only 1 in 5 individuals who possess such literature actually abuse children. However, the alarming aspect of this crime is the extent of the population involved (Long, McLaughlin, & McCaffrey, 2002). The police have discovered many individuals "who you would never expect to be involved in such a crime" (Long et al., 2002). There are numerous legal questions brought before the court, concerning issues such as what constitutes pornography and what investigative tactics can be used to find those in possession of such material. The law has been continually evolving over the past few years in this area, and will continue to do so in years to come.

FEMALE SEXUAL OFFENDERS

Female sexual offenders constitute a considerably underreported and underresearched proportion of the sex offender population (Righthand & Welch, 2001; Travin, Cullen, & Protter, 1990). There are several reasons why victims may not report sexual abuse by females. Many female-perpetrated offenses are incestuous, and incestuous acts of abuse are the least reported sexual offenses. Also, women are traditionally seen as caregivers, nonviolent nurturers who are either not willing or not capable of harming children. Many adult and adolescent males are also reluctant to report abuse because of the shame of being a victim. Alternatively, they may not view the actions against them as abuse (Elliot & Briere, 1994). Kasl (1990) states that underreporting is the result of a social taboo, and that the stigma caused by female sexual abuse must be abolished.

As a result of this underreporting, there is a dearth of information on why females sexually offend and what is the best way to treat and supervise them. The research that does exist is comprised of studies with small samples, many of which produce conflicting results. What we do know is that female sexual abuse is reported less than male sexual abuse (Travin et al., 1990), the age of onset is generally young (Ray & English, 1995), female sexual offenders usually have young victims (Fehrenbach & Monastersky, 1988), and their offending behavior is often linked to abusive backgrounds and/or psychological disorders (Bumby & Bumby, 1997).

Most studies on female sexual offenders have small sample sizes because there are so few females convicted and treated for sexual offenses. Because of the small sample sizes, most studies of female sex offenders are case studies (for example, see Hunter et al., 1995). As such, they produce valuable qualitative information about the female offenders, but this information is not necessarily generalizable to the larger female sex offender population.

Because of the underreporting of female sexual offending, the true level of offending is unclear. Females can commit any type of sexual offense, from sexual assault to rape. One common finding across most studies is that the age of onset for sexual offending in females tends to be young (Brown, Hull, & Panesis, 1984; Fehrenbach & Monstersky, 1988; Miccio-Fonesca, 1998; Ray & English, 1995). The percentage of sex offenders that is female increases as age decreases. Thus, whereas females make up approximately 3 percent of the adult sex offender population (Correctional Service of Canada, 1996), they make up approximately 10 percent of adolescent offenders (13–18 years of age) and nearly 20 percent of child offenders (12 years of age and under) (Ray & English, 1995).

The Correctional Service of Canada (1996) conducted one study that contradicts the finding that most female sexual offenders are young. Of the 19 female offenders they interviewed, they found that the average age of first offenses was 33 and the youngest age at which they began offending was 17. Some findings in this study did support other studies, however. For instance, most of the females had a low educational level (none had a college-level education); they had low IQs (bordering on mental retardation) (Lewis & Stanley, 2000); they were primarily of low socioeconomic status; and many had substance abuse problems. Half the sample claimed to have abused only one victim, but they averaged 2.44 victims per offender. The majority of the victims were female, children, and frequently the biological children of the female offender. This differs from studies on female adolescent offenders, which indicate that the most common victims are children whom the offender is babysitting (Fehrenbach & Monastersky, 1988).

Female offenders also tend to come from chaotic households, and Lewis and Stanley (2000) showed that female offenders have a high likelihood of past sexual and physical victimization and ongoing physical victimization. Some researchers found that all the female offenders in their study were abused (Hunter et al., 1995); others claim that almost all female adolescent and child sexual offenders were abused (Fehrenbach & Monastersky, 1988); and yet others found an abuse rate of approximately 75 percent (Jennings, 2000). Travin and colleagues (1990) found that not only are most female sexual offenders abused, but also they are abused quite severely—a fact that must play a role in their treatment. Adolescent females who abuse were often abused when they were young and by more than one offender (Righthand & Welch, 2001).

Though it is more common for them to be abused by males, adult females also sexually abused many girls who began offending as adolescents (Righthand & Welch, 2001). Adult female offenders also appear to be responsible for abusing a large number of males. Briggs (1995) found that adult women were responsible for abusing many young boys who later became adult child molesters. Women may commit many offenses against boys and men, including rape. Groth and Burgess (1980) showed that 19 percent of their sample of sexual offenders was female. Whether adult or child, male or female, female offenders almost always know their victims and have a previous relationship with them.

Though female sexual offenders differ in many ways from their male counterparts, they do have some similar characteristics (Matthews, Matthews,

Table 12.1 Female Typologies of Offenders

Typology	Description
Teacher/Lover	Initiate sexual abuse of adolescent males and seek loving relationships with them; have significant CDs of justification and minimization of harm; do not regard their actions as abuse.
Male Coerced/Male Accompanied	Influenced by male abusers to sexually offend; have low self-esteem; often abuse drugs and/or alcohol; are often in an abusive relationship with the male who coerces them to offend
Predisposed	Initiate the sexual abuse; most common victims are their own children; history of sexual and physical abuse; deviant and/or violent sexual fantasies; seeking power and control; may have serious psychological disorders

SOURCE: Matthews et al. (1989)

& Speltz, 1989). For instance, both have cognitive distortions (CDs). Just like males, female sex offenders tend to deny, minimize, and justify their abusive actions (Wolf, 1985). However, Matthews (1998) claimed that female offenders have fewer cognitive distortions and are more likely to be receptive to treatment and motivated to change their behavior. Female sex offenders may also have paraphilias, but far fewer than do male abusers. Female adolescent sex offenders have similar psychosexual disturbances to male adolescents, but the females were often abused more severely and for a longer period of time than the males.

Researchers have attempted to classify female sex offenders into typologies, though these typologies differ significantly from typologies of male offenders. Matthews et al. (1989) constructed three typologies of adult female sex offenders: teacher/lover, male coerced/male accompanied, and predisposed (see Table 12.1). The *teacher/lover* typology is composed of women who initiate sexual abuse of adolescent males. These females tend to have severe cognitive distortions, particularly in denial of the harm they cause to the victims. They are often seeking a loving relationship and, like fixated male child molesters, see their actions as loving and caring. They often do not regard their abuse of the victim as harmful, but rather see themselves in relationship with the children they are abusing.

The *male-coerced/male-accompanied* typology of female sexual offenders consists of females who are influenced by male abusers to sexually offend. These women tend to have low self-esteem, are often unassertive, have poor social and relationship skills, are dependent upon others, and often abuse substances. Their male partners who coerce them to offend are often abusive and violent, and there is likely a history of domestic violence among the partners. Many (approximately half of the adult female sexual offenders in most samples) are coerced into abusing by male partners. Nathan and Ward (2002) found that many of the females in the male-coerced typology were motivated by anger, rejection, and revenge. Though the male-coerced/male-accompanied typology is common among adult females, female adolescent offenders are rarely coerced into offending by male partners (Fehrenbach & Monastersky, 1988).

The *predisposed* female offender is the most dangerous and abusive classification of offender. These females initiate the sexual abuse, often against their own children or other family members. Nearly all of these offenders were abused as children, both physically and sexually. They are often angry and may have deviant sexual fantasies in terms of both sexual attraction and violence (for example, sadism). They are often seeking power and control, and are the most likely of the female offenders to have serious psychological disorders.

Because these typologies may not be all encompassing, the Correctional Services of Canada (1996) added two categories to this classification system: the angry-impulsive offender (who expresses anger and the need for power and control similarly to the predisposed offender, but has fewer psychosocial disorders) and male–accompanied familial and nonfamilial (to differentiate between incestuous and nonincestuous abusers, because nonincestuous abusers tend to be more serious in terms of number of victims and types of offenses).

This information can all be considered preliminary, because so little is known about the female sex offender population. It will be difficult to conduct more comprehensive studies on female sex offenders until the rates of reporting increase; until that time researchers must accept information that is largely qualitative, from small samples, and not generalizable.

SEXUAL ABUSE IN THE CHURCH

Though it is not a new phenomenon, the sexual abuse of women and children by clergy has emerged as a critical issue that needs to be analyzed from a legal, structural, and psychological perspective (Isley, 1997). Many factors make this topic difficult to assess, including the underreporting of offenses, the secretive nature of the abuse, and in many cases the lack of a formal response by the church (Flynn, 2000). Most of the studies that have been conducted relate to a single parish or treatment program for the offending priests. These studies are rarely generalizable because they have small sample sizes of either victims or offenders and are often based on anecdotal information or self-reports. Table 12.2 shows examples of some methodologies used in these studies.

Nature and Scope of Child Sexual Abuse in the Church

Though no studies yet provide a thorough accounting of the causes and context of child sexual abuse in the Catholic Church, one study does provide a thorough accounting of the numbers of abusive priests and their victims. This study, conducted by researchers at John Jay College of Criminal Justice, is based on reports from the universe of records for all priests and deacons in the United States from 1950 to 2002. This study was commissioned by the United States Conference of Catholic Bishops pursuant to the Charter for the Protection of Children and Young People, which was adopted by the bishops

Table 12.2 Some Published Studies on Sexual Abuse in the Church (since 1990)

Author(s), Year	Sample	Method
Andrews (1999)	Four congregations of clergy and parishioners	Self-reports
Flynn (2000)	25 sexually abused women	Self-reports
Goetz (1992)	374 ordained pastors to find out how many had affairs	Self-report surveys
Irons and Laaser (1994)	25 sexually abusive priests who are in treatment	Assessment scales to determine sexual and other addictions
McDevitt (1999)	Three groups of Roman Catholic priests to determine the extent of their own personal abuse	Self-reports
McLaughlin (1994)	Pilot study with adults and children to find out the difference in effects of abuse on their spirituality	Spirituality scale and self-reports
Mendola (1998)	277 Catholic priests and religious brothers referred for psychiatric evaluation	Retroactive study examining archival data
Pritt (1998)	115 Mormon women who reported sexual abuse	Questionnaire examining spirituality, concept of God, and optimism and pessimism
Rosetti (1995)	1,810 Catholics to determine the significance in victim trauma based on age and gender	Questionnaire
Rosetti (1997)	1,810 Catholics to determine the effect of abuse accusations on their faith in church and God	Questionnaire

at their annual meeting in June 2002. The aim of the study (John Jay, 2004) was to provide a descriptive analysis of the nature and scope of the problem of child sexual abuse in the Catholic Church. Specifically, the mandate was fourfold, requiring the researchers to

1. Examine the number of allegations and nature of alleged offenses of child sexual abuse by priests and deacons between 1950 and 2002 in the United States

2. Collect information about priests and deacons who had allegations of abuse, including their characteristics and the number and type of victims they abused

3. Collect information about the characteristics of the alleged victims, such as age, gender, and victim–perpetrator relationship, and the type of offenses

4. Collect information about the financial impact of the sexual abuse scandal on the church

This was a descriptive study, providing a better understanding of the number of offenders, victims, and money paid by the church. The main findings of the study were as follows:

Prevalence

- Victims made allegations against 4,392 priests, accounting for approximately 4 percent of priests who were active in ministry between 1950 and 2002.
- In this same time period, 10,667 victims made allegations of abuse against priests and deacons.
- Abuse cases peaked in the 1970s; however, because of the significant delay in reporting of abuse cases, it is fair to assume that more victims will come forward and report abuse in the future.
- The cases of abuse occurred across the United States consistently, with an average of 3–6 percent of priests per region having allegations of abuse made against them. It was also consistent by size of diocese, again ranging from 3 to 6 percent.

Costs

- At the time of the study, the church had paid out more than $572 million for victim compensation, treatment for the victim and priest, and attorney costs (though more recent reports indicate that this total is likely more than $700 million now).

Priests

- The majority of abusers were diocesan priests (69 percent), and most had the duties of pastor (25 percent) or associate pastor (42 percent) at the time of the abuse.
- The priests with allegations of abuse ranged in age from 18 to 90 at the time they committed their first act of abuse.
- The majority of priests (56 percent) had one victim, though 149 priests (3.5 percent of abusers) were responsible for abusing 2,960 victims (26 percent of the total).

Victims

- The majority of victims (81 percent) were male and between the ages of 11 and 14.
- Approximately 6 percent of the victims were under age 7. This is the only age group where there were more female than male victims.

Offenses

- Most priests committed more than one type of offense against an individual victim. Overall, they had allegations of more than 20 types of offenses.

- The most common offenses alleged against priests were touching under the victim's clothes (57 percent), touching over the victim's clothing (57 percent), victim disrobed (28 percent), cleric performing oral sex (27 percent), and penile penetration or attempted penile penetration (25 percent). However, few priests committed only the most minor acts such as touching over the victim's clothes.

The abuse most frequently occurred in the home of the priest.

Response to the Abuse

- Approximately 40 percent of priests with allegations of sexual abuse participated in some type of treatment program, the most common of which was a sex offender-specific treatment program.

- Victims reported approximately 14 percent of abuse allegations to the police, most of which were investigated. Thus, 3 percent of all priests against whom allegations were made were convicted and about 2 percent received prison sentences to date.

Causes of Child Sexual Abuse in the Church:
Current Hypotheses

Sexual abuse in the church has become particularly topical since 2002, largely as a result of the case of John Geoghan. A defrocked priest who was convicted of assault and was eventually murdered in prison, Geoghan was accused of abusing more than 100 children over a period of three decades. He was convicted in a criminal court on one count of indecent child assault, but has 84 civil suits pending. Though such abuse was not uncommon, this case was extreme for many reasons. First, it is rare for those who were abused to report the abuse, particularly as so many of Geoghan's victims did. Geoghan abused most of these victims decades ago, however, and they were willing to come forth to stop the possibility of future abuse of other children. Additionally, many cases are handled informally. Rather than charge a priest with criminal misconduct, the church often handles the cases informally, through treatment for the offender, economic restitution to the victim, or relocation of the priest to a different parish. Third, priests are rarely found guilty of sexual misconduct. Rather, the church may boast of treatment success and explain that the offender has repented his sins and been forgiven.

The most important issue that emerged from this case was the acknowledgment that abuse within the church is often hidden, and those at the highest level of the church hide it. Cardinal Bernard Law, the head of the Boston archdiocese while Geoghan was abusing children, knew about the abuse. Several individuals reported his misconduct, and the church's response was to remove

Geoghan temporarily and treat him. Unfortunately, like many of the "pedophile priests," he was then reinstated into a position of authority within the church, where he continued to abuse. It was this informal and inappropriate handling of the case that allowed the abuse to proliferate.

The questions regarding sexual abuse in the church are many. First, it is necessary to look at the clergy who are offending and ask who they are and why they are abusing. Second, it is important to look at victims to find out who is targeted for abuse and the effect this abuse has on the victims. Third, it is important to look at the organizational structure of the church to determine if and how it has facilitated such actions. Previous studies have primarily focused on the first two of these three issues, though at least one study has theorized about the role of celibacy and the patriarchal power structure of the church as potential causes of abuse (Sipe, 1995).

As with all sexual offenders, clergy offenders begin sexually abusing women or children for a variety of reasons. Those who abuse women may be naïve about their position in the church and their position of trust over the parishioners (Francis & Turner, 1995). At the other extreme, these offenders may have severe personality disorders or paraphilias that render them likely to sexually abuse. Those who abuse children may fit the typology of fixated or regressed offenders. They may be sexually attracted to children and clinically diagnosed as pedophiles. Alternatively, the abusive clergy may not be sexually attracted to children but regress to abusing children in their care for any number of reasons. Here control rather than prevention strategies are important; these include treatment, supervision, and removal of the offending clergy from positions of authority in the church.

Whether the offenders would be classified as fixated or regressed offenders, it is clear that they use their position of authority and trust over the children and incorporate this into their abusive behavior. Some have compared abuse in the church to abuse within the family because of its secretive nature and the reluctance of the victims to report the abuse (Flynn, 2000). Clergy have access to boys because of their proximity to them and their trusted position in these boys' lives (Isley, 1990), and they often use belief in God as an emotional grooming tactic or silencing strategy (Farrell & Taylor, 2000) in a way that abusive parents groom their children through emotional blackmail.

Some priests admit that they need help but are reluctant to seek out treatment because they believe it would jeopardize their position within the church (Goetz, 1992). Like all sex offenders, however, clergy should receive treatment, and one study of 25 abusive clergymen indicated that the offenders were assessed as having extensive treatment needs (Irons & Laaser, 1994). Their treatment programs should not only include the fundamental cognitive-behavioral treatment techniques, but should also include emphasis on the authoritative and spiritual role of the clergy (Farrell & Taylor, 2000; Kelly, 1998). Some suggest that treatment programs for clergy should resemble the 12-step process of substance abuse programs, which require the offenders to take responsibility for their actions and manage their own behavior (Valcour, 1990). Unfortunately, this 12-step process might not address all of the social, psychological, and cognitive issues that would be addressed in an extensive cognitive-behavioral treatment program.

Like the clergy who abuse them, victims of sexual abuse in the church constitute a unique group of individuals. They not only experience the same consequences as all sexual abuse victims (for example, posttraumatic stress disorder, depression), but many also experience additional problems in relation to their faith in God and the church. The abuse may have a psychological and spiritual impact, creating theological, spiritual, and existential conflict (Farrell & Taylor, 2000). Rosetti (1995) conducted a study to measure levels of spirituality and faith in God, and his results indicated that primary victims' faith in God might decline. Specifically, his study found that male victims' faith in God did not decline, but that of female victims of sexual abuse in the church did decline. When comparing the impact of sexual abuse on children versus adults, McLaughlin (1994) found that spirituality declines more for children abused by clergy than for adults abused by clergy. However, both adults and children abused by clergy attend church less frequently after the abuse occurs.

Secondary victims of sexually abusing clergy include not only the victims' families but also the abusive priest's congregation. Rosetti (1997) examined the attitudes of Catholics to determine whether their faith in God declined as a result of clergy abuse in their parish. He found that although their faith in God did not waiver, the parishioners' faith in the church and the priesthood did decline significantly (Rosetti, 1997). Andrews (1999) supported this assertion by stating that members of the congregation experience shock, grief, anger, and a feeling of being personally wounded by the experience.

Though the media has recently focused on the sexual abuse of children in the church, adults are also victims of sexual abuse. In fact, until the mid-1990s, known victims of sexual abuse in the church were almost exclusively adult women. Adult female victims who are abused may be seeking help from the church with problems, thereby presenting themselves as vulnerable (Francis & Turner, 1995). Because the church is reluctant to reprimand and blame the priest involved, the church (including officials and members of the congregation) tend to blame the victim for initiating such actions (Francis & Turner, 1995). One study looked at the effects of sexual abuse on Mormon women who were abused as children (Pritt, 1998). This study showed similar findings to those of Catholic victims; namely, treatment of the victims must address spiritual issues because the victims showed strongly negative measures regarding their spiritual well-being.

Adding to the psychological trauma of the victims is the lack of recognition of the problem by the church organization. Until the case of Geoghan emerged in the media, the church seemed to focus much more on protecting itself than the victims of abuse. This lack of institutional recognition of the problem allowed for sexually abusive behavior to proliferate, as cardinals and bishops in the hierarchy simply moved priests from one parish to another. Sipe (1999) cites denial of the problem by church authorities and those in the parish as key problems in the facilitation of sexual abuse. He points out that in order to decrease the abuse, church authorities must acknowledge and address the problem and institute a stricter degree of ethical standards for sexual behavior in the priesthood. Lane (1995), who explored the role of the church in the facilitation of abuse, claimed that the patriarchal ideology of the church socializes the clergy to be dominant and powerful, with little accountability. This lack of accountability allows the perpetrators of abuse to continue abusing, and the lack of action from the church further victimizes the victims (Lane, 1995; Smith, 1994). It is this lack of early formal intervention by the church authorities that seems to lead to crises in the church (Andrews, 1999; McDevitt, 1999).

Despite the informal nature of how the church handles many complaints, there are laws mandating reporting of child sexual abuse to the police. As a result, members of the church are required by law to report child sexual abuse. The victims of abuse can sue the church in order to rout the secretive nature of such abuse (Smith, 1994), which is what has happened since the beginning of the 21st century.

Among the key issues that need to be discussed is the mandate of celibacy by the clergy. Though it is impossible to prove that the priesthood dogma of celibacy leads to increased chances of sexual abuse, at least one author suggests that researchers must open up discussions on this topic (Sipe, 1995). He explains that it is this issue of celibacy, in addition to the patriarchal structure of church hierarchy, that should be examined in order to determine what factors lead to the etiology and facilitation of abuse in the organizational structure of the church.

For information on continuing work in the Church to address the problem of child sexual abuse, see websites for the United States Conference of Catholic Bishops (http://www.usccb.org), Voice of the Faithful (http://www.votf.org), Bishop Accountability (http://www.bishopaccountability.org/resources.html), and the Survivors Network for Those Sexually Abused by Priests (http://www.snapnetwork.org).

CHILD PORNOGRAPHY, THE INTERNET, AND CHILD PREDATORS

The dangers of child pornography and the Internet are threefold: children are being exploited for pornographic images, children are accessing pornographic images, and children are being solicited online to meet sexual predators. Child pornography is the depiction of sexually explicit behavior involving a minor under the age of 18 years. According to U.S. Code, Title 18 § 2256, this behavior includes actual or simulated: vaginal intercourse, oral or anal intercourse, bestiality, masturbation, sexually sadistic or masochistic behavior, and exhibition of the genitals. States have also included offenses such as penetration of the vagina or rectum digitally or with foreign objects, and excretory functions performed in a lewd manner. Images are also considered pornographic if the child is the focal point of a sexually suggestive setting; is in an unnatural pose or inappropriate attire; the depiction suggests coyness or willingness to engage in sexual activity; or the depiction is intended to elicit a sexual response in the viewer.

Several laws have been passed to protect children from pornographic exploitation. The Missing and Exploited Children website, quoting Medaris (1995), explains seven laws that help to safeguard children. The Sexual Exploitation of Children Act of 1977, among other things, prohibits the use, selling, and transportation of children for pornographic productions. The Child Protection Act of 1984 specified that a minor is a child under 18, and any sexually explicit material of minors is child pornography. In 1986, the Child Sexual Abuse and Pornography Act accomplished two tasks: it banned the advertisement of child pornography and increased penalties for recidivist child pornographic offenders. The Child Protection and Obscenity Enforcement Act of 1988 explicitly prohibited the possession, sale, and distribution of child pornography via the Internet. In 1990, Congress clarified this stipulation, making it illegal to possess three or more pornographic images of children. The Telecommunications Act of 1996 made it illegal for adults to send sexual images to or persuade children to engage in sexually explicit behavior through the Internet. In 1996, the Child Pornography Prevention Act made it illegal to possess or distribute any images that appear to sexually exploit minors. In 1998, Congress passed the Child Online Protection Act, which requires commercial pornographers to have users verify they are over 18 before entering an adult pornographic website.

Despite all the precautions taken by legislation to prohibit child pornography, the Internet is responsible for its significant increase in circulation. The primary reason for this increase, and the primary problem with policing it, is the anonymity of the Internet. There has been an explosion of pornography sites—consisting primarily of adult images—but this medium has also allowed for the escalating distribution of child images with little information about who supplies these images. The National Coalition for the Protection of Children and Families (NCPCF, 2002b) explains that there are now more than 300,000 pornographic websites on the Internet (that is approximately 60 percent of all websites), and in January 2002 alone, more than 27 million individuals visited these websites. NCPCF (2002a) summarizes statistics from several empirical studies regarding pornography and the Internet. Citing *Newsweek* magazine, it explains that the Federal Bureau of Investigation opened up approximately 700 cases relating to child pornography in 1998, and this number quadrupled to 2,856 in 2000. It also cites the National Center for Missing and Exploited Children website as stating that approximately 1 in 5 children who use the Internet received a sexual solicitation within the past year.

In an effort to skirt the legal consequences of possessing and distributing child pornography, some individuals have begun to create "virtual" children for their pornographic images. The issue of "virtual child pornography" has been one of both legal and ethical contention. This is where images appear to depict minors engaging in sexual activity, but the images are produced by some means other than the use of real children (such as computer-generated images of children or images of adults who look like children). Virtual, or fictitious, children are not protected by the Child Pornography Prevention Act of 1996, purportedly to protect the right of free speech. In the case of *Ashcroft v. Free Speech Coalition* (2002), the Court said that acts banning virtual child pornography are constitutionally vague and they violate the free speech clause of the First Amendment. The Court did recognize the dangers in allowing such material to be produced, but it also acknowledged that the virtual images are not fundamentally related to sexual abuse of children. Shortly after the Court announced its decision to protect virtual child pornography, several senators (led by John Ashcroft) began revising the law so that images that are "virtually indistinguishable" from minors engaging in sexual activity will not be protected. These revisions have yet to be tested by the courts.

It is difficult to track the possession, distribution, and circulation of child pornography because of the anonymity of the Internet. It is even unclear as to who should be investigating particular offenses, as "jurisdiction" generally refers to physical geography, and there is no geographical boundary for the World Wide Web. Some local agencies have the duty to investigate cyber-crime, though jurisdiction will usually fall on federal agencies. This is because much of the crime in cyberspace crosses state and even international boundaries, and therefore many of the crimes are cross-jurisdictional.

There is little physical evidence on the Internet like that available at a "true" crime scene, so investigators must target offenders through their "conversations" and electronic "fingerprints." Any computer, computer system, computer network, or any software or data owned by the suspect that is used during the commission of any public offense involving pornography (or any other cyber-crimes) or that is used as a repository for the storage of illegal software is subject to forfeiture. Unfortunately, there are few established boundaries as to how cyber-searches can legally take place and what type of searches would be considered constitutional under the Fourth Amendment.

In order to conduct searches of computers, officers can use wiretaps that are similar to those used on telephones. In order to obtain a wiretap order, it must either be issued where the interception occurs or it must be consensual. For consensual wiretaps, the party must consent, not the service provider. The service provider can monitor information in order to protect itself, however. Additionally, the provider can disclose information that it inadvertently came across if the information pertains to a crime. In terms of the Fourth Amendment, computers are equivalent to "containers"; the user does not have a special expectation of privacy, even though data can be erased (*Commonwealth of Pennsylvania v. Copenhefer,* 1991). As with a container, the officer must have probable cause to search the computer, which usually requires a warrant specifying exactly what is to be searched and what the officer is searching for. Once the officers look for material beyond the scope of their specified search, they violate the individual's Fourth Amendment rights. For instance, in the case of *United States v. Carey* (1999), the officers had a warrant to search the suspect's computer for drug-related information. Upon finding images of child pornography, the officers continued to search for further such images in the .jpeg files. The Court invalidated the search, claiming that the officers should have stopped the search and obtained a warrant once they found the pornographic images.

CONCLUSION

Our knowledge of sexual offenses and offenders is continually expanding. Empirical studies help to explain why people commit acts of abuse, how victims cope with the abuse, and how effective our treatment programs and legislation are at preventing recidivism. While treatment for offenders has progressed continually over the past 20 years, legislation for this population has come full circle. We have nearly the same laws today regarding sex offenders that we had in the 1930s, despite our increased knowledge about sexual offending.

Despite all our research, we cannot definitively say why people offend. We cannot definitively say that one type of treatment is superior to others. We cannot say that one system of management is sufficient for everyone. Sexual abuse has occurred for centuries, even millennia, and there is no legislation that can prevent it completely. We must utilize our knowledge, based on empirical research, to treat, manage, and supervise offenders as best we can so that we reduce the number of potential victims who will have to live with the scars of sexual abuse for the rest of their lives.

CHAPTER SUMMARY

- Though research has advanced our knowledge of adult male sex offenders significantly in the past few decades, our knowledge of female sex offenders continues to be limited.

- By the end of the 1990s, a new typology of child molester seemed to emerge: the "pedophile priest." Though a problem long before that, there seemed to be a sudden explosion of cases involving sexual abuse in the church, with thousands of alleged victims reporting abuse.

- Like with most types of crime, there are a small number of priests responsible for a large percentage of allegations of child sexual abuse. The John Jay Study showed that 149 priests were responsible for abusing more than 2,600 victims.

- Also like the general population of child sexual abusers, the priests with allegations of sexual abuse tended to have close relationships with the victims and their families (participating in "grooming" behavior).

- Globalization in the 1990s brought out a new problem: increased possession and distribution of child pornography on the Internet. Exacerbating this problem is the fact that offenders are difficult to track, and the law is constantly evolving to adapt to new forms of transmission and types of images.

DISCUSSION QUESTIONS

1. What are some of the similarities and differences between female and male sex offenders? How do you think that reporting of offenses may differ between victims of male and female offenders? Why?

2. What factors led to the child sexual abuse "crisis" in the Catholic Church? What should be done with perpetrators of child sexual abuse who are priests? How is this the same or different from actions taken against other perpetrators of child sexual abuse?

3. What kind of effect has the Internet had on child pornography? Other sexual offenses against children? Why?

4. What are the difficulties in implementing legislation related to Internet pornography?

NOTE

After his conviction and incarceration, Geoghan was killed by a fellow inmate in July 2003.

❖

Bibliography

PRINT AND ONLINE SOURCES

Abel, G. G., Becker, J. V., & Cunningham-Rathner, J. (1984). Complications, consent, and cognitions in sex between children and adults. *International Journal of Law and Psychiatry*. 7: 89–103.

Abel, G. G., Becker, J. V., Cunningham-Rathner, J., Mittelmen, M., & Rouleau, J. L. (1988). Multiple paraphiliac diagnoses among sex offenders. *Bulletin of the American Academy of Psychiatry and the Law*. 16: 153–168.

Abel, G. G., Becker, J. V., Mittelmen, M. S., Cunningham-Rathner, J., Rouleau, J. L., & Murphy, W. D. (1987). Self-reported sex crimes of nonincarcerated paraphiliacs. *Journal of Interpersonal Violence*. 2: 3–25.

Abel, G. G., Becker, J. V., & Skinner, L. (1980). Aggressive behavior and sex. *Psychiatric Clinics of North America*. 3: 133–151.

Abel, G. G., & Blanchard, E. B. (1974). The role of fantasy in the treatment of sexual deviation. *Archives of General Psychiatry*. 30: 467–475.

Abel, G. G., Blanchard, E. B., & Becker, J. V. (1978). An integrated treatment program for rapists. In R. T. Rada (ed.), *Clinical Aspects of the Rapist*. New York: Grune & Stratton.

Abel, G. G., Lawry, S. S., Karlstrom, E., Osborn, C. A., & Gillespie, C. F. (1994). Screening tests for pedophilia. *Criminal Justice and Behavior*. 21: 115–131.

Abel, G. G., Mittelmen, M. S., & Becker, J. V. (1985). Sexual offenders: Results of assessment and recommendations for treatment. In M. H. Ben-Avon, S. J. Hucker, & C. D. Webster (eds.), *Clinical Criminology: The Assessment and Treatment of Criminal Behavior*. Toronto: MandM Graphics.

Abel, G. G., Osborn, C. A., & Twigg, D. A. (1993). Sexual assault through the lifespan: Adult offenders with juvenile histories. In H. E. Barbaree, W. L. Marshall, & S. M. Hudson (eds.), *The Juvenile Sex Offender*. New York: Guilford.

Abel, G. G., & Rouleau, J. L. (1990). The nature and extent of sexual assault. In W. L. Marshall, D. R. Laws, & H. E. Barbaree (eds.), *Handbook of Sexual*

Assault: Issues, Theories and Treatment of the Offender. New York: Plenum.

Abel, G. G., & Rouleau, J. L. (1995). Sexual abuses. *Clinical Sexuality.* 18: 139–153.

Abel, G. G., Rouleau, J., & Cunningham-Rathner, J. (1986). Sexually aggressive behavior. In W. Curran, A. McGarry, & S. Shah (eds.), *Psychiatry and Psychology: Perspectives and Standards for Interdisciplinary Practice.* Philadelphia: FA Davis.

Ahlmeyer, S., Heil, P., McKee, B., & English, K. (2000). The impact of polygraph on admissions of victims and offenses in adult sexual offenders. *Sexual Abuse: A Journal of Research and Treatment.* 12: 123–138.

Akerstrom, M. (1986). Outcasts in prison: The cases of informers and sex offenders. *Deviant Behaviour.* 7: 1–12.

Alaska Department of Corrections Offender Programs. (1996, August). *Sex offender treatment program: Initial recidivism study. Executive summary.* Available at http://www.uaa.alaska.edu/just/reports/9602

Alexander, R. (1993). The civil commitment of sex offenders in light of Foucha v. Louisiana. *Criminal Justice and Behavior.* 20: 371–387.

Allard-Dansereau, C., Haley, N., Hamane, M., & Bernard-Bonnin, A. C. (1997). Pattern of child sexual abuse by young aggressors. *Child Abuse and Neglect.* 21: 965–974.

Allard-Dansereau, C., Hebert, M., Tremblay, C., & Bernard-Bonnin, A. C. (2001). Children's response to the medical visit for allegations of sexual abuse: Maternal perceptions and predicting variables. *Child Abuse Review.* 10: 210–222.

Allison, J. A., & Wrightsman, L. S. (1993). *Rape: The Misunderstood Crime.* Newbury Park, CA: Sage.

American Academy of Pediatrics, Committee on Child Abuse and Neglect. (1991). Guidelines for the evaluation of sexual abuse of children. *Pediatrics.* 87: 254–260.

American Civil Liberties Union. (1998). *Lifestyle Discrimination in the Workplace: Your Right to Privacy under Attack.* New York: ACLU.

American Psychiatric Association. (1994). *Diagnostic and Statistical Manual of Mental Disorders: DSM-IV* (4th ed.). Washington, DC: APA.

American Psychiatric Association. (1999). *Dangerous Sex Offenders: A Task Force Report of the American Psychiatric Association.* Washington, DC: APA.

Amir, M. (1971). *Patterns in Forcible Rape.* New York: Columbia University Press.

Andrews, D. A., Bonta, J., & Hoge, R. D. (1990). Classification for effective rehabilitation: Rediscovering psychology. *Criminal Justice and Behavior.* 17: 19–52.

Andrews, D. A., & Kiessling, J. J. (1980). Program structure and effective correctional practices: A summary of the CaVIC research. In R. R. Ross & P. Gendreau (eds.), *Effective Correctional Treatment.* Toronto: Butterworth.

Andrews, D. A., Zinger, I., Hoge, R. D., Bonta, J., Gendreau, P., & Cullen, F. T. (1990). Does correctional treatment work? A clinically relevant and psychologically informed meta-analysis. *Criminology.* 28: 369–397.

Andrews, D. J. (1999). *Healing in Congregations in the Aftermath of Sexual Abuse by a Pastor.* Dissertation from Hartford Seminary; available through University Microfilms International, Ann Arbor, MI.

Araji, S. (1997). *Sexually Aggressive Children: Coming to Understand Them.* Thousand Oaks, CA: Sage.

Arata, C. M. (1998). To tell or not to tell: Current functioning of child sexual abuse survivors who disclosed their victimization. *Child Maltreatment: Journal of the American Professional Society on the Abuse of Children.* 3: 63–71.

Awad, G. A., & Sanders, E. B. (1989). Adolescent child molesters: Clinical observations. *Child Psychiatry and Human Development.* 19: 195–206.

Awad, G. A., & Sanders, E. B. (1991). Male adolescent sexual assaulters: Clinical observations. *Journal of Interpersonal Violence.* 6: 446–460.

Bagley, C., Wood, M., & Young, L. (1994). Victim to abuser: Mental health and behavioral sequels of child sexual abuse in a community survey of young adult males. *Child Abuse and Neglect.* 18: 683–697.

Baker, T., Skolnik, L., Davis, R., & Brickman, E. (1991). The social support of survivors of rape: The difference between rape survivors and survivors of other violent crimes and between husbands, boyfriends, and women friends. In A. W. Burgess (ed.), *Rape and Sexual Assault III: A Research Handbook.* New York: Garland.

Baker, A. J. L., Tabacoff, R., Tornusciolo, G., & Eisenstadt, M. (2001). Calculating number of offenses and victims of juvenile sexual offending: The role of posttreatment disclosures. *Sexual Abuse: Journal of Research and Treatment.* 13: 79–90.

Bancroft, J. (1971). The application of psychophysiological measures to the assessment and modification of sexual behaviour. *Behaviour Research and Therapy.* 9: 119–130.

Bancroft, J. (1978). The relationship between hormones and sexual behavior in humans. In J. Hutchison (ed.), *The Biological Determinants of Sexual Behavior.* Chichester: Wiley.

Barbaree, H. E., Hudson, S. M., & Seto, M. C. (1993). Sexual assault in society: The role of the juvenile offender. In H. E. Barbaree, W. L. Marshall, & S. M. Hudson (eds.), *The Juvenile Sex Offender.* New York: Guilford.

Barbaree, H. E., Seto, M. C., & Peacock, (2001). Evaluating the predictive accuracy of six risk assessment instruments for adult sex offenders. *Criminal Justice and Behavior.* 28: 490–521.

Barbaree, H. E., Seto, M. C., Serin, R. C., Amos, N. L., & Preston, D. L. (1994). Comparisons between sexual and non-sexual rapist subtypes: Sexual arousal to rape, offense precursors and offense characteristics. *Criminal Justice and Behavior.* 21: 95–114.

Bartholomew, A. (1968). A long-acting phenothiazine as a possible agent to control deviant sexual behavior. *American Journal of Psychiatry.* 124: 917–923.

Bartholomew, K. (1990). Avoidance of intimacy: An attachment perspective. *Journal of Social and Personal Relationships.* 7: 147–178.

Bass, E., & Davis, L. (1988). *The Courage to Heal.* New York: Harper & Row.

Baxter, D. J., Marshall, W. L., Barbaree, H. E., Davidson, P. R., & Malcolm, P. B. (1984). Deviant sexual behavior: Differentiating sex offenders by criminal and personal history, psychometric measures, and sexual response. *Criminal Justice and Behavior.* 11: 477–501.

Becker, J. V. (1990). Treating adolescent sex offenders. *Professional Research Psychology and Practice.* 21: 362–365.

Becker, J. V. (1998). What we know about the characteristics and treatment of adolescents who have committed sexual offenses. *Child Maltreatment.* 3: 317–330.

Becker, J. V., Cunningham-Rathner, J., Kaplan, M. S. (1986). The adolescent sexual perpetrator: Demographics, criminal history victims, sexual behaviors and recommendations for reducing future offenses. *Journal of Interpersonal Violence.* 1: 421–445.

Becker, J. V., & Hunter, J. A. (1997). Understanding and treating child and adolescent sexual offenders. In T. H. Ollendick & R. J. Prinz (eds.), *Advances in Clinical Child Psychology.* New York: Plenum.

Becker, J. V., Hunter, J. A., Stein, R. M., & Kaplan, M. S. (1989). Factors associated with erection in adolescent sex offenders. *Journal of Psychopathology and Behavioral Assessment.* 2: 355–363.

Becker, J. V., Kaplan, M. S., Tenke, C. E., & Tartaglini, A. (1991). The incidence of depressive symptomatology in juvenile sex offenders with a history of abuse. *Child Abuse and Neglect.* 15: 531–536.

Becker, J. V., & Stein, R. M. (1991). Is sexual erotica associated with sexual deviance in adolescent males? *International Journal of Law and Psychiatry.* 14: 85–95.

Beneke, T. (1995). Jack and Ken. In P. S. Searles & R. J. Berger (eds.), *Rape and Society.* Boulder, CO: Westview.

Benoit, J. L., & Kennedy, W. A. (1992). The abuse history of male adolescent sex offenders. *Journal of Interpersonal Violence.* 7: 543–548.

Berger, R. J., Searles, P., & Neuman, W. L. (1995). Rape-law reform: Its nature, reform and impact. In P. S. Searles & R. J. Berger (eds.), *Rape and Society*. Boulder, CO: Westview.

Berlin, F. S. (1989). The paraphilias and Depo-Provera: Some medical, ethical and legal considerations. *Bulletin of the American Academy of Psychiatry and the Law*. 17: 233–239.

Berlin, F. S., & Meinecke, C. F. (1981). Treatment of sex offenders with antiandrogen medication: Conceptualization, review of treatment modalities, and preliminary findings. *American Journal of Psychiatry*. 74: 596–601.

Berliner, L., & Conte, J. R. (1995). The effects of disclosure and intervention on sexually abused children. *Child Abuse and Neglect*. 19: 371–384.

Berliner, L., Schram, D., Miller, L. L., & Milloy, C. D. (1995). A sentencing alternative: A study of decision making and recidivism. *Journal of Interpersonal Violence*. 10: 487–502.

Berson, N. L., Herman-Giddens, M. E., & Frothingham, T. E. (1993). Children's perceptions of genital examinations during sexual abuse evaluations. *Child Welfare*. 72: 41–49.

Blume, E. S. (1990). *Secret Survivors: Uncovering Incest and Its Aftereffects in Women*. New York: Ballantine.

Blumer, D., & Migeon, C. (1975). Hormone and hormonal agents in the treatment of aggression. *Journal of Nervous and Mental Disorders*. 160: 127–137.

Bolen, R., & Scannapieco, M. (1999). Prevalence of child sexual abuse: A corrective meta-analysis. *Social Service Review*. 73: 281–313.

Boney-McCoy, S., & Finkelhor, D. (1995). Psychosocial sequelae of violent victimization in a national youth sample. *Journal of Consulting and Clinical Psychology*. 63: 726–736.

Bowden, P. (1991). Treatment: Use, abuse and consent. *Criminal Behaviour and Mental Health*. 1: 130–141.

Bowers, L. (1996). *An Evaluation of the Effectiveness of the First Version of the Core Programme for Rapists*. Prepared for the SOTP Accreditation Panel, London.

Bradford, J. (1990). The antiandrogen and hormonal treatment of sex offenders. In W. L. Marshall, D. R. Laws, & H. E. Barbaree (eds.), *Handbook of Sexual Assault: Issues, Theories and Treatment of the Offender*. New York: Plenum.

Bradford, J., & MacLean, D. (1984). Sexual offenders, violence and testosterone: A chemical study. *Canadian Journal of Psychiatry*. 29: 335–343.

Bradley, A. R., & Wood, J. M. (1996). How do children tell? The disclosure process in child sexual abuse. *Child Abuse and Neglect*. 20: 881–891.

Brannon, J. M., & Troyer, R. (1995). Adolescent sex offenders: Investigating adult commitment-rates four years later. *International Journal of Offender Therapy and Comparative Criminology*. 39: 317–326.

Brehm, S. S., & Brehm, J. W. (1981). *Psychological Reactance: A Theory of Freedom and Control*. New York: Academic.

Breiner, S. J. (1990). *Slaughter of the Innocents: Child Abuse through the Ages and Today*. New York: Plenum.

Briggs, F. (1995). *From Victim to Offender: How Child Sexual Abuse Victims Become Offenders*. St Leonards, NSW, Australia: Allen & Unwin.

Brochman, S. (1991). Silent victims: Bringing male rape out of the closet. *The Advocate*. 582: 38–43.

Brody, S., & Tarling, R. (1980). *Taking Offenders Out of Circulation*. Home Office Research Study 64. London: HMSO.

Brown, M. E., Hull, L. A., & Panesis, L. K. (1984). *Women Who Rape*. Boston: Massachusetts Trial Court.

Brownmiller, S. (1975). *Against Our Will: Men, Women and Rape*. New York: Bantam.

Bumby, K. M., & Bumby, N. H. (1997). Adolescent female sexual offenders. In B. K. Schwartz & H. R. Celini (eds.), *The Sex Offender, Vol. II: New Insights, Treatment Innovations and Legal*

Developments. Kingston, NJ: Civic Research Institute.

Bumby, K. M., & Hanson, D. J. (1997). Intimacy deficits, fear of intimacy, and loneliness among sex offenders. *Criminal Justice and Behavior.* 24: 315–331.

Bund, J. M. (1997). Did you say chemical castration? *University of Pittsburgh Law Review.* 59: 157.

Bureau of Justice Statistics. (1998). *Child Victimizers: Violent Offenders and Their Victims.* Washington, DC: U.S. Department of Justice.

Bureau of Justice Statistics. (1999). *Felony Sentences in State Courts, 1996.* Washington, DC: U.S. Department of Justice.

Burgess, A. W. (Ed.). (1991). *Rape and Sexual Assault III: A Research Handbook.* New York: Garland.

Burgess, A. W. (1995). Rape trauma syndrome. In P. S. Searles & R. J. Berger (eds.), *Rape and Society.* Boulder, CO: Westview.

Burgess, A. W., Hartman, C., Ressler, R. K., Douglas, J. E., & MacCormack, A. (1986). Sexual homicide: A motivational model. *Journal of Interpersonal Violence.* 1: 251–272.

Burgess, A. W., & Holstrom, L. L. (1974). Rape trauma syndrome. *American Journal of Psychiatry.* 131: 981–986.

Burt, M. (1980). Cultural myths and supports for rape. *Journal of Personality and Social Psychology.* 38: 217–230.

Burton, D. L. (2000). Were adolescent sexual offenders children with sexual behavior problems? *Sexual Abuse: Journal of Research and Treatment.* 12: 37–48.

Burton, D. L., Miller, D. L., & Shill, C. T. (2002). A social learning theory comparison of the sexual victimization of adolescent sexual offenders and non-sexual offending male delinquents. *Child Abuse and Neglect.* 26: 893–907.

Cairns, K. (1999). *Surviving Paedophilia: Traumatic Stress after Organised and Network Child Sexual Abuse.* Staffordshire: Trentham.

Calder, M. C., Hanks, H., Epps, K. J., Print, B., Morrison, T., & Henniker, J. (2001). *Juveniles and Children Who Sexually Abuse: Frameworks for Assessment.* Dorset: Russell House.

Calhoun, K. S., & Atkeson, B. M. (1991). *Treatment of Rape Victims: Facilitating Psychosocial Adjustment.* Elmsford, NY: Pergamon.

Campis, L. B., Hebden-Curtis, J., & DeMaso, D. R. (1993). Developmental differences in detection and disclosure of sexual abuse. *Journal of the American Academy of Child and Adolescent Psychiatry.* 32: 920–924.

Canada. (1984). *Sexual Offenses against Children.* Ottawa: Canadian Government Publishing Centre.

Canestrini, K. (1999.) The method of risk assessment used for the New York State Sex Offender Registration Act. *National Conference on Sex Offender Registries.* Proceedings of a BJS/SEARCH conference.

Caputo, A. A., Frick, P. J., & Brodsky, S. L. (1999). Family violence and juvenile sex offending: The potential mediating role of psychopathic traits and negative attitudes toward women. *Criminal Justice and Behavior.* 26: 338–356.

Carpenter, D. R., Peed, S. F., & Eastman, B. (1995). Personality characteristics of adolescent offenders: A pilot study. *Sexual Abuse: A Journal of Research and Treatment.* 7: 195–203.

Center for Sex Offender Management. (2000, January). *Community Supervision of the Sex Offender: An Overview of Current and Promising Practices.* Available at http://www.csom.org/pubs/supervision2.html

Center for Sex Offender Management. (2000, October). *The Collaborative Approach to Sex Offender Management.* Available at http://www.csom.org/pubs/collaboration.html

Center for Sex Offender Management. (2002, January). *Time to Work: Managing the Employment of Sex Offenders under Community Supervision.* Washington, DC: U.S. Department of Justice, Office of Justice Programs.

Champion, D. J. (1994). *Measuring Offender Risk: A Criminal Justice Sourcebook.* Westport, CT: Greenwood.

Chaneles, S. (1976). Prisoners can be rehabilitated—Now. *Psychology Today.* 129–133.

Charles, G., & McDonald, M. (1996). Adolescent sex offenders. *Journal of Youth and Child Care.* 11: 15–25.

Child Maltreatment Report. (2001). Washington, DC: Children's Bureau, Administration on Children, Youth and Families.

Christiensen, K., Elers-Neilson, M., LeMaire, L., & Sturup, G. K. (1965). Recidivism among sexual offenders. *Scandinavian Studies in Criminology.* 1: 55–85.

Cipolat, U. (1996). *Rape before the International Criminal Tribunal for the Former Yugoslavia: The Tadic/ "F" Case.* LL.M. dissertation, Yale Law School.

Claiborne, R. (2002, January). *Protected Priest: Archdiocese Admits Priest Should Have Been Reported for Molesting Children.* Retrieved from http://abcnews.go. com/sections/wnt/DailyNews/ pedophile_priest020125.html

Clark, D. (1996). *Behavioural Changes Following Completion of the Core Programme.* Prepared for the SOTP Accreditation Panel, London.

Clarke, J. (1997). *HM Prison Service's Sex Offender Treatment Programme: An Overview.* Treating Sex Offenders in a Custodial Setting, HMP Brixton.

Clarke, N. K. (1993). Sex offenders: An overview. In N. K. Clarke & G. M. Stephenson (eds.), *Sexual Offenders: Context, Assessment and Treatment.* Division of Criminological and Legal Psychology Paper No. 19. London: Home Office.

Cohen, M. L., Garofolo, R., Boucher, R., & Seghorn, T. (1971). The psychology of rapists. *Seminars in Psychiatry.* 3: 307–327.

Connell, R. (1990). The state, gender, and sexual politics: Theory and appraisal. *Theory and Society.* 19: 507–544.

Conte, J. R. (1991). The nature of sexual offences against children. In C. R. Hollin & K. Howells (eds.), *Clinical Approaches to Sex Offenders and Their Victims.* West Sussex: Wiley.

Conte, J. R., Wolf, S., & Smith, T. (1989). What sexual offenders tell us about prevention strategies. *Child Abuse and Neglect.* 13: 293–301.

Cooper, C. L., Murphy, W. D., & Haynes, M. R. (1996). Characteristics of abused and non-abused adolescent sexual offenders. *Sexual Abuse: Journal of Research and Treatment.* 8: 105–119.

Correctional Service of Canada. (1996). *Case Studies of Female Sex Offenders.* Ottawa: Correctional Service of Canada.

Coyne, J., & Berry, A. (2000). *Rape as an Adaptation?* Retrieved September 27, 2003, from http://www.eurowrc.org/ 06.contributions/1.contrib_en/11. contrib.en.htm

Criminal Law Revision Committee. (1984). *Sexual Offences: Fifteenth Report.* London: HMSO.

Cuklanz, L. M. (1996). *Rape on Trial: How the Mass Media Construct Legal Reform and Social Change.* Philadelphia: University of Pennsylvania Press.

Cullen, F. T., & Gendreau, P. (1989). The effectiveness of correctional rehabilitation. In L. Goodstein & D. L. MacKenzie (eds.), *The American Prison: Issues in Research Policy.* New York: Plenum.

Cumming, G., & Buell, M. (1997). *Supervision of the Sex Offender.* Orwell, VT: Safer Society Press.

Danni, K. A., & Hampe, G. D. (2002). An analysis of predictors of child sex offender types using pre-sentence investigation reports. *International Journal of Offender Therapy and Comparative Criminology.* 44: 490–504.

Darke, J. L. (1990). Sexual aggression: Achieving power through humiliation. In W. L. Marshall, D. R. Laws, & H. E. Barbaree (eds.), *Handbook of Sexual Assault: Issues, Theories and Treatment of the Offender.* New York: Plenum.

Davis, G., & Leitenberg, H. (1987). Adolescent sex offenders. *Psychological Bulletin.* 101: 417–427.

Davis, M. H. (1983). Measuring individual differences in empathy: Evidence for a multidimensional approach. *Journal of Personality and Social Psychology.* 44: 113–125.

Devoe, E. R., & Coulborn-Faller, K. (1999). The characteristics of disclosure among children who may have been sexually abused. *Child Maltreatment: Journal of the American Professional Society on the Abuse of Children*. 4: 217–227.

Dickens, B. (1985). Prediction, professionalism, and public policy. In C. D. Webster, M. H. Ben-Aron, & S. J. Hucker (eds.), *Dangerousness: Probability and Prediction, Psychiatry and Public Policy*. New York: Cambridge University Press.

Dietz, P., Hazelwood, R., & Warren, J. (1990). The sexually sadistic criminal and his offenses. *Bulletin of the American Academy of Psychiatry and the Law*. 18: 163–178.

DiGiorgio-Miller, J. (1994). Clinical techniques in the treatment of juvenile sex offenders. *Journal of Offender Rehabilitation*. 21: 117–126.

DiGiorgio-Miller, J. (1998). Sibling incest: Treatment of the family and the offender. *Child Welfare League of America*. 78: 335–346.

Dorsett, K. (1998). Kansas v. Hendricks: Marking the beginning of a dangerous new era in civil commitment. *DePaul Law Review*. 48: 113–159.

Dover, K. J. (1978). *Greek Homosexuality*. Cambridge, MA: Harvard University Press.

Dunn, C. (1940). Stiloestral induced gynacomastatia in the male. *Journal of the American Medical Association*. 115: 2263–2264.

Eby, K. K., Campbell, J. C., Sullivan, C. M., & Davidson, W. S. (1995). Health effects of experiences of sexual violence for women with abusive partners. *Health Care for Women International*. 16: 563–576.

Ehrenkranz, J., Bliss, E., & Sheard, M. (1974). Plasma testosterone: Correlation with aggressive behavior and social dominance in man. *Psychosomatic Medicine*. 36: 469–475.

Elliot, D., & Briere, J. (1994). Forensic sexual abuse evaluations of older children: Disclosures and symptomology. *Behavioral Sciences and the Law*. 12: 261–277.

Elliot, M., Browne, K., & Kilcoyne, J. (1995). Child sexual abuse prevention: What offenders tell us. *Child Abuse and Neglect*. 19: 579–594.

Ellis, E. M., Atkeson, B. M., & Calhoun, K. S. (1981). Sexual dysfunction in victims of rape. *Women and Health*. 5: 39–47.

Ellis, H. (1899/1942). *Studies in the Psychology of Sex* (2 vols.). New York: Random House.

Ellis, L. (1989). *Theories of Rape: Inquiries into the Causes of Sexual Aggression*. New York: Hemisphere.

English, K., Pullen, S., & Jones, L. (1997). *Managing Adult Sex Offenders in the Community: A Containment Approach*. NIJ Research in Brief. Washington, DC: Department of Justice, National Institute of Justice.

Epps, K. (1993). A survey of experience, training, and working practices among staff working with adolescent sex offenders in secure units. In N. K. Clarke & G. M. Stephenson (eds.), *Sexual Offenders: Context, Assessment and Treatment*. Division of Criminological and Legal Psychology Paper No. 19. London: Home Office.

Epps, K. J. (1999). Causal explanations: Filling the theoretical reservoir. In M. C. Calder (ed.), *Working with Young People Who Sexually Abuse: New Pieces of the Jigsaw Puzzle*. Dorset: Russell House.

Erooga, M., & Masson, H. C. (Eds.). (1999). *Children and Young People Who Sexually Abuse Others: Challenges and Responses*. London: Routledge.

Estrich, S. (1987). *Real Rape*. Cambridge, MA: Harvard University Press.

Evans, D. R. (1968). Masturbatory fantasy and sexual deviation. *Behaviour Research and Therapy*. 6: 17–19.

Ewing, C. (1985). Preventive detention and execution: The constitutionality of punishing future crimes. *Law and Human Behavior*. 15: 139–163.

Fagan, J., & Wexler, S. (1988). Explanations of sexual abuse assault among violent delinquents. *Journal of Adolescent Research*. 3: 363–385.

Farrell, D. P., & Taylor, M. (2000). Silenced by God: An examination of unique characteristics within sexual abuse by the clergy. *Counselling Psychology Review.* 15: 22–31.

Farrell, G. (1995). Preventing repeat victimization. In M. Tonry & D. P. Farrington (eds.), *Crime and Justice: A Review of Research. Vol. 19: Building a Safer Society: Strategic Approaches to Crime Prevention.* Chicago: University of Chicago Press.

Federal Bureau of Investigation. (2000). *Crime in the United States, 2002.* Washington, DC: U.S. Department of Justice.

Federal Bureau of Investigation. (2003). *Crime in the United States, 2002.* Washington, DC: U.S. Department of Justice.

Fehrenbach, P. A., & Monastersky, C. (1988). Characteristics of female adolescent sexual offenders. *American Journal of Orthopsychiatry.* 58: 148–151.

Fehrenbach, P. A., Smith, W., Monastersky, C., & Deisher, R. W. (1986). Adolescent sex offenders: Offender and offense characteristics. *American Journal of Orthopsychiatry.* 56: 225–233.

Fenichel, O. (1945). *The Psychoanalytic Theory of Neurosis.* New York: Norton.

Ferrara, M. L., & McDonald, S. (1996). *Treatment of the Juvenile Sex Offender: Neurological and Psychiatric Impairments.* Northvale, NJ: Jason Aronson.

Finkelhor, D. (1980). Sex among siblings: A survey report on its prevalence, its variety, and its effect. *Archives of Sexual Behavior.* 9: 171–194.

Finkelhor, D. (1984). *Child Sexual Abuse: New Theory and Research.* New York: Free Press.

Finkelhor, D. (1986). *A Sourcebook of Child Sexual Abuse.* London: Sage.

Finkelhor, D., Hotaling, G., Lewis, I. A., & Smith, C. (1990). Sexual abuse in a national survey of adult men and women: Prevalence, characteristics, and risk factors. *Child Abuse and Neglect.* 14: 19–28.

Finkelhor, D., & Jones, L. M. (2004). *Sexual Abuse Decline in the 1990s: Evidence for Possible Causes.* Washington, DC: U.S. Department of Justice, Office of Juvenile Justice Programs.

Finkelhor, D., & Ormrod, R. (2001, September). *Crimes Against Children by Babysitters.* Washington, DC: Juvenile Justice Bulletin.

Floud, J., & Young, W. (1981). *Dangerousness and Criminal Justice.* S. L. Radzinowicz, series ed. Cambridge Studies in Criminology. London: Heinemann.

Flynn, K. A. (2000). *Clergy Sexual Abuse of Women: A Specialized Form of Trauma.* Dissertation from Claremont Graduate University; available from University Microfilms International, Ann Arbor, MI.

Foote, R. (1944). Hormone treatment of sex offenders. *Journal of Nervous and Mental Diseases.* 99: 928–929.

Ford, M. E., & Linney, J. A. (1995). Comparative analysis of juvenile sexual offenders, violent nonsexual offenders, and status offenders. *Journal of Interpersonal Violence.* 10: 56–71.

Francis, P. C., & Turner, N. R. (1995). Sexual misconduct within the Christian Church: Who are the perpetrators and those they victimize? *Counseling and Values.* 39: 218–227.

Frank, et al. (1985). Induced abortion operations and their early sequelae. *Journal of the Royal College of General Practitioners.* 35: 175–180.

Fredrickson, R. (1992). *Repressed Memories: A Journal to Recovery from Sexual Abuse.* New York: Simon & Schuster.

Freeman-Longo, R. E. (1996). Feel good legislation: Prevention or calamity. *Child Abuse and Neglect.* 20: 95–101.

Freeman-Longo, R., & McFadin, B. (1981). Sexually inappropriate behavior: Development of the sexual offender. *Law and Order.* 29: 21–23.

Freud, S. (1905). My views on the part played by sexuality in the aetiology of the neuroses. In S. Freud (1959), *Collected Papers, Vol. II.* New York: Basic Books.

Freud, S. (1907). Sexual enlightenment of children. In S. Freud (1959), *Collected Papers, Vol. II.* New York: Basic Books.

Freud, S. (1905/1953). *Three essays of the theory of sexuality. The Complete Psychological Works of Sigmund Freud* (Standard ed., vol. 7). London: Hogarth.

Freud, S. (1959). *Collected Papers, Vol. II.* New York: Basic Books.

Freund, K. (1963). A laboratory method of diagnosing predominance of homo- and heteroerotic interest in the male. *Behavior Research and Therapy.* 1: 85–93.

Freund, K. (1990). Courtship disorder. In W. L. Marshall, D. R. Laws, & H. E. Barbaree (eds.), *Handbook of Sexual Assault: Issues, Theories and Treatment of the Offender.* New York: Plenum.

Freund, K., & Kuban, M. (1994). The basis of the abused abuser theory of pedophilia: A further elaboration on an earlier study. *Archives of Sexual Behavior.* 23: 553–563.

Freund, K., McKnight, C. K., Langevin, R., & Cibiri, S. (1972). The female child as a surrogate object. *Archives of Sexual Behavior.* 2: 119–133.

Frick, P. J. (1998). *Conduct Disorders and Severe Antisocial Behaviour.* New York: Plenum.

Frohmann, L. (1995). Discrediting victims' allegations of sexual assault: Prosecutorial accounts of case rejections. In P. S. Searles & R. J. Berger (eds.), *Rape and Society.* Boulder, CO: Westview.

Furby, L., Weinrott, M., & Blackshaw, L. (1989). Sex offenders recidivism: A review. *Psychological Bulletin.* 105: 3–30.

Gabor, T. (1990). Looking back or moving forward: Retributivism and the Canadian Sentencing Commission's proposals. *Canadian Journal of Criminology.* 32: 537–546.

Ganzar, V. J., & Sarason, I. G. (1973). Variables associated with recidivism among juvenile delinquents. *Journal of Consulting and Clinical Psychology.* 40: 1–5.

Garland, R., & Dougher, M. (1990). The abused/abuser hypothesis of child abuse: A critical review of theory and research. In J. R. Feierman (ed.), *Pedophilia: Biosocial Dimensions.* New York: Springer-Verlag.

Garland, R., & Dougher, M. J. (1991). Motivational intervention in the treatment of sex offenders. In W. R. Miller & S. Rollnick (eds.), *Motivational Interviewing: Preparing People to Change Addictive Behaviour.* New York: Guilford.

Geberth, V. J. (1996). *Practical Homicide Investigation: Tactics, Procedures, and Forensic Techniques.* Boca Raton, FL: CRC.

Gebhard, P., Gagnon, J., Pomeroy, W. (1965). *Sex Offenders: An Analysis of Types.* London: Heinemann.

Gendreau, P., Goggin, C., & Paparozzi, M. (1996). Principles of effective assessment for community corrections. In R. P. Corbett & M. K. Harris (eds.), A review of research for practitioners. *Federal Probation* 60: 64–70.

Gendreau, P., & Ross, R. R. (1979). Effective correctional treatment: Bibliotherapy for cynics. *Crime and Delinquency.* 25: 463–489.

Gendreau, P., & Ross, R. R. (1987). Revivification of rehabilitation: Evidence from the 1980s. *Justice Quarterly.* 4: 349–408.

Glaser, D. (1969). *The Effectiveness of a Prison and Parole System.* Indianapolis: Bobbs-Merrill.

Glaser, D. (1974). Remedies for the key deficiency in criminal justice evaluation research. *Journal of Research in Crime and Delinquency.* 11: 144–154.

Gleuck, S., & Gleuck, E. T. (1950). *Unravelling Juvenile Delinquency.* Cambridge, MA: Harvard University Press.

Goetz, D. (1992). Is the pastor's family safe at home? *Leadership.* 13, 38–44.

Golding, J. M. (1996). Sexual assault history and women's reproductive and sexual health. *Psychology of Women Quarterly.* 20: 101–121.

Good, O. S. (2001, July 24). Public hears pitch for group home: Advocate says facility for young sex offenders would be safest in state. *Rocky Mountain News.* 20A.

Gottfredson, M. R., & Hindelang, M. J. (1977). A consideration of telescoping and memory decay biases in victimization surveys. *Journal of Criminal Justice.* 5: 205–216.

Grace, S., Lloyd, C., & Smith, L. J. F. (1992). *Rape: From Recording to*

Conviction. Home Office, Research and Planning Unit Paper No. 71. London: HMSO.

Grant, C., & McDonald, M. (1996). Adolescent sexual offenders. *Journal of Child and Youth Care.* 11: 15–25.

Grant, H., & Terry, K. J. (2001). *Report on the Management and Care of Sex Offenders in New York City.* Presentation to the Sex Offender Management Team.

Grant, H., & Terry, K. J. (2005). *Law Enforcement in the 21st Century.* Boston: Allyn & Bacon.

Graves, R. B., Openshaw, D. K., Ascione, F. R., & Ericksen, S. L. (1996). Demographic and parental characteristics of youthful sexual offenders. *International Journal of Offender Therapy and Compara-tive Criminology.* 40: 300–317.

Gray, A. S., & Pithers, W. D. (1993). Relapse preventions with sexually aggressive adolescents and children: Expanding treatment and supervision. In H. E. Barbaree, W. L. Marshall, & S. M. Hudson (eds.), *The Juvenile Sex Offender.* New York: Guilford.

Gray, S. H. (1982). Exposure to pornography and aggression towards women: The case of the angry male. *Social Problems.* 29: 387–398.

Green, R. (1994). Recovered memories of sexual abuse: The unconscious strikes back or therapist induced madness? *Annual Review of Sex Research.* Mt. Vernon, IA: Society for the Scientific Study of Sex.

Greenfeld, L. A. (1997). *Sex Offenses and Offenders: An Analysis of Data on Rape and Sexual Assault.* Washington, DC: U.S. Department of Justice, Bureau of Justice Statistics.

Greenland, C. (1984). Dangerous sex offender registration in Canada, 1948–1977: An experiment that failed. *Canadian Journal of Criminology.* 26: 1–12.

Greer, J. G., & Stuart, I. R. (Eds.). (1983). *The Sexual Aggressor: Current Perspectives on Treatment.* New York: Van Nostrand Reinhold.

Gries, L. T., Goh, D. S., & Cavanaugh, J. (1996). Factors associated with disclosure during child sexual abuse assess-

ment. *Journal of Child Sexual Abuse.* 5: 1–20.

Griffin, S. (1979). *Rape: The Power of Consciousness.* New York: Plenum.

Grisso, T., & Appelbaum, P. S. (1992). Is it unethical to offer predictions of future violence? *Law and Human Behavior.* 16: 621–633.

Grisso, T., & Appelbaum, P. S. (1993). Structuring the debate about ethical predictions of future violence. *Law and Human Behavior.* 17: 482–485.

Groth, A. N. (1979). *Men Who Rape: The Psychology of the Offender.* New York: Plenum.

Groth, A. N. (1983). Treatment of the sexual offender in a correctional institution. In J. G. Greer & I. R. Stuart (eds.), *The Sexual Aggressor: Current Perspectives on Treatment.* New York: Van Nostrand Reinhold.

Groth, A. N., & Burgess, A. W. (1977). Motivational intent in the sexual assault on children. *Criminal Justice and Behavior.* 4: 253–264.

Groth, A. N., & Burgess, A. (1980). Male rape: Offenders and victims. *American Journal of Psychiatry.* 137: 806–810.

Groth, A. N., Hobson, W. F., & Gary, T. S. (1982). The child molester: Clinical observations. In J. Conte & D. A. Shore (eds.), *Social Work and Child Sexual Abuse.* New York: Haworth.

Groth, A. N., Longo, R. E., & McFadin, J. D. (1982). Undetected recidivism among rapists and child molesters. *Crime and Delinquency.* 28: 102–106.

Groth, A. N., & Loredo, C. M. (1981). Juvenile sex offenders: Guidelines for assessment. *International Journal of Offender Therapy and Comparative Criminology.* 25: 31–39.

Grubin, D., & Gunn, J. (1990). *The Imprisoned Rapist and Rape.* London: Home Office.

Grubin, D., & Prentky, R. (1993). Sexual psychopathy laws. *Criminal Behaviour and Mental Health.* 3: 381–392.

Grubin, D., & Thornton, D. (1994). A national program for the assessment and treatment of sex offenders in the

English prison system. *Criminal Justice and Behavior.* 21: 55–71.

Grubin, D., & Wingate, S. (1996). Sexual offence recidivism: Prediction versus understanding. *Criminal Behaviour and Mental Health.* 6: 349–359.

Gurley, G. (March, 2001). Pleasures to the fur. *Vanity Fair.* 174–196.

Gutheil, T. G. (2000). Preventing critogenic harms: Minimizing emotional injury from civil litigation. *Journal of Psychiatry and the Law.* 28: 5–18.

Guy, E. (1992). The prison service's strategy. In Prison Reform Trust (ed.), *Beyond Containment: The Penal Response to Sex Offending.* London: Prison Reform Trust.

Hagan, M. P., Gust-Brey, K. L., Cho, M. E., & Dow, E. (2001). Eight year comparative analyses of adolescent rapists, adolescent child molesters, other adolescent delinquents, and the general population. *International Journal of Offender Therapy and Comparative Criminology.* 45: 314–324.

Hagan, M. P., King, R. P., & Patros, R. L. (1994). The efficacy of a serious sex offenders treatment program for adolescent rapists. *International Journal of Offender Therapy and Comparative Criminology.* 38: 141–150.

Hallack, S. L., & White, A. D. (1977). Is rehabilitation dead? *Crime and Delinquency.* 23: 372–382.

Hammer, E. F. (1957). A psychoanalytic hypothesis concerning sex offenders. *Journal of Clinical and Experimental Psychology.* 18: 341–360.

Hanley, R. (2000, March 17). Psychologists fired after disputed release of rapist. *New York Times.* B:1.

Hanley, R. (2000, March 23). Freed rapist traveled openly by bus across east and south during nationwide manhunt. *New York Times.* B:5.

Hanson, R. F., Saunders, H. S., Saunders, B. E., Kilpatrick, D. G., & Best, C. (1999). Factors related to the reporting of childhood rape. *Child Abuse and Neglect.* 23: 559–569.

Hanson, R. K., & Bussiere, M. T. (1996). *Sex Offender Risk Predictors: A Summary of Research Results.* Available at http://www.csc-scc.gc.ca/crd/forum/e082/e

Hanson, R. K., & Bussiere, M. T. (1998). Predicting relapse: A recta-analysis of sexual offender recidivism studies. *Journal of Consulting and Clinical Psychology.* 66: 348–362.

Hanson, R. K., Gizzarelli, R., & Scott, H. (1994). The attitudes of incest offenders: Sexual entitlement and acceptance of sex with children. *Criminal Justice and Behavior.* 21: 187–202.

Hanson, R. K, & Harris, A. (1998). *Dynamic Predictors of Sexual Recidivism.* Ottawa: Office of the Solicitor General of Canada.

Hanson, R. K., & Thornton, D. M. (1999). *STATIC 99: Improving Actuarial Risk Assessments for Sex Offenders.* Ottawa: Public Works and Government Services.

Hare, R. D., & Jutai, J. W. (1983). Criminal history of the male psychopath: Some preliminary data. In K. T. Van Dusen & S. A. Mednick (eds.), *Prospective Studies of Crime and Delinquency.* Boston: Kluwer-Nijhoff.

Hare, R. D., & MacPherson, L. M. (1984). Violent and aggressive behavior by criminal psychopaths. *International Journal of Law and Psychiatry.* 7: 35–50.

Harlow, C. W. (1999). *Prior Abuse Reported by Inmates and Probationers* (NCJ 172879). Washington, DC: U.S. Department of Justice.

Harris, J., & Grace, S. (1999). *A Question of Evidence? Investigating and Prosecuting Rape in the 1990s.* Home Office Research Study 196. London: Home Office.

Harris, V. (2000). The antecedents of young male sex offenders. In G. Boswell (ed.), *Violent Children and Adolescents: Asking the Question Why* (pp. 138–150). London: Routledge.

Hart, T. C., & Rennison, C. (2003). *Reporting Crime to the Police, 1992–2000.* Washington, DC: U.S. Department of Justice, Bureau of Justice Statistics.

Hartley, C. C. (1998). How incest offenders overcome internal inhibitions through the use of cognitions and cognitive distortions. *Journal of Interpersonal Violence.* 13: 25–39.

Hastings, T., Anderson, S. J., & Hemphill, P. (1997). Comparisons of daily stress, coping, problem behavior, and cognitive distortions in adolescent sexual offenders and conduct-disordered youth. *Sexual Abuse: A Journal of Research and Treatment.* 9: 29–42.

Hayashino, D. S., Wurtele, S. K., & Klebe, K. J. (1995). Child molesters: An examination of cognitive factors. *Journal of Interpersonal Violence.* 10: 106–116.

Haywood, T. W., Grossman, L. S., & Kravitz, H. M. (1994). Profiling psychological distortions in alleged child molesters. *Psychological Reports.* 75: 915–927.

Hays, S. E. (1981). The psychoendocrinology of puberty and adolescent aggression. In D. A. Hamburg & M. B. Trudeau (eds.), *Biobehavioral Aspects of Aggression.* New York: A. R. Liss.

Hazelwood, R. (1983, September). The behavior-oriented interview of rape victims: The key to profiling. *FBI Law Enforcement Bulletin.*

Hazelwood, R. R., Dietz, P. E., & Burgess, A. W. (1983). *Autoerotic Fatalities.* Lexington, MA: Lexington Books.

Heim, N. (1981). Sexual behavior of castrated sex offenders. *Archives of Sexual Behavior.* 10: 11–20.

Hemphill, J. F., Hare, R. D., & Wong, S. (1998). Psychopathy and recidivism: A review. *Legal and Criminological Psychology.* 3: 139–170.

Herman, J. L. (1990). Sex offenders: A feminist perspective. In W. L. Marshall, D. R. Laws, & H. E. Barbaree (eds.), *Handbook of Sexual Assault: Issues, Theories and Treatment of the Offender.* New York: Plenum.

Heyman, B. (1997). *Risk, Health and Healthcare: A Qualitative Approach.* London: Edward Arnold.

Hicks, R. D. (1991). *In Pursuit of Satan.* New York: Prometheus.

Hillbrand, M., & Waite, B. M. (1994). The everyday experience of an institutionalised sex offender: An idiographic

application of the experience sampling method. *Archives of Sexual Behavior.* 23: 453–463.

Hilliker, D. R. (1997). *The Relationship between Childhood Sexual Abuse and Juvenile Sexual Offending: Victim to Victimizer.* Dissertation from Ohio State University; available through University Microfilms International, Ann Arbor, MI.

Hogue, T. E. (1995). Training multidisciplinary teams to work with sex offenders: Effect on staff attitudes. *Psychology, Crime and Law.* 1: 227–235.

Hollin, C. R., & Howells, K. (1991). *Clinical Approaches to Sex Offenders and Their Victims.* West Sussex: Wiley.

Holmes, R. M. (1991). *Sex Crimes.* Newbury Park, CA: Sage.

Holmes, R. M., & Holmes, S. T. (2002). *Sex Crimes: Patterns and Behavior.* Newbury Park, CA: Sage.

Homes, M. M., Resnick, H. S., Kilpatrick, D. G., & Best, C. L. (1992). Rape-related pregnancy: Estimates and descriptive characteristics from a national sample of women. *American Journal of Obstetrics and Gynecology.* 175: 320–324.

Hood, R., & Shute, S. (1996). Protecting the public: Life sentences, parole, and high risk offenders. *Criminal Law Review.* 788–800.

Houston, J., Wrench, M., & Hosking, N. (1995). Group processes in the treatment of child sex offenders. *Journal of Forensic Psychiatry.* 6: 359–368.

Howard League Working Party. (1985). *Unlawful Sex.* London: Waterlow.

Howells, K. (1981). Adult sexual interest in children: Consideration relevant to theories of aetiology. In M. Cook & K. Howells (eds.), *Adult Sexual Interest in Children.* London: Academic.

Hucker, S. J., & Bain, J. (1990). Androgenic hormones and sexual assault. In W. L. Marshall, D. R. Laws, & H. E. Barbaree (eds.), *Handbook of Sexual Assault: Issues, Theories and Treatment of the Offender.* New York: Plenum.

Hunter, J. A., Jr., & Becker, J. V. (1994). The role of deviant sexual arousal in juvenile offending: Etiology, evaluation and treatment. *Criminal Justice and Behavior.* 21: 132–149.

Irons, R., & Laaser, M. (1994). The abduction of fidelity: Sexual exploitation by clergy—Experience with inpatient assessment. *Sexual Addiction and Recovery.* 1: 119–129.

Isley, P. (1997, March). Child sexual abuse and the Catholic Church: An historical and contemporary review. *Pastoral Psychology.* 45, 227–299.

Isley, P. J. (1991). Adult male sexual assault in the community: A literature review and group treatment model. In A. W. Burgess (ed.), *Rape and Sexual Assault III: A Research Handbook.* New York: Garland.

Isley, P. J., & Isley, P. (1990, November). The sexual abuse of male children by church personnel: Intervention and prevention. *Pastoral Psychology.* 39: 85–99.

Jacobs, W. L. (1999). *The Utilization of Offense Characteristics in the Classification of Male Adolescent Sexual Offenders.* Dissertation from Florida State University; available through University Microfilms International, Ann Arbor, MI.

Jacobs, W. L., Kennedy, W. A., & Meyer, J. B. (1997). Juvenile delinquents: A between-group comparison study of sexual and nonsexual offenders. *Sexual Abuse: A Journal of Research and Treatment.* 9: 201–217.

Janus, E. S. (1997). The use of social science and medicine in sex offender commitment. *New England Journal on Criminal and Civil Commitment.* 23: 347–386.

Janus, E. S., & Meehl, P. E. (1997). Assessing the legal standard for predictions of dangerousness in sex offender commitment proceedings. *Psychology, Public Policy, and Law.* 3: 33–64.

Jehu, D. (1988). *Beyond Sexual Abuse: Therapy with Women Who Were Childhood Victims.* Chichester: Wiley.

Jennings, K. T. (2000). *Female Sexual Abuse of Children: An Exploratory Study.* Dissertation from the University of Toronto; available through University Microfilms International, Ann Arbor, MI.

Jenkins, P. (1998). *Moral Panic: Changing Concepts of the Child Molester in Modern America.* New Haven: Yale University Press.

Jenkins, P., & Maier-Katkin, D. (1991). Occult survivors: The making of a myth. In J. Richardson, J. Best, & D. Bromley (eds.), *The Satanism Scare.* New York: Aldine & Gruyter.

John Jay College. (2004). *The Nature and Scope of Sexual Abuse of Minors by Catholic Priests and Deacons in the United States, 1950–2002.* Washington, DC: USCCB.

Johnson, J. T. (1992). *Mothers of Incest Survivors: Another Side of the Story.* Bloomington: Indiana University Press.

Kahn, T. J., & Chambers, H. J. (1991). Assessing reoffense risk with juvenile sexual offenders. *Child Welfare.* 70: 333–344.

Karpman, B. (1954). *The Sexual Offender and His Offenses: Etiology, Pathology, Psychodynamics and Treatment.* New York: Julian.

Kasl, C. D. (1990). Female perpetrators of sexual abuse: A feminist perspective. In M. Hunter (ed.), *The Sexually Abused Male, Vol. 1: Prevalence, Impact and Treatment.* New York: Lexington Books.

Kavoussi, R. J., Kaplan, M., & Becker, J. V. (1988). Psychiatric diagnoses in adolescent sex offenders. *Journal of the American Academy of Child and Adolescent Psychiatry.* 27: 241–243.

Kear-Colwell, J., & Pollock, P. (1997). Motivation or confrontation: Which approach to the child sex offender? *Criminal Justice and Behavior.* 24: 20–33.

Keary, K., & Fitzpatrick, C. (1994). Children's disclosure of sexual abuse during formal investigation. *Child Abuse and Neglect.* 18: 543–548.

Kelly, A. F. (1998). Clergy offenders. In W. L. Marshall & Y. M. Fernandez (eds.), *Sourcebook of Treatment Programs for Sexual Offenders.* New York: Plenum.

Kemshall, H. (2001). *Risk Assessment and Management of Known Sexual and Violent Offenders: A Review of Current Issues.* Police Research Series, Paper 140. London: Home Office.

Kinsey, A. (1948). *Sexual Behavior in the Human Male*. Philadelphia: Saunders.

Knight, R. A., & Prentky, R. A. (1990). Classifying sexual offenders. In W. L. Marshall, D. R. Laws, & H. E. Barbaree (eds.), *Handbook of Sexual Assault: Issues, Theories and Treatment of the Offender*. New York: Plenum.

Knight, R. A., & Prentky, R. (1993). Exploring characteristics for classifying juvenile sex offenders. In H. E. Barbaree, W. L. Marshall, & S. M. Hudson (eds.), *The Juvenile Sex Offender*. New York: Guilford.

Knight, R. A., Prentky, R. A., & Cerce, D. D. (1994). The development, reliability and validity of an inventory for the multidimensional assessment of sex and aggression. *Criminal Justice and Behavior*. 21: 72–94.

Knight, R. A., Prentky, R. A., Schneider, B., & Rosenberg, R. (1983). Linear causal modeling of adaptation and criminal history in sex offenders. In K. T. Van Dusen & S. A. Mednick (eds.), *Prospective Studies of Crime and Delinquency*. Boston: Kluwer-Nijhoff.

Knopp, F. H. (1984). *Retraining Adult Sex Offenders: Methods and Models*. Syracuse, NY: Safer Society Press.

Knopp, F. H. (1985). *The Youthful Sex Offender: The Rationale and Goals of Early Intervention and Treatment*. Syracuse, NY: Safer Society Press.

Kobayashi, J., Sales, B., Becker, J. V., Figueredo, A. J. et al. (1995). Perceived parental deviance, parent/child bonding, child abuse and child sexual aggression. *Sexual Abuse: Journal of Research and Treatment*. 7: 25–44.

Koss, M. P., & Harvey, M. R. (1991). *The Rape Victim: Clinical and Community Interventions* (2nd ed.). Newbury Park, CA: Sage.

Koss, M., Gidycz, C., & Wisniewski, N. (1987). The scope of rape: Incidence and prevalence of sexual aggression in a national sample of higher education students. *Journal of Consulting and Clinical Psychology*. 55: 162–170.

Kraemer, B. D., Salisbury, S. B., & Spielman, C. R. (1998). Pretreatment variables associated with treatment failure in a residential juveniles sex offender program. *Criminal Justice and Behavior*. 25: 190–202.

Krafft-Ebbing, R. V. (1886/1965). *Psychopathia Sexualis*. New York: Putnam.

Kreutz, L. E., & Rose, R. M. (1972). Assessment of aggressive behavior and plasma testosterone in a young criminal population. *Psychosomatic Medicine*. 34: 321–332.

Kruttschnitt, C., Uggen, C., & Shelton, K. (2000). Predictors of desistance among sex offenders: The interactions of formal and informal social controls. *Justice Quarterly*. 17: 61–87.

La Fond, J. Q. (1999). Can therapeutic jurisprudence be normatively neutral? Sexual predator laws: Their impact on participants and policy. *Arizona Law Review*. 41: 375.

La Fontaine, J. S. (1990). *Child Sexual Abuse*. Cambridge, UK: Polity.

La Fontaine, J. (1994). *The Extent and Nature of Organised and Ritual Abuse*. London: HMSO, Department of Health.

Lamb, S., & Edgar-Smith, S. (1994). Aspects of disclosure: Mediators of outcome of childhood sexual abuse. *Journal of Interpersonal Violence*. 9: 307–326.

Lane, N. J. (1995). *The Abuse of Power by Church and Society toward Women with Disabilities: The Theological and Spiritual Implications of Sexual Abuse of the Vulnerable by the Powerful*. Dissertation from the Union Institute; available through University Microfilms International, Ann Arbor, MI.

Lane, S. L. (1997). Assessment of sexually abusive youth. In G. D. Ryan (ed.), *Juvenile Sexual Offending: Causes, Consequences, and Correction*. West Sussex: Wiley.

Langan, P. A., & Harlow, C. W. (1992). *Child Rape Victims, 1992*. Washington, DC: U.S. Department of Justice, Office of Justice Programs, Bureau of Justice Statistics.

Langan, P. A., & Harlow, C. W. (1994). *Child Rape Victims, 1992*. Crime Data Brief. Washington, DC: U.S. Department of Justice.

Langevin, R. (1983). *Sexual Strands: Understanding and Treating Sexual Abnormalities in Men*. Hillside, NJ: Erlbaum.

Langevin, R., Bain, J., Ben-Aron, M., Coulthard, R., Day, D., Handy, L., Heasman, G., Hucker, S. J., Purins, J. E., Roper, V., Russon, A. E., Webster, C. D., & Wortzman, G. (1985). Sexual aggression: Constructing a predictive equation. A controlled pilot study. In R. Langevin (ed.), *Erotic Preference, Gender Identity and Aggression in Men: New Research Studies*. Hillsdale, NJ: Erlbaum.

Langevin, R., & Lang, R. A. (1985). Psychological treatment of paedophiles. *Behavioral Sciences and the Law*. 3: 403–419.

Langevin, R., Lang, R.A., & Curnoe, S. (1998). The prevalence of sex offenders with deviant fantasies. *Journal of Interpersonal Violence*. 13: 315–327.

Langevin, R., Wright, P., & Handy, L. (1988). Empathy, assertiveness, aggressiveness, and defensiveness among sex offenders. *Annals of Sex Research*. 1: 533–547.

Langstrom, N., & Grann, M. (2000). Risk for criminal recidivism among young sex offenders. *Journal of Interpersonal Violence*. 15: 855–873.

Lanning, K. (1986). *Child Molesters: A Behavioral Analysis for Law Enforcement Officers Investigating Cases of Sexual Exploitation*. Washington, DC: National Center for Missing and Exploited Children.

Lanyon, R. I. (1991). Theories of sex offending. In C. R. Hollin & K. Howells (eds.), *Clinical Approaches to Sex Offenders and Their Victims*. West Sussex: Wiley.

Largen, M. A. (1991). Confidentiality in the sexual assault victim/counselor relationship. In A. W. Burgess (ed.), *Rape and Sexual Assault III: A Research Handbook*. New York: Garland.

Laws, D. R., Hanson, R. K., Osborn, C. A., & Greenbaum, P. E. (2000). Classification of child molesters by plethysmographic assessment of sexual arousal and a self-report measure of sexual preference. *Journal of Interpersonal Violence*. 15: 1297–1312.

Lawson, L., & Chaffin, M. (1992). False negatives in sexual abuse disclosure interviews: Incidence and influence of caretaker's belief in abuse in cases of accidental abuse discovery by diagnosis of STD. *Journal of Interpersonal Violence*. 7: 532–542.

Lazebnik, R., Zimet, G. D., Ebert, J., Anglin, T. M., Williams, P., Bunch, D. L., & Krowchuk, D. P. (1994). How children perceive the medical evaluation for suspected sexual abuse. *Child Abuse and Neglect*. 18: 739–745.

Lees, S. (1996). *Carnal Knowledge: Rape on Trial*. London: Hamish Hamilton.

Leiter, R. A. (Ed.). (1999). *National Survey of State Laws* (3rd ed.). Farmington Hills, MI: Gale.

Levine, J. P. (1976). The potential for crime overreporting in criminal victimization surveys. *Criminology*. 14: 3.

Lewis, C. F., & Stanley, C. R. (2000). Women accused of sexual offenses. *Behavioral Sciences and the Law*. 18, 73–81.

Lidz, C. W., & Mulvey, E. P. (1995). Dangerousness: From legal definition to theoretical research. *Law and Human Behavior*. 19: 41–48.

Lieb, R., & Matson, S. (1998). *Sexual Predator Commitment Laws in the United States: 1998 Update*. WA: Washington State Institute for Public Policy.

Lightfoot, L. O., & Barbaree, H. E. (1993). The relationship between substance use and abuse and sexual offending in adolescents. In H. E. Barbaree, W. L. Marshall, & S. M. Hudson (eds.), *The Juvenile Sex Offender*. New York: Guilford.

Lindsey, R. E., Carlozzi, A. F., & Eells, G. T. (2001). Differences in the dispositional empathy of juvenile sex offenders, non-sex offending delinquent juveniles and nondelinquent juveniles. *Journal of Interpersonal Violence*. 16: 510–523.

Lipton, D., Martinson, R., & Wilks, J. (1975). *The Effectiveness of Correctional Treatment*. New York: Praeger.

Lipton, D., McDonel, E. C., & McFall, R. M. (1987). Heterosocial perception in rapists. *Journal of Consulting and Clinical Psychology.* 55: 17–21.

Lisak, D., & Ivan, C. (1995). Deficits in intimacy and empathy in sexually aggressive men. *Journal of Interpersonal Violence.* 10: 296–308.

Littel, K. (2000). *Engaging Advocates and Other Victim Service Providers in the Community Management of Sex Offenders*. Washington, DC: U.S. Department of Justice, Office of Justice Programs.

Littel, K. (2001). *Sexual Assault Nurse Examiner (SANE) Programs: Improving the Community Response to Sexual Assault Victims*. Washington, DC: U.S. Department of Justice, Office for Victims of Crime.

Litwack, T. R. (1993). On the ethics of dangerousness assessments. *Law and Human Behavior.* 17: 479–482.

Lloyd, C. (1991). The offense: Changes in the nature and pattern of sex offences. *Criminal Behavior and Mental Health.* 1: 115–122.

Loftus, E. (1993). The reality of repressed memories. *American Psychologist.* 48: 518–537.

Loftus, E. (1994). Therapeutic recollection of childhood abuse. *The Champion—National Association of Criminal Defense Lawyers.* 18: 5–10.

Loftus, E. F., & Davies, G. M. (1984). Distortions in the memory of children. *Journal of Social Issues.* 40: 51–67.

Longo, R. (1983). Administering a comprehensive sexual aggressive treatment program in a maximum-security setting. In J. G. Greer & I. R. Stuart (eds.), *The Sexual Aggressor: Current Perspectives on Treatment*. New York: Van Nostrand Reinhold.

Long, McLaughlin, & McCaffrey, (2002).

Looman, J., Gauthier, C., & Boer, D. (2001). Replication of the Massachusetts Treatment Center child molester typology in a Canadian sample. *Journal of Interpersonal Violence.* 16: 753–767.

Lundberg-Love, P. K. (1999). The resilience of the human psyche: Recognition and treatment of the adult survivor of incest. In M. A. Paludi (ed.), *The Psychology of Sexual Victimization: A Handbook*. Westport, CT: Greenwood.

MacLeod & Sarago (1987). Family secrets: Child sexual abuse. *Feminist Review.* 7.

MacMillan, H. L., Fleming, J. E., Trocmé, N., Boyle, M. H., Wong, M., Racine, Y. A., et al. (1997). Prevalence of child physical and sexual abuse in the community: Results from the Ontario Health Supplement. *Journal of the American Medical Association.* 278: 131–135.

Mair, K. J., & Stevens, R. H. (1994). Offending histories and offending behaviour: A ten-year follow-up of sex offenders tried by sheriff and district courts in Grampian, Scotland. *Psychology, Crime and Law.* 1: 83–92.

Malamuth, N. (1981). Rape proclivity among males. *Journal of Social Issues.* 37: 138–157.

Malamuth, N. (1986). Predictors of naturalistic aggression. *Journal of Personality and Social Psychology.* 50: 953–962.

Mann, R., & Thornton, D. (1997). *The Evolution of a Multi-Site Sex Offender Treatment Programme*. London: HM Prison Service, Programme Development Section.

Mapes, B. E. (1995). *Child Eyewitness Testimony in Sexual Abuse Investigations*. Brandon, VT: Clinical Psychology Publishing.

Marques, J. K. (1999). How to answer the question "Does sex offender treatment work?" *Journal of Interpersonal Violence.* 14: 437–451.

Marques, J., Day, D. M., Nelson, C., & West, M. (1994). Effects of cognitive-behavioral treatment on sex offender recidivism: Preliminary results of a longitudinal study. *Criminal Justice and Behavior.* 21: 28–54.

Marques, J., Nelson, C., West, M. A., & Day, D. M. (1994). The relationship between treatment goals and recidivism among child molesters. *Behavior Research and Therapy.* 32: 577–588.

Marquis, J. N. (1970). Orgasmic reconditioning: Changing sexual object choice through controlling masturbation fantasies. *Journal of Behavior Therapy and Experimental Psychiatry.* 1: 263–271.

Marshall, W. L. (1989). Intimacy, loneliness and sexual offenders. *Behavior Research and Therapy.* 27: 491–503.

Marshall, W. L. (1993). The role of attachment, intimacy, and loneliness in the etiology and maintenance of sexual offending. *Sexual and Marital Therapy.* 8: 109–121.

Marshall, W. L. (1994). Treatment effects on denial and minimization in incarcerated sex offenders. *Behavior Research and Therapy.* 32: 559–564.

Marshall, W. L. (1996). Assessment, treatment and theorizing about sex offenders: Development during the past twenty years. *Criminal Justice and Behavior.* 23: 162–199.

Marshall, W. L., Anderson, D., & Fernandez, Y. (1999). *Cognitive Behavioral Treatment of Sexual Offenders.* Toronto: Wiley.

Marshall, W. L., & Barbaree, H. E. (1990a). An integrated theory of the etiology of sexual offending. In W. L. Marshall, D. R. Laws, & H. E. Barbaree (eds.), *Handbook of Sexual Assault: Issues, Theories and Treatment of the Offender.* New York: Plenum.

Marshall, W. L., & Barbaree, H. E. (1990b). Outcome of comprehensive cognitive-behavioral treatment programs. In W. L. Marshall, D. R. Laws, & H. E. Barbaree (eds.), *Handbook of Sexual Assault: Issues, Theories and Treatment of the Offender.* New York: Plenum.

Marshall, W. L., Barbaree, H. E., & Eccles, A. (1991). Early onset and deviant sexuality in child molesters. *Journal of Interpersonal Violence.* 6: 323–336.

Marshall, W. L., Barbaree, H. E., & Eccles, A. (1993). A three-tiered approach to the rehabilitation of incarcerated sex offenders. *Behavioral Sciences and the Law.* 11: 441–455.

Marshall, W. L., & Eccles, A. (1991). Issues in clinical practice with sex offenders. *Journal of Interpersonal Violence.* 6: 68–93.

Marshall, W. L., & Eccles, A. (1993). Pavlovian conditioning processes in adolescent sex offenders. In H. E. Barbaree, W. L. Marshall, & S. M. Hudson (eds.), *The Juvenile Sex Offender.* New York: Guilford.

Marshall, W. L., Eccles, A., & Barbaree, H. E. (1991). Treatment of exhibitionists: A focus on sexual deviance versus cognitive and relationship features. *Behavior Research and Therapy.* 29: 129–135.

Marshall, W. L., Hudson, S. M., Jones, R., & Fernandez, Y. M. (1995). Empathy in sex offenders. *Clinical Psychology Review.* 15: 99–113.

Marshall, W. L., Laws, D. R., & Barbaree, H. E. (1990a). Present status and future directions. In W. L. Marshall, D. R. Laws, & H. E. Barbaree (eds.), *Handbook of Sexual Assault: Issues, Theories and Treatment of the Offender.* New York: Plenum.

Marshall, W. L., Laws, D. R., & Barbaree, H. E. (1990b). Issues in sexual assault. In W. L. Marshall, D. R. Laws, & H. E. Barbaree (eds.), *Handbook of Sexual Assault: Issues, Theories and Treatment of the Offender.* New York: Plenum.

Marshall, L. E., & Marshall, W. L. (2002). The role of attachment in sexual offending: An examination of preoccupied-attachment-style offending behavior. In B. Schwartz (ed.), *The Sex Offender: Current Treatment Modalities and Systems Issues.* New York: Civic Research Institute.

Marshall, W. L., & Pithers, W. D. (1994). A reconsideration of treatment outcome with sex offenders. *Criminal Justice and Behavior.* 21: 10–27.

Martinson, R. (1974). What works? Questions and answers about prison reform. *Public Interest.* 35: 22–54.

Matthews, J. K. (1998). An 11-year perspective of working with female sexual offenders. In W. L. Marshall,

Y. M. Fernandez, S. M. Hudson, & T. Ward (eds.), *Sourcebook of Treatment Programs for Sexual Offenders*. New York: Plenum.

Matthews, J. K., Matthews, R., & Speltz, K. (1991). Female sexual offenders: A typology. In M. Q. Patton (ed.), *Family Sexual Abuse: Frontline Research and Evaluation*.

Matthews, N. A. (1994). *Confronting Rape: The Feminist Anti-Rape Movement and the State*. J. Urry, series ed. International Library of Sociology. London: Routledge.

Matthews, R., Hunter, J. A., & Vuz, J. (1997). Juvenile female sexual offenders: Clinical characteristics and treatment issues. *Sexual Abuse: Journal of Research and Treatment*. 9: 187–199.

Matthews, R., Matthews, J. K., & Speltz, K. (1989). *Female Sexual Offenders: An Empirical Study*. Orwell, VT: Safer Society Press.

McDevitt, P. J. (1999). *Priests as Victims of Childhood Sexual Abuse: The Effects of Disclosing a History of Childhood Sexual Abuse on the Capacity for Empathy*. Dissertation from Loyola College, MD; available through University Microfilms International, Ann Arbor, MI.

McGrath (1994). Sex offender risk assessment and disposition planning: A review of clinical and empirical findings. *International Journal of Offender Therapy and Comparative Criminology*. 35: 328–350.

McGuicken, G. K., & Brown, J. (2001). Managing risk from sex offenders living in communities: Comparing police, press, and public perceptions. *Risk Management: An International Journal*. 3: 331–343.

McGuire, R. J., Carlisle, J. M., & Young, B. G. (1965). Sexual deviations as conditioned behavior: A hypothesis. *Behavior Research and Therapy*. 3: 185–190.

McGuire, R. J., & Vallance, M. (1964). Aversion therapy by electric shock: A simple technique. *British Medical Journal*. 2: 594–597.

McKibben, A., Proulx, J., & Lusignan, R. (1994). Relationships between conflict, affect and deviant sexual behaviors in paedophiles and rapists. *Behavior Research and Therapy*. 32: 571–575.

McLaughlin, B. R. (1994). Devastated spirituality: The impact of clergy sexual abuse on the survivor's relationship with God and the church. *Sexual Addiction and Compulsivity*. 1: 145–158.

McMullen, R. J. (1992). *Male Rape: Breaking the Silence on the Last Taboo*. London: GMP.

Medaris, M. (1995). *Child Sexual Exploitation: Improving Investigations and Protecting the Victims*. Washington, DC: U.S. Department of Justice, Office of Juvenile Justice and Delinquency Prevention.

Medea, A., & Thompson, K. (1974). *Against Rape: A Survival Manual for Women*. New York: Farrar, Straus & Giroux.

Megargee, E. I. (1981). Methodological problems in the prediction of violence. In J. R. Hays, T. K. Roberts, & K. S. Soloway (eds.), *Violence and the Violent Individual*. Lancaster, UK: Spectrum.

Mendola, M. J. (1998). *Characteristics of Priests and Religious Brothers for Evaluation of Sexual Issues*. Dissertation from Antioch University, the New England Graduate School; available through University Microfilms International, Ann Arbor, MI.

Meyer-Bahlberg, H. (1987). Commentary on Bain's "Hormones and sexual aggression in the male." *Integrative Psychiatry*. 5: 89–91.

Mezey, G. C., & King, M. B. (Eds.). (2000). *Male Victims of Sexual Assault* (2nd ed.). Oxford: Oxford University Press.

Miccio-Fonseca, L. C. (1998). Adult and adolescent female sex offenders: Experiences compared to other female and male sex offenders. *Journal of Psychology and Human Sexuality*. 11: 75–88.

Miller, W. R., & Rollnick, S. (1991). *Motivational Interviewing: Preparing People to Change Addictive Behavior*. New York: Guilford.

Minden, P. B. (1991). Coping with interpersonal violence and sexual victimization: Perspectives for victims and care providers. In A. W. Burgess (ed.), *Rape and Sexual Assault III: A Research Handbook*. New York: Garland.

Miner, M. H. (2002). Factors associated with recidivism in juveniles: An analysis of serious juvenile sex offenders. *Journal of Research in Crime and Delinquency*. 39: 421–436.

Miner, M. H., & Dwyer, S. M. (1997). The psychosocial development of sex offenders: Differences between exhibitionists, child molesters and incest offenders. *International Journal of Offender Therapy and Comparative Criminology*. 41: 36–44.

Mohr, J. W., Turner, R. E., & Jerry, N. B. (1964). *Pedophilia and Exhibitionism: A Handbook*. Toronto: University of Toronto Press.

Monahan, J. (1981). *Predicting Violent Behavior: An Assessment of Clinical Techniques*. Beverly Hills, CA: Sage.

Mondimore, F. M. (1996). *A Natural History of Homosexuality*. Baltimore: Johns Hopkins University Press.

Money, J. (1970). Use of androgen depleting hormone in the treatment of male sex offenders. *Journal of Sex Research*. 6: 165–172.

Money, J., Wiedeking, C., Walker, P. A., & Gain, D. (1976). Combined antiandrogen and counselling program for treatment of 46, XY and 47, XYY sex offenders. In E. Sachar (ed.), *Hormones, Behavior and Psychopathology*. New York: Raven.

Moore, B. S. (1990). The origins and development of empathy. *Motivation and Emotion*. 14: 75–79.

Moore, K. A., Nord, C. W., & Peterson, J. L. (1989). Nonvoluntary sexual activity among adolescents. *Family Planning Perspectives*. 21: 110–114.

Morrison, T. (1999). Is there a strategy out there? Policy management perspectives on young people who sexually abuse others. In M. Erooga & H. C. Masson (eds.), *Children and Young People Who Sexually Abuse Others: Challenges and Responses*. London: Routledge.

Mullvihill, M., Wisniewski, K., Meyers, J., & Wells, J. (2003). Losing track: Florida's sex offenders flock to Mass., then disappear. *Boston Herald*.

Murphy, W. D. (1990). Assessment and modification of cognitive distortions in sex offenders. In W. L. Marshall, D. R. Laws, & H. E. Barbaree (eds.), *Handbook of Sexual Assault: Issues, Theories and Treatment of the Offender*. New York: Plenum.

Nathan, P., & Ward, T. (2002). Female sex offenders: Clinical and demographic features. *Journal of Sexual Aggression*. 8: 5–21.

National Adolescent Perpetrator Network. (1993). The revised report from the National Task Force on Juvenile Sexual Offending. *Juvenile and Family Court Journal*. 44: 1–120.

National Center for Victims of Crime. (1997). *Male Rape Information Sheet*. Available at http://www.rapecrisiscenter.com/Male%20Rape%20Infor%20Sheet.html

National Coalition for the Protection of Children and Families. (2002a). *Current Statistics*. Available at http://www.nationalcoalition.org/safety.phtml?ID=53

National Coalition for the Protection of Children and Families. (2002b). *Pornography and the Internet*. Available at http://www.nationalcoalition.org/safety.phtml?ID=18

National Institute of Justice. (1992). *When the Victim Is a Child* (2nd ed.). Washington, DC: U.S. Department of Justice, Office of Justice Programs.

National Report Series. (2000). Children as Victims. *1999 National Report Series, Juvenile Justice Bulletin*. Washington, DC; U.S. Department of Justice, Office of Juvenile Justice and Delinquency Prevention.

Nelson, S. (2001). Physical symptoms in sexually abused women: Somatization or undetected injury? *Child Abuse Review*. 11: 51–64.

New York City Alliance Against Sexual Assault. (2001). *Comprehensive Sexual Assault Treatment Programs: A Hospital-Based Model*. New York: NYC Alliance.

Nicholaichuk, T. P. (1996). *Sex Offender Treatment Priority: An Illustration of the Risk/Need Principle.* Available at http://www.csc-scc.gc.ca/crd/forum/e082/e

O'Brien, M., & Bera, W. H. (1986). Adolescent sexual offenders: A descriptive typology. *Preventing Sexual Abuse: A Newsletter of the National Family Life Education Network.* 1: 2–4.

O'Connell, M. A., Leberg, E., & Donaldson, C. R. (1990). *Working with Sex Offenders: Guidelines for Therapist Selection.* Newbury Park, CA: Sage.

Odem, M. E. (1995). *Delinquent Daughters: Protecting and Policing Adolescent Female Sexuality in the United States.* Chapel Hill: University of North Carolina Press.

Office of the Legislative Auditor. (1994). *Sex Offender Treatment Programs.* St. Paul, MN: Office of the Legislative Auditor.

Office for Victims of Crime. (2001). *First Response to Victims of Crime 2001.* Washington, DC: U.S. Department of Justice, Office for Victims of Crime.

Olweus, D., Matteson, A., Schalling, D., & Low, H. (1980). Testosterone, aggression, physical, and personality dimensions in normal adolescent males. *Psychosomatic Medicine.* 42: 253–269.

O'Reilly, G., Morrison, T., Sheerin, D., & Carr, A. (2001). A group-based module for adolescents to improve motivation to change sexually abusive behavior. *Child Abuse Review.* 10: 150–169.

Orlando, D. (1998). Sex offenders. *Special Needs Offenders Bulletin.* Washington, DC: Federal Judicial Center.

Pallone, N. J. (1990). *Rehabilitating Criminal Sexual Psychopaths: Legislative Mandates, Clinical Quandaries.* New Brunswick, NJ: Transaction.

Palmer, T. (1975). Martinson revisited. *Journal of Research in Crime and Delinquency.* 12: 133–152.

Paludi, M. A. (1999). *The Psychology of Sexual Victimization: A Handbook.* Westport, CT: Greenwood.

Parker, S. G. (2001). *Establishing Victim Services within a Law Enforcement Agency: The Austin Experience.* Washington,

DC: U.S. Department of Justice, Office for Victims of Crime.

Pelka, F. (1995). Raped: A male survivor breaks his silence. In P. S. Searles & R. J. Berger (eds.), *Rape and Society.* Boulder, CO: Westview.

Perkins, D. (1991). Clinical work with sex offenders in secure settings. In C. R. Hollin & K. Howells (eds.), *Clinical Approaches to Sex Offenders and Their Victims.* West Sussex: Wiley.

Perry, N. W., & Wrightsman, L. S. (1991). *The Child Witness: Legal Issues and Dilemmas.* Newbury Park, CA: Sage.

Persky, H., Smith, K. D., & Basu, G. K. (1971). Relations of psychologic measures of aggression and hostility to testosterone in man. *Psychosomatic Medicine.* 33: 265–277.

Phan, D. L., & Kingree, J. B. (2001). Sexual abuse victimization and psychological distress among adolescent offenders. *Journal of Child Sexual Abuse.* 10: 81–90.

Piper, A. (1993). Truth serum and recovered memories of sexual abuse. *Journal of Psychiatry and Law.* 21: 447–471.

Pirke, K. M., Kockott, G., & Dittmar, F. (1974). Psychosexual stimulation and plasma testosterone in men. *Archives of Sexual Behavior.* 3: 577–584.

Pithers, W. D. (1994). Process evaluation of a group therapy component designed to enhance sex offenders' empathy for sexual abuse survivors. *Behavior Research and Therapy.* 32: 565–570.

Pithers, W. D., Kashima, K. M., Cumming, G. F., Beal, L. S., & Buell, M. M. (1988). Relapse prevention in sexual aggression. In R. A. Prentky & V. L. Quinsey (eds.), *Human Sexual Aggression: Current Perspectives.* New York: New York Academy of Science.

Pithers, W. D., Marques, J. K., Gibat, C. C., & Marlatt, G. A. (1983). Relapse prevention with sexual aggressives: A self-control model of treatment and maintenance of change. In J. G. Greer & I. R. Stuart (eds.), *The Sexual Aggressor: Current Perspectives on Treatment.* New York: Van Nostrand Reinhold.

Pithers, W., Beal, S., Armstrong, J., & Petty, J. (1989). Identification of risk factors through clinical interviews and analysis of records. In D. R. Laws (ed.), *Relapse Prevention with Sex Offenders.* New York: Guilford.

Police Responses to Crimes of Sexual Assault. (2002). Available at http://www.vaw,umn.edu/finaldocuments/consac3.htm

Polizzi, D. M., MacKenzie, D. L., & Hickman, L. J. (1999). What works in adult sex offender treatment? A review of prison and non-prison based treatment programs. *International Journal of Offender Therapy and Comparative Criminology.* 43: 357–374.

Porter, R. (Ed.). (1984). *Child Sexual Abuse within the Family.* London: Tavistock.

Potas, I. (1982). *Just Deserts for the Mad.* Canberra: Australian Institute of Criminology.

Prentky, R. A. (1994). The assessment and treatment of sex offenders. *Criminal Justice and Behavior.* 21: 6–9.

Prentky, R. A., & Burgess, A. W. (1988). *Rehabilitation of Child Molesters: A Cost-Benefit Analysis.* Unpublished manuscript. Massachusetts Treatment Center.

Prentky, R. A., & Burgess, A. W. (1990). Rehabilitation of child molesters: A cost-benefit analysis. *American Journal of Orthopsychiatry.* 60: 80–117.

Prentky, R. A., Burgess, A. W., Rokous, F., Lee, A., Hartman, C., Ressler, R., & Douglas, J. (1989). The presumptive role of fantasy in serial sexual homicide. *American Journal of Psychiatry.* 146: 887–891.

Prentky, R., Harris, B., Frizzell, K., & Righthand, S. (2000). An actuarial procedure for assessing risk in juvenile sex offenders. *Sexual Abuse: A Journal of Research and Treatment.* 12: 71–93.

Prior, V. (2001). Invited comments to: Children's response to the medical visit for allegations of sexual abuse: maternal perceptions and predicting variables. *Child Abuse Review.* 10: 223–225.

Prison Reform Trust. (1990). *Sex Offenders in Prison.* London: Prison Reform Trust.

Prison Reform Trust. (1991). *The Woolf Report: A Summary of the Main Findings and Recommendations of the Inquiry into Prison Disturbances.* London: Prison Reform Trust.

Pritt, A. F. (1998). Spiritual correlates of reported sexual abuse among Mormon women. *Journal for the Scientific Study of Religion.* 37: 273–285.

Prochaska, J. O., & DiClemente, C. C. (1982). Transtheoretical therapy: Toward a more integrative model of change. *Psychotherapy: Theory, Research and Practice.* 19: 276–288.

Programme Development Section. (1997a). *The Prison Service Sex Offender Treatment Programme.* Prepared for the SOTP Accreditation Panel, London.

Programme Development Section. (1997b). *Sex Offender Treatment Programme Accreditation Criteria 1997–8.* Prepared for the SOTP Accreditation Panel, London.

Pryor, D. (1996). *Unspeakable Acts: Why Men Sexually Abuse Children.* New York: New York University Press.

Quinsey, V. L., Chaplin, T. C., & Varney, G. (1981). A comparison of rapists' and non-sex offenders' sexual preferences for mutually consenting sex, rape, and physical abuse of women. *Behavioral Assessment.* 3: 127–135.

Quinsey, V. L., Khanna, A., & Malcolm, P. B. (1998). A retrospective evaluation of the regional treatment centre sex offender treatment program. *Journal of Interpersonal Violence.* 13: 621–644.

Quinsey, V. L., Lalumiere, M. T., Rice, M. E., & Harris, G. T. (1995). Predicting sexual offences. In J. C. Campbell (ed.), *Assessing Dangerousness: Violence by Sexual Offenders, Batterers and Child Abusers.* Thousand Oaks, CA: Sage.

Quinsey, V. L., Rice, M. E., & Harris, G. T. (1990). *Psychopathy, Sexual Deviance and Recidivism Among Released Sex Offenders.* Research Report Vol. 7, No. 5. Pentanguishine, ONT: Mental Health Centre.

Quinsey, V. L., Steinman, C. M., Bergerson, S. G., & Holmes, T. F. (1975). Penile circumference, skin conductance and ranking responses of child molesters and "normals" to sexual and non-sexual stimuli. *Behavior Therapy*. 6: 213–219.

Quinsey, V. L., Warneford, A., Pruesse, M., & Link, N. (1975). Released Oak Ridge patients: A follow-up study of review board discharges. *British Journal of Criminology*. 15: 264–270.

Rada, R. T. (1978). Classification of the rapist. In R. T. Rada (ed.), *Clinical Aspects of the Rapist*. New York: Grune & Stratton.

Rada, R. T., Laws, D. R., & Kellner, R. (1976). Plasma testosterone levels in the rapist. *Psychosomatic Medicine*. 38: 257–268.

Rada, R. T., Laws, D. R., Kellner, R., Stiristava, L., & Peake, G. (1983). Plasma androgens in violent and non-violent sex offenders. *Bulletin of the American Academy of Psychiatry and the Law*. 11: 149–158.

Rape and Rape Prevention. (1999). Available at http://www.estronaut. com/a/avoiding_rape.htm

Rape Crisis Federation. (2002, February 25). *Rape!* Notingham, UK: Rape Crisis Federation of Wales and England.

Ray, J. A., & English, D. J. (1995). Comparison of female and male children with sexual behavior problems. *Journal of Youth and Adolescence*. 24: 439–451.

Redding Police Department. (1996, July 29). *Parolees and Sex Offenders*. Available at http://ci.redding.ca.us/rpd/rpdoff. htm

Reiss, D., Grubin, D., & Meux, C. (1996). Young "psychopaths" in special hospital: Treatment and outcome. *British Journal of Psychiatry*. 168: 99–104.

Rennison, C. M. (2001). Criminal victimization 2000: Changes 1999–2000 with trends 1993–2000. *National Crime Victimization Survey*. Washington, DC: Bureau of Justice Statistics.

Rennison, C. M., & Rand, M. R. (2003). *Criminal Victimization, 2002*. Washington, DC: U.S. Department of Justice, Bureau of Justice Statistics.

Resnick, H. S., Acierno, R., & Kilpatrick, D. G. (1997). Health impact of interpersonal violence: Medicinal and mental health outcomes. *Behavioral Medicine*. 23: 65–78.

Ressler, R. K., Burgess, A. W., & Douglas, J. E. (1988). *Sexual Homicide: Patterns and Motives*. New York: Lexington Books.

Rhodes, A. (2002). Fifth grade rapist exposes woeful lapse in bureaucratic communication. Retrieved from http://www. wgac.com/austin/ 01-16.html

Rice, M. E., Quinsey, V. L., & Harris, G. T. (1991). Sexual recidivism among child molesters released from a maximum-security psychiatric institution. *Journal of Consulting and Clinical Psychology*. 59: 381–386.

Rich, L. L. (1995). Right to privacy in the information age. *Publishing Law Center*. Available at http://publaw.com/ privacy.html

Righthand, S., & Welch, C. (2001). *Juveniles Who Have Sexually Offended: A Review of the Professional Literature*. Washington, DC: U.S. Department of Justice, Office of Juvenile Justice and Delinquency Prevention.

Rizzo, N. D. (1981). Can everyone be rehabilitated? *International Journal of Offender Therapy and Comparative Criminology*. 25: 41–46.

Robson, B. (1999). *A Prison by Any Other Name*. Available at http://www. citipages.com/databank/18/863/ article3579.asp

Roesler, T. A., & Weissmann-Wind, T. A. (1994). Telling the secret: Adult women describe their disclosures of incest. *Journal of Interpersonal Violence*. 9: 327–338.

Rogers, C. M., & Terry, T. (1984). Clinical interventions with boy victims of sexual abuse. In I. Stewart & J. Greer (eds.), *Victims of Sexual Aggression*. New York: Van Nostrand Reinhold.

Rosetti, S. J. (1995). The impact of child sexual abuse on attitudes toward God and the Catholic Church. *Child Abuse and Neglect*. 19: 1469–1481.

Rosetti, S. J. (1997). The effects of priest-perpetration of child sexual abuse on the trust of Catholics in priesthood, church and God. *Journal of Psychology and Christianity*. 16: 197–209.

Rosman, J., & Resnick, P. (1989). Sexual attraction to corpses: A psychiatric review of necrophilia. *Bulletin of the American Academy of Psychiatry and the Law*. 17: 153–163.

Ross, D. F., Miller, B. S., & Moran, P. B. (1987). The child in the eyes of the jury: Assessing mock jurors' perceptions of the child witness. In S .J. Ceci, M. P. Toglia, & D. F. Ross (eds.), *Children's Eyewitness Testimony*. New York: Springer Verlag.

Ross, R. R., & Gendreau, P. (Eds.). (1980). *Effective Correctional Treatment*. Toronto: Butterworth & Company.

Ross, R. R., & McKay, B. (1980). Behavioral approaches to treatment in corrections: Requiem for a panacea. In R. R. Ross & P. Gendreau (eds.), *Effective Correctional Treatment*. Toronto: Butterworth & Company.

Russell, D. E. H. (1975). *The Politics of Rape: The Victim's Perspective*. New York: Stein & Day.

Russell, D. E. H. (1984). *Sexual Exploitation: Rape, Child Sexual Abuse and Sexual Harrassment*. Beverly Hills, CA: Sage.

Russell, D. E. H. (1986). *The Secret Trauma: Incest in the Lives of Girls and Women*. New York: Basic Books.

Ryan, G. (1999). Treatment of sexually abusive youth. *Journal of Interpersonal Violence*. 14: 422–437.

Ryan, G. D. (1991). Historical responses to juvenile sexual offences. In G. D. Ryan & S. L. Lane (eds.), *Juvenile Sexual Offending: Causes, Consequences and Correction*. Lexington, MA: Lexington Books.

Ryan, G., Miyoshi, T. J., Metzner, J. L., Krugman, R. D., & Fryer, G. E. (1996). Trends in a national sample of sexually abusive youth. *Journal of the American Academy of Child and Adolescent Psychiatry*. 35: 17–25.

Sampson, A. (1992). Treatment programs: From theory to practice. In Prison Reform Trust (ed.), *Beyond Containment: The Penal Response to Sex Offending*. London: Prison Reform Trust.

Sanday, P. R. (1981). *Female Power and Male Domination*. New York: Cambridge University Press.

Sanderson, R. (1960). Clinical trial with millenil in the treatment of schizophrenia. *Journal of Mental Science*. 106: 732–741.

Saunders-Wilson, D. (1992). The need for sexual glasnost. In Prison Reform Trust (ed.), *Beyond Containment: The Penal Response to Sex Offending*. London: Prison Reform Trust.

Scaramella, J. J., & Brown, W. A. (1978). Serum testosterone and aggressiveness in hockey players. *Psychosomatic Medicine*. 40: 262–265.

Scarce, M. (1997). *Male on Male Rape: The Hidden Toll of Stigma and Shame*. New York: Insight Books.

Schlank, A. M., & Shaw, T. (1996). Treating sexual offenders who deny their guilt: A pilot study. *Sexual Abuse*. 3: 371–380.

Schneider, A. L., & Sumi, D. (1981). Patterns of forgetting and telescoping. *Criminology*. 19: 3.

Schwartz, B. K. (1995). Characteristics and typologies of sex offenders. In B. Schwartz (ed.), *The Sex Offender: Corrections, Treatment and Legal Practice, Vol. 3*. Kingston, NJ: Civic Research Institute.

Schwartz, B. K. (1999). The case against involuntary commitment. In A. Schlank & F. Cohen (eds.), *The Sexual Predator: Law, Policy, Evaluation and Treatment, Vol. 2*. Kingston, NJ: Civic Research Institute.

Schwartz, B., & Cellini, H. (Eds.). (1997). *The Sex Offender*. Kingston, NJ: Civic Research Institute.

Scott, L. K. (1997). Community management of sex offenders. In B. Schwartz & H. Cellini (eds.), *The Sex Offender*. Kingston, NJ: Civic Research Institute.

Scott, M. B., & Lyman, S. M. (1968). Paranoia, homosexuality, and game theory. *Journal of Health and Social Behavior*. 9: 179–187.

Scully, D. (1990). *Understanding Sexual Violence: A Study of Convicted Rapists.* Cambridge, MA: Unwin, Hyman.

Scully, D., & Marolla, J. (1984). Convicted rapists' vocabulary of motive: Excuses and justifications. *Social Problems.* 31: 530–544.

Scully, D., & Marolla, J. (1985). "Riding the bull at Gilleys": Convicted rapists describe the rewards of rape. *Social Problems.* 32: 251–263.

Sealy, G. (2002, February). *The Talk in Church: Some Experts Say Abuse Cases Could Open Up Religious Sexual Discussions.* Available at http://abcnews.go.com/sections/us/DailyNews/churchsex020222.html

Sebba, L. (2001). On the relationship between criminological research and policy: The case of crime victims. *Criminal Justice.* 1: 27–58.

Seghorn, T. K., & Cohen, M. (1980). The psychology of the rape assailant. In W. Cerran, A. L. McGarry, & C. Petty (eds.), *Modern Legal Medicine, Psychiatry and Forensic Science.* Philadelphia: FA Davis.

Seghorn, T. K., Prentky, R. A., & Boucher, R. J. (1987). Childhood sexual abuse in the lives of aggressive sexual offenders. *Journal of the American Academy of Child and Adolescent Psychiatry.* 26: 262–267.

Seidman, B. T., Marshall, W. L., Hudson, S. M., & Robertson, P. J. (1994). An examination of intimacy and loneliness in sex offenders. *Journal of Interpersonal Violence.* 9: 518–534.

Seifert, R. (1993). War and rape: A preliminary analysis. In A. Stiglmayer (ed.), *Mass Rape: The War against Women in Bosnia-Herzegovina.* Lincoln: University of Nebraska Press.

Seling, M. (2000). *A Treatment Program Overview.* Steilacoom, WA: Special Commitment Center.

Serin, R. C. (1991). Psychopathy and violence in criminals. *Journal of Interpersonal Violence.* 6: 423–431.

Serin, R. C., Malcolm, P. B., Khanna, A., & Barbaree, H. E. (1994). Psychopathy and deviant sexual arousal in incarcerated sexual offenders. *Journal of Interpersonal Violence.* 9: 3–11.

Serrill, M. S. (1975). Is rehabilitation dead? *Corrections.* 3: 21–26.

Shaw, J. A., Lewis, J. E., Loeb, A., Rosado, J., & Rodriguez, R. A. (2000). Child on child sexual abuse: Psychological perspectives. *Child Abuse and Neglect.* 24: 1591–1600.

Simkins, L. (1993). Characteristics of sexually repressed child molesters. *Journal of Interpersonal Violence.* 8: 3–17.

Simkins, L., Ward, W., Bowman, S., & Rinck, C. M. (1989). The Multiphasic Sex Inventory: Diagnosis and prediction of treatment response in child sexual abusers. *Annals of Sex Research.* 2: 205–226.

Simon, L. M. J., Sales, B., Kaskniak, A., & Kahn, M. (1992). Characteristics of child molesters: Implications for the fixated-regressed dichotomy. *Journal of Interpersonal Violence.* 7: 211–225.

Simon, T., Mercy, J., & Perkins, C. (2001, June). *Injuries from Violent Crime, 1992–98.* Washington, DC: U.S. Department of Justice, Bureau of Justice Statistics.

Sipe, A. R. (1995). *Sex, Priests and Power: Anatomy of a Crisis.* New York: Brunner/Mazel.

Sipe, A. R. (1999). The problem of prevention in clergy sexual abuse. In T. G. Plante (ed.), *Bless Me Father for I Have Sinned: Perspectives of Sexual Abuse Committed by Roman Catholic Priests.* Westport, CT: Praeger.

Sipe, R., Jensen, E. L., & Everett, R. S. (1998). Adolescent sexual offenders grown up: Recidivism in young adulthood. *Criminal Justice and Behavior.* 25: 109–124.

Skinner, B. F. (1953). *Science and Human Behavior.* New York: Macmillan.

Skogan, W. G. (1975). Measurement problems in official and survey crime rates. *Journal of Criminal Justice.* 3: 1.

Smith, A. B., & Berlin, L. (1977). Can criminals be treated? *New England Journal on Prison Law.* 3: 487–502.

Smith, D. W., Letourneau, E. J., & Saunders, B. E. (2000). Delay in disclosure of childhood rape: Results from a national survey. *Child Abuse and Neglect.* 24: 273–287.

Smith, H., & Israel, E. (1987). Sibling incest: A study of dynamics of 25 cases. *Child Abuse and Neglect.* 11: 101–108.

Smith, L. M. (1994). Lifting the veil of secrecy: Mandatory child abuse reporting statutes may encourage the Catholic Church to report priests who molest children. *Law and Psychology Review.* 18: 409–421.

Smith, M., & Pazder, L. (1980). *Michelle Remembers.* New York: Congdon & Lattes.

Smith, W., & Monastersky, C. (1986). Assessing juvenile sex offender's risk of reoffending. *Criminal Justice and Behavior.* 13: 115–140.

Smith, W. R. (1988). Delinquency and abuse among juvenile sexual offenders. *Journal of Interpersonal Violence.* 3: 400–413.

Smith, W. R., Monastersky, C., & Deishner, R. M. (1987). MMPI-based personality types among juvenile sexual offenders. *Journal of Clinical Psychology.* 43: 422–430.

Snaith, P. (1983). Exhibitionism: A clinical conundrum. *British Journal of Psychiatry.* 143: 703–710.

Snyder, H. N. (2000). *Sexual Assault of Young Children as Reported to Law Enforcement: Victim, Incident, and Offender Characteristics, NIBRS Statistical Report.* Washington, DC: U.S. Department of Justice, Office of Justice Programs Bureau of Justice Statistics.

Solicitor General of Canada. (1990). *Management and Treatment of Sex Offenders.* Ottawa: Minister of Supply Services.

Soothill, K. L., Jack, A., & Gibbens, T. C. N. (1976). Rape: 22 year cohort study. *Medicine, Science and the Law.* 16: 26–39.

Sorenson, T., & Snow, B. (1991). How children tell: The process of disclosure in child sexual abuse. *Child Welfare.* 70: 3–15.

State of New York. (1999). Governor Pataki announces latest criminal justice reform; Civil commitment of sexually violent predators protects New York families. Press release. Albany: Press Office.

Steadman, H. J. (1972). The psychiatrist as a conservative agent of social control. *Social Problems.* 20: 263–271.

Stermac, L. E., & Segal, Z. V. (1989). Adult sexual contact with children: An examination of cognitive factors. *Behavior Therapy.* 20: 573–584.

Stermac, L. E., Segal, Z. V., & Gillis, R. (1990). Social and cultural factors in sexual assault. In W. L. Marshall, D. R. Laws, & H. E. Barbaree (eds.), *Handbook of Sexual Assault: Issues, Theories and Treatment of the Offender.* New York: Plenum.

Stone, A. (1985). The new legal standards of dangerousness: Fair in theory, unfair in practice. In C. D. Webster, M. H. Ben-Aron, & S. J. Hucker (eds.), *Dangerousness: Probability and Prediction, Psychiatry and Public Policy.* New York: Cambridge University Press.

Strahan, T. (1991). Women increasingly receive public assistance as abortion is repeated. *Association for Interdisciplinary Research in Values and Social Change Newsletter.* 4: 3–7.

Sturman, P. (2000). *Drug Assisted Sexual Assault.* London: Home Office, Police Research Award Scheme.

Summit, R. C. (1983). The child sexual abuse accommodation syndrome. *Child Abuse and Neglect.* 7: 177–193.

Sutherland, E. (1950). The diffusion of sexual psychopath laws. *American Journal of Sociology.* 50: 142–148.

Sykes, G. M., & Matza, D. (1957). Techniques of neutralization: A theory of delinquency. *American Sociological Review.* 22: 664–670.

Tappan, P. W. (1950). *The Habitual Sex Offender: Report and Recommendation of the Commission on the Habitual Sex Offender.* Trenton: Commission on the Habitual Sex Offender.

Taslitz, A. E. (1999). *Rape and the Culture of the Courtroom*. New York: New York University Press.

Terry, K. J. (1999). *Analysing the Effects of Motivation on Sex Offenders in a Cognitive-Behavioural Treatment Programme*. Unpublished doctoral dissertation, Cambridge University, Cambridge, UK.

Terry, K. J. (2000). *Sustaining Employment: Factors Associated with Job Retention Among Ex-Offenders*. New York: Report for the Center for Employment Opportunities.

Terry, K. J., & Furlong, J. (2003). *Sex Offender Registration and Community Notification: A "Megan's Law" Sourcebook*. Kingston, NJ: Civic Research Institute.

Terry, K. J., & Mitchell, E. W. (1999). The impact of voluntariness on treatment efficacy: Is motivation necessary? *Forensic Update*. 59: 7–12.

Terry, K. J., & Mitchell, E. W. (2001). Motivation in sex offender treatment efficacy: Leading a horse to water *and* making it drink? *International Journal of Offender Therapy and Comparative Criminology*. 45: 663–672.

Thomas, T. (2000). *Sex Crime: Sex Offending and Society*. Devon: Willan.

Thompson, K. M., Wonderlich, S. A., Crosby, R. D., & Mitchell, J. E. (2001). Sexual victimization and adolescent weight regulation practices: A test across three community based samples. *Child Abuse and Neglect*. 25: 291–305.

Thornhill, R., & Palmer, C. (2000). *A Natural History of Rape: Biological Bases of Sexual Coercion*. Cambridge, MA: MIT Press.

Tracy, F., Donnelly, H., Morgenbesser, L., & MacDonald, D. (1983). Program evaluation: Recidivism research involving sex offenders. In J. G. Greer & I. R. Stuart (eds.), *The Sexual Aggressor: Current Perspectives on Treatment*. New York: Van Nostrand Reinhold.

Travin, S., Cullen, K., & Protter, B. (1990). Female sexual offenders: Severe victims and victimizers. *Journal of Forensic Sciences*. 35: 140–150.

Turner, S. (2000). Surviving sexual assault and sexual torture. In G. C. Mezey & M. B. King (eds.), *Male Victims of Sexual Assault*. Oxford: Oxford University Press.

Uniform Crime Report. (2002). *Crime in the United States*. Available at http://www.fbi.gov/ucr/cius_02/html/web/appendices/07-append02.html

Valcour, F. (1990). The treatment of child sex abusers in the church. In S. J. Rosetti (ed.), *Slayer of the Soul: Child Sexual Abuse and the Catholic Church*. Mystic, CT: Twenty-third Publications.

Vallerie, V. (1997). Relationships between alcohol, expectancies and sexual offenses in convicted offenders. In B. Schwartz & H. Cellini (eds.), *The Sex Offender*. Kingston, NJ: Civic Research Institute.

Veneziano, C., & Veneziano, L. (2002). Adolescent sex offenders: A review of the literature. *Trauma, Violence and Abuse*. 3: 247–260.

von Hirsch, A., & Ashworth, A. (1996). Protective sentencing under section 2(2)(b): The criteria for dangerousness. *Criminal Law Review*. 175–183.

Walker, E. A., Katon, W. J., Hansom, J., Harrop-Griffiths, J., Holm, L., Jones, M. L., Hickok, L., & Jemelka, R. P. (1992). Medical and psychiatric symptoms in women with childhood sexual abuse. *Psychosomatic Medicine*. 54: 658–664.

Walker, S. (1989). *Sense and Nonsense about Crime: A Policy Guide*. Pacific Grove, CA: Brooks/Cole.

Walrath, C., Ybarra, M., & Holden, E. W. (2003). Children with reported histories of sexual abuse: Utilizing multiple perspectives to understand clinical and psychosocial profiles. *Child Abuse and Neglect*. 27: 509–524.

Ward, C. (1995). *Attitudes towards Rape: Feminist and Social Psychological Perspectives*. S. Wilkenson, series ed. Gender and Psychology: Feminist and Critical Perspectives. London: Sage.

Ward, C., & Inserto, F. (1990). *Victims of Sexual Violence: A Handbook for Helpers*. Kent Ridge: Singapore University Press.

Ward, T., Hudson, S., & McCormack, J. (1997). Attachment style, intimacy deficiencies and sexual offending. In B. Schwartz & H. Cellini (eds.), *The Sex Offender*. Kingston, NJ: Civic Research Institute.

Ward, T., & Keenan, T. (1999). Child molesters' implicit theories. *Journal of Interpersonal Violence*. 14: 821–838.

Watkins, B., & Bentovim, A. (2000). Male children and adolescents as victims: A review of current knowledge. In G. C. Mezey & M. B. King (eds.), *Male Victims of Sexual Assault*. Oxford: Oxford University Press.

Watkins, J. G. (1993). Dealing with the problem of false memory in clinic and court. *Journal of Psychiatry and Law*. 21: 297–317.

Weinrott, M. R. (1996). *Juvenile Sexual Aggression: A Critical Review*. Portland, OR: Center for the Study and Prevention of Violence.

West, D. J. (1985). Helping imprisoned sex offenders: Discussion paper. *Journal of the Royal Society of Medicine*. 78: 928–932.

West, D. J. (1987). *Sexual Crimes and Confrontations: A Study of Victims and Offenders*. A. E. Bottoms, series ed. Cambridge Studies in Criminology. Aldershot, UK: Gower.

Wexler, D. B. (1999). Introduction to the Therapeutic Jurisprudence Symposium. *Arizona Law Review*. 41: 263.

Whitehead, J. T., & Lab, S. P. (1989). A meta-analysis of juvenile correctional treatment. *Journal of Research in Crime and Delinquency*. 26: 276–295.

Wilks, J., & Martinson, R. (1976). Is treatment of criminal offenders really necessary? *Federal Probation*. 40: 3–8.

Williams, L. M., & Finkelhor, D. (1990). The characteristics of incestuous fathers: A review of recent studies. In W. L. Marshall, D. R. Laws, & H. E. Barbaree (eds.), *Handbook of Sexual Assault: Issues, Theories and Treatment of the Offender*. New York: Plenum.

Williams, S. M. (1996). *A National Strategy for Managing Sex Offenders*. Available at http://www.csc-scc.gc.ca/crd/forum/e082/e

Wolf, S. C. (1985). A multi-factor model of deviant sexuality. *Victimology: An International Journal*. 10: 359–374.

Wormith, J. S., & Ruhl, M. (1986). Preventive detention in Canada. *Journal of Interpersonal Violence*. 1: 399–430.

Yalom, I. D. (1985). *The Theory and Practice of Group Psychotherapy* (3rd ed.). New York: Basic Books.

Zahn-Waxler, C., & Radke-Yarrow, M. (1990). The origins of empathic concern. *Motivation and Emotion*. 14: 107–130.

Zgourides, G., Monto, M., & Harris, R. (1997). Correlates of adolescent male sexual offense: Prior adult sexual contact, sexual attitudes and use of sexually explicit materials. *International Journal of Offender Therapy and Comparative Criminology*. 41: 272–283.

LEGAL CASES

Addington v. Texas, 441 U.S. 418 (1979).

Artway v. Attorney General of New Jersey, 81 F.3d 1235, 1267 (3rd Cir. 1996).

Ashcroft v. Free Speech Coalition 122 S. Ct. 1389 (2002).

Brown and others, 94 Cr. App R 302 CA, [1994] IAC 212 HL(1992).

Commonwealth of Pennsylvania v. Copenhefer, 587 Atl. 2d 1353 (Pa. 1991).

Connecticut Department of Public Safety v. Doe, 123 S. Ct. 1160 (2003).

Doe v. Pataki, 940 F. Supp. 603, 620 (S.D.N.Y. 1996).

Doe v. Poritz, 283 N.J. Super. 372, 661 A.2d 1335 (1995).

E. B. and W. P. v. Verniero, 119 F.3d 1077 (3rd Cir. 1997).

Foucha v. Louisiana, 504 U.S. 71 (1992).

Hammer v. Hammer, 418 N.W.2d 23, 27 (Wis. Ct. App. 1987).

In re Campbell, 986 P.2d 771 (Wash. 1999).

In re Linehan, 518 N.W.2d 609, 614 (Minn. 1994).

In re Turay, 986 P.2d 790 (Wash. 1999).

In re Young 857 P.2d 989 (Wash. 1993).

Jackson, 406 U.S.

Jacobson v. Massachusetts, 197 U.S. 11, 26, 49 L. Ed. 643, 25 S. Ct. 358 (1905).

Kansas v. Hendricks, 521 U.S. 346 (1997).

O'Connor v. Donaldson, 422 U.S. 563 (1975).

Opinion of the Justices to the Senate, 423 Mass. 1201, 698 N.E.2d 738 (1996).

Paul v. Davis, 424 U.S. 693 (1976).

People v. McClellan, 6 Cal.4th 367, 24 Cal Rptr. 2d 739 (1994).

Ramona v. Isabella, Cal. Sup. Ct. C61898 (1994).

Rise v. Oregon, 59 F.3d 1556 (9th Cir. 1995).

Roe v. Wade, 410 U.S. 113 (1973).

Rowe v. Burton, 884 F. Supp. 1372 (D. Alaska 1994).

Russell and Sterns v. Gregoire, 124 F.3d 1079 (9th Cir. 1997).

Seling v. Young, 121 S. Ct. 727 (2001).

Skinner v. Oklahoma, 316 U.S. 535 (1942).

Smith v. Doe, 123 S. Ct. 1140 (2003).

Snyder v. State, 912 P.2d 1127 (Wyo. 1996).

State ex rel. Pearson v. Probate Court of Ramsey County, 205 Minn. 545, 555, 287 N.W. 297, 302 (1939).

State v. Cameron, 185 Ariz. 467, 916 P.2d 1183 (Ct. App/ Div. 1 1996).

State v. Skroch, 883 P.2d 1256 (Mont. 1994).

State v. Ward, 123 Wash. 2d 212, 737 P.2d 250 (1987).

Tyson v. Tyson, 727 P.2d 226, 229 (Wash. 1986).

United States v. Carey, 172 F.3d 1268 (1999).

United States v. Salerno, 481 U.S. 739, 95 L. Ed. 2d 697, 107 S. Ct. 2095 (1987).

Young v. Weston, 192 F.3d 870 (9th Cir. 1999).

Index

A

Abel, Gene, 43
absconding, 201
abuse. *See* child sexual abuse; cycle of abuse theory; rape
academics. *See* schools and school performance
acceptance and healing, 115–116, 131
acquaintances. *See* victim-offender relationship
actuarial risk assessment, 193, 194–195*t,* 209
addictive behaviors, 156
Addington v. Texas (1979), 214
adjudication process. *See* courts and adjudication process
adolescent offenders. *See* juvenile offenders
affective disorders. *See* depression
age, offense victims, 10, 112, 233
age of consent. *See* consent
agencies. *See* government agencies
aggression
    juvenile offenders, 72, 104
    power and control-focused rapists, 74
    sadistic rapists, 73
    testosterone effects, 40
Alaska
    registration of offenders, 196

alcohol and drug abuse
    juvenile offenders, 99
    restrictions on offenders, 175
    triggering factors, 67–68, 172
    See also medications and drugs
Alves, Raymond, 210
American Civil Liberties Union (ACLU), 165*n*
Amytal, 33
androgens, 39
anger. *See* negative emotional states
animals
    bestiality, 90
    used to lure children, 173
anxiety. *See* negative emotional states
apparently irrelevant decisions (AIDs), 53, 160
arrests and prosecutions
    child pornography cases, 239
    civil commitment, 208
    cleared by arrest, 19*n*
    consistent public policy, 177
    criminal procedure, 120, 125–128
    England, 69*n*
    management of offenders, 168
    New York City, 28
    political motivation, 29
    registration laws, 184, 189